Pandora's Box

To You, Adam Crawford...
I have five things to say.

Pandora's Box

By

George Bennett Fain

ISBN: 978-0-6151-4135-0

Publisher
KronosKemet Press
Huntington, WV

Marketing and Distribution
KronosKemet Press
508 Marcum Terrace
Huntington, WV 25705
Telephone: 304-617-7881
Email: blueschilde@yahoo.com

Printed by Lulu.com
United States of America

First Edition 2007

Pandora's Box Soundtrack is a collection of songs that were included in the story. No disrespect intended to the songwriters or the musicians who created or performed these songs. Each one was copyrighted elsewhere and is not the property of KronosKemet Press.

Disc One:

The Cruxshadows --Winterborn
Tool --Prison Sex
Garbage --#1 Crush
Goran Bregovic --Kai An Se Thelo
Rihanna --Turn the Music Up
Steve Pierson --Secrets
Cake --I Will Survive
Joaquin Phoenix --Home of the Blues
Garth Brooks --To Make You Feel My Love
Tom Waits --How's It Gonna End
Heather Nova --Gloomy Sunday
Sting --Shape of My Heart
INXS --Never Tear Us Apart
Mandy Patinkin --Oyfn Pripetshik

Disc Two:

Vanessa Mae --Toccata and Fugue
Los Lobos --Someday
Jason Jobe --Freedom to Stay
Grayson Capps --Lorraine's Song
Rufus Wainwright --Hallelujah
Eric Clapton --Born in Time
Warren Zevon --Mister Bad Example
Cibo Matto --Sugar Water
Squirrel Nut Zippers --Blue Angel
Melissa Etheridge --Refugee
Lorna Vallings --Taste
Cruxshadows --Deception
Tracy Chapman --The Promise
Steve Miller Band --Abracadabra remix
White Town --Your Woman
Toad the Wet Sprocket --Pray Your Gods

Acknowledgements:
My soul sings for you

Adam Crawford. Many things must be left unsaid, because it's late, but whatever conversation we haven't had tonight, we'll have tomorrow.

Chris Worth. Just because.

Dennis Look, Todd Cox and Ronnie Stapleton, Amanda Spearman. Erik Fessette, Arthur Fryer, the bartenders at the now-defunct Driftwood Lounge. Some of the Drag Queens at the Polo Club---you know who you are. Tommy Setliff who asked me why I was wasting my talents by not even attempting to publish.

Marty Laubach---my boss---my professor and mentor. You've become my friend at a time in my life when I needed one of those more than anything else in the world.

Lena Hall Fain---my mum. We should all have a mum so cool. She has believed in me even when I didn't feel so very tough or brave or smart. I might exasperate the hell out of this woman, but she also knows that there is ***nothing*** I cannot do when I set my mind to it and that when it comes to my family, there's nothing I won't do.

My daughters---Jackie and Kenzie, the lights of my life and the candles in my window. They're my best friends. Over the years they have put up with a lot from me, as a writer and a parent. It's the curse of a writer's children that they must repeatedly hear 'Just one more hour, please, just until I get to the end of this scene…'

Alannah---my niece, who came along at the moment when I was ready to be an aunt.

The writers of The Rest Is Silence online writing list and the Neon Silence writing list; perhaps the lists are defunct now, but if not for your love and thoughtful help, I wouldn't have perfected my style.

Sasscat Fitchett.

P. L. Nunn, the artist who designs my cover-art. I've been in love with her work for years, both the written and the graphic. Thank you, Pam, for taking care of my characters and making them look the way I imagine they must. To see the artist's work, please visit www.bishonenworks.com

Jim Fain. Who will probably never even know this book exists. By being my psycho-emotional obstacle, my father provided me with the balls and the determination that one must have for writing. It is not my job, but it is my ***true vocation***---thanks, Dad, for making me so bull-headed by giving me something I ***had*** to prove.

Glossary:

malakh: The genetic descendants of fallen angels.

benu: A malakh who possesses the ability to heal from almost every kind of wound. They are created either by genetic alteration or born to manifest. They do not age and the only way to kill them is by destroying their spinal cord or their brain. They are, by nature, the consummate hunter.

tchatchau: A malakh who can go invisible through the mirage created by their sweat and body heat index. They are mortal and fiery in nature and have quickened biological clocks, desiring to breed young and often. They are warriors, at heart.

sakau: A malakh who can pick up on the emotions of others, an empath.

husa-hekau: A malakh who can influence others with his emotions, even temporarily altering the reality of those around them. It is a chemical they produce in their brains and pheromones. They can kill with this chemical, if it runs out of control.

hekau: A malakh who can influence others with his voice.

sa-hekau: A malakh who possesses empathy and can influence others with his voice.

saihu: A malakh who possesses the ability to connect to human consciousness in dreams.

saihu-heb: A Dreamer malakh who has spent their life deliberately dreaming, as in a priesthood.

asetau: A malakh who can shift their shape at will, becoming anyone they can visualize.

thalocian: Another name for the shapeshifter malakh.

benandanti: 'good walkers', comprised of men and women born with a caul on their face, they were compelled to serve and protect their villages during the night. Benandanti possessed the ability to leave their bodies, during sleep, to do battle with the forces of evil. Benandanti were witches and healers. After their nightly battles with evil, they woke with an intense thirst. They were compelled also to be back in their bodies by the morning. The benandanti were considered soldiers of the spirit.

Maahes: Ancient Egyptian god of war. He was believed to help Pharaoh in battle. Usually depicted as a lion-headed man carrying a knife or a sword. Maahes sometimes wore the crown of a king. Occasionally, he was depicted as a lion devouring a captive. He was thought to be the guardian of sacred places, protecting the innocent. He was connected to Ma'at, the goddess of harmony and balance. Maahes punished those who violated Ma'at. He was called Lord of the Massacre, Avenger of Wrongs, and The Scarlet Lord. Among his cult centers was the Nubian city of Meroe.

Sekhmet: A lion-headed goddess associated with war and retribution and plague. Her priests were often physicians and surgeons. She is depicted with the sun disk and uraeus serpent headdress. Her names were Powerful One, the Mistress of Dread, and The Red Lady. A legend about her states that she was a blood-drinker and was brought up out of the South---

Upper Egypt or perhaps even Nubia.

Apedemak: Ancient Nubian god of war. The counterpart to Maahes. His main temple was located in the Nubian city of Meroe. A legend claims that he might have been the real father of Sekhmet.

Nubia, Ta-seti: The ancient land of the south.

Kemet: The ancient name used to describe the fertile land on either side of the Nile; often is used to describe the entire land of Egypt.

Seidi: Pure blood Egyptian culture from Upper Egypt.

Misrene: Egyptian natives from any quarter of the land.

Misr: A name used for Egypt.

Medjay: Society and culture associated with the Pan-Grave People of Nubia. After Egypt's conquer over Nubia, many Medjay came to work as guards and policemen in the cities of Egypt. They practiced scarification and tattooing.

Dry your eyes and quietly bear this pain with pride
For heaven shall remember the silent and the brave
And promise me, they will never see, the fear within our eyes
We will give strength to those who still remain
So bury fear for fate draws near and hide the signs of pain
With noble acts, the bravest souls endure the heart's remains
Discard regret, that in this debt a better world is made
That children of a newer day might remember, and avoid our fate.
And in the fury of this darkest hour we will be your light
You've asked me for my sacrifice and I am Winter born
Without denying, a faith is come that I have never known
I hear the angels call my name and I am Winter born
Hold your head up high-for there is no greater love
Think of the faces of the people you defend
And promise me, they will never see the tears within our eyes
Although we are men with mortal sins, angels never cry
So bury fear for fate draws near and hide the signs of pain
With noble acts, the bravest souls endure the heart's remains
Discard regret, that in this debt a better world is made
That children of a newer day might remember, and avoid our fate.
And in the fury of this darkest hour we will be your light
You've asked me for my sacrifice and I am Winter born
Without denying, a faith in God that I have never known
I hear the angels call my name and I am Winter born
And in the fury of this darkest hour I will be your light
A lifetime for this destiny. For I am Winter born
And in this moment...I will not run, it is my place to stand
We few shall carry hope within our bloodied hands
And in our Dying we're more alive-than we have ever been
I've lived for these few seconds for I am Winter born
And in the fury of this darkest hour we will be the light
You've asked me for my sacrifice and I am Winter born
Without denying, a faith in man
That I have never known
I hear the angels call my name
And I am Winter born
Within this moment now
I am for you, though better men have failed
I will give my life for love
For I am Winter born
And in my dying I'm more alive, than I have ever been
I will make this sacrifice for I am Winter born

(Winterborn by The Cruxshadows)

Proem

Twelve thousand years ago, when I left the battlefields of Heaven, I fell.

But, as I crossed the barrier between this and the realm where humans live, I called matter to myself. I did it to create a body that most closely resembled my true form. But, as I did so, choosing flesh, a large piece of my spirit was broken away, split like an atom. The scream that tore free of me created the flesh which harbored my Light.

In choosing free will and creating a body of my own, I lost the Light of this Universe, my father and my mother. That Light, my divinity, was the better part of me which could easily translate the music of Heaven. In this state, I was incomplete and I felt an emptiness such as had never existed before. It was a hunger for the Light I had lost. My wings became darkened and I could no longer hear the Universe's song in its true form. I became hungry, needing to be joined with my lost Light.

All the Midael and Grigori and other elohim who fell with me, they knew the same---this was our fate as a group and as individuals. The love of flesh was formed when the Grigori chose humans over divinity, but we, as Midael, answering their sin with a sin of our own, didn't realize what would come of it until we made flesh for ourselves from the nothing. We were split into two, Light and Dark. Neither Light nor Dark is pure; Light possesses some darkness and Dark possesses some gleaming of light. It is the tiny part which calls out in the void, seeking to be found...seeking to be made whole.

I found the hunger for the flesh in an unspoken knowledge that my Light was in flesh, that this missing piece of my whole was bound in blood, in breath. I hungered for flesh, to join with flesh, to worship flesh...to be with my Light. It came from within that loss, the split. I sought Nemat, who might make me complete again...my eternal self. I devoured flesh in every way possible and there are so many possible hungers for the flesh, from the most animal to the most divine, from the teeth to the carnality of copulation. The torment, it was hell. Like a fire, my Light burned brightly within the flesh.

It was easy to find, at first, despite the fact that my Light was mortal, could die. It died, returned, died again, returned once more...cycle after cycle, I tracked it, within the dark of my mind and from the ethereal. Each time it returned to the flesh, I had no trouble finding my Light---I was forever the same and could not die, so my memory of it was untainted. My Light could remember me, then, and all I ever needed to do was remind Nemat of its destiny...of what Nemat possessed in its flesh that I could not bear to be parted from.

It was glorious, when we could re-Join. To be so whole that Heaven's music kept me dazzled and drunken with pleasure. I was patient, I learned to accept what I could be given...we were not truly one, but with Nemat, my agony was lessened. With Nemat, I didn't feel the hunger so strongly, didn't crave the darkest of pleasures...that which was found in the degradations and hellish punishments of any human who crossed my path in that millennia. I hunted them on occasion, when Nemat was not mine...I hunted them, punished them for being so wondrous and for not being Nemat.

With Nemat, I felt as if I could bear to exist outside Heaven's song. When Nemat was not with me, I sought the frail humans I could destroy in revenge...for with each death, I heard less of the song. I believed it might be better to not hear the music anymore, in any way. I believed it could be better to be deaf to Heaven than to suffer outside that great song, able to hear and yet unable to hear.

If I must be shut away from the Light, let me not hear The Song.

Nemat felt no pain from the fall, for it was Light and its human flesh muffled the music of

Heaven even while echoing that eternal, perfect chorus. I mated with humans, created children who carried in their hybrid forms my angelic knowledge and part of my angelic body. They also possessed something I didn't...a soul. For my soul was Nemat, forever circling further and further away from me with each cycle it lived.

Nine thousand years ago, a war broke out between my brothers and myself. It was pure chaos. Angels against angels. We almost destroyed this world and all the people in it. Things shifted and, at last, I brought order by imprisoning the darkest of my siblings. I imprisoned the greatest of them, Semjaza, in a holy place where only I can walk unscathed.

I made a pact with the Universe, through my Light. I imprisoned my brothers, those who wanted to enslave humans as pets and sheep, and accepted the price this Universe demanded. I was to be placed in a citadel, trapped by song magics, forever known as protector and partisan of mankind. It was a citadel of my own creation, designed to hold me half-asleep until the day when I might awaken to the clarion call of the Universe once again.

I was imprisoned in mortal flesh at last. The Guardians, my own children, did this, in the land once known as Kush and Ta-seti. They imprisoned my immortal body and hid it in my home far to the north, near the delta. They thrust my sleeping spirit into the body of my youngest androgyne daughter, a shape-shifting nephilim who would become known as a fierce, pitiless god in the lands of both Ta-seti and Kemet for the angelic gifts she possessed---this child's strength and hunger and power would make her into a deity to be loved and feared from White Wall to Meroe.

Her name? Sekhmet. Maahes. Apedemak.

I was chained to a child who might die---perhaps after thousands of years---and return again, forever carrying me in the blood. I slept in my citadel, living over and over with this special, chosen one.

I stirred when my beloved Nemat was near. The song from Nemat's Light caused me to shift in my prison, to seek out my only hope. I could not rest. I sought Nemat through the ages, with each drowsy lifetime I lived as a mortal. When it was possible...when I was malakh and possessed some magic or angelic gift, I sought Nemat through the ethereal. I found my Light and endeavored to re-Join in whatever manner was possible.

But, there was distortion; we were both bound in the mortal flesh, which can hide much...Nemat didn't recognize me every time. More than once, I didn't recognize Nemat.

In the cycles when Nemat loved me, I felt the pain lessen. That love soothed the darkness in me and those were good times. I used the hunger to create beauty, to guide and teach and heal. I am forever a warrior; it is what I was, in my creation. This showed itself in thousands of cycles.

When Nemat loved me, came together with me in our pale shade of re-Joining, I gave my hunger to the Light. When Nemat didn't know me, didn't love me...the emptiness was a torment I couldn't bear. I destroyed love, destroyed life. All in the craving to have the nameless thing which belongs to only humans and their malakh cousins, my children.

This nameless thing often goes by the words of God, Love, Hope. It is the flame of a soul. When Nemat loves me, it is possible for me go on fighting to protect the nameless thing which fills Nemat but which is not in me. My wings seek out the Light, to grow warm in the divinity of Nemat's soul, for Nemat is the embodiment of my Light, the divine love I gave up in my determination to become flesh.

Can you imagine my immortal form? I am locked in a fragile flesh prison...so frail when compared to the angelic form I once had. It cannot be destroyed; it was entombed in the deepest cave of a place now lost to human reckoning. It waits there, for me. Forever young and forever full of power. Forever vibrating at the lowest of frequencies that only I can identify, that only I can hear.

The weapons and knowledge I imparted to my chosen children, the Guardians, those things have been cared for with such devotion and fear. I gave them to the ones I trusted to protect those gifts. I did this with the knowledge that, somewhere along the way, I would come into the flesh of a descendent who possessed certain potentials and I would again be powerful enough to wield my legacy and my weapons in the interests of protecting the

humanity I both love and hate.
It was a promise I made to the Universe.
My name is Israfil Arakelba, Guardian of Life.

Call me Judas.

I came to this city of iniquity nearly four years ago and made it my own hunting ground, as my kind often do. We do not share easily, vampires. It is not the way of a predator to willingly allow poaching in the forest it has chosen for itself. We might allow a childe of our making to hunt in the chosen wilderness, but even this is often a difficult matter.

This city is known for its connection to the supernatural, the demonic and the angelic; it is a city in love with death and decay. I believe this must be the reason for why so many of my kind attempt to move in; vampires are most comfortable with demons and angels and prefer a hunting ground where the kill can be hidden without great effort...or written off as something else entirely.

New Orleans, the birthplace of the blues...a haven for magic of all kinds.

Where else would there be a guild dedicated to the underground, black market world of crime? I came here, following my instincts and my instructions for watching the Chosen, and made the decision that this city's murder rate could support me...me and my sensuous childe.

I am the Guardian of the Sang-rael al-Mahdi; this reason alone is why I have survived the centuries. I was born outside the walls of Jerusalem in the year 1122; before my death, I was a stable-boy and a priest and a Knight.

My name is Joseph Louis Rheims Snowden, but you may call me Judas.

I am a bane to the existence of my own kind and a curse on the lips of those who once trusted me, as a mortal man, to protect and keep the truth of a sacrament most dear to The Poor Fellow Soldiers of Christ and the Temple of Solomon. How can a creature such as myself be the protector and guardian to such a miraculous gift as the Sang-rael al-Mahdi? How can God allow a monster to protect and keep watch on the bloodline of His own chosen warrior?

Nevertheless, I have found no one who might be strong enough to inherit---I searched, believe me---and, in its own perversity, it is fitting that I should be the last of my people, the last Watcher of Scion. For who better than a creature of darkness to exist through the centuries, on watch without blinking, to keep track of a bloodline just as holy as the bloodline of Yeshua bar Yosef?

You might consider it blasphemy, to hear this; the claim that there could be a blood as pure and powerful as the blood of that teacher, that messiah. I tell you this: I have seen wonders in this world the likes of which shall never be witnessed by any other soul---Undead or mortally alive. I have continued to allow my own existence for that sole purpose---the observation and guardianship of the Sang-rael al-Mahdi.

There was once a Lamb, there was once a Lion. The Lamb was the right hand son of God, chosen to walk among the mortals as a teacher. This Lamb died, killed by the very people he came to teach. But, the prophesies also spoke of a Lion...a Lion whose whole purpose was the protection and cleansing of the world and its people. He was the left hand son of God, a Master of the Sephiroth, a warrior of the spirit. He came before the Lamb and he shall come again. So claim the prophesies.

He is here, among us...but, he is not what he seems. He has chosen a different form, a different clay. He was once a mortal man with malakh blood and malakh power. Now, he is not.

I call myself Judas. I am a killer, a monster. I live by the blood of the guilty and the innocent. I walk at night because my unclean body cannot endure the good sunlight. The vampire in me is bone-deep, a disease of the blood and spirit that hales from demons as old as this world. I kill my own kind, as well, cleaning them from the living world as a surgeon

21

must clean a putrefied wound. I keep this city fairly clean of reckless, outlaw vampires, protecting it from evil with evil.

I have fought hard, through the centuries, to find a balance. I have despaired and railed against my existence...I have denounced myself and all those who are of my ilk. I have punished my beloved childe for how this state exalted and perfected him---he is a delicious creature; I both hate and love him, his Undead body and Undead soul.

Yet, I have often crowed at and reveled in my base, brutal Undead nature.

How can a monster such as myself still fight and struggle to maintain the watch and the guard? Why should a monster do such things? If I am of darkness and death, how can I be the Watcher and the Guardian of the Sang-rael al-Mahdi, that which is the very essence of life and sound and light? How can I be the one destined to watch her?

Yes...call me Judas.

Chapter One

My name's Tennyson and I'm a gardener.   Sounds like the start of a kid's book, doesn't it?

Yeah, well.

Tennyson Beaulieu. No middle name.   It wasn't something my mom gave a lot of thought to. I chose a middle name for myself, for all the times when it's needed on official documents. Tennyson Ashwin Beaulieu.

Ashwin. That's one of the only things I know about my dad. His name was Ashwin. I also know that he wasn't American, either, but born someplace in the Middle East. Supposedly, Arabic on his mom's side.   My mom says she doesn't know much about it, except that my dad's paternal family were English. My mom's name is D'Ann Beaulieu. My parents met at school in Los Angeles; my mom was a student out there in California, and my dad was earning pay as a teacher in an Anthropology class.

It was a scandal, of course, the whole thing.   Instead of getting a real degree for business, my mom got a liberal arts degree. Then, to add insult to injury, Mom wasn't supposed to fall in love with a scholar, even one so handsome as my dad, and she was a 'bad' daughter, choosing to run off with her boyfriend.   When she was heavy-pregnant with me, my dad was killed in a drug store robbery by a stray bullet meant for the pharmacist. My mom told me it was just an accident, but, as a kid, I liked to imagine Ashwin was being a hero, using himself to shield the innocent pharmacist.

After he was dead, his family came to retrieve the body and my mom never saw them again---she came back to New Orleans and started teaching art studies at UNO.   She said Ashwin's family wasn't too hyped on the idea of an American Creole mulatto in the family, but they send money every month for me.   I still get a monthly allowance from my dad's people; I don't know their names and the checks are always written on a solicitor's account, some bank in London. People called King-Hobbs. Part of the agreement, before I was born, was that my mom would never contact the solicitors for anything other than money and she could never tell me who my dad's people were.

I don't even know if Ashwin was his first name or his last name. I wouldn't have known that much about his name if it weren't for the ring my mom wears. She has a pretty, ancient-looking ring with a funky black scarab stone that she only takes off when bathing or washing dishes; I snatched it up once, when I was ten, and discovered that the inside of the gold band was inscribed with a single name.   Ashwin.   Asking my mom, she admitted that my dad gave her the ring.

My mom comes from a long line of doctors in New Orleans; our family's kinda famous for that. The Beaulieu. We're descended from free blacks who made a name for themselves after the Civil War. We're Creole. We're a freedom-loving people and hate restrictions and to us, duty and possession are matters only for the family.   Not many people in the family know that I date mostly women because I keep it on the down-low---I think they're waiting for the day my mom sends out the wedding invitations for me and some lucky, rich boy from the Garden District.

I don't wanna get married...and forget about babies.

Who needs a baby, anyway? This is the modern world and there's no reason to keep any bloodline rules. *Right*?

So, now you ask: how does a woman like me fit into a place like Pandora's Box? Well, the answer's simple: Life here's a crazy soap opera and I'm the one who tries to make sense of it all. The one who is neither cast nor audience nor author. Except, that's not very accurate. I'm part of this. Only, I'm not a member of the club---I'm not one of the players here. I mean, look around you, honey. This is not your average night club. It's not even close.

Since you made it through the door, you must be okay. They're careful here. Let me fill you in. Just so you know what you're dealing with. Not everyone here is a player and not every player shows his face. It's a place for terminal civility, for this is neutral territory reigned over by an ice-blooded bitch of a genii.

She's behind the bar, just in case you wondered. The tall, skinny blonde with no tits. Yeah, the one wearing a shirt and tie. Her name's Mattie Curran, but the story goes that she's a retired CIA agent. This is her club, a place where dirty deeds are networked out to the best possible operative. She runs it kinda like a little, secular agency. Rumor has it, she used to be a *real* Femme Nikita.

To look at her, you get two impressions. One, she doesn't look old enough to have the reputation, and, two, she might be a he. Maybe. She's got this look about her, like a mix of Annie Lennox and that English chick who played in the movie 'Orlando'. All androgynous and sword-sharp.

You noticed. I've heard it said, by people who know Mattie, that she used to be a normal person. She had long hair and wore dresses on occasion and had a husband, a family. She's got three sons. One of them is just her step-son, but she raised him from diapers, so I guess she has the right to claim him. Dante, Rugby, and the baby, Gabe---he's almost a year old. Dante is her step-son, Rugby is her son by her dead husband, and Gabe's dad is...well, Gabe's dad is Rhys. You don't know him, yet, but he was a member of Mattie's team for almost ten years. In the CIA. He's a member of the club here, a player.

Story goes, Mattie belonged to an aristocratic mafia's assassin guild in England when she was a teenager. She came to America in her early twenties and ended up working for the CIA, out in California. She got stupid and got married and everything, but when her husband died in the line of duty right in front of her eyes, she went back to men's clothes and the---oh, she's older than she looks. She's in her fifties, I think. She just looks like she's in her early thirties.

Look around you, honey. This place is as far from *normal* as it gets. A quarter of the usual patrons and club members are like her. They don't show their age and a lot of them worked for the CIA, the same as Mattie Curran. This place is a haven for malakh and other things not human. It's like Magazine Street can be seen by the non-humans from all over the world---a big neon sign that points the way to home. They're drawn to Pandora's Box because of the club's nature and because that's how they are. Particularly malakh. Malakh love humans, but they prefer the company of their own kind. I've heard it said that it's the scent; they can *smell* each other from across the room. Identification pheromones, maybe.

Malakh? Well, they're not like us, that's for sure. Malakh are the descendents of angels. Human and angel hybrid offspring. Some have wings, some don't, but the ones that do have wings...you probably won't see the wings right off the bat. The wings tend to stay invisible. For the most part, malakh pass for human...on the surface.

Sometimes, I think someone should write a handbook for their breed...a clear, concise way to understand all the subtle, scary details. I've been dealing with the malakh here a few years. Since I first stepped foot in this bar. That was back before I was legal to drink and the only things the bartenders would let me have were coffee and juice and soda pop. Well...except for when Rembrandt worked the bar for Mattie; Rembrandt let me have beer, sometimes.

Of course, that was back before I understood why Rembrandt was being careful, looking around before he poured me a cold one. I didn't know what this place was, then. I just thought it was a safe gay bar, someplace non-threatening where I could be among my own kind. Back then, I didn't understand that, in Pandora's Box, I was only nominally okay and the bartenders were watching out for me without being obvious, and I was *not* among my own kind. An empath or a telepath, working as a network agent for Mattie, could be sitting within 'listening' distance and might pick up on the fact that Rembrandt just gave 'the kid' a beer and then Rembrandt would be in stir with Mattie. If the network agent told on him.

Is Mattie Curran one? Yeah. She's malakh. She also happens to have a little empath talent. She's almost impossible to kill, doesn't age, and has a singing voice that could put the sweetest diva to shame. To *shame*, sugar---I've heard her. Look around at the people in this room. There's enough light, you can see the children of angels. Look for the ones who seem to *glow* from under the skin, as if nothing can soil them.

Don't you just love this place? So old-class New Orleans, but cleaner than some of the dives you'll find here. And it's open sexuality, which means anything goes, but always with a lot of politeness. Did you know it's a coffeehouse during the day? Yeah. Mattie's partners, Jim and Russ, run the coffeehouse, and she runs the bar with Rembrandt, who has lived in this neighborhood his whole life.

Have you been to the temple, yet? It's huge; a friend of mine said that Mattie had three rooms of this place opened up, to make the temple. And outside, in the backyard, out that door there, there's a garden with tables. But, the dance floor is fixed to look like an ancient non-secular temple. It's got statues and everything. That's why they call it a temple.

This is just a big, old house that Mattie and her family turned into a bar. Here, we have the two front rooms opened for the bar. And, soundproofed on the other side of that wall, it's the temple. The kitchen's open, too, if you ever want something to eat. Upstairs, that's private. Offices and stuff.

Anything you want, aboveboard or underground, you just talk to Mattie or Rembrandt, and they can find you the perfect man or woman or malakh for the job. The club members pay a due and that gives them the right to do business here. Some of them even have offices. That hallway over there, past the billiards tables? It goes up the stairs and leads to a bunch of rooms where the business goes down. Real QT, you know?

Oh, anything you want. Hackers, assassins, B&E artists, accountants, smugglers, and lawyers. If it can be networked, Mattie Curran handles it. Everything but prostitutes and drugs. She doesn't network those, but if your job calls for the use of either, the player who works for you can probably handle the details of that, too.

Okay, you've got good eyes. That short Mexican guy at the end of the bar, he's Javi. He used to be CIA. Most of Mattie's old team works here. Handsome, don't you think? I like his hair; you can't really tell in this light, but his hair is the color of cinnamon. And so curly. And I love the way he smiles. From what Rhys told me, Javi was one of the last members of Mattie's CIA recon team. He just joined the club recently. Jack of all trades type, you know? He's a shape shifter, what the malakh call tholocian or asetau. He and Rhys used to be partners in the team the way Daniel and Mattie were partners.

Am I a member of the club? No. I'm just me. I've got a free pass to come in here any time I like, though. I'm sometimes in here with Dante, Mattie Curran's step-son. He's the main DJ. He used to work for the government, too, as a computer analyst. Basically, he's a hacker. Well, what I mean by 'with' is that we're friends and we hang out. He's bi and funny---very funny. He has the wit of a catty, culturally-warped libertine. Right now, he's dating this hot little lawyer boy named Jules. They make a cute couple.

Well, to be honest, Dante's not the real reason why I'm allowed in here without question. My best friends also work here. Valeska and Rhys. They're here, tonight. In the temple. You can't miss them. They're the ones that all the girls love.

Come on, I'll show you. Grab your drink. You don't wanna miss *this*.

Rhys was dancing with Valeska an evil, sexy tango to the sounds of a song by Voronlight. The two svelte, pretty boys moved in circles now under the rolling strobes, as if stalking prey. Each was held tightly by the eyes of the other. They came together once more, drawn by the fierce energy of the drum, and swayed, naked hands finding the shift of slender, leather-clad hips as they wrestled in sensual battle.

'He is, without a doubt, the only one of his kind in the known world.'

At that thought, Daniel smiled to himself and lifted his drink for a sip of cold bourbon. His dark eyes were on Rhys, where they often stayed. When Rhys danced, he found himself unwilling to do anything but *watch*. Someday, his garcon would become aware of the unholy love he felt and, then, surely, Rhys would pity him. Yet, he could not help himself. He watched Rhys and mused on the idea of how desperate and impossible his affections were.

He was French. Musing on the tragic comedy of life was innately in his blood.

Along with the hateful curse of his genetic legacy.

He was the oldest person in the temple and the bar...with the exception of Joseph Snowden. Joe, always chilly and often brutal, also sat in the shadows. Doubtless, the knight's eyes were also on the two sleek dancers who dominated the stage---Valeska belonged to Joe.

He had come here, as usual, with the idea of perhaps finding work. It was not a dire necessity, but he found that keeping himself busy was a way to lessen the pain of his grief. If he could work, he did not dwell on his beloved wife, his Creole fleur. She was on his mind more often these days; she came to him in his dreams and she smiled and she reached to touch him and it was precious, but it was madness, too. A part of him knew---he would have to leave New Orleans to escape the largest part of his grief. New Orleans---her city.

It had been four years since she had left him, taken by death. The cancer had not been merciful or quick and his fleur had worn herself to the bone with the therapies and medicines. Death, when it came at last, had turned into a mercy. He had, at first, not seen it as such; it had taken Rhys' strange wisdom to help him understand and accept his loss.

'Mon ami is insufferable, but I love him nonetheless. It is the way he moves; his careless, unconscious grace. It is his smile, which can never be truly imitated; he could, I imagine, give Mona Lisa a lesson in the art of being mysterious. His is the dark beauty of a sword, sharp and lethal and double-edged. He is unaware, for the most part, of how he affects those he must come into contact with. But, I love the garcon with everything I possess in my soul. I return to him in endless circles at the mere twist of fate's noose. Death has no hold on him; it is what he understands best.'

The shadows hid him well, in a corner of the club's dance room...the temple. Here and there, in the darkness, he saw the flicker of eyes and of lit cigarettes, of a gleam upon the lifted glass as it moved from table to parted lips. These were the denizens of the dark, those like himself and the others whose life or unlife were similar.

'He is a heathen. He dances with his delicious college boys, his luscious college girls, as if he is the head priest...a god made flesh and blood for their rituals of sound and light. He is an object of worship to them; I do not mistake it, a good half of those children would give their soul to possess him. They would willingly give up a limb or two for the pleasure of a night with Rhys.'

His young partner was lean and muscular, a rapier created of flesh and bone. He curled his upper lip at how Rhys' brown hair now slipped free of its pigtail, loosened by the agile fingers of the Undead gypsy thief. Under the flashing strobes, his garcon's olive-tan face was now half-hidden by the long sienna-brown waves, revealing a different side of Rhys' beauty. The quick glint of strong white teeth in a sly, dangerous smile. The Arabic curve of high, broad cheekbones and a flashing glimpse of drowsy bedroom eyes the unlikely bi-color of sky and sand. Rhys was in his element as the tribal rites music thumped through every inch of every body in the temple.

Daniel felt a pang at a new thought. *'Mattie must surely despise me...but, it was her choice. Non? She might have kept my garcon and she chose to shut him out of her bed and away from her heart.'* His smile returned, cooler and full of self-recrimination. *'She believes we are lovers and I do nothing to dissuade her, nothing to appraise her of the truth. Why should I? Let the woman believe what she wishes---she has her child from him. It is more than I have gained in Rhys.'*

He let it go, the thoughts. Instead, he watched the dark ones who could slide from shadow to shadow. The temple was the dance-show floor of his ex-partner's club. He had dubbed it such, upon seeing how Rhys had chosen to decorate. Mattie had bought the house and renovated it, creating a French salon bar in the fashion of the last century; his thin, blonde friend had decided it would be a business investment for herself and for Rhys---who, at the time, was Mattie's barely-legal lover, at eighteen.

With this freedom and a decent sum of cash, Rhys had decorated the dance-show floor to his own unusual tastes. The room resembled nothing so much as a temple, to his mind, as it contained life-sized statues of ancient gods from several pantheons and each wall rippled with a mesh of gold lame and Moroccan rugs and linens both white and black. The tables were teak and cypress, an extravagance he barely believed and could adore. Rhys, like himself, had royal tastes, even as they were both accustomed to living on a budget of only a few francs or dollars.

Most of the people who came to Pandora's Box were young and beautiful, college students from the local universities. It was an open environment, where the homosexual and the heterosexual could mingle without fear of reprisals. No such prejudices could exist in Pandora's Box; Mattie would *not* allow violence or hate on her territory, for this was neutral ground.

Herein sat many players who could not afford to have the authorities breathing down their necks. This club, it was a safe haven for retired CIA kite operatives who had managed to escape the ultimate retirement plan of death, which was so often the last gift from their previous employer, Uncle Sam. Pandora's Box held other surprises, too, in the form of mutants and malakh and monsters, alive and Undead both. Many were networking their skills through Mattie Curran, who ran a very tight ship for the sake of safety and profit.

As he watched Rhys dance with Valeska, among the lovely flowers of New Orleans' youth, he thought back on the years of his work for the American government. He had come to this country a half-century before and found work in a butcher shop not so very far from this very club---the butcher shop that his Vivienne's papa had owned. Before long, he had started an apprenticeship to a vampire assassin and made a name for himself as an efficient and fastidious killer.

But, in 1972, he had found himself sitting across a table from a gentleman who worked for the CIA; this man had brought an irrefutable deal to him. He could go to prison under the yoke of multiple murders, as an assassin, or he could ply his trade for the country that offered amnesty. He had taken the deal, wishing to keep his young wife and children from ignoble poverty. His choice had not come without its own selfish reason---he would never have survived another sixty-year stint in prison; he had been incarcerated before, in his first century.

Once in the CIA, he had been placed with the BDS, an elite corp of kite operatives who were partnered off into teams all over the world. They might be required to kill on occasion, but their duties were multifold and often much more mundane. He had found himself partnered with a young British woman whose real name was unfamiliar to him, but whose reputation under an assumed identity had rung true chords with his memory. Through the sixties, a young man in England had cast a tall shadow in the whispered stories of international players. Thom Curran was a name he knew well, from the tales and rumors.

Unfortunately, upon being introduced to his new, boyishly female partner, he could little have guessed that Thom Curran and Mattie Curran were the one and the same. It was only after a joint session with their team's psychiatrist that he had been given the truth about the woman to whom he was meant to trust his life. He had been sorely reminded, then, that appearances were often deceiving; he could never have imagined Mattie being the cold and cruel assassin of those ugly tales.

For...what did Thom and Mattie have in common? Thom Curran had loved no one, had once killed his own sneak-boy to protect the silence of an assigned murder, and Mattie had a family...oui? Mattie had two brothers and their wives and their children; Mattie had Rob and Rob's infant son and she smiled like sunlight breaking through sullen, gray clouds. Mattie laughed like a young girl and was easily moved to tears---she seemed the least likely candidate for work as a CIA kite operative.

27

Their psychiatrist had revealed the truth as Mattie sat with gray eyes steady upon the fold of her freckled hands in her lap, at his side. Lorraine had spared him nothing, had said these things so that he might have a better grasp on what his young partner was capable of. Mattie Curran might have a lover, might live in a white-picket fence world, but she was of his ilk and it was forever within reach under her nutmeg-speckled skin, behind her smiling face. She was, according to the gene tests, of his own kind, but not yet manifesting the same ability. If she should die by some means other than a shot to the head or a break of her spinal cord, Mattie may awaken from that death into the world of a benu malakh.

This conversation had occurred in 1973; he had given it much thought, since. Especially in the days of darkness which had come to them in 1985. With the births of both Rugby Thomas Webster and Josiah Rhys Rose in 1984, the world had seemed safe enough, despite what he was contracted to do for the American government.

It had not mattered to any of them that L'Enfant Rose possessed mutant abilities that he should not have been born with. It had not mattered that the garcon was something outside their mental grasp; they accepted what they were told by the charismatic doctors of the Malakh Principles team. The situation was under control, according to both Pierre Lorraine and Steven Rose, the two who had created the Malakh Principles experiments in 1973. Steven had altered his own DNA and passed a new legacy on to his child, Josiah Rhys, who had received malakh abilities from both his mama and papa.

But, in 1985, came the death of Mattie's lover and husband, Rob, and the deaths of both Steven and Roan, Rhys' parents---his dear friends. At the time, it was believed that Rhys had died with them, in a terrible accident. Mattie, before he could do anything to protect the young ones involved, gave away both Dante and Rugby, Rob's sons, to differing members of their family. Dante had been shuttled off to a Webster in San Diego and Rugby had been sent to Edinburgh, to foster with Mattie's brother, Pierce.

Upon doing so with her children, his partner had disappeared into a lab in northwestern Nevada for the chance to play Russian Roulette with her own genes; Steven's and Lorraine's projects had included a gene therapy which could switch on the DNA of certain latent malakh, bringing forth their true, manifesting potentials. Mattie Curran had gone into the Chiron bunker labs with a dead heart, intending to die in the Tubs, a testament to failed experimentation, and had emerged a creature like him, manifested. A true benu, like himself...able to die and shake it off like a brief illness, able to heal unnaturally fast from almost any wound.

Mattie had not intended to survive the procedure, had become everything that the Malakh Principles experiments had predicted, and he had witnessed the rebirth of Thom Curran in the following years, after the Chiron gene therapy. The Golden Wolf, as she was known to the CIA, became a shining star of the BDS teams, having manifested as more than a benu. She had awoken in the Tubs as an empath, able to read and pick up on the emotional thoughts of others---a sakau benu malakh. She was, in that first ten years, the ultimate warrior and agent, and he had ridden the dark road at her side, letting himself do as she did.

His wife and children, safe here in New Orleans, had lived as much as six months of the year without him, but that was the duty he had been called for. Mattie had abandoned Rob's sons to their respective guardians and thrown herself into the cold void of a monster's world. Her husa-hekau step-son, Dante, was old enough and knew the truth, but Rugby had grown nearly to a man believing Mattie was only his tante...his aunt.

Then, in 1995, something changed; something had come to light which changed the nature of his existence as a kite operative. Someone on the inside of the CIA's experimentation programs had alerted Internal Affairs to a certain project that was being conducted in the hills outside Cold Springs, California. A child, raised with a group of similar children in a clandestine outpost bunker, had drawn attention with a presentation to the BDS Council...the scientist doing the presentation was the scientist responsible for the experiment, the man who had raised these children to become the prototypes of malakh soldiers.

The Malakh Principles experiments had never died, had continued silently and out of his sight during the decade he had worked so untiring and without regret as Mattie Curran's partner. Lorraine had raised a dozen malakh children to become weapons of great potential and terrible skill---called DeathAngels---yet only one of these children possessed the obvious markings of a tchatcha, the rarest malakh breed.

When the information leaked to Internal Affairs, an investigation was started. Mattie was pulled from their assignment to work on the team conducting the secret investigation. Within a week after starting this new mission, his partner had called him on the other side of the world with alien panic and ragged tears, emotion which ripped the clean and crisp British tones of her voice. She had discovered Lorraine's on-going project and the truth behind why Internal Affairs was concerned.

One child in the compound, a biological weapon of incredible potentials, was only eleven years old and possessed an ability to go invisible. Immediately, he had known what Mattie was intimating with such a claim; they had only known two people who were capable of such a feat. Steven, their dead scientist friend, and his young child...Josiah Rhys. Steven and Josiah Rhys were both dead.

Non?

Non.

Rhys, having secretly survived the accident which killed his parents, had been adopted by Lorraine and was taken to Cold Springs to live behind razor wire in a large lab complex, had been raised without moral or ethical comprehension, without any knowledge of what a child should have as basic, inalienable rights in life. Lorraine had brought Rhys up to eleven years old as his own son, training the garcon to a warrior's world with other malakh children of differing potentials. Rhys, at eleven years old, was fast and highly intelligent and lethal...was capable of killing men with whatever could be grasped in his young hands.

Mattie had called him, demanded he do something to help her with the matter. They could not allow this to continue. Lorraine had to be stopped, killed...and Rhys had to be saved. He had agreed, but chosen to take a secretive path. He would help Mattie make arrangements to have Rhys removed from the lab and then he would take the boy to his homeland, moving his entire family in the process. He would ensure Rhys' safety, if it was possible...and he would do anything necessary to make it possible. Mattie had found a helpmate on the inside, in the lab. A young researcher who was appalled at the situation---the very same scientist who had blown the whistle.

In the summer, only six months after discovering Rhys' whereabouts, the young researcher had smuggled the garcon out in a closed box of shredded papers and into the wooded area beyond the razor wire and the fences. There, he had met the scientist and taken custody of his dead friends' child, the garcon he had not seen in a decade. He could imagine what the soft-faced researcher had thought, seeing him; he had a reputation for death and chilly stoicism. What could he possibly do with a child like Rhys?

In less than a week, he had boarded a plane to his homeland and taken Rhys as his 'nephew', legal papers in order. Lorraine had disappeared in that same week and he had his suspicions as to the method of that disappearance. Mattie, when provoked, was a creature of unrelenting, undying hate. He had never asked his partner about it, her possible involvement.

On the stage, Rhys swung free from Valeska; the gypsy reached for and caught his garcon's forearm below the snug half-sleeve of glittering black Lycra. He imagined what it felt like, the sizzle of cold fingers pressing hard to fever-hot muscles. Silken skin the golden hue of cafe latte trapped by the olive-dusky steel of the Undead hand. Demon Undead dancing the ageless tango of desire with the super-alive malakh descendent of angels. Could there be a more poignant, apt view of the world?

Chapter Two

His childe danced with the heathen tchatcha as hard, pounding music filled the club's dance room with the rough sounds of heavy metal remixed. The throb of bass and drum re-created the dangerous song and reminded him of battle. Battle was something he understood and he understood the sentiment in the words that growled from every speaker embedded in the walls and every amp.

'I've got my hands bound, my head down, my eyes closed, and my throat wide open. Do unto thee what has been done to me. Do unto others what has been done to you.'

It was nearly unbearable to watch the two dancers and he sliced into his own tongue with the tip of a fang which distended in jealousy ownership. The taste of blood only heightened his arousal. In an effort to keep himself sober-minded, he washed away the chilled, slick copper with a swallow of warm import beer.

'You're breathing, so I guess you're still alive even if signs seem to tell me otherwise.'

He could admit his jealousy; Nico was an unholy beauty and belonged to him, but he could not make his gypsy boy shine in the manner that Rhys was capable of. He could not dance, he could not sing, he did not present something forbidden to his childe. For Nico, Rhys was a creature of similar intent, yet hot-blooded and very alive...these aspects alone were enough to entice Nicolai.

He had not fed tonight. He had not fed in two days. His last kill had consisted of a murderous addict whose blood tasted of cheap gin and greasy take-out chicken and withdrawal. He had chosen a criminal, out of habit; when in his right mind and careful of his duty, he preferred to not eat innocent humans, if it was possible to make a distinction.

Two days ago, on his way to the club, he and Nico had stopped to put gas in their automobile and interrupted a robbery in progress. The ragged white thief had stood at the register, shaking a stolen gun at the young black man behind the counter. The clerk had been trying to fulfill the demand for cash, eyes like twin circles of terror in his sable face.

Going inside to pay for the gasoline, he had walked back through the convenience store, watching the drama as it unfolded. At last, coming to the counter himself, he'd stepped behind the angry-frightened addict. He could still smell the strange burning scent of the vagabond's skin, in his memory. But, it was the clerk's face that stayed the clearest, for him.

He had taken the shaking gun without hesitation, sliding it into his coat pocket, and then broken the fragile stalk of the vagabond's neck. While the clerk babbled his thanks and dialed the telephone to summon the police, he had stood under the unnatural light and taken the still-warm blood that he craved.

Before the black clerk could turn back around to look at him, putting down the telephone, he'd let the body drop to the dirty tiles. Laying his money on the counter, he had walked out of the store and back into the windy chill of the night. Nico had laughed at him, in the car, as he made a face at the horrible taste of the addict's blood and pulled back out onto the halogen-lit street.

His Rom childe's droll voice, in the memory, made him smile now, as he thought of it.

'You shouldn't pick up food at a gas station, Joseph---it's bad for you.'

Joseph lifted his glass of warm beer for another sip, still smiling.

'Got your hands bound, your head down, your eyes closed. You look so precious now.'

The tchatcha wore black leather trousers with boots that matched and a short-sleeved black shirt that could have been only malachite and antimony paint for how it moved with the boy's torso. Nicolai, his childe, wore the same, obviously enjoying a chance to be uniformed in the manner of his friend.

As they prowled and wrestled on the dance stage among the lovely children who dared to step into the club, the two killers could have been mistaken for lovers by any present who were unaware of the truth. For, yes, it was in the way Nico and Rhys smiled...it was in the way they came together, their bodies finding a familiarity which should have been profane and impossible. But, the players among the crowd knew...Nico belonged to Joseph Snowden and Rhys belonged to no-one but himself.

No, that was not accurate. The players and employees of the club believed Rhys Lorraine belonged to Daniel D'Loup; it was only the Undead and the tchatcha who could identify otherwise, going on scent. Daniel D'Loup said nothing to dissuade any rumor, but he knew that the benu malakh was not bedding the boy. He would have smelled the claim upon the young, fiery malakh. More importantly, he would have smelled the boy's unique stench upon the dark-haired benu. He did not scent these things; not in a manner to suggest a sexual union. Daniel and Rhys were not lovers and Rhys was not Daniel's boy, even if the majority here believed otherwise.

Still, such a erring belief did not stop the more daring, in this place. Rhys was courted by many, as was Nicolai. Nico flirted, in response, but never strayed from him; Rhys Lorraine did as he pleased, but was exceptionally prudent. This was for the sake of Mathilda Curran, of course; there was no one more likely to be hurt by such flagrant whoring than the abandoned mother of that tchatcha's son and he was aware of what seemed to elude even Mathilda's notice. Rhys might do as he pleased, but he was certainly careful and discreet; Mathilda only knew or suspected the tchatcha of a small handful among the dozens.

He did not need light to see the denizens of the temple-styled dance room. Shadows hid nothing from his eyes. He was fully aware, with a flick of his eyes, that Daniel D'Loup was intently watching the dancers---in particular, the benu was watching Rhys and Nico with steady eyes that burned in the dark. He could smell the lust from where he sat, several meters away. Everywhere, all around him, there was the odor of need and want, and the Helvetian malakh's ever-changing scent was one he understood best. It was difficult to ignore the smell and feel of flesh-trapped sunshine.

Joseph gave thought to his past, letting his mind wander.

He had lived his early life in a village just outside the walls of Jerusalem, born to a woman of Aramaic descent, and suffered a stammer that made normal speech almost impossible. He believed her story, for he'd had no other voice to heed; she told him he was born in a year the Christians named 1122, when the magnificent Hugh dePayens was in charge of the very young militia templi, also known as the Knights of the Temple. He'd never known his father, but his mother had claimed that he came from royal blood---the blood of the first Crusaders. He was part European, but had no inkling if this alien part of him was Frank, Teutonic, or Anglo-Saxon.

He could remember the first time he'd left his home in the barren hills outside the city walls. His mother had taken him to the commanders who lived at the Temple of the Well at the age of eight or perhaps nine, in the year 1131. This was a mere three years after the Knights' Rule was adopted at the Council of Troyes. At this time, he knew nothing of such things. All he was aware of was that these tall, fierce men were *The Poor Fellow Soldiers of Christ and the Temple of Solomon.* He was given to them as a stable-boy after a heated, semi-private conversation between two of the elder knights and his mother.

He'd often considered the idea that his father must be among these bearded warriors who wore white and whose most secular and public beliefs seemed to be much more rigid and faithful and mystical than the beliefs and behaviors of other knights he had seen. Of course, he had never been given much opportunity to watch any knights for more than a minute or two as they passed through the nearly decimated village of his childhood. He thought the militia templi were special because of their devotions; they did not act like the other Christians he had encountered in his early life.

It was while working in the Temple Mount stables with the giant warhorses and donkeys and camels that he had first become aware of the whispers and the music, in the year 1133.

It was spring and already quite hot and he was a mere eleven year old boy, trying to clean in the stone-vaulted stables. He was kicked in the chest one day by a particularly high-spirited donkey mare whose name translated into Aramaic as Amares, *'God Has Promised'*. The donkey's hoof left a strange mark on his chest, cut deep into the flesh above his breast. The distorted shape of the mark was remarkably like a large heart, smooth and etched as by a branding iron, and it lay directly in the center of his chest.

Bleeding and dazed and breathless, he laid upon the straw and realized that, with his doubled vision, he could see things beyond the range of normal sight. Spirits and angels and demons walked among them---and they were right in the stables! The other stable-boys ran to get the priests and the physicians from the House, squalling that Yusef Bar-Ya'el was dead and bleeding terribly.

The music he heard, in his ringing ears, it was the music of the celestial spheres and he became aware, as he lay silent in his agony, that all the voices of the world created this music. Dissonant or perfect, every voice was part of the choir and without it, the Universe was not in harmony. He became aware of a whisper in his ear that seemed to have no point of origin outside himself; the whisper was without sex and spoke of how discordant the world was, how terrible the music sounded. The whisper spoke of the Lamb and the Lion, the Bar-Kochba, the Sephiroth, the Paean Tree...he had only heard of one or two of these sacred things, the others were rumors only.

He saw, as the whisper went on and the world swam and buzzed in his sight, an endless scrubby dune. There was a tree at the bottom, off to one side, but it was burned by the sun and destroyed by the drought. Blinking did not make these visions go away. Then, as he despaired and listened to both the whisper and the sound of his fellow stable-boys still running around and screaming for help, a figure appeared in his sight. In the peripheral of his awareness, a figure came from beyond the dune and the tree and began to approach him in a casual manner. As the figure sauntered, the dune sprouted grass and flowers and the tree came back to life, producing pomegranates as big as a boy's head.

In his ear, the whisper came: *'First came the Lion, whose very blood creates life where no life can be sustained. The Lion shall return to you and you shall follow the Lion, for your heart is of his flesh and will burn as an eternal beacon. You will live to see the Lion return.'*

The figure came onwards but he could not clearly see its face.

When he came fully aware again, he was startled by the appearance of a tawny, bearded face leaning over him where he lay. Immediately, his first thoughts were of being devoured by the creature. His second thoughts were of how blameless he would die, as he had worked hard to follow the Hebrew faith he'd been born to and to accept the Christian faith of the Knights who had taken him in. He gasped and the words that escaped him were a superstitious prayer that his mother had taught him: *'al-Mahdi Asad Bomani!'*

The whispers were still there, faint and fading, but his mind was taken from the awareness by the pain and the voices. He was in agony from the wound in his chest and the voices which talked above him spoke of healing. He was taken to one of the refectories nearby and his wound was treated. Indeed, as he looked back on it, he realized that, from the very start, he was given better treatment than another stable-boy would have received.

The priests and lay brothers of the militia templi would not answer many of his questions, during those first days, and treated him with a strange and silent behavior that seemed to be one part awe and one part fear. It was only on the third day that he began to get answers for the unique manner in which he was handled.

The same great man, with the tawny hair and pale hazel eyes, came to him in the stone refectory and offered him a cup of diluted wine---not strong enough to make him insane with drunkenness, but enough to slake his constant thirst and enable him to speak without stammering. For the first time in his life, he could talk without despair, for his words were easily understood by the man who sat by his narrow, white bed.

This man was Sir Arthur Rheims Caledonia Snowden, of Britain, and he dressed in plain dun robes and trousers with worn, scuffed boots as he sat in the refectory, under an open window, and talked with Yusef. He would never wear his white coat and gloves while not in his vigilance as a Knight Brother and this was no matter of being vigilant to the Rule. Among the Knights and the Temple House, this man was known simply as Snowden, but he told the wounded boy in the bed that they were to be friends and so...it was Arthur and Joseph. Arthur said that the name must be Joseph, not Yusef, for the sake of keeping to the Christian way.

Arthur Snowden spoke of what must happen now...for Joseph had seen a vision in the stables and God had left a mark on Joseph, as proof of the boy's purpose in life. Did he not know of what he said, while in the throes of that divine communication? Arthur did, for Arthur had been the witness to it, and Arthur was speaking on his behalf before the other Knights and the priests.

Joseph was to become his squire, to bear arms at his side in preparation of battle, and to care for those belongings which were his to handle, under the Rule. This included a warhorse, two donkeys, and his armaments. This also meant that Joseph wouldn't work in the stables anymore.

Arthur had explained, as he lay there in the refectory with his narrow chest heavily bandaged in white linen, that it was forbidden for a boy so young to become part of the Order, even as a squire. That, until he was grown into a man and able to work as the squire of a Knight Brother, he must attend school and be educated. He would be educated as a warrior and a priest and given the same wages as a stable-boy, with which to help his mother.

When he asked for the reason why---why would he be given such an honor, when he was not baptized a Christian?---Arthur Snowden told him that there was a story in the history of the Saracen and Jewish faiths which spoke of the Lion. It was a story that many discounted but which certain men among the Knights held sacred...nearly as sacred as they held Christ Himself. It was the story of a man not yet born whose spirit was so great and powerful as to encompass the Temple and all its mysteries. In the story, this man was the sole possessor of a sacred word---the great unknown and ineffable name of God. The same story told of how this man, the Lion, carried the All-Seeing Eye within his own beating heart.

This legendary man was perhaps of no religious conviction, but he would lead all warriors of a pure faith to live in brotherhood. This was to say, the Saracen would bow to the man, for the story of this Lion came from the Jewish and Islamic history of Egypt.

If this great man were to come to the world among the Knights of the Temple, the war against inequity would be won and the Saracens would see the Christians as brothers. It was a belief that the Holy Church itself did not hold, but which these few, certain men among the Knights had come to see as important; as important as caring for their fellow mankind. For that was what this great man was meant to do---bring about an age of harmony in the name of mankind.

This great man had come before the Lamb, in the time of Christ...and yet, the story was older than that. The great man had appeared in ancient times, living in Egypt during the time of Jewish slavery. This was where the tale began: the Jews had carried the story with them of a Lion whose valor was beyond that of kings and priests. The story had passed down into Islamic faith, speaking of this same Lion of Kemet who lived in the time of an ancient and powerful Egyptian king.

It was believed that this Lion had lived many times, always when an oppressed people needed him the most. It was believed he would return, for the stories spoke of such...and was it not written in the holy places?

Yusef, renamed Joseph, had not known of words written in holy places, but he knew something of the Lion. His mother had talked of that to him, when he was very young, and this was where his prayer found its wellspring. *'al-Mahdi Asad Bomani'*. Protector Lion. His mother had told him that they were of the al-Mahdi Asad, sacred in ancient times and no longer revered or acknowledged in this time of Christians with blood on their hands.

Arthur Snowden told him he was to become a squire and, later, a Knight Brother, because of what had been heard and seen by those present in the stables in the aftermath of Joseph's wounding. The wound had glowed like fire, its shape much like a fiery heart, and Arthur himself had heard the words of Joseph's prayer to the Protector Lion. Arthur himself had heard Joseph speak of the Lion and a renewing of the land.

He was considered a holy relic unto himself and therefore, he must be raised carefully and with the proper education, for the Knight Brothers believed him to be a sign of the Lion's favor. Arthur Snowden had claimed the right to be father and guardian to Joseph; he would no longer be known by the name his mother had given him of Yusef Bar-Ya'el but by the name of Joseph Louis Rheims Snowden.

Yusef had accepted these things; what else could he do? To not work so hard in the stable, taking the brunt of abuse from Christian boys and men, was a blessing. He would learn what the Knights wished him to learn and he would give his life to their cause.

Previously uneducated, Joseph had suddenly found himself immersed in learning several languages and the history of the world from the Scion point of view. Secretly, the Scion priests of the militia templi did not think the Church's view on history was complete. The Church believed that nothing but Christian history mattered and that all else was evil; the Scion knew that the world of Christianity had started in other faiths and other histories and they struggled to include these, while upholding Christian might and valor. This was done for the sake of understanding their enemy better, but it was in those histories that the mysteries began to surface. These were mysteries declaimed by the Church as evil, even as Christian faith had their sources in them. Such was the Ark of the Covenant and the Ark of Grace and the Lion, the al-Mahdi Asad, with his sacred words and the All-Seeing Eye in his heart.

As a squire, he learned warrior craft and became very skilled with a sword and the horse. He kept his hair clipped short, as many of the Knights did, and let his beard grow. In the early mornings, before the world became alive with the sun's return, he lay half-awake and listened to the whispers in his ear and heart...the whispers that revealed mysteries to him which the Scion was eager to hear of.

His existence and his ability to talk of such secret and sacred truths only made him more important. It was believed he must live among the Knights and take part in the Scion mysteries, to ensure that the Lion's return would be recognized. For the militia templi were men and they were wise enough to see the truth of history. If Christ's appearance among the Jews had gone unrecognized by so many, what of the Lion, who had returned much more often? Could he appear among them and not be realized? It was possible---and so Joseph's life was tied to the militia templi and Arthur Snowden, for Joseph was the one soul most likely to recognize the Lion of the Temple.

Upon reaching the age of majority and being accepted as a man of worth, having been adopted and trained by Arthur Snowden, Joseph became a Knight Brother at the age of twenty-three in the year 1145, having taken the vows of chastity and poverty and obedience.

But, war came again; he left Jerusalem in 1146 to ride into battle at Arthur Snowden's side. It was two years later, in 1148, that his life took its turn and he discovered the true meaning behind the whispers that claimed he would live to see the Lion's return.

Outside Damascus, the plains were embattled. Through the war, he had served as priest and Knight Brother, working as both warrior and healer. Yet, he did these things only in loyalty to his fellow Knights and the Temple, for he knew the cause was lost. The whispers that came to him every morning in the early gray dawn spoke of how wrong these wars were...of how they were doomed to fail because of the war's method. The knights of all orders were killing not only warriors but women and children and the Universe would not abide such a horror.

He didn't speak of this failure to any but Arthur Snowden, for it would be considered a treason and a heretical belief. Arthur Snowden, wiser than most of his Brother Knights, realized the truth in Joseph's private words and did what he could to prevent the slaughter of innocents.

In a great and terrible battle, on July 25 of 1148, Joseph was struck down just after noon. He fell to the sword of his enemy because the sun blinded him. But, at dusk, the plains lay silent as the battle was finished, and Joseph Snowden was still alive but only barely. As he wept from pain, half-dead under the body of his slaughtered enemy, something crept from the hills nearby the city of Damascus by the dark of night. This something was intent on enjoying the spoils of war; it was a blood-drinker, a lamia, a child of Lilit. A vampire.

The vampire found him and he'd struggled, trying to keep it from taking him. In the struggle, the vampire was wounded badly...and the unclean blood soaked into his exposed wounds and even into his mouth. The vampire left him there, dead...but, the change had already begun. Just before dawn, he'd awakened again and felt a sense of great and irrational panic at the knowledge of the rising sun. His wounds were healed and he was able to escape the crush of dead bodies with ease, fleeing quickly to find shelter.

Digging under the scrubland dirt, he'd hid himself from daylight and wakened again at dusk with a terrible hunger that he couldn't understand. He was of a thought that the blood loss had left him unhinged, for nothing appeared the same; the world looked and sounded entirely different. He hadn't given thought to how he'd managed to live, after being attacked by something so obviously a monster.

Heading for the camp of his brethren Knights, he found wine and food and succor with the militia templi survivors. But, it wasn't wine or bread he wanted. The wine tasted delicious, but it didn't help his thirst...and the bread tasted of ashes on his tongue. The sight and smell of someone preparing to roast a haunch of meat sent the priestly Knight into paroxysms of fury and trembling.

But, raw meat wasn't what he needed or wanted, despite his attempts to assuage the hunger with these. He disgusted and frightened his fellow Knight Brothers and the priests and all the warriors by devouring the bloody meat straight from the spit. When they tried to restrain him, he turned upon them and murder was done. He couldn't be injured, he couldn't even be slowed; he killed a squire with his bare hands. The surprise of this brought him to a stop. He allowed himself to be put in chains while the Knights and priests decided on what should be done. The blood on his hands, the blood of the squire, was too much to resist. He licked his fingers clean while on his knees at the fire, to the absolute horror of those men he had called brothers.

After the other soldiery and warriors had left, heading away from the city walls after four days of defeat, Joseph's own camp stayed, pondering his transformation. It was decided by those who studied such things among the militia templi that he had become an abomination---they knew of such things as vampires and demons and malakh---and realized that there was no cure. No amount of praying or fasting or study would help Joseph Snowden. They sought a way to kill him, instead. They gave him no more blood and no meat and put him in stronger chains; chains specifically forged for the Undead and for demons and malakh.

It was his howling which brought the other Undead to the camp.

After two or three days in a black tent, locked within chains he couldn't break, his hunger grew so strong that he began to scream and his screams weren't like the shrieks of a human. In the hills, the vampires heard him---they hunted the city of Damascus. It was this city the Knights had come to, with the other warriors who would fight to preserve Christianity in the Holy Land. After three nights of listening to Joseph's newborn vampire howls, the other Undead came down from the hills.

He had not known then---he quickly learned---that vampires were not notoriously clan-like. They were loners and preferred to hunt in small packs of two and three, if they did not hunt alone. This was a group numbering six, existing together only by the common denominator of one vampire Master, who was Sire to them. It was this Sire's wish alone which kept them as a mob in the same area.

It was their Sire who decided to find the newborn fledgling who was disturbing the four-legged game in the hills with his screams. He led his family down to the camp after dark and left them there, out of sight, while he approached the tent, hidden in a glamour which prevented the human militia templi and Crusade-warriors from seeing anything amiss. There, in the tent, Joseph told the story to this Sire, told of how he'd been nearly killed in battle and then fought off the strange creature after the sun went down. The Sire heard of what had happened since---Joseph Snowden hadn't understood, even then, what he was or why his fellow Knight Brothers kept him locked in a black tent.

Hearing the story, the Sire recognized that it was one of his own clan who had accidentally created the newborn. He decided to free Joseph from the Knights. What began as a small operation to break the chains and lead him away from the encampment turned into a horrific battle when the Knights and soldiery realized that there was something unnatural and unclean in their midst---something much more powerful in its intent than Joseph.

Five vampires and their Sire wiped out the remaining camp of humans, leaving none alive. The key to the magic-forged chain was produced from the body of a dead monk and Joseph was taken by the Undead to live in the hills above the city of Damascus and the plain where so many humans had died in the name of religious intolerance, ignorance, and greed.

It was there, with his new 'family', that he stayed for exactly two full moons. Two calendar months. He had quickly seen the darkness and the evil for what they were; the human part of his mind was horrified, being a trained and devoted Knight Brother. The vampire part of his mind, being much more in control of his body, possessed gifts and understandings which he had not before suspected could exist.

He had learned very quickly, studying his 'family' and himself...he was dead, forever dead, but he could not lay in the good earth and rot. Instead, he must prowl in the night and sleep during the day, hungry for the blood and flesh of living mortals. He was a thing unholy, cast from God's sight. But, he did recognize what it was, at last, for had his mother not told him stories of Lilit's children? Had he not studied within the Scion and the Temple, to recognize the two different kinds of offspring from Lilit?

Better than the knowledge he carried, from his days in the militia templi, he had found that, as a vampire, he did not necessarily *have* to sleep and he no longer needed any food but blood. His 'family' slept during the day, but he did not always follow their pattern. Indeed, his body only required a few hours of sleeping rest and was voraciously endowed with energy and strength.

On the last night he prowled Damascus with his 'family', he decided upon his course of action. Before dawn, when their Sire and all five of his Undead siblings, including the one whose blood had un-created him, lay torpid in the cave that served as their barracks, Joseph drew his sword and beheaded every last one. It was a difficult thing---the sun's slow rising made him drowsy and he lacked the demonic strength only the night could bring. But, having set his mind upon freedom, he did what he found necessary and rid himself of the others. They were foul and did not recognize God in anything, not even their victims.

Once they were dispatched and existed as nothing more than dust that glittered and smelled of exotic spices, he lay down and slept the hours of daylight away. Awake once more at twilight, he went into Damascus and began to work at surviving without the company of others like himself. He did not feel an emotional need for the vampires, but it was understood that, to be safe, he might need someone to guard his rest. He had learned this, among them, and believed it for how weak he felt in the daylight.

He didn't dare sleep among mortals for they might spy out the truth of him and he didn't dare buy just any slave to play guard and servant for a slave might revolt or gossip. But, more than anything at all, he wished to see Jerusalem again and to speak with his mother. She would surely not be aware of what her son had become, as long as he governed his hunger and kept his wits about him. She was aged and going blind.

He'd set out for Jerusalem, traveling only at night, and hiding himself in the ground like a scorpion or a snake during the hours when the sun made everything hot and bright. He wore the heavy robes of the Muslim, covering his face, and painted his face and hands with the brown dye found in the roots of certain plants. Thus, he'd disguised the pale flesh that death had brought to him and thus did he protect himself without a watchful guard during all hours.

In Jerusalem, he went to his mother's house and discovered that the blind have a power that the seeing mortal doesn't possess; they can become aware of the truth without words or eyes. His mother suspected what he was and he made a confession to her. She told him to go to the Priory at the Temple and talk with the elders among his Scion compatriots, but that first he must go to the wise men of their village---the ones who were still alive, after the coming of Christian warriors. These things he did.

The wise men told him that, if he was alive and yet not alive, then he was a monstrosity...if he could not procreate as the Universe and the Father demanded of all his creations, then he was not a man any longer. But, if he was still aflame with the desire for the purpose of his life, then he must be something more than evil.

The Scion elders, monks and priests, were frightened of him, but they were more aware of his visions and the whispers he had spoken of, as a youth. If he was still alive and yet not alive, then it must be God's will...and he must devote himself once more to the Mysteries and make of himself what God wished. If his purpose was to see the coming of the Lion of God, then this must be the reason for his continuing existence, even if his existence was blood-driven. He must truly be the Wandering Jew. For it had been said, in his youth, when he had the vision in the stables, that his destiny was in the blood.

If he could master his hunger, then he could live in the Temple's depths and study; in this way, he could carry on the mission for the militia templi's Scion with each generation that passed. They would endure the monster of him if he would work to hear more of the whispers.

He had lied, to the priests of the Scion, in order to win their help; they had let him stay in the Temple, hidden from the world, on the belief that he could still hear the whispers of God in his heart...the heart that no longer beat below the scar on his chest. He could not hear the whispers or the music; he was deaf to the innate knowledge of the Mysteries which had once been his. He could only pay lip service to these Mysteries, even as he continued to watch and serve.

Still thinking on his past, Joseph poured himself more beer from the pitcher that sat before him. He took a drink of its warm froth and frowned, bitterly, watching Nicolai and Rhys.

Chapter Three

Daniel, a retired kite operative born in the year 1613, could not stop the muscles between his shoulders as they gave a spasm at the way Valeska drew Rhys close. The two boys writhed, swaying as a cobra might sway. Valeska and Rhys stood, nose to nose and hip to hip, wearing their mutual passion as a second skin.

Dieu.

The spasm grew, returning to knock at the back door of his brain. It gained admittance without conscious thought and traveled the length of his spine. Now, he trembled in the dark, knowing he had no choice but to ignore the steady thump of blood in his chinois.

It would be emotional suicide to admit his love to Rhys; with such knowledge in his grasp, the garcon had taken Mattie's heart to pieces with only a few, well-placed---but devastating---attacks. Gabe, of course, being the largest and most permanent. Twelve years ago, on the night he had taken custody of Rhys, he had not imagined the frail-seeming child would live to see maturity. Rhys had exceeded his imagination, within the first year, showing an unfathomable depth of comprehension for the world. Social innocence aside at such a tender age, the garcon had already owned a savvy grace for the finer arts of covert operative work.

His sin, his terrible *love*...it should not exist. He knew it should not exist. Had he not taken Rhys as his 'apprentice', even allowing Steven's lab-grown son to work for the BDS under an assumed identity? Rhys had shown a true talent for the job of a kite operative, revealing how very well he was trained. Even as he and Mattie had used the garcon for the genetic skills Rhys alone possessed, he had felt a serious qualm at the fact of how they put a teenaged boy in the field, as an undercover agent, but did nothing to rectify the situation in the face of how often Rhys succeeded when no other person could.

Truly, Rhys was not only Steven's son; Lorraine had put his indelible mark upon the tchatcha, impossible to forget or miss.

For the last twelve years, he had taught Rhys how to love the world; he had taught Rhys all the social skills the garcon had been denied by the nature of his childhood. In the last eight years, Rhys had worked with him as his apprentice and, after they had retired from the CIA, his partner. Yet, even now, at twenty-three, Rhys could not survive on his own. His garcon needed a master, someone with the ability to harness the *frightening* creature that existed behind Rhys' laughing gaze.

Mattie had tried, giving into the unusual desire she felt, taking the garcon as her lover...but, after two years of Rhys, his ex-partner had given up. Rhys could not be leashed by the blonde Brit; instead of managing any control, Mattie had broken her own heart and withdrawn from the relationship in the last months of a gravid state. She had tried to deny Rhys in his hunger to become a father, but the garcon was devious and had given Mattie a son despite all her precautions. Gabriel Todd Curran was nearly a year old now and bore several traits which suggested to him that Rhys' genetic legacy would, with time, reveal itself in Mattie's youngest son. The child was a budding sakau, already able to pick up on the emotional thoughts of the adults around him.

These days, Mattie ran her business and networked the players. She allowed Rhys free access to their son, remained a friend, and overtly seemed to hold nothing against him or against Rhys. Yet, he felt a sense of concern for what had been destroyed; he suspected Mattie would have kept Rhys forever, except for one niggling detail...Rhys was loyal to none that he had ever laid eyes upon. Mattie could not accept second-place in love and Rhys had never put anyone upon a pedestal. True, the garcon was loyal to work partners and to friends, but he had yet to see the lover who could capture Rhys' heart wholly. Rhys loved no one in the deep, abiding manner of a mate; there were none to ever live in that singular, holy place in his garcon's heart.

He imagined Mattie believed them to be lovers, he and Rhys. They had lived together in the same house since the chilled, rainy night Golden Wolf had thrown Perseus Shadow out. Pregnant and tired of Rhys' dominant malakh behaviors, a year ago, Mattie had decided that she would rather not live with the garcon; Rhys had come home one evening to find himself shut out of the blonde Brit's bed and heart. Leaving in the hurricane-like thunderstorm which raged over New Orleans that night, Rhys had walked from the corner of Esplanade and Chartres to his house on Tchoupitoulas.

Daniel finally closed his eyes on the sight of his garcon dancing with the vampire gypsy and leaned back in the wooden chair, falling deeper into the shadows, as he remembered the night in his thoughts. He slept hard and deep, by nature, and had woken to find Rhys standing over his bed in the dark, clothes soaked through and shivering from the chill. His partner had entered his house through the upstairs balcony door, having climbed the wrought iron trellis which stretched from bottom porch to top porch on the front side of his two-story Italianate house.

There was a smell which came unbidden to mind, the scent of that night. Rhys' skin stayed at a feverish temperature and, when soaked with cold rain, steamed the odd tchatchau malakh odor of copper and fading stargazer lilies, that scent which made him think sometimes of the more familiar acacia-wood and lotus. In the dark, Rhys had stood at the foot of his bed and trembled from the cold and thorn-bridled grief.

The garcon's breath had sounded ragged in the silence between the spatters of growing thunder; Rhys' gaze on him in the dark of his bedroom had felt heavier than a mountain and hotter than the blue heart of a flame, but his partner had done nothing but breathe and shiver...until he himself had whispered and the whisper had startled Rhys, making the garcon blink with a stupefied, open-mouthed gape. It was as if he had sent an arrow or a bullet to the very core of his partner, a sudden and terrifying reminder of their strange, unlikely bond.

He had whispered. *'Stop weighing your soul against the stones of Hell. You need no invitation, mon cher.'*

They had their own rooms, their own space within the house, but often, for no other reason than mutual comfort and safety, they shared his bed with all due chastity. He frequently woke to find Rhys crawling into the blankets at his side, shivering with silent emotions that could never find a way to be expressed. For whatever reason Rhys might have, coming from a life unlike any other, his garcon often could not bear to sleep alone.

To this very night, he did not understand why those words had come from his tongue. He believed the sentiment might have its birth in the bond itself and how the bond had come to exist. Being given the custody of a lethal child in the budding of puberty, he had prepared himself for what might possibly happen. Rhys was not like other children; Rhys was a well-trained weapon who retained psychological triggers and a lack of human morals. He had believed Rhys to be dangerous, naturally, and prepared himself for the duty of deactivating Lorraine's masterpiece. What he had not given allowance for was how he would come to rely on the garcon's skills...or how easily he would fall into affection.

From the very first night, on that moonlit wooded hillside, he had felt the bond begin; Rhys needed him, he needed Rhys, and they danced the waltz of two souls who revolved around each other in mutual commitment. He could no more abandon the garcon than he could abandon his own heartbeat. It had started with the moment they looked at each other, that first night, and had endured every night since.

One moment, he had been only Daniel D'Loup, benu malakh and CIA kite operative, and, the next moment, looking down into the young face of his charge, he had become something entirely else. For, meeting that young-old, wise stare, he had found himself lost in the infernal abyss that was Rhys. With eyes the mixed and muddied color of sky and sand, the garcon had seen past his face and his brain and into his soul...and with the tiny flick of a curving, shy smile, had forgiven him for every sin he had ever committed in his *long* life.

He had let Rhys sleep in his bed when necessary from the very start, when the boy seemed to need the comfort of a living creature to share the quiet of rest.

His affections were not paternal, by any stretch of imagination; they had changed a number of years ago, before Rhys reached the American ideal of adulthood. At only seventeen, Rhys had captured his more sensual imagination and held it in chaste devotion. He kept his own council for that sinful affection, but he knew Mattie was aware of it. Rhys might have no concept for what he felt---being unable to read his emotions on the deeper levels---but Mattie was aware. Little escaped Golden Wolf. Doubtless, she believed they were lovers now, for the nature of their bond had only deepened in the last year. Did she hate him for it? Did she hate him for accepting what she had turned aside?

Daniel slitted his eyes now to watch Rhys, once again. He lifted his glass to drain the last swallow of bourbon, enjoying the icy burn. Upon the heels of that action, he lit a cigarette from the packet on his table, and relaxed with a careless, Gallic movement of shoulders and hips. He was three hundred and ninety-two years old and, in only six months, that would increase by one more year. He was nineteen times older than his young partner, the one who---pitiless and unknowing---held his heart. Nineteen times twenty-one and this was only a few years older than he carried in his bones. He could remember what it had felt like to be Rhys' age; he had, at twenty-three, already owned more responsibility than he had wanted, and was that so different from the garcon? Rhys had owned responsibility since early youth, in the lab, and never failed to shoulder a new burden when it appeared. Let Rhys dance with the deadly gypsy creature, let Rhys enjoy the night. Rhys had few real pleasures and yet seemed to never lack for joy of one sort or another.

As he watched, Rhys tipped his head back with laughter at some murmured comment from Valeska, uncaring for the crowd of young dancers who moved and jostled them under the rolling strobe lights. When his garcon's throat was revealed, the Undead one gave a sharp-toothed smile and nuzzled at the fiery, thin flesh gleaming with perspiration.

He drew his breath in; the air burned jagged and sharp in his lungs and he held it as he saw the kiss turn bloody. Only a knowledgeable observer would be aware of Valeska's nature, would know what the gypsy vampire did *now* to Rhys. He knew...he watched with jaded eyes and knew that, in the shadows of the temple, Joseph Snowden watched the same show. Valeska was feeding on the fevered, sweet blood of a tchatcha malakh...the only one of his kind in the world.

Only a creature like Valeska would dare to do this; vampires were usually careful in their dealings with malakh...even a malakh such as Rhys, whose scent and heat seemed to draw them like moths to a candle's flame. Only Valeska would dare to touch Rhys so openly, taking blood in public---and Rhys thought nothing of it, for his garcon loved death and enjoyed the scalpel sharp pain of such a sacrifice. For Rhys, this public feeding was a ritual between himself and the most beautiful vampire they had yet to encounter...an undead thing worthy of his garcon's generosity.

He knew...Joe was watching, Joe could see the ritual. He did not know what Joe thought of such a display, for he had yet to speak of it with the ancient Templar. This was only the latest ritual in a long line spanning the last year, since Rhys had come to live in his house.

He frowned as Valeska licked at the wounds, forcing them shut, and then he saw nothing more as his attention was drawn away from the stage and the dancers. Through the crowd of university students who moved around the tables came a pair of humans who seemed to be headed in his direction. Daniel blew smoke from his nose and studied them, his gaze shuttering as he let his malakh senses take over.

The woman was inconsequential, for all her beauty...and she was a true beauty. Yet, she had the vapid, empty expression of a toy. This one was nothing to him, could do nothing; there was not even the hint of a mask about her demeanor. With bottle-blonde hair that fell about her shoulders like a thin veil, she was exactly what she presented herself to be, dressed in three inch heels and a strapless black sheath that hugged her lean thighs as she followed the man.

The man, on the other hand...this one was a *puzzle*. Tall and Saxon-lean, the man owned a dancer's grace. Powerfully built with muscles well-hidden under charcoal Armani, the figure glided through the shadows and the carnival strobe lights with the air of a feline. This was a predator masquerading in the disguise of a businessman. Unlike the woman, the man's hair was a natural golden blonde and straight, cut short; the front was brushed back from his clear, unmarked brow in a boyish manner than suggested lush nonchalance about appearances. Yet, he knew...this was not the case. It was contrived, from top to bottom.

Daniel took another drag from his cigarette and flicked the ashes into the clear glass ashtray that sat in the center of his table. Never did he take his eyes from the pair as they approached...and they did approach, headed in a beeline for him. The man carried two glasses and a wine bottle with the careless attitude of one who was unbothered by the impromptu, bohemian situation. Money would never be a problem for such a man...and he felt his interest piqued. A client? But, as the man reached his table, he realized his mistake; this man was no human. The cigarette smoke and heat had disguised a viable, important element of his ability to scent out malakh...this was a benu with some added ability he could not discern. Hence the appearance and the smooth grace...non?

He gave a thin smile of greeting that did not rise beyond his mouth.

"You're L'Epee D'Mort." The French title slid sleekly from the man's voice and it was suddenly easy to hear two things immediately; the malakh was British---cultured English, to be precise---and spoke French with a natural accent, which suggested he may have been taught the language from childhood. "Seigneur D'Loup."

He tilted his head to the side, letting his sable-dark, pigtailed hair slide against the shoulder of his white, collarless work shirt. With a raising of his left eyebrow, he spoke in a low voice that was nearly lost in the music. "Oui. Would you care to join me, m'sieur?"

The pair sat down across from him; the man pulled out the chair for the woman, having set the bottle and the glasses on the table's well-polished surface. Then, for a long moment of silence, he and the other malakh studied each other. He quickly discerned, from scent, that this was indeed a benu. But, there was more to it than this...something in the man's scent suggested a greater legacy than that of the benu...something he could not place.

He let his gaze flow off the man and he looked closely at the woman; she was, as he suspected, perfectly human and apparently harmless. She was wide-eyed, gazing around the temple in open wonder. He chuckled, at last finding the place to begin. "You have never seen such a place, ma chere?"

She shook her blonde head and smiled back, showing even, white teeth. "No."

"Maya doesn't go to clubs...not clubs such as this one, anyway." The man was pouring the wine, handing him a glass. "I spoke with the bartender and she told me I could find you here. She recommended that you might be the man I need to talk with."

"Perhaps." He answered, noncommittal, as he took the glass of dark red merlot. "If you pass Golden Wolf's inspection and she makes a recommendation, then you may assume she knows what she speaks of. Why would she suggest that we speak, m'sieur?"

For a moment, he suspected a trap; he always did, it was part of his nature.

The man took a sip of the merlot and smiled, more at ease---or seemingly so. "My name is Sterling. Waric Sterling. I'm looking for a handful of particular items and they have eluded my grasp...but, your bartender suggested you might have a special understanding of how to retrieve such."

He took a sip from his own glass. It was an excellent merlot with a hint of cherries in the bouquet. He looked away from the table, towards the stage, and let his gaze slide over Rhys and Valeska, who were now dancing with a nubile human fille, a shared 'girlfriend' whose name was Tennyson. The two garcons sandwiched the dark-skinned fille between them, a sexy slide of limbs and hips and chest that he understood well. At last, he answered, not taking his eyes from the trio of dancers. "I do not do retrievals, m'sieur. You might find what you seek with one of the others here."

"Your bartender, she seemed convinced you would be the perfect one for such a job."

The man named Sterling insisted with a shark-cruel smile, his accent clean and Oxford collegiate. "The retrieval itself is no matter...a simple thing. But, it's the place that needs your touch. The bartender said that you have a special understanding of the Middle East. Egypt in particular. What I need is a man who can go under the wires and around the local authorities and accomplish what has to be done with a minimum of fuss or notice. For something of that nature, a native works best...and the lovely woman behind the bar said you were the man to see."

Daniel had to admit to himself that this was perhaps the truth. He raised his glass for another sip of wine, musing on the matter at hand. Through more than a century and a half's experience in the Sahara desert and among the Berber, the Bedouin, and the Seidi and Misrene, he was perhaps the only man for the job, if the job required finesse and a knowledge of Egyptian culture and society. Yet, he wanted to investigate the 'job' more carefully. He couched it in the language Sterling would appreciate. "Tell me about these items, m'sieur...perhaps I shall be properly intrigued."

"Would you rather find a quiet room to discuss the..." Sterling had to force his voice louder to be heard over the raucous applause and laughter of the crowd on the stage-floor. For a long minute, the blonde Englishman blinked and looked around in surprise at the volume, which was louder than the music it concluded.

Daniel smiled to himself, not allowing it to show on his face, as Rhys sauntered off the stage, his arms wrapped around the shoulders of both Valeska and Tennyson, who were grinning wild in the way of their kind. They accepted their accolades with pride and gracious words, moving through the knot of people. The three needed nothing from the college children who offered drinks and telephone numbers and sly, glancing strokes from hands that would give more pleasure if it was wanted. All his garcon might do was drop a hint that he might enjoy...and anything Rhys wanted, these hedonists would provide.

When the three managed to reach the table, he said nothing as Rhys kissed first Valeska and then Tennyson, raw boy hands far more gentle than they appeared to be. Valeska gave a laugh and glided off, the clean aloe scent of his Undead flesh leaving a strange perfume in the air as it moved past him. From the corner of his eye, he watched the gypsy vampire disappearing into the shadows where Joe Snowden sat, hidden from sight. The Childe returned to its master, its Sire.

Tennyson lingered, being held in place by Rhys, who whispered in her ear, raw-boned fingers cupping the Creole girl's face on one side. He saw how Tennyson's green-gray eyes flashed momentarily with silent laughter, he could not look away as the garcon's hand slid from chocolate velvet cheek to long coal-shiny braids with their gold beads and to a thin shoulder before sleeking over the red silk of Tennyson's shirt. He wondered, idly, if Rhys had seduced the girl yet. It would be like his garcon...to slide past the defenses and sensibilities of a woman who seemed to be a femme lesbian, to see where his sensual ambitions could take him.

Then, Tennyson was moving away, headed for the doorway that led back into the bar, her round hips swaying from side to side with an erotic grace. She moved like a woman on a mission, all business and fiery toss of her plaited hair; it was a rhythm all her own, the Creole sense of self.

He did not bother to rise, introducing his garcon. "M'sieur Sterling, this is Rhys...he is my partner. Garcon, sit...M'sieur Sterling has a proposition for us, a job that we might consider." As an afterthought, he nodded at the woman. "This is M'sieur Sterling's friend, Maya."

Rhys did as he suspected the garcon would; with a flowing step all his own, Rhys bowed to the woman and took her hand from the table's edge, kissing it with the genteel courtesy of a man born a century ago. Sienna brown hair, damp with sweat, slid against olive-fawn throat and cheeks, framing the soft face; his garcon's voice was a husky murmur, barely audible. "Ma chere, you are *an enchantment* for the eyes."

He did not need to hear it from Rhys to know that his partner was aware of what Sterling was; it was in the predatory smile that the garcon gave, now, shaking the Englishman's hand.

Sterling took the fore once again and suggested, still grasping Rhys' hand. "Perhaps we can retire to some quieter room, to discuss this matter?"

"Yeah. Sounds cool." Rhys withdrew, straightening up; as he watched from under his lashes, he saw how the garcon turned half away, as if to show them his back. But, he was aware of what drew Rhys' attention. Something moved in the shadows of the furthest corner, where Joe Snowden and Valeska sat. Rhys' predatory smile curved into a slow smirk and then, with no effort at all and a flicker of those quick eyes, the danger was past and his garcon was the genteel host. "Let me get my drink from Tennyson and I'll join you upstairs, okay?"

Ah. So, that was where Tennyson Beaulieu had disappeared to---l'fille went to the bar to fill a drink order. Daniel nodded and stood, suggesting it to their 'guests'. "M'sieur, ma chere, we have an office here, in the upstairs. If you would..."

They followed him through the back of the temple, past the shadowed corners and the DJ's booth, to the stairs that led up to the second story, where the offices were located. He carried his glass and Sterling carried the bottle, Maya following like the obedient toy she seemed to be. He wondered what he could ask for a job that required him to steal; he was not accustomed to taking such assignments, preferring to leave such petty work to others. Rhys had no qualms about theft, but it was really beneath his standards.

Yet, *Egypt*? Might he make the journey to see his son Alexander and the oasis and the people of the village he had left behind? To finally visit the grave of his dead wife, Muhjahri, and pay the respects he had failed to pay in her declining years? To breathe the open desert air of his own chosen homeland once more? To walk in the trees and fields by the most magnificent river in the world? He could certainly make a side-trip, to the Faiyum, once the job was finished, and force Alexander to speak with him, face to face.

Ah, oui, he would like to see Egypt again.

Chapter Four

As he watched them dance, he became aware of Daniel D'Loup once more. Daniel's attention was shifting from the stage. He flicked his eyes sideways and watched as two figures approached through the rolling strobe lights. They were headed for the benu malakh's table. The ruggedly handsome Helvetian child of angels had company, it seemed. He frowned harder, his brows drawing together, as he watched the two.

The man was a benu malakh of a rare breed and didn't appear, on the surface, as he did under. Not a shape shifter, yet...something more insidious. His face was the true face, but he was much older than he appeared to be; but, yet, differently than a benu. He was of the benu, for there was a whiff of sunlight on his well-dressed body, but it was far more than simply benu. His scent, indeed, was difficult to place in a darkened room full of sweating mortals and malakh and mutants, all of which smelled of a feast to him. Was this a witch, then? A benu gifted in glamours?

He decided it must be so and turned his attention to the woman.

The woman was...mystery. As he watched the blonde woman walk in her short red dress, he lost sight of her several times. She was clearly in his sight and then...she was gone, disappearing only to reappear within less than a second. Too fast for mortal or malakh eyes, it was odd. She had no scent, no mortal gleam about her skin. It was as if she was not really there at all. Could she be a glamour? A true glamour, existing only in and from the spell?

Joseph straightened his shoulders against the chair he sat in, feeling the cold wood on the naked spots his sleeveless undershirt exposed. Now, he slouched, sliding further down so that he could watch without being noticed by D'Loup. It was not that he cared whether or not he elicited jealousy or concern or enmity---he cared not---it was for the sake of watching. He wanted to know something of these two and what they might possibly want from the benu malakh that he could hardly call his elder, even if Mathilda Curran trusted the Helvetian as she trusted few others.

He did not take his eyes off them nor give his wayward childe any attention on the dance stage until Tennyson Beaulieu showed herself in the room. Joseph smelled the dark-skinned girl before he was aware of it; she had a unique perfume and one that pleased him.

Now, he homed in on her with the voracious awareness of a predator. He could willingly sell his soul for this one, if he had a soul left to sell, yet he did nothing to show it in any manner. It wouldn't be seemly if she became knowledgeable of his desires or understanding; for he did understand her better than she could imagine. For he knew what she was; he knew who she was, in the deepest well of her spirit.

He might disdain Rhys Lorraine's affections for Nicolai, but he welcomed Tennyson Beaulieu's. He did not mind if Tennyson occasionally cast lustful eyes on his childe and mate, Nico...for who better than Tennyson Beaulieu to entrust his lover with? Tennyson might, on the occasion, desire Nicolai, but neither of the two would act on such lust.

He would not care if she occasionally passed out in his home, sleeping naked under Nico's arm. He would never care if she did, for she was a sacred mortal, wasn't she? She carried the mark of the Chosen One. She was the very creature for which he'd waited eight hundred and eighty-three years. He would forbid her nothing, yet never show his affections. He could not allow Tennyson to know that he was carefully watching, to protect the holy one from those who might mis-use or abuse her. His love was pure.

In this moment, he did not care that his childe danced with the unnatural little malakh boy, Rhys; for Tennyson was with them, between their lithe and beautiful bodies, consecrating the sacrilegious communion of vampire and malakh. The two boys, looking so young despite their years, danced with the voluptuous dark-skinned Creole girl, turning their strange and homoerotic ritual into a sacrificial ménage a trois.

They were unique, the three of them; he could admit that.

Rhys, in black Spandex and leather, was the only living tchatcha in the world and had light brown hair with blue eyes and olive-toned skin and features that held a hint of the Arab in them; this lavicious malakh was a living proof of how dangerous the sin-eaters were, that whole extinct race. The tchatchau had the hungers of a vampire and a desire to procreate that might put the common hare to shame.

Tennyson, in red silk and black leather, had long black plaits. Her flashing gray-green eyes were nearly the same color as his own, but he imagined that mortals lost themselves in her gaze faster than in his hypnotic stare. In the club, she wore clothes that showed off all the fertile curves that God had chosen to bestow upon her, but he much preferred the flowing skirts and blouses of her greenhouse clothes. He knew that her family must be very proud of the way she'd grown, the manner in which she carried herself; she was neither male nor female in behavior. That was as it was meant to be, for wasn't the Lion of God often spoken of in androgynous terms?

Any self-respecting girl would run in horror at the thought of what lurked in the shadows of Pandora's Box, but Tennyson was far from merely mortal. She was more than human. Something more dangerous. And completely ignorant of herself.

The beauty of the two mortals was never in dispute. Rhys Lorraine was enough to bewitch humans and Undead alike. He imagined that the boy's angel ancestors must have possessed this same unholy gleam. Tennyson, on the other hand, was the epitome for females of her species---he believed this, his opinion only. Perhaps he was biased. These two mortals were, in his bias, polar opposites of light and dark nature. It was his childe, dancing with them, that provided an offset to this contrast.

Nico, at two hundred and thirty-three years old, was the object of his hellish devotions. His vampire offspring drove him to utter despair a great deal of the time. With his womanish hair and lithe form, Nicolai delighted in finding new ways to make him gnash his teeth and bite his tongue.

And when he could manage to be stoic...

Nico delighted in the punishments he could devise.

'I would die for you, I would die for you. I've been dying just to feel you by my side. To know that you're mine. I will cry for you, I will cry for you. I will wash away your pain with all my tears. And drown your fear. I will pray for you, I will pray for you. I will sell my soul for something pure and true. Someone like you.'

Together, the three danced to a sexy Garbage song full of pornographic moaning. It made every hair on his body rise in sensual agreement; whatever else the DJ hacker might be, Dante Webster understood music on its most primitive and malakh levels.

'See your face every place that I walk in. Hear your voice every time I am talking. You will believe in me and I will never be ignored. I will burn for you, feel pain for you. I will twist the knife and bleed my aching heart. And tear it apart. I will lie for you, beg and steal for you. I will crawl on hands and knees until you see...you're just like me.'

The warm beer felt marvelous, going down his throat. He turned his thoughts to why he was in New Orleans, working at such a level of the underworld. It had all begun with the arrest of militia templi, of course, in 1307.

'Violate all the love that I'm missing. Throw away all the pain that I'm living. You will believe in me and I can never be ignored.'

In the year 1214, the elders of the Scion decided that he must leave the quiet sanctuary of their libraries. Too many of the younger priests and monks and Knights were aware of his existence---the questions continually mounted. He must go from Jerusalem and head for Egypt, where the order possessed some land. This was, of course, where the Blood came from and the Scion charged him with a special task. He must seek out the Blood and protect it, ever watchful for the potential rising of that one they sought. They now believed that the Chosen One would spring from a pure source of the Blood.

When Philip the Fair had declared the Knights of the Temple to be heathens and heretics in 1307, he had almost immediately fallen in his charge. Even now, in the early years of the twenty-first century, he could not quite decide what evil had taken root in his head---causing his lapse. He suspected it was some lack of morality or simply a cruel fact of his vampire self. He suspected it was a defiance for the loss of the whispers which he had heard in his youth, after being kicked by the donkey.

But, for whatever reason, he slid from his duty in the year of 1309. He had awoken one night, after a day's worth of dreamless sleep, and left his crypt for the teeming city of Cairo. Here, instead of carefully choosing a victim who deserved death, he killed an innocent. He chose a child who wandered the alleys after dusk, lost and afraid. Dressed as a Muslim, he promised succor and help for the frightened girl and then, upon drawing her into the deepest shadows of a mosque's back wall, he devoured her blood and licked his fingers clean with great satisfaction.

This had been the first genuine realization of what he truly was, as a creature of darkness. From that night onward, he had existed for an Unlife which burned with evil.

He left Egypt for Europe, intent upon learning the modern world.

For him, in the following centuries, humanity served as little more than cattle and sheep and he was the wolf that hunted their sweet blood and their soft flesh; the more innocent his victim, the greater his pleasure in killing. God was dead and the Devil reigned in the ashes of Eden and he was a monster. Love was a lie and his destiny was in the blood.

This was what he'd already believed in 1351 when he found Misha in Kiev and stole the dead rabbi's child away from the Christian mob who persecuted her family while dying of the plague. He'd wanted a slave, someone to watch over him as he slept...someone with whom he might have intelligent conversation. He was lonely, in his own way, and had wanted a companion. Who better than one of his own people, a child who could be taught? Ukrainian and Jewish, the daughter of a rabbi who'd occasionally worked as teacher and personal secretary to the nearest war-lord, Misha had never known the world beyond the forest and town of her youth, but she was quick-witted and intriguing. She was, at the time of their first meeting, only fourteen.

He'd taken her away from Kiev disguised as a boy, for her own safety. Two years later, he had taken her to be his wife. As his wife, Misha had flourished---she hadn't feared him, once she understood the depths of evil mere mortals were capable of. By comparison to the monstrosity of acts done by Christian people in a murdering rage of fear, a vampire of obvious education and practical logic hadn't seemed a terrible thing.

Only three years later, he'd made her into his eternal and immortal bride.

He'd loved her...

Yet, even with love in his heart for Misha, he'd tortured and killed and terrorized mortals.

This was what he'd existed for, in the year 1795, when he found Nicolai in Spain. He'd been fascinated by the Russian gypsy whose birthplace was so very close to Kiev, the very town where he'd found Misha.

He had continued his reign of Undead horror until he found himself being stalked via telephone and post card by a young man from the States. This young man, in the late nineteen-sixties, had asked him for help concerning a story obscured in Templar history. He had carefully checked the young man out and then decided that it couldn't hurt to share what he knew of the legend he had once protected so strenuously.

This young man had sent him to London first and then to Cairo, to meet with people who were of the Blood. These were educated people extremely interested in meeting with a creature of his calibre and knowledge. These were people not afraid of his nature, for they understood the world and its many species. A renewal of his faith came and he remembered his duty. He no longer killed humans for pleasure or out of greed.

He had never met the young American man, face to face, but he'd heard great things concerning Steven Rose and Nasir Asad al-Din. This long-distance conversation had continued until that man's death, in 1985. He would never have known that Steven Rose had died, if not for the cool, distant voice of a stranger on the line at the last occasion he attempted to call his American contact.

'Doctor Rose no longer lives at this address, monsieur. He and his wife both passed away last week in an automobile accident...oui, it is a terrible tragedy. A special heritage

has been lost, for their son died with them.'

Upon hearing this, he immediately contacted Nasir Asad al-Din and was informed that these things were true. Steven Rose was dead and yet this did not mean his duty had ended. For, even as he grieved for the death of a stranger he'd never met---a mortal!---he was asked to do something, in Steven Rose's memory. He must go to New Orleans and create a residence there; once every three months, he must go on vacation to this city and watch a certain young girl.

This young girl was of the Blood and believed to be the Chosen One. Only he would know for certain, of course, as he had the most understanding of what could be hidden in mortal life.

But, then, just over three years ago, he had observed that his prey visited a certain club--- newly opened---almost every night of the week. Immediately, he had inquired to the nature of the club and found himself intrigued. He joined, dragging Nico with him. To Mathilda Curran, he had explained their natures and insisted that she and every other player call him Joe...a nice, solid, ordinary American name.

Nico scoffed at the idea of his 'nickname', but he knew that it was necessary for him to be able to blend in, exist within the new century and by the new rules. A club of the underworld, a guild of infamous faces and names, this was a perfect place for the likes of him; yet, he could not understand why the girl visited nearly every night.

Until he met Rhys Lorraine and, through the tchatcha, Daniel D'Loup.

Tennyson Beaulieu visited Pandora's Box, in the early days, because of her friendship with a very young, ex-CIA operative named Perseus Shadow...better known to the small world of this club as Rhys. It was a strange love affair, of course; he saw no indication of sexual behaviors between them, which was a true comfort.

It was Nicolai who had brought him the knowledge of his prey. By nearly killing the girl in a pique of blood-lust, his childe had discovered the mark of a Chosen One, a chosen child.

Tennyson was marked. It only proved what he had observed already; she was the Lion of God, the reincarnation of an ancient warrior whose sole purpose for existing was the protection of humanity from the darkness.

She was the only reason he stayed in New Orleans, working here.

As he mused on that, his childe came to him out of the flashing lights and into the darkness of his corner. Nicolai lifted his left hand and kissed it on the knuckles, dark eyes full of laughter; he could smell the sweat and blood-scent coming from his beloved.

It aroused his hunger, once more, and reminded him that he had not fed in two days.

He would have to remedy that, soon.

The upstairs was full of potted plants, the sort of vegetation that could normally be found only in the jungle. The air was humid, despite the weather outside still being chilly for New Orleans in late winter. The walls and floor were dark redwood and the furnishings were forest green brocade, heavy chairs and divans that were designed to resemble their ancestors from a century ago. The sandy cream ceilings had a scalloped texture.

At the top of the stairs, in the landing, he came to the single, true inhabitant of the Magazine Street club residence. Genevieve Maigny ran the offices and managed the house when there was no one else available; she was, in truth, the life blood of Pandora's Box. She was the daughter of an old friend of his---the friend he had brought with him from Europe in his immigration to America during the late fifties---and had come to work for Mattie, well-trained in the ways of such business.

She stood up from her desk and smiled warmly as he led his 'guests' in the direction of his office. "Bon jour, Oncle." With her dark brown hair cut into an inverted bob, Genevieve was the picture of modern French fashion in gray silk. She held out a manila file folder. "I have a requisition form for you to sign. Rhys wants your permission to charge a

47

new weapon and ammunition to the business account."

Not glancing at his 'guests', Daniel opened the folder and scanned the form in question. He murmured to the young Maigny fille. "L'garcon is *insane*. What would he need a grenade launcher for? We represent skill and finesse and discretion, but mon garcon wants a grenade launcher..." He found the last item on the list and raised his eyes in disbelief. *"And fifty kilos of C4 plastique?"*

Genevieve met his startled gaze and shrugged, her demeanor one of quiet bemusement as she looked from him to Sterling and Maya. Her eyes, the color of warm claret, sparkled. "Your partner, he claims there are mice nesting in the baseboards here. Perhaps he intends to exterminate?"

He lifted his wine glass and drank from it, laughing. "Your sense of humor, chere, is delicious." Closing the folder, he laid it on the desk. "I will attend to this business when I have spoken with my partner on the matter." He motioned to his office door. "T'plait, m'sieur, ma chere, you must join me here."

The rooms he had chosen for his office were two that overlooked the back garden with its wrought iron fence and overgrown hosta plants, its lush elephant ear palms and jasmine and Queen's Wreath and oleander. Honeysuckle and bougainvillea twined and twisted on every available surface of tree-trunk and fence.

The rooms were designed to resemble an apartment, with the office doubling with a kitchenette and the bedroom had its own water closet. There was a bar and a large wooden desk that sat in the middle of the main room; to his credit, there was nothing incriminating ever left in this place. Before the pale, polished oak desk sat several chairs and a fainting couch, all done in creamy ecru brocaded silk.

Rhys had done the decorating for every wall; paintings and poster-sized photographs hung at odd levels and angles, showing his garcon's eclectic tastes. Potted vines and exotic trees sat on the floor between tables and in every corner; there was a long, counter-like table on one wall that held a series of computers---Rhys' personal database system. There was also a television set into a scroll-carved wall cabinet.

"Make yourself comfortable, t'plait." He nodded at the furniture, polite with the 'guests', as he moved to sit down in one of the overstuffed leather chairs. "My partner will join us momentarily."

Through the floor, he continued to hear the bass and drum as it played in the temple. He sat in one of the chairs and shared the wine with Sterling as they talked of more pleasant things, such as the current economics and how the ECU's influence in America's future might have a greater impact than previously predicted by this country's political animals. Sterling's friend, Maya, had little to say, but smiled in her bland fashion as she walked around the office, examining pictures and photographs as if she was touring an art gallery.

Thirty minutes later, he was pouring a third glass of wine for both himself and Sterling when Rhys opened the door of their office and entered with a roguish grin, once again in order from head to toe; there was no hair out of place in Rhys' re-worked queue and somewhere, between temple and office, the garcon had carefully washed away all traces of glitter and lipstick. He did not need to smell the aroma of cannabis to be fully aware of where his garcon had stopped, on the way to his side. No doubt Tennyson Beaulieu had enticed Rhys with a tin of hydroponic, greenhouse-produced 'medicine'.

His partner carried a tall glass in one hand; he knew, with the instinct of his kind, what Rhys was drinking now. The odor was pungent enough for him to catch a whiff. A spiced bloody Mary. If he was not much mistaken, there was probably blood in the tomato juice. If so, it was a willing donation from Tennyson or some other human who thought nothing of opening a vein for vampires...or for the world's only known tchatcha.

"I apologize for the wait, folks. I couldn't keep the lady waiting anymore. Previous engagements and all that." Rhys came to the brocade fainting couch and flopped down onto its silky cushion with the grace of a jungle cat. In a smooth slide, his partner went from sitting up to a sprawl. He was the very image of a discotheque twink in black Lycra and butter-soft leather and scuffed Doc Martins. "Let's talk business."

He smiled, indulgent, and watched Sterling and the young woman, Maya. They were both highly impressed by Rhys' unorthodox behavior. He imagined that Sterling had never dealt with a garcon of Rhys' age in conjunction with such dangerous, difficult work. He knew...he would never bother to explain all the other idiosyncrasies that came with Rhys. Such as the blood drinking or the invisibility or the occasional Cimmerian mien that found its way into his garcon's blue hazel eyes.

More than one aspect of Rhys' childhood had endured, despite his best efforts at civilizing Steven's son. He knew, from the information he was given on the Malakh Principles experiments, that a great number of traits which Rhys showed came from the genetic phenotypes inherent to tchatchau malakh. Steven had shown those same traits in the last years of his life, after being altered on the genetic level, non?

Tchatchau malakh were physiological shooting stars, compared to the benu.

Sterling began by setting his wine down in order to withdraw a brown envelope from the inner pocket of his suit's jacket. The blonde Englishman spoke in a frank, casual tone, his hands moving with the slowness of a man who was in no hurry to do anything.

"A month ago, an archaeological dig in the wadis east of Dendara, Egypt, revealed something extraordinary. These items may well be the find of a century, in that esoteric field, but their worth to me is far greater than a king's ransom. My interest in these items is that of a scholar, not a treasure-seeker. But, I need a skilled man with native sensibilities to retrieve certain artifacts from the Museum in Cairo before they are placed on display. I am looking for someone who can blend into the background of that city, find the items in question, and get them to me with a minimum of fuss. I was told that you, Mister D'Loup, could well be that someone."

He nodded, taking the packet that Sterling offered. Inside were a number of matte-finished photographs in black and white. He began looking through them as their 'guest' continued to speak.

"My interest in these particular artifacts began when I attended school with a group of boys, in London. Their fathers were Egyptologists and they knew stories about that country which are not often found in any written journal or narrative. Many of these were, of course, fables and hearsay, but one story in particular captured my imagination."

"Goody. I need a bedtime story." Rhys drawled, arching one brow in snarky humor.

Sterling behaved as if he had not heard the comment. "The tale claimed that the ancient Egyptian and Nubian gods were, in fact, the fallen angels mentioned in Hebrew, Islamic, and Christian texts, and that one of their number was a warrior who had the reputation for being a savior of sorts. When in god form, with the Egyptian pantheon, he was called Sekhmet, the Eye of Ra, who was a bloodthirsty antidote to evil. With the Nubian pantheon, he was Apedemak. You might liken this character to any legendary hero, but the stories claim that he's returned in the flesh a number of times, in the interests of protecting mankind from its greatest enemies."

Immediately, he already knew the story.

Daniel examined the photographs; they were five by sevens and showed a dig site such as the ones he had seen in the last century, when living in Egypt, but with modern equipment involved. Then, at last, he came to the pictures that showed a carved tomb's open doorway, the stones shifted to reveal a dark cavern-like recess. Behind these were photos of a table that held a number of interesting items...a set of bronze scroll cases that showed the dull gleam of age, a pair of large wrist braces that seemed be carved of metal---perhaps gold---with glyphs incised into the surface, a throat torque of the same metal with similar markings, and a mask.

The mask captured his imagination---he was correct in his guess, concerning the story. The photograph trembled as his hand moved of its own volition; something about this mask made the skin on his back crawl in an unspeakable emotion. He had seen this thing before, in his dreams, but any deeper knowledge was lost, leaving behind only the gnawing thought that...the wearer of this mask was a dark god whose rites had demanded blood.

The mask itself was unusual for an artifact of any Egyptian dynasty. It was formed to fit the upper half of a face, leaving the bottom half open to sight. There was the smooth plane of brow and arched cheekbones, of a strong nose...but, where the lower cheeks, mouth, and jaw should be, the mask did not cover. He imagined the lips of the man who could wear such a mask would be curved and thick and like silk to the touch, but capable of uttering terrible evil.

In the center of the brow, where a man's eyebrows should meet, there was a symbol carved. A glyph he recognized in his soul. The glyph was not a pure Egyptian sigil, but above it was the feather of Ma'at standing on the Eye of Ra.

This was the mask of Bomani, the legendary warrior Misrene and Bedouin tribesmen spoke of in whispers. It simply must be; was this not the sigil he had seen traced into the sand before a campfire, long ago? He had dreamed of this mask for more than a century, had dreamed of the man who wore this mask. It could be nothing else, if his gut instincts were correct. A century ago, when he had roamed the desert and oases with the tribes, he had heard these stories and thought them only fairytales, fables...but, now he wondered.

For had they not described this mask in detail?

"Tell me, m'sieur, what these things mean to you." Daniel spoke in a flat and direct tone, not looking up from the photograph he held. "Tell me why you want this to be done. Is it purely for the sake of the artifacts or do you have some inkling for what these things were meant to be? If you have heard the stories surrounding such a warrior, you must have some knowledge of what his legacy contained, in all probability."

"That certainly does remain to be seen, don't you think?" Sterling's question was not meant to be answered.   "I have, indeed, heard the stories concerning a legacy of the Guardians or whatever it is they were called. I don't believe in the magical aspect of those stories, Mister D'Loup, but I do know fully well that such a find could spark debate and perhaps, in the most extreme end, even a re-writing of all major faiths. In a way, I hope to keep such nonsense to a whisper..." The middle-aged Englishman smiled crookedly at him, debonair and sly. "After all, we are men of reason, not heathens."

'Speak for yourself' He sneered in his mind, keeping the thought to himself as he turned his gaze downward, to study the photograph of the unusual mask. *'You may know some small piece of the story, but you cannot possibly understand what you are seeking.   There are things, m'sieur, still living in the dark and lost places of this world...things that cannot die, things that crave retribution in the same manner a drunkard craves his first mouthful of spirits.   They hate us with all the power of their immortal bodies...and for the fallen who are half-conscious in their malakh prisons, sleeping fitfully in the genetic code of their descendants, the very world itself is a hellish nightmare they cannot awaken from.   I would know more of why you want the mask of that cursed warrior...'*

"I wanna know something...where *exactly* was this stuff found?" Rhys asked, breaking him loose of his private commentary.   His partner was looking through the photographs he had laid down on the coffee-table.   The tall glass was held in two precarious fingers against the bare skin of exposed, tan abdomen where Rhys' metallic black Lycra shirt had ridden upwards.

Sterling chuckled, turning his attention on the younger malakh.   "I'm glad you asked. The tomb was found in the wadis to the east of Dendara, in a small necropolis. According to the information I was able to gather, through a few young Egyptologists who are working on the site, this tomb belonged to a priest of Sekhmet...a scribe. If the inscriptions and contents of the tomb are accurate, this lector priest was supposedly a son of the Lion of Kemet, a warrior for Pharaoh. The symbol on the mask...it was found carved on the stones in several tombs of this necropolis.   It suggests this was the resting place of the Lion's descendants, those who lived near Dendara."

"But, this stuff...this was all found in one tomb, right?" Rhys frowned, taking a drink of his bloody mary.   The garcon's upper lip was rimed with a red froth that begged to be licked away; he would never become insane enough to do such a thing...especially with the faintest scent of human blood coming from the glass.

"Yes." Sterling was refilling their wine glasses, ignoring Maya's presence in the room;

the benu was focused entirely on the young tchatcha. "From what I've gathered, the tombs that are marked with the Lion of Kemet's symbol all contain a strange side-step for the time period when this scribe-priest was supposed to have lived. The mummies are nearly intact but seem to have been heavily pickled and wrapped in cartonnage linen and papyrus and then, oddly enough, are tied into a fetal position and laid to rest on their left side. From what I was informed of, this was a very ancient habit, stemming from the funerary practices of early Nubia."

"Nearly intact?" He raised his curious eyes and studied the Englishman. "What do you mean by *'nearly intact'*?"

"They were never treated the way the average body was treated, being mummified." Sterling explained; it was becoming obvious that this malakh was a fairly knowledgeable student of the ancient civilization. "In the case of the Guardian mummies, the bodies are being revealed as nearly whole. These people didn't shave the hair from their heads and when they died, only one organ was removed before the embalming process began."

"The heart." Rhys whispered it and gave a little, odd smile. "They were sin-eaters and couldn't allow a loved one to disappear into the dark beyond death...you had to take the heart into yourself, preserve the soul from the nothing."

Daniel, taking a drink of his merlot, swallowed hard and nearly choked with shock.

It was Sterling who laughed, nodding. "Yes. This is what the carvings on the tomb walls suggest. These people had their own versions of The Book of the Dead and The Book of Gates, vastly different than the texts conventionally found in other tombs of the same era. It's a major find. The texts that can be translated are starting to suggest a sub-group of people who may have come out of Nubia at some point, who have escaped notice or mention until now...and this lector priest's tomb seems to indicate that he, at the very least, lived and died during the reign of Ramses the Second." Now, their 'guest' grew curious, pinning Rhys with a narrowed gaze. "May I ask what inspired your speculation on the nature of devouring the heart?"

He watched the garcon from under lowered lashes, intent on Rhys' expression. He could see the rising shadows as they came to change the very beauty of his partner's face; it was an eclipse of the soul, familiar to him. He had seen this many times in the decade he had known Rhys. The very hue of the tchatcha's eyes evolved, grew darker.

"I just...knew." Rhys murmured, not glancing up from the last photograph, that of the Lion's mask. Then, as fast as the veil of night had fallen, it lifted from his garcon's eyes. Rhys tossed the photograph on the table and settled again on the fainting couch, laying down. "Okay. What about the museum? Where this stuff is. Who's in charge of the crap coming in from this dig?"

Sterling pulled another photograph from his Armani coat pocket. It was handed to him first and he studied it before passing it on to Rhys as their 'guest' answered. "Doctor Ibrihim Marwah. He comes from a four generation line of Egyptologists. This dig was---is---his personal project. He's the man responsible for the money. He managed to drum up quite a bit of it, in fact, from a private investor. He's spent most of his career being the black sheep of his field due to an obsession with the Lion of Kemet. The dig at Dendara will secure him a place in history, of course, and great prestige."

"You talk as if you're his friend." Rhys' tone was inflectionless, without bias.

"He is a friend, I suppose." Sterling sipped at the merlot in his glass, pale eyes following the lovely Maya as she studied another photograph on the wall. "Or perhaps a friendly rival...that would be more to the truth. I have no intention of robbing him of the fame involved, but he does not need these particular items in order to stake his claim. Not truly. Enough people have already photographed and examined them---if they were lost, the proof of their existence is still yet solid."

"What kinda man is your friend, Doctor Marwah?" Relaxed, Rhys' lazy eyes was slitted, showing only a hint of blue. "Does he like women or boys? Does he drink? Does he have vices that we can...*use*?"

Daniel relaxed, letting his garcon handle this matter. It was what Rhys did best, truly, devising plans even as the details were provided.   He himself could not do better.   As he squared his shoulders against the chair's soft leather, he examined Sterling more closely. This was a malakh of some unique ability, one that he could not quite decide upon; something more than an manifested benu.

"Ibrihim has a fondness for modern women...women with a mind of their own.   The more intelligent, the more he likes them."   Waric Sterling said with a low chuckle, swirling the glass of wine in one hand so that the dark red merlot left a melting parabola on its perfect crystal.

"Blonde or brunette?"   Rhys pushed; the accent---a French-American slur---made itself easier to hear.   "Should he find a woman enticing, would she be Muslim and behind the veil or does he like European women...or from the States, maybe?"

"Most definitely those who don't live behind the veil."   Their 'guest' leaned forward over the coffee-table, as if sharing a secret.   "Highly educated women."

"Hobbies?"   Rhys tossed the last picture back onto the smooth surface, next to the wine bottle.

Sterling laughed again, but with more vigor---as if this was a game and he was winning. "He likes plants and ancient civilizations, lad.   More than that, we never really delved into. His private life's never shown any inkling of stain.   Nothing that you can use, I think."

For a long moment, there was nothing said or done, and Daniel turned to glance at Rhys. His garcon stared at nothing, as if seeing a world beyond the visible one.   He opened his mouth with the intention of explaining to Sterling that they would take the job, but before he could speak, Rhys nodded, as if making up his mind about some idea.

He smiled behind the rim of his glass, letting his partner take the floor.

"There's probably students coming and going all the time there, in the museum. Especially with this new exhibit in the works."   The young, brown-haired tchatcha said in a soft voice, speculating.

"I imagine so."   Sterling allowed.

He chose now to speak.   "If we do this for you, m'sieur, I would expect the fee to be generous.   The fee for something of this magnitude, with the potential of becoming an international incident, must be comparable to the fee for wet work."

Sterling agreed.   "More than generous, Mister D'Loup.   It will more than compensate you for the work involved.   A hundred thousand dollars, a third of it before you leave America.   Once you have accomplished the job, you can have your bartender give me a call...then, we shall meet in this club and settle the difference."

It sounded fair and honest enough---as honest as these deals could be, when theft or murder was bargained for.   Yet, it was too easy and he fought a frisson of concern at the mere idea of what he was preparing to steal---the mask of a legendary warrior of angelic descent.   A warrior he had dreamed of, on a regular basis, when living in the desert.   A warrior whose life had always felt personal to him---and with the dreams he had endured, a sense of the personal was no great surprise.

"I will provide you with the deposit number for an account in Zurich."

"Excellent. I need you to be in Egypt and working on this within the week.   The exhibit is three weeks from now and I would prefer to have it finished before the museum is flooded with heightened security measures."   Sterling began gathering the photographs, sliding them back into their brown envelope.

"I believe I do understand."   He lifted the edge of his mouth into a curving smirk.   "You can make the deposit and we shall be on a flight to Cairo in two days.   If I know my partner, he has already started forming a most unique plan and is anxious to begin."

He glanced at Rhys and found his garcon had slumped back onto the fainting couch, one slim arm over his young face, the bloody mary abandoned on the coffee-table.   All that could be seen of Rhys' face, now, were one arched brow and a wicked grin.

The tchatcha spoke with an arrogant drawl.   "Just call me your budding neophyte Egyptologist."

Chapter Five

It was a good night. A really good night.

He licked his teeth and found the after-taste of tchatcha there; it sent a sexy shiver through him. Fire and sugar and sex and gold...that was what it was like. He was the only one who ever tapped the tchatcha, the only one who ever dared. Not that his Sire ever let any other bloodsucker into the club.

The darkness and strobing colors mingled, heady and psychedelic.

They sat at their usual table, with the lamp off, and watched the parade of cutie-pie college kids who flirted and danced, unaware of how dangerous the environs could be. In a way, it was like sitting in the middle of a giant buffet that he wasn't allowed to touch. The smell alone was enough to make him feel off-kilter, but he behaved himself within the confines of the club.

It was a rule, started on the day he and Joseph had taken the contract from Golden Wolf. They would keep the vampires out of Pandora's Box, help control the vampire population in The Big Easy, and keep their fangs off the mortals who visited the club. They couldn't eat the children or attack the players.

The only living person in the whole place who refused to hold to Golden Wolf's rule was the tchatcha he called his friend. Rhys. It was a game and a ritual with them, the breaking of that rule. He and Rhys danced together, lost in the sway and pull of a timeless battle---a battle where no sword or bullet could do as much damage as the seductive smile or the offering kiss. The only weapon he possessed, in the battle, was his fangs. For Rhys, the only weapon was a strange comprehension that spanned a farther distance than even Joseph could claim.

He had never told his Sire of this. How could he explain the terrible wisdom he saw in Rhys' gaze, as they danced? He said nothing, instead; Joseph didn't forbid his choice to behave in such a way and he maintained the mystery of his friendship with the world's only tchatcha malakh.

He'd never told his Sire of the single time he'd crossed the boundaries and fucked Rhys, only a month after Mattie Curran had thrown the tchatcha out. To tell Joseph was an invitation to death---Joseph would never accept or sanction such a thing. If the elder vampire knew of what he'd done, a year ago, with the tchatcha, there was no question of what would happen. Rhys would die. And he would wish he could do the same. He knew something about Rhys that only a *real* lover would recognize---Rhys wasn't like other boys, by any stretch of the imagination. It was a secret he had to carry; he couldn't tell anyone, not even Tennyson, for fear that it would reach his Sire's ears.

He sat with his back to the open floor and its milling mortals; Joseph's back was against the linen-swathed wall. Joseph sipped warm Guinness, but he didn't drink anything---he didn't want to lose the taste of Rhys' blood in his mouth until he had no choice.

The music had gone down a notch in volume; Dante Webster was playing more eclectic mixes, heavy in Eastern European and Moorish influences. *His* kind of music. Like the Goran Bregovic piece that was currently swirling through the amps and speakers. It made his unbeating heart twist and clutch.

Nicolai Valeska became aware of his mortal hag coming along the wall, in the shadows, approaching the table. Then, he caught sight of her. She looked stoned and woozy; not a surprise, since she'd disappeared through the smoke room door with Rhys.

As she reached the table, Tennyson grasped a nearby chair from the black, cloth-muffled wall, and swung it around. In a singularly dyke move, she straddled the wooden seat, her arms in their red silk finding a folded perch on the chair's back.

Joseph said nothing; he was minutely aware of his Sire's gaze, though. His Sire's hawk-like stare was on the dark-skinned Creole, flat and without judgment of any kind. He took the lead, smiling as he leaned sideways in his chair. Closer to her face and the long braids that lay loose upon her shoulders, Nicolai spoke.

"Did you leave him in a stupor back there, babydoll?"

She made a sour expression, taking a drink of the glass she carried. It smelled like a slow comfortable screw, orange juice and Southern Comfort. Her full-lipped mouth pouted as she narrowed her eyes to see him in the dark. "No. He had to go upstairs. Business."

His hag had been bled. He smelled it. With a quick glance, he found the bandage on her wrist. Right at the place where hand and forearm joined, on the outside. No arteries, no major veins...but a good bleeder. Apparently, Joseph smelled it, too.

"You should not give him your blood so freely, girl."

Tennyson shrugged; her gray-green eyes were dilated and almost unfocused. Her voice slurred a little. "It's okay. He doesn't drink blood that often. I think he gets high from it. He doesn't take much, maybe half a cup at the most."

Joseph reached for the black-shaded metal lamp on their table and flicked it on. Now, they were illuminated and his eyes adjusted with a twinge. He studied his hag and his Sire; Tennyson was relaxed and half out of her brain with cannabis and booze, but Joseph was sober and stern.

"It does not matter how much you give him, girl." Joseph frowned hard, lifting the glass of warm, frothy beer that sat on a plain white napkin. With a drink that left just the tiniest hint of moisture behind on his Sire's upper lip, Joseph's dark brows knit together. The voice of his Master was passionless. "Give a creature your blood, you give him a taste for your death. You give him power. A creature like Lorraine, he might betray you without warning."

Nicolai didn't bother to remind Joseph that *he* was the first creature to have ever tasted Tennyson's blood; instead, he tugged at the metallic black Spandex on his ribs, adjusting it as he studied his mulatto hag. She was nodding, accepting what his Sire said without actual agreement. He knew what that meant; she *didn't* agree and respected Joseph's position as a player too much to put up an argument. What would be the point? Joseph had been around too long and...one never knew when his Master might decide to rip someone's head off, to prove a point.

In this case, that someone *might* be Rhys.

No, it wasn't a good idea to remind Joseph about his own little experience of tasting Tennyson's blood. It was bad enough that he tasted Rhys so much---once or twice a week, sometimes more. To remind his ancient Sire of his *own* fuck-up, with Tennyson, was kind of like begging for a bad night.

He winced, inside, able to remember the beating he'd taken over it, the first time. When he'd told Joseph that he'd nearly killed Tennyson in the ugly rest-room of a greasy spoon diner, his Sire had gone absolutely ape-shit on him. Particularly when he'd mentioned the tattoo. Joseph really didn't like the idea of him feeding on Tennyson; he couldn't decide if it was jealousy or what and didn't want to ask questions for a chance at clarification. All he needed to know was: Tennyson was off limits to his fangs and his need for blood. If he was starving to death and she slit her own wrists for mercy, he'd better refuse like a gentleman and then run like hell.

Doing it just once, by accident, had gotten him the worst beating of his Undead life.

Nicolai decided it was time to change the subject. He reached into the pocket of his coat, slung over the back of his chair, and pulled out a battered pack of cards and his smokes. He needed a cigarette and a game of spades. With a grin, he lit up and let it droop off his lower lip as he shuffled the cards, breaking the uneasy silence between his hag and his Master, who were staring each other down like two Alpha dogs ready to go to war over a meat-juicy bone.

He made his statement. "It's not worth fighting about. Tennyson has the right to shed her blood if she wants and Joseph has the right to be worried if he wants."

Tennyson snorted, obviously and non-verbally sarcastic at the idea of Joseph being worried about a mortal woman. She believed his Sire hated her; it was another secret he had to keep---that Joseph really liked Tennyson and considered her special in some way. He really didn't understand all of it---Joseph didn't have much use for women, period, except as food. The only female he'd seen Joseph talk with, spend any real time with, was Misha--- and look what good that did. Made Joseph a crazy mess, right? Not that anyone in this club would ever believe the things he knew about his Sire. They all thought he was a cold-blooded, Undead monster made of steel. They didn't know Joseph like he did.

Joseph was nothing but a big fucking *pussy*. A drama queen, even.

He cut the deck and gave a lop-sided grin, the cigarette hanging from the corner of his mouth. "Besides, if I didn't know it would do some *serious* damage to his chances of staying a mortal, I'd open a vein for Rhys any old day of the week."

Instantly, he knew he'd said something wrong. Joseph's eyes went cold and flat and animal. His Sire chose to say nothing here, in front of Tennyson, but Nicolai knew that there was another tally on the wall. He was never entirely sure how many times he could say something or do something outside of Joseph's rules before the ancient Undead knight decided to re-teach him the lesson of obedience.

"Deal the cards, honey, before I slip into a coma over here." Tennyson suggested, bringing some warmth back to the table. A glance at his hag's stoned-happy smile and he winked at her, agreeing. She knew that Joseph was a hard bastard and forgave it as much as any mortal was likely to.

She'd claimed several times that what Joseph did to him was spousal abuse and he didn't have to take it; but, she didn't understand vampire psychology or the rules a childe learned to play by. She didn't understand that he wasn't Joseph's spouse. Joseph had a wife. *He* was slave and childe and lover all rolled into one. Mortal marital laws could not apply. He was determined, for her own protection, that she would never have to see any of the truth firsthand.

Cards dealt, he sat back and played the game, letting Joseph keep track of the bids with a chewed up ink pen on a piece of scratch paper. Nothing to worry about and when Rhys got done with business, they could dance again. He needed that.

It was hard to describe to just anyone what dancing with Rhys was like. Not just anyone would get the idea. He was a musician---he'd always been a musician, addicted to tones and rhythms. He was Rom, from a proud Russian blood and a proud clan; there had always been a band of musicians among the cousins. He was simply the most long-lived one of the family. The music in Pandora's Box was better than the music in any other club in New Orleans---better than any other club in the world---and he knew the secret that so few grasped.

The DJ in Pandora's Box was a malakh of rare talent and awesome power who loved to create new sounds that only the Undead and the malakh could appreciate. In the moments when Dante Webster's laughter whipped out over the crowd of dancers, coming from a dozen different amps, introducing the next mix, he always knew...it would be special and remind him of when he was *alive* and able to feel his blood move in time with the music.

He loved to dance with Rhys because the tchatcha could keep up with him; Joseph said that this was because the tchatcha were blood-drinkers of the ancient world who thrived on the most primitive side of their natures. Joseph said that Rhys Lorraine had inherited those same primal urges and behaviors from his tchatcha ancestors. Personally, he didn't care what the reason could be---he loved to dance with Rhys and it was even better when Tennyson joined them in the center of the strobe-lit dance floor.

His hag could dance and there was something earthy and impossibly sweet about her. She danced best with him and with Rhys---except for that one girl who showed up, now and then, to captivate Tennyson for a night or two. But, that girl wasn't a problem; she never stuck around for more than a weekend and then was gone again, leaving him his hag still intact.

Personally, he had an idea that she needed to find a woman and *soon*.

She was spending too much time with Rhys.

Valeska and Joe don't really seem to fit...you know? They're such opposites. I think of Valeska as one of my best friends, but Joe...that's a totally diff story. Let me tell you a little about them and maybe you'll get the picture of what's going on here. Cause, they are one of the most fascinating couples I've ever known, straight *or* gay.

Nicolai Valeska---almost everyone calls him Valeska; Joe calls him Nico and Rhys calls him Nick---is a Rom whose family is originally from Kiev. A Rom who was born during the late eighteenth century. I think that was during the time of the French Revolution. Of course, he had nothing to do with all that. Valeska's tribe was traveling way out of their normal territory due to some political upheaval; they went to Granada, Spain, for horse-trading, and decided to stay for a few years. It was in Granada that Valeska met Joe.

Valeska himself was born in Kiev, but he was in his early teens when he first danced the flamenco. He had learned the violin from his grandfather's knee and was earning money with its sweet wailing song, adding a new instrument to the street bands who played anything a payo wanted to hear for a few pieces of copper. At fourteen, he was considered a man and expected to help the tribe with the daily work of life. He was the only Rom violinist who dared to try playing with the gitano guitarists and he took beatings for the payment, sometimes, but soon the payos were asking for him, when they came to the taverns, and Nicolai was earning the equivalent of a few silver pieces every week. He was valuable to his tribe, then.

It was in one of those taverns that a certain payo customer saw Valeska playing and kinda fell in love. I think *lust* would be more realistic. Joe seems to have a thing for Russian beauties, male and female. Joseph Snowden was already a lot of centuries old and had traveled all over the world, never staying in one place for very long.

His taste for young men and half-grown boys was, of course, kept quiet, but he was known for his money. He was already wealthy, by then, having kept his ties to the remaining sects of what he'd come from, as a mortal man. In Granada, he went around in the robes and turban of the Muslims, but that was for his protection more than for any religious tolerance. White men in Granada, at that time, weren't very welcome, and he was only grudgingly accepted. Money opens a lot of doors.

In the tavern, Joe kept a room while doing business with the local merchants. He was, at that time, working as an importer-exporter. He brought things from all over the known world to Spain's big markets and then sold them, buying Spanish merchandise to sell elsewhere. Spices, rugs, animals, glassware, et cetera. Even people. Yeah. Joe dealt under the table in slaves between Granada and Morocco and Algiers and Cairo---he even took them further east than that.

Every evening, while he entertained his merchant clients, he heard the little Rom who played the violin like a boy who'd sold his soul to the devil. Any Russian music that lived inside of Valeska had already, after a handful of years, taken on a very Moorish sound. Talk about Arabic violin...that's how Valeska sounds on those strings. He's even modified his violin to use a fifth string which has a low, moaning cry when stroked by the bow. He claims that's his soul-string.

Anyway. Valeska caught Joe's attention in Granada at a bad time for gitanos and gypsies. Back then, there was a law that stated *'if a gitano is caught roaming away from a town where he can claim residence, then any free man may take him as a slave for his own moral good'*. What a load of crap, but that was the way of the royal politics, back then.

Joe befriended the teenaged Russian Rom boy and paid him twice as much as what most musicians made...and then waited for his opportunity. He asked Valeska to do him a favor, taking a particular item from Granada to one of the outlying villages. It was a special item; a wine flask encrusted with jewels and gold. It was supposedly a gift from Joe to a wine-seller, being given as a way to warm the path between the two merchants.

It was a two day journey and Valeska started out with the wine flask hidden on his person, wrapped in a rare cloth. Halfway there, he was overtaken by the guards from Granada; he was wanted for theft. A merchant in Granada was claiming the Rom boy had taken advantage of him, stolen a priceless item, and then taken off. Valeska was dragged back to Granada and put in the gaol, where he was soon placed for sale among other prisoners for sale as a slave.

You guessed it. Joe bought the teenaged Rom boy, despite Valeska's declarations of innocence, and put his name on the newly purchased slave. He wanted Valeska for music and for a human guard, someone who could watch over him as he slept...it didn't take Valeska long to figure out what Joe Snowden was.

Valeska was introduced to Joe's partner in Rome---a girl forever nineteen years old; a Russian Jewess named Mishenka who had nearly died in the Plague, a victim of religious persecution in Kiev. She had spent a few years as Joe's human guard and companion before becoming a member of his 'family'.

The three of them made a family; Valeska adapted to his new life. He was only a slave in name, after all. Joe didn't restrict him, at first, giving the Rom boy room to do what needed to be done for the sake of protecting what was theirs. And what is a Rom without the road? With Joe, he got to travel and see the world and play his music all the time without having to worry about struggling for coins or food. Plus, there was Misha---he and Misha became friends, despite the fact that she was a vampire and he was a mortal gypsy. I think they were more than friends, but don't quote me on that.

But, over time---a few years---Joe became jealous of the attentions that came from other corners. Men and women both loved the young Rom who played violin and danced for them in both low taverns and in high society ballrooms. Valeska's beautiful, you've seen that. While Joe probably hadn't touched the boy yet, it was obviously destined to happen at some point...at least, that was probably *Joe's* thoughts. The jealousy turned to a new lust, the lust to possess something that always remained just out of reach.

The sexual side of their relationship began over something Misha did. Misha left them in Rome, only five years after Valeska joined their family. Joe, furious, searched for the missing member of his little clan, but didn't find her. The anger built into a fire that needed to be quenched and, one night, after drinking heavily of both blood and wine, Joe went back to Valeska in the villa that he kept in Rome, and instead of falling into his windowless room for a day's worth of sleep, he caught Valeska down in the cool-stone wine cellar and tied the mortal Rom spread-eagle over a huge barrel. It was a rough seduction.

From that point onward, every one of Valeska's mornings were spent either in the cellar or locked into Joe's private rooms, where no sunlight could intrude. More than a few nights were spent in the villa's garden, Joe educating Valeska to the arts of sex and how to express himself sensually.

But, that kinda love isn't healthy...it breeds madness, even for normal people. Joe's *far* from normal, you realize, and being nearly nine hundred years old can't be okay for any shreds of humanity that could still exist in the vampire psyche. Joe loved Valeska and, Valeska found himself loving Joe in return. He understood Joe and that made it possible. You hear about this kinda stuff in abnormal psychology; people who have been kept hostage begin to identify with their captor...especially when there is any kindness and attraction involved. Valeska began to fall in love with the surly vampire madman who treated him like gold most of the time.

Unfortunately, Joe's mental instability bred a fear in the vampire part of his brain. What if Valeska didn't love him? What if Valeska left him, as Misha had? What if Valeska took advantage of his affections and crept in to kill him as he slept? What if Valeska used some residual resentment over his treachery in Granada to do him in and what if he allowed it, being blinded by love? He decided the boy had to die, to ensure Valeska would never betray him.

One night, he sunk his fangs into Valeska while fucking him silly in the windowless bedroom.   He was so into what he was doing, that whole year, he'd failed to notice something.   His semen had blood in it and he'd been tying Valeska to him through the taint. Valeska was alive; his heart beat and his soul was intact, but he was changing at a very slow but definite rate.   The night Joe killed Valeska, he drained the Russian Rom dry while fucking him into a screaming, quivering lump of jelly.

When Joe woke up, as the sun was going down, he probably didn't know what to think. He was laying in the bed with the corpse of his dead boy.   Who didn't stay dead very long. As Joe was preparing to bury the body in the garden and burn his villa to the ground, Valeska woke up and attacked him, hungry and needing blood.

Now, they were joined forever, through that tie...and it was a whole new level of existence.   Joe couldn't get rid of Valeska, loved him even more at the same time he hated the creature he'd brought forth, while Valeska...Valeska was suddenly capable of things his young mind had never fathomed possible.   Joe's insanely jealous and Valeska plays with that, keeping Joe's attention on him.   It's a dangerous combination.

They've been together, ever since, for better and for worse.

The club's dance floor was still thumping, but Dante---who was playing DJ---had turned it down a notch or two for the sake of...whatever reason Dante found.   She was on her second drink since leaving the smoke-room and feeling pretty damn mellow.

They were playing spades and really needed one more person, but three was okay. Under her chair, she had pushed off her dancing shoes to relieve the cramp in her arches. After taking a sip of her slow comfortable screw, Tennyson tossed down the next card and grinned as it trumped the other two.   She gathered the book and laid the cards face down on the table's edge.

Joe and Valeska gave each other a look that showed more than love or animosity.   They were trying to 'read' each other, the way a married couple might.   She folded her cards close to the table's edge as she rubbed at the bandage on her wrist.   To have Rhys cut her with a penknife where her thumb joined at the wrist was so cold and calculating---especially while sitting together on the loveseat in the narrow, closed-off hallway that served as the smoke-room.   Even if she did enjoy the twisted knowledge of what the guy was doing with her blood.

She played out the game with her vampire friend and his Sire, watching them.   They really were the odd couple.   Joe with his short, coffee-dark hair and intense green eyes---he was six feet in his socks, from what she could guess with her internal measuring stick.   He was the original knight in shining armor, if you didn't notice that he was a bloodsucker and liked to kill his own kind for fun on a regular basis.   On the downside, he was moody and sullen and made Angel from that TV show look like a real party animal.   He was also vicious and possessive and didn't really like her all that much.   She was pretty sure that Joe put up with her just because Valeska insisted she was family and that meant no one could kill her, even for sport.

How comforting.

Joe preferred nice, expensive things.   The finest suits and cars.   When he went casual, it was in designer chic-slumware.   Tonight, the elder vampire was wearing faded, worn denim and a white wifebeater that showed off his beautiful physique.   He was all muscle, but it was a healthy, well-done muscular.   She knew it was from his life as a knight, in the Templar. When he'd had a lot of blood to drink, his skin was darkened enough to make him appear alive.   He liked being clean and neat; his hair and his nails were never unkempt.   He was an anomaly, among the Undead, from what Valeska had told her.

Her Rom vampire friend, though, was the opposite.   Valeska didn't care what he looked like, even though he was remarkable.   She'd always thought he looked kinda like Johnny Depp.   Petite at only five foot six and pretty enough to be a girl---or so she sometimes thought. With black hair hanging to his shoulders straight and thick and black eyes that sparkled with intense animal intelligence, Nicolai Valeska was a whirlwind of motion when he decided to be quick...but, for the most part, when not on the offensive or the dance floor, the younger vampire was sedate and sleek and wiry, like a cat.

Tennyson gathered the cards in her slim, mulatto hands and began to shuffle them for another game as she smiled, remembering the night when she'd realized the Undead truth about Valeska. When they'd realized the truth about each other.

At that time, she'd been coming to the club for a good three months and had gotten to know both Rhys and Valeska. She stayed about half in love with Rhys---it was something dark and intense. If there was a guy alive she might actually *love*, it was Rhys, and that was dangerous all by itself. But, then, one night, she'd had too much to drink and let Valeska drive her home. Only, they hadn't gone home. First, they'd stopped at a diner for coffee and a bite to eat.

Halfway through the meal, she'd gotten up and staggered to the toilet. Before she could close the door behind her, Valeska had stepped in and taken care of the lock. Then, the cute little Rom had pressed her to the wall for a cool, wet kiss and she had let it happen, too drunk to say no and too much in awe of him to protest.

His mouth had tasted like the rib-eye steak and grilled onions, like the coffee, like sin itself...and she'd moaned, happy. His lips, so chilly, had slipped from hers to open at her throat. Without a thought, she had let him flip her around on the wall and pull at the collar of her shirt in the back. His mouth, his teeth on the nape of her neck...damn. Pressed tight on the wall, her cheek on the cold tiles, she'd wondered why her last girlfriend hadn't possessed a mouth like this one.

She'd closed her eyes and let it happen, thinking...it wouldn't be so bad to take Valeska home...wouldn't be so bad to wake up with this body next to hers, in the morning. Was a *man* worth that? Could she stand to be touched by a man, for that?

The answer in her head, that night, was yes...until Valeska put his fangs into her throat from behind and she'd gone crazy from the pain-pleasure of it, the awareness that this man holding her so firmly was not a man at all but something else. She hadn't screamed, but she'd growled and fought to get loose. Something primal in her head had snarled a warning: *'Get free or die, bitch---this is the beast at the top of the food chain.'*

Valeska had torn her shirt, trying to re-pin her to the wall without breaking bones. And it was the final straw, the ripping of those buttons. She'd turned on him, slamming hard at his crotch. Down on his knees, the pretty-boy vampire had revealed his fangs, the twist of his darker nature as it showed through his face. But, in that moment, Valeska had also apparently lost his desire to take blood...when his eyes fell on the mark she bore on the front curve of her left shoulder, the hunger disappeared as if it had never existed.

He'd begged her forgiveness, there, on the dirty floor of the diner's restroom, with real tears in his black gaze. He was of the Rom and he remembered stories of children who were marked from early childhood with a certain tattoo. The children who bore that mark were special to the gods, to God. It was a covenant with the earth itself. They were royalty among the tribes of all nations in the world.

All she knew about the mark was...refusing to answer any questions, Mom had paid a man in the Quarter to use a tattoo gun on her the week after her very first period, when she was only twelve. It wasn't a particularly nice or cute tattoo, but she supposed it was okay. Valeska seemed to think it was important enough and had refrained from having her as dinner. The whole thing, when she looked at it now, was weird as hell.

But, if Valeska's reaction was strange, Rhys' reaction had alarmed her.

The first time Rhys had spotted the tattoo, the tchatcha malakh had gotten a lethal darkness around the eyes and a strange, almost ugly smile. The guy had slid along a wall to her, always smiling that same way, and then slung his arm around her waist, asking in a whisper where she'd gotten the cool tat, which was visible because of the halter top she'd worn that night. Once she'd explained the tattoo's existence, Rhys had bent over and brush-kissed the mark with his fiery-wet lips, murmuring to the thing itself. It made her shiver, to think about the words.

'One of them.'

He'd made *'them'* sound like some horrid curse.

Wasn't as if the damn thing was all that *interesting* to look at. Black ink under her skin in the shape of a nine-point Enneagram with a dot in the dead center. She'd thought, after discovering religions and their symbols, that it was some kinda fucked-up Star of David. But, it was more. She'd found out that it was a Sufi symbol for The Presence of God. The Nasq Kabir. It was *more*, though, if Rhys and Valeska both found something to revere in the mark. At least, Valeska revered it...Rhys acted like he wanted to carve it from her flesh with that damned pen knife of his.

Who knew what he'd do with her tattoo, after he did something so drastic?

Maybe he'd eat it.

She dealt out the cards, enjoying the feel of slick cardboard under her fingers as she watched the vampires from under her lashes. They were touching each other without touching---it was in the way their eyes moved. Valeska was opening himself there, sitting on the chair like a princeling, as if Joe's gaze was a chilly fingertip sliding over smooth, cool flesh. They were feral, like this, and she *loved* to watch...it was the voyeur in her. It was part of what she loved in spending time with Valeska or Rhys. Getting to watch a survivor in action.

As Tennyson picked up her cards to decide on the possible books in it, a hand fell on her shoulder and she nearly jumped from the chair in surprise. Craning her head quickly, her beaded braids clicking, she found Rhys' partner, Daniel, standing there.

The brawny player looked only at her, his deep blue eyes like black sapphires in the dimness. His accented voice was a husking slur as he spoke, not bothering to lean close. "He has requested your presence in the office."

As she blinked at the idea, she saw how Daniel's gaze rose and finally flicked from Valeska to Joe before a thin smile slipped onto that cat-like curve of mouth. She could see the glitter of stubble on his cheeks and jaw, the way his long ponytail stuck to his collar when he shifted position. She had seen his hair down, before---it hung past his shoulders and was thickly wavy, almost like a woman's. And so dark, like brown-black sable. He wore blue jeans and an old-fashioned work shirt with no collar and it really seemed right for the guy.

He was malakh, she knew, and there was always something in his handsome face that made her feel fluttery in the pit of her stomach...not desire, but worry. As if she'd done something wrong and he was somehow aware of the details. The black leather gloves he wore just reminded her of what Daniel did for money---what Daniel had been doing for a *very long time*.

She swallowed and gave a nod, excusing herself as she slipped her shoes back on. Picking up her glass, she ducked her head as she went past Daniel. She didn't look back; she knew that Daniel was now sitting down in her seat, ignoring the card game that was now null and void.

Chapter Six

Tennyson steeled her nerves as she moved down the small, dimly lit hallway and towards the stairs that led up to the offices. She'd never been invited to this office---not by Daniel or Rhys. She hoped she wasn't in for some kinda trouble. After all, she'd seen the pair of strangers with Daniel, before. Clients, probably...*no*, most likely. And Rhys had gone up, too, leaving her woozy and stoned on the loveseat in the smoke-room.

Adjusting her ruby silk blouse, she thought about the pair of players who shared the office she was headed for. She'd known Rhys since her first night in the club; Rhys was Daniel D'Loup's partner. She didn't even know his real last name, even after three years; Dante said that Rhys went by Lorraine, but that it *wasn't* the name Rhys was *born* with. Didn't matter; she liked Rhys and she could admit to herself that part of the attraction was physical, but the only reason she could think of was that the physical aspect came from how girly he was. He was *really* femme, sometimes. She really just loved having him for a friend because he was smart and funny and what in the hell could Rhys want her in the office for?

When she reached the top of the stairs, she didn't have to ask the receptionist for directions---she'd been to Nicolai's and Joe's office a few times and her Rom friend had pointed out the other office. Genevieve knew her on sight and nodded, polite. Instead of going to the office door she was familiar with, she turned and went to the other. There were other rooms, but these were the two main offices of Pandora's Box.

Tennyson opened the door and entered, taking a deep breath.

It was larger than she'd imagined, lush with potted trees and vines, and warm. The room looked like a cross between a den and an office. Rhys laid on a funky-shaped couch, smoking a joint and drinking his bloody mary. He looked pleased to see her; he gave a little nod and a smirk. She didn't speak to him, instead choosing to examine the office first.

The walls were covered in poster-sized photos and paintings. In fact, there was a series of sepia-toned photographs done of the same young woman---a voluptuous mulatto girl with cafe latte skin and pale eyes and high cheekbones and long curls. Most of the photos were of that young woman lounging in window seats or out in a garden overgrown with tropical plants. She wore nothing but a sheet of either silk or transparent linen. Her gaze was soft, unfocused, trained on something beyond the photographer. Other than the cloth that only enhanced her perfect skin and bone structure, the figure of beauty wore a strand chain of some metal that wound around her throat, over her slim arms, on her waist and voluptuous hips, and disappeared out of sight under the arch of folded knee or tiny foot.

Hmmm...*interesting.*

One photograph, not in sepia tones, caught her attention and she moved across the office towards the door that had to lead into the second room. She stopped in front of it, mesmerized, forgetting altogether that Rhys was in the office with her.

It was a picture of the desert---an oasis, probably. Tennyson took a drink of her tart cocktail, enthralled. There was so much to be seen, in the picture. In the background, the short sand-colored buildings of a village or town could be seen. A few green trees were present, between the buildings and the objects of interest. She found the camouflaged, leaf-shaded shapes of camels in the greenery.

But, in the foreground, a man stood...he leaned against the side of a sandy, beat-up, dust-coated Jeep. Behind him, in the Jeep, she spotted an assault rifle and a bandolier of ammo. In his late twenties, he had tan skin and an expressive mouth. He had a strong, straight nose and smooth brow that was only partially to be seen under the line of a black burnoose. He looked like...he looked as if he might belong there. He was slender, a white man in the long, flowing robes of the native Bedouin. And he had the most amazing blue eyes. They glowed, startlingly sky-like, in that sweet boy face.

Then, she realized who the man looked like and her jaw dropped.

Rhys. He looked like Rhys.

Those eyes, in that dusty, bronzed face...so breathtaking.

"Wow." She whispered.

"I always liked that picture." Rhys spoke up, his quiet accent a little thicker than usual. He'd been raised by Frenchmen, he had told her once, and so he kept a polyglot accent, almost a patois dialect. It was somewhere close to Daniel's accent, really. She didn't turn to look at him as he laughed, low and sexy, going on. "My partner doesn't mind me wanting to keep it here. Just like I don't mind the pictures of his wife."

The mulatto woman...that had to be Daniel's dead wife, then. She'd died of cancer. She knew that, from conversations with Dante. She knit her brows together, shifting to glance at her friend; he was still on his strange couch, watching her with drowsy eyes. "Why do you want a picture of yourself hanging up? Is it just sentimental, for the sake of a memento? I mean...it *is* you, right?"

Rhys' smile grew broader and she felt herself warming to it; he seemed genuinely amused.

"That's not me." The malakh sat up, then, carefully balancing his glass in one hand as he stubbed out the joint he'd smoked down to a nub. His voice was almost a whisper as he blew smoke from his flared nostrils. "That's my dad. Daniel gave me the original picture back when he and I first got to know each other, when I was a kid. He knew my parents---he and my dad were good friends."

"Your dad?" She turned to study the picture again.

Okay, yeah. The skin color was different---Rhys was darker, almost mulatto. The mouth of this young man was thinner than Rhys' full, pretty lips. And there was a difference in the eyes. A slight one. Rhys' gaze was more slanted and...had tan-brown in them. And...Rhys had that scar, didn't he? Right there, barely noticeable in the fold of his left eye.

"His name was Steven. Steve." Rhys sounded contemplative behind her, on the couch. And she recognized the crazy-gentle meaning of this moment; the malakh was sharing secrets with her. "He was a scientist for the CIA, but he also worked in the field as an agent, sometimes, the last few years of his life. That picture was taken while he was in college, in Egypt. He was like me, from what Mattie and Daniel say. They claim that it was one of the ways Mattie knew who I was, the first time she saw me. It wasn't just what I could do, it was how I looked. I mean...I look at the picture and I see the differences first. I don't see me 'til I look at them both, both my mama and my papa."

Tennyson stepped backwards and shifted, going to the couch. She sat down beside him. She'd known, for a while, that Rhys had grown up an orphan, raised by some friend of his family's, but this was the first time she had gotten the chance to hear him talk about it. He never talked about his family, about the way he'd grown up...what she had heard about his past had come from Dante.

"Do you have a picture of her? Your Mom?" She relaxed against the end of the couch, half-turned to face the black-clad twink malakh. She couldn't help but see the strangely dark expression that rose into his eyes then and she compensated, back-pedaling. "I mean, I don't wanna pry. It's just...you sound like you need to talk about this stuff. I carry pictures of my parents, both of them. My Dad died before I was born, but I feel like I know *something* about him when I look at the picture."

The darkness was slow to leave Rhys' face, but then he rolled his eyes and gave a cocky smirk. "Yeah, actually I do. I carry their pictures in my wallet. Maybe I'm not so different from other guys, huh?"

She didn't tell him how very different she believed he was, from other guys.

"Can I see?" She dared.

Rhys rolled to one side and pulled out the wallet he carried in the back pocket of his leather pants. Still on the chain, he opened it and slid two little photos out. One was a smaller version of the photograph hanging on the wall behind a frame. Rhys' dad. The other was a black and white photo of a young woman who looked like she was either mulatto or Arabic. She wasn't an especially pretty girl, but there was a strength in her face that really jumped out. An odd wisdom that could be seen in her eyes, in the curving, full lips. Yeah. She could see Rhys in the woman. It was easy to see, in fact.

"She worked for the CIA, too. She was part of the same team, with Daniel and Mattie. Her name was Roan Bashiyra Ata'din. My papa told me that my parents met there in Egypt, while Steve was in college. Mattie said that Roan's parents were Egyptian. From what I understand, they're both still alive, living somewhere. Over there. I've just never met them. My grandparents."

Tennyson couldn't believe that her secretive malakh friend would share so much. She smiled, gentle, and made a suggestion. "Maybe you should change that, when you get a chance...go meet your family."

"Nah." Rhys was quick to dismiss the idea as he put the photos away, slipping his wallet back into the pocket he'd dragged it from. The chain clink-chimed for a second and went silent again. Her friend drained the bloody mary then, shaking his head as he set the empty glass down on the table's surface. "I'm not like them. From what I've been told...neither was she. My mother. That's why she joined the CIA's elite teams---so she could use those differences for a cause she might believe in. She was, everyone thought, some kinda mutant, but it was more. She was a throw-back. A malakh. Like Steve and like Mattie and like Daniel. Like me. She didn't fit in with her tribe and neither would I."

"You don't think so?" She pondered it, suddenly realizing how much alike they were. She'd never known anything about her Dad's family. She voiced it. "I've always wondered what it'd be like to meet my Dad's family. I've only seen a few pictures and I get money from them, as an inherited allowance, every month, but they made my Mom promise that there wouldn't be any contact between us---them and me. I don't even know if my grandparents are alive---my Dad's parents. I've learned to accept that, but I still...I wish I could know something."

They went quiet, then, lost in the thoughts of dead family. She wondered again about the name Ashwin and why it always came back to her when she least expected it. Why she felt like she needed to know the truth about her dead father. Didn't Rhys want the same thing?

Finally, he spoke again and when he did, he reached out and touched her wrist with his bare fingers. They scorched, like a red-hot iron. "Daniel and I have to leave the country. We're going to Egypt, actually, making with the tourist thing...wanna go on vacation with us?"

Tennyson opened her mouth in amazement and then closed it, *snap*. Her brain fizzled, trying to imagine what it meant, an invitation like that. Egypt. Where Rhys' mother's family was from. She had forgotten why she was asked to the office in the first place. Daniel had said that Rhys needed to see her.

She blinked a few times, staring at her malakh friend, and then shook her head, flabbergasted. "I like you a lot, Rhys, but I don't think..."

The sleek, dangerous player was back. He gave a bemused laugh, squeezing her wrist; his accented voice teased. "Non, princess, I'm not asking you to go along for a sexy vacation. I need you to come along on an assignment. A job. If you feel up to the work, I need someone to play a distraction for our mark."

It hadn't even occurred to her that it could be a hit---that she could be helping her friend set a man up to die. She knit her brows together in thought, then asked. "Is it *dangerous*? Could we get caught?"

"Always." Rhys winked, licking away the last traces of his drink from the lower curl of his mouth. With one hand, he reached up to the nape of his neck and tugged at his light brown ponytail, as if straightening the polished waves. "We have to do something and I need a gorgeous, intelligent woman who can distract a man without getting bogged down by any attraction of her own. You know? Someone who won't lose her head over a guy."

"You could get anyone, I'm not femme fatale material...I don't..." She let it fall away, left unfinished.

What the hell was Rhys doing to her? It was as if she was under some sleepy, cotton-soft spell.

He leaned close then, his lips coming close to her cheek as he murmured, his drawling voice mixing tease with plea. One lock of his hair had fallen out of place and was tantalizing at his cheekbone. "I can't get just *anyone*. My distraction has to be gorgeous and intelligent and impervious to the wiles of men. She has to be a garden person, someone who can woo a mark using the art of plants. Someone smart enough to follow my lead, in doing the cover-story. Not just anyone's gonna cut it, Tenny...it has to be you."

It seemed like too much of a coincidence. It had to be a set-up. She backed up a few inches to look him in the eye, serious. But, then Rhys gave her a winsome smile, so tender it made her heart clench. It was the smile of a boy who genuinely wanted her help and was willing to beg, if he needed to.

Tennyson started to protest and decline.

He whispered, then, husking the words against her lips, the threatening offer of a kiss she was powerless to refuse. "If you do this, Tenny, I'll give you anything you want."

Okay. That cinched it. It was a dangerous game, playing with a player. Wow. Her Mom would never believe she'd been so crazy, to make a deal with a man who could kill with a smile.

She nodded her agreement, breathing the words, feeling weak under his fiery-wet mouth as he cupped her face in both his large hands. "Fine, yes. I'll do this...but, you owe me, Rhys. I can't believe I'm saying yes. You better not get me killed or thrown in jail."

Nicolai pushed a few strands of dark hair away from his eyes and studied the cards he held. Four potential bids, which meant that Tennyson and Joseph were also holding decent hands. *Hmm.* He lost himself in the cards and didn't realize there was someone approaching the table until it was too late.

It was Tennyson's quick jump that made him look up and around to see that Daniel D'Loup stood at the table. The regal-looking benu malakh stood with his gloved hand on Tennyson's shoulder and no expression on his strongly handsome face. He wore faded blue jeans and a long-sleeved work shirt without a collar---it gleamed like snow in the darkness. The gloves only served as a reminder of what this creature was, as a player.

The benu had a delicious accent. "He has requested your presence in the office."

Tennyson glanced at him with her pale, agate-like eyes and then at Joseph before nodding, laying her cards face-down on the table. Taking her glass of slow comfortable screw along, his hag headed for the door that led upstairs to the offices. He could see the golden beads in her braided hair long after he lost sight of her dark trousers and blood-red shirt.

Daniel D'Loup, without being invited, sat down in the empty chair.

"May I speak with you alone, Snowden?" It was polite and indifferent; Daniel's gaze went past him without hesitation. To the malakh, he didn't exist in this moment. But, Joseph did; Daniel wanted to talk with his Sire. The benu malakh tilted his head, the tail of his tied-back hair falling against the flat collar and shoulder of that clean, white shirt. "I must have your ear for a few moments."

Joseph could say no, could suggest another time and place, but he knew it wouldn't happen. His lover nodded to Daniel and then reached to give his hand a touch---just the barest hint of a touch---the permission to leave.

Getting up, Nicolai licked at his teeth again and let the after-taste of Rhys' blood glow on his tongue as he slid his sunglasses into place. Without a backwards glance, he headed for the bar. He could finally have a drink, maybe have a conversation. He'd seen a few players in the bar, earlier; they were probably still sitting there.

The bar was a large room, lined with book shelves and tables. Against one wall ran the high counter of cypress-wood. It gleamed golden-red in the muted light. Here, he couldn't hear the noise of the dance-floor. It was far less crowded, too. The jukebox was playing a Steve Pierson song and he stood at the end of the bar, listening, while waiting for Mattie to notice him.

'Something in the air, so dark I can't see. Everybody knows what's going on, everybody but me. Oh these secrets...you know, you know they're killing me. Yes, they say the truth will set you free, aw, but I can't believe all these secrets.'

"What do you want?" Mattie Curran asked, her voice clipping the words short. She'd finally come to this end of the bar and sounded irritated. But, he was accustomed to it; she almost always sounded irritated.

Bringing his attention around to the freckled bitch, he gave her a broad smile that revealed his fangs. He lowered his chin enough to show his eyes over the rim of his dark sunglasses. "A vampire martini, please."

Mattie grunted non-commitally at him and rolled up her left sleeve once more, to reveal her elbow, as she turned away. He pulled himself up onto the closest barstool and lit another cigarette. The smoke in the bar-room was thick and blue and hung at face level, but he didn't necessarily have to breathe, so...he could care less. It wasn't as if he could die of cancer.

The blues song continued to wail from the jukebox as he studied the patrons who usually didn't venture out of this part of the club. A few middle-aged fags on the prowl, a few tough dykes...a handful of players who didn't like the dance-floor. Four of them were shooting pool under the funky off-kilter lamp that flooded the green-felt table like a prison spot-light, their faces shadowed as they moved. He knew them all on sight, but didn't care; they weren't friends or comrades or even interesting.

But, two stools down from him...Javi. Javi the shape-shifter asetau, talking to Rembrandt from across the bar. Rembrandt was the yellow-skinned Creole bartender who worked with Mattie at night. Now, there...there, he might find some conversation. At least, he could talk with two mortals who knew the score of Pandora's Box.

Nonchalantly, he moved to sit next to the asetau malakh.

Javi Clay was wearing blue flannel pajama pants and flip-flops with an over-sized white tee-shirt. He looked like he'd just crawled out of bed and walked to the club, still half-asleep. He could smell the odd chocolate scent that rose from the malakh player's warm skin. It made him feel hungry again.

Mattie brought him his martini before the Mexican asetau even realized he was sitting there, so close. Javi jumped, his caramel brown eyes growing wide. He offered a gentler version of the smile he'd given to Mattie and silently nodded at the shape-shifter. Rembrandt straightened up on his side of the bar and moved away, damp bar-rag in one big hand.

"How's it going, Clay?" He asked, to be polite.

The asetau shrugged and buried his answer in the mug of amber beer he lifted to his strange, goatish upper lip. It sounded like an 'okay'. He lifted his own glass, fragile and thin, to sip at the cocktail. The four cherries in it bobbed up and down like disembodied heads in a sea of fresh blood.

Mmm. Cherry vodka, vermouth, grenadine, and cranberry juice. Chilled.

It slid over his tongue and cleaned away the last traces of copper and sex from Rhys' blood. He licked his lower lip and took a drag off his cigarette, rolling his head to the side so that his hair would glide off his brow without help.

"Anybody new in your life?" He dared, flicking his gaze towards Rembrandt before pinning the petite shape-shifting malakh with his full stare. Over the rim of his sunglasses, he knew what his eyes looked like...he knew what Javi saw, staring back at him. Dark, almost black, with a tiny hint of red-gold fire...the mark of something less than human, something more than demon.

"No, not really." Javi Clay shrugged now.

He made a suggestion. "Maybe you're just not looking in the right places."

If he wasn't too far off his mark, the asetau was lying to him. There was someone new and that someone was in the bar tonight...in this room. The scent of malakh pheromones was one he knew pretty damn well. But, it wasn't Rembrandt. He could see that much.

"How's going with you and..." Javi's voice faded on the last; the asetau wouldn't say Joseph's name unless it couldn't be helped.

"Unlife's wonderful. We're going on a clean-up in a few nights, take out some trash that's been hanging around the Quarter. We keep picking up on them---they're the kind that feeds on the tourists here for Mardi Gras. Joe's got some new weapons he wants to try out." He tossed his Sire's player nickname out casually. "Wanna go with us?"

"To clean out vampires?" Javi nearly choked on his beer and wiped the spill away with a crumpled paper napkin. The cinnamon-curled malakh went pale under his bronzed Latino skin. With a shake of his head, Javi refused. "I can't. I don't know anything about killing vampires."

"It's easy." He laughed, taking another drink of the martini. Now, he stubbed out his cigarette and shifted on the stool, to face the asetau. "All you do is put a stake through their heart or cut off their head. *Poof*, they're dust in the wind."

"Easy for you." Javi frowned, looking down at the napkin he still held in his square hand; it was getting worried to shreds. "You're one of them and...doesn't it take a lot of strength? More strength than I've got."

Nicolai Valeska leaned in closer, confidingly, knowing that his presence unnerved the malakh. "Oh, come on. If Perseus Shadow can kill vampires, you can. He goes out with us sometimes. It can be a lot of fun. We won't let anything bad happen to you."

"He's got plans, you Undead shite." Mattie was in front of them; she interrupted, reaching for the ashtray that sat on the bar. Dumping it, she wiped up the small section of bar and then put the square glass back in its space, directly between him and Javi. "He can't go on one of your crazy hunts. Dorado's got another job to do...right, Dorado?"

The Mexican malakh's CIA nom de guerre made him sit up and take notice. And it showed on Javi's face; he didn't mind that Mattie had interrupted. So, Dorado had a job to do, for the club. Well, that was fine.

He said so. "It's okay. You can go with us some other time. You don't even have to kill them, Clay. You can serve as our sneakboy and watchdog. Sometimes, we get stopped by the cops and it's better if we have someone to run interference for us."

Mattie snorted and he shifted his gaze to her, staring up at the evil blonde. She looked like a boy, sometimes, and he knew she was older than she looked. She was benu malakh, altered on the genetic level, and she was often cruel. But, she was a fair boss and he didn't mind the work. In her shirt and tie, she could've passed for a college boy...as long as the observer didn't study her eyes too hard. Or the cut of her mouth.

Cruel, bitter bitch.

Her stare was like steel and clouds and her face was boyishly soft; if it weren't for the expression in her eyes and the flat line of her mouth, she'd be pretty...very pretty, for a benu malakh. It was easy to see what Rhys loved, but it was just as easy to see where Rhys had gotten himself sliced to pieces.

Hard to believe that his friend was still mourning this lost lover.

She didn't have any tits, from what he'd seen. And her hips were as narrow as a man's. There was nothing very appealing about her body, as far as he could see...nothing fertile or earthy or voluptuous about Mattie Curran.

Yet, for all that...Joseph liked Mattie. Joseph said Mattie was a rare woman.

Whatever.

After she moved off and away once more, he stared into his martini and studied the bobbing cherries. He poked at one with the tip of his finger and then...then, he became aware of the changing scent from the asetau who sat beside him. The dark, semi-sweet chocolate smell was growing stronger.

Nicolai lifted his eyes to the side, to watch Javi without being noticed.

Javi Clay's stare was planted squarely on Mattie Curran and there was a crazy smile on the shape-shifter's Mexican face.   Mattie was unaware of it, of course, but...damn.   He couldn't help it; he chuckled to himself at the mess of Javi's affections.

The asetau was falling in love with a benu malakh who had a reputation as a world-class ball-buster.   Other than Rhys, he'd never heard so much as even a whisper about Mattie's love life.   Dante Webster said that she didn't have one and if anyone would know, it'd be Dante...Mattie's step-son, the person she was closest to, emotionally.

So.   Javi was going head over heels for Rhys' ex-lover, the mother of Rhys' son.   Now, that could prove ugly...if Rhys decided to be a bastard about his claim on the situation.   It was something he really wanted to see.   The vampire in him wanted to watch, to see what would happen.

He mused on it for a moment, leaving Javi Clay alone, before turning his mind inwards to a different consideration.   He was convinced that Tennyson was a demi-malakh and just as equally convinced that she didn't know.   It was just something she had said, something Rhys had said.   They could smell each other, his two friends.   Could smell the scent that only vampires, demons, and the descendants of angels could pick up on.

Accidental-like, Rhys had mentioned it first---that he could find Tennyson in a room full of people, blind-folded.   Her scent was that unique.   Tennyson's confession had been something else, more embarrassed than anything.   She'd confided in him that she found Rhys' sweat to be one of the sexiest things she'd ever smelled.

He knew she wasn't demon and she wasn't Undead.   So...malakh.   Which would account for the light coming from her skin, the slinky-crazy light.   He pretended he didn't know what Joseph was talking about when his Sire got into expounding on malakh attributes, but he knew.   He knew.

He'd decided early to not tell Tennyson what he'd figured out about her; if she knew, she'd let him know eventually.   It didn't *really* matter, around here, right?   That led him to considering malakh and vampires and the source of their origins, according to Rhys and according to Joseph.

Joseph had told him a bizarre story which wasn't too far from what his own ancestors had said.   Vampires were supposedly the children of Lilit, the first woman on earth.   And, yet, so were malakh.   According to Joseph, Lilit was simply a term to be used for independent women who didn't need a man in order to survive in the world...it was rather modern and free-thinking of his Master to say so and, yet...

Lilit, in legend, was Adam's other half.   Man and woman had been created together, as one androgyne being.   When they were separated, the trouble began.   Lilit refused to give Adam complete dominion and left his home.   She met up with angels and corrupted them with her beauty, wit, and intelligence.   She bore these fallen angels children.   Some were monstrous---vampires and demons.   Others were benu and asetau and hekau and sakau.   But, one child was tchatchau---more like vampires than not, yet mortal and able to go invisible.

According to Joseph's stories, these children were looked upon at first by other humans as monsters or protectors.   The distinction began to be entangled and warped; the malakh were often seen as monsters, because they weren't completely human and possessed abilities that made them different.   Over time, they found ways to hide among humans and evolve.

Then, as thousands of years passed, there were fewer and fewer of them...and, now, there was perhaps two thousand malakh in the whole world.   Joseph's broad count, of course, since no one could be sure.   The count was based on the idea that, for every one million babies born, a malakh might show itself...and even that was probably being overly generous to their birth rate.

According to Joseph's stories, the vampires recognized malakh by scent because of some common disposition that went beyond living and unliving.   Particularly with Rhys.   Joseph couldn't be sure, because Rhys was the only tchatcha they knew---and probably the only one in the whole world---but his Sire claimed that Rhys was irresistible to vampire senses through that common disposition.

For, as Joseph said, there was another legend which claimed that the vampires came from a mix of demon and tchatchau. That legend talked of how tchatchau were the original blood-drinkers in the world and they got mixed up with some demon that could take over a body after it was dead, incorporating memory and psychology. The demon passed itself on within the blood---an ordinary human could die and become Undead, if he was given vampire blood. But, the legend said that this all began with an unholy mix of tchatchau and demon.

Nicolai Valeska drank his martini and ordered another, smoking cigarettes as he changed gears in his mind and thought about what Rhys had told him of malakh genetics and how they'd evolved. To him, something in Rhys' explanation made much more sense than Joseph's.

Malakh had started out as half-angel cousins to ordinary mortals, smarter and faster and stronger. At one time, they'd been on the fast track of the quicker, more potent evolution; they'd have wiped humans out as Cro-Magnon had wiped out his predecessors. It was simply the way of evolution. Over three-fourths of them born were androgyne, hermaphrodite; of these three-fourths, half would be able to reproduce as either male or female.

All malakh breeds had a distinct look and scent and these were used for recognition and breeding; in the beginning, there were ten very different types of malakh. But, over time, they were condemned as demons and monsters and so, their second evolution began. Their scents became more elusive and the wings became unseen; only the ones who could hide what they were might manage to live long enough to find mates and produce children. If a malakh couldn't hide what he was, he didn't survive and his bloodline was finished. But, the scent always gave them away---to another malakh. Even demi-malakh could pick up the odors---if aware of what it meant, that different smell.

Behind him, the jukebox made a cough-grinding noise and started playing something new---something besides baleful electric blues. The music was electric, but alternative and hot.

"Hey, Goldie! This one's for you!" A familiar voice shouted, breaking off into a crazed laugh that he recognized intimately.

Nicolai whipped around on the stool, nearly toppling off. He'd gotten drunk fast---after only five vampire martinis---and there, in the open space by the jukebox, stood Rhys Lorraine, who looked sly and cruel and everything else the tchatcha was able to be with just a crooked smile.

'At first I was afraid. I was petrified. I kept thinking I could never live without you by my side. But then I spent so many nights just thinking how you'd done me wrong. I grew strong. I learned how to get along. And so you're back from outer space. I just walked in to find you here without that look upon your face. I should have changed my fucking lock. I would have made you leave your key if I'd have known for just one second you'd be back to bother me.'

It was Cake, coiling free of the jukebox, and he groaned. He knew this song---he'd heard it too damn much, recently. But, Rhys wasn't going to let up. After assaulting the jukebox, the sleek malakh boy began to stalk toward the cypress-wood bar with open arms, obviously challenging Mattie Curran to stop him.

And it went on, the show. Rhys didn't sing, now, but lip-synched perfectly.

'Oh now go. Walk out the door. Just turn around now. You're not welcome anymore. Weren't you the one who tried to break me with desire? Did you think I'd crumble? Did you think I'd lay down and die? Oh not I. I will survive. As long as I know how to love, I know I'll be alive. I've got all my life to live. I've got all my love to give. I will survive. I will survive.'

Rhys drunk and stoned was a wild sight; even in slick clothes and without a hair out of place, the tchatcha was feral. Before he could move out of the way, he found his shoulders being used as a spring-board for his friend's attack on the bar. Rhys went up past him, over the bar-stools, and onto the bar's golden-warm surface.

Up and down the bar, skinny-muscular Rhys paraded; not a single glass was toppled.

Black shit-kicker boots moved as delicately as if on point in a ballet and Mattie Curran did nothing. She stood back, against the rear counter, with her arms folded against the nearly flat expanse of her ribs. Her mouth was thinned out and her eyes were like stone gimlets. Pandora Box's owner and manager was not amused in the least by her ex-lover's rock star antics.

'It took all the strength I had just not to fall apart. I'm trying hard to mend the pieces of my broken heart. And I spent oh so many nights just feeling sorry for myself. I used to cry. But now I hold my head up high. And you'll see me with somebody new. I'm not that stupid little person still in love with you. And so you thought you'd just drop by, and you expect me to be free. But now I'm saving all my lovin' for someone who's lovin' me.'

Rembrandt, on the other hand, was already in motion. He had to give the Creole credit---Rembrandt didn't try to pull Rhys off the bar. Instead, the barman spoke to Javi, who watched the tchatcha with something akin to bemusement in his open-mouthed expression. But, then, that was to be expected. Rhys and Javi had been partners, in the CIA team that Mattie had led...right?

"Dorado." Rembrandt had to work, getting Javi's attention. The Creole barman slapped the bar in front of the asetau. "Dorado! Go get D'Loup. Tell him he's gotta come get his boy off the bar, now. The crazy fool's goin' too far again."

The ex-CIA malakh operative moved fast, headed away to get 'help'.

Rhys swaggered and danced to the trumpets and guitars, his face lit by the low-hanging lamps that swayed dangerously close to him. There was something going on here, he could see...Rhys didn't usually do this kind of insane crap in the club. Rhys was psycho, but there was a limit where the club was concerned. This was beyond the limit. So, what was happening? Had something happened with Tennyson, in the office?

The idea of that made him bristle with jealousy.

'Oh now go. Walk out the door. Just turn around now. You're not welcome anymore. Weren't you the one who tried to break me with desire? Did you think I'd crumble? Did you think I'd lay down and die? Oh not I. I will survive. As long as I know how to love, I know I'll be alive. I've got all my life to live. I've got all my love to give. I will survive. I will survive.'

He felt his Sire approaching. Nicolai managed to take his eyes off the show, turning to look at the doorway that led into the 'temple' dance-room part of the club. Above him, to the left, Rhys continued to parade on the bar. In a few moments, he smelled the other two--- Daniel and Tennyson. And then, Dorado.

Daniel came through the door first, wine glass in his gloved hand. The dark-haired Swiss benu looked much more amused than Golden Wolf had, seeing Rhys on the bar-top among the ashtrays and glasses. Tennyson was right on the malakh's heels, her braided hair clicking with each move she made; she looked surprised. His Sire came behind them, followed by Javi Clay. Javi looked embarrassed, his Sire didn't. Joseph wore no expression at all.

"Make him get down, D'Loup." Rembrandt said to Daniel, loud enough to be heard over the jukebox. Everyone in the bar had stopped what they were doing previously and were watching Perseus Shadow. The Creole barman shook his graying head with disgust. "He's got no business doin' shit like this here, drunk or not."

Mattie was the only one who had stayed truly silent; she hadn't moved or spoken. With her shirt sleeves rolled up and her tie loosened just the tiniest bit, she was smooth. Even the sheaf of strawberry blonde hair that fell out of place on her brow was just as it should be.

It wasn't Perseus Shadow's partner who stepped forward, to take command. Daniel stood still, with an expression akin to Mattie's. No, it was Tennyson---his hag---who pushed close to the bar, coming to stand directly beside him. Her voice was low and husky, her tone insistent. "Come down, Rhys. You've made your point. I don't think anyone's gonna deny you the crown."

Without any indication that he'd heard Tennyson, Rhys jumped down off the bar. The tchatcha assassin landed in front of Daniel and, uncharacteristically, stumbled. Daniel caught Rhys around the waist and held the boy close, for balance. Nicolai Valeska, on the sidelines, saw the expression on the two benu malakh' faces. Storm-cloud gray Brit and deepest sapphire Swiss. Mattie and Daniel stared at each other, now smiling their vaguely bemused smiles...and silently vowed murder.

Oh, *yes*. It was there. Anyone with a taste for death could see the murder as it was promised. Once the very best of friends and partners, they still trusted each other implicitly, from what he'd seen, but Mattie hated Daniel and Daniel hated Mattie...and all because of Rhys.

Chapter Seven

It was Joseph who broke the silence---the jukebox had stopped playing, but no one else was talking. His Sire began clapping slowly and evenly, showing his lack of interest with the sarcasm that sliced through the comment. "Nicely done, boy. Let me be the one to buy your next drink. I'll even put five dollars in for your music."

He watched, trepidation filling his gut, as his ancient Master slid a five dollar bill into the jukebox's mouth. Joseph stood there, in his modern-day clubbing clothes---wife-beater and jeans and boots---as if vampires had a right to exist in the same world as angels and innocents. It made him shiver inside, the realization of how wrong it really was. His gypsy heart might not beat anymore, but it still knew wrong from right.

The dykes and the fags were going back to their own business and Rembrandt was pouring drinks. Tennyson plopped down onto the bar stool next to him, where Javi had been sitting before, and ordered another slow comfortable screw. The scent of orange juice and Southern Comfort was wafting off her, almost as strong as the cannabis and pheromones.

Dorado didn't seem to mind that his seat had been taken; the curly-headed satyrine asetau simply took the next stool down.

He kept himself turned sideways, so that he could see the other players in this domestic drama. Mattie still hadn't moved and she was still locking stares with Daniel, who hadn't turned loose of Rhys yet. And that black-gloved hand looked right, curled around the tchatcha's skinny, Spandex-covered ribs.

Joseph came to the bar, now, moving like a nightmare of sex and muscles and sex and darkness. His Sire's smile was as human and sardonic as it ever got, covering up the fangs which would give the game away. "Mathilda, if you please. Give D'Loup and his boy another of whatever they are drinking...on me."

He lost sight of Daniel and Rhys, as his attention was drawn back to his hag. She flipped the edge of her beaded braids back over the shoulder of her blood-red silk shirt and gave him a startlingly bright smile that showed the dimples which were hidden most of the time. Her skin was delicious to look at...like creamed and sugared coffee.

"So. What've you been up to? I came back downstairs and you were nowhere. Joe said he didn't know where you went. Any idea what he and Daniel were talking about?" The questions rattled off Tennyson's tongue fast and he felt dizzy, half from the booze and half from the gleam that came from his hag's body.

The jukebox began playing again and he was only vaguely aware of the music. It didn't seem very important as he stared, tipsy, at the mulatto girl. He could see the veins in her throat as they pulsed. He could smell the blood, too, and it was heady.

"I...I sat here. I drank." He mumbled, finally breaking the spell by force. Out of the corner of his eye, he saw Rembrandt. The barman was asking him if he wanted another vampire martini. He shook his head at the Creole without looking away from Tennyson. Lifting his fingers, he rubbed away the hair that stuck to his cheek and ear on the left side. Words spilled out and he spoke his mind without thought. "I really think I need to eat. I'm falling in love with you again---"

He had gotten so lost in Tennyson's skin and eyes that he failed to notice his Sire. Joseph's big hand came down on his shoulder just then and nearly caused him to lose his position on the bar stool. Turning too fast, he looked up into his Master's green-gray gaze and swallowed the squeak of fear that bubbled into his chest and throat. But, Joseph was smiling at him---his terror was unwarranted, this time.

"Do you want something more to drink, Nico?" The pet name brought him back to his sane mind. It was as if Joseph hadn't heard his mad words to Tennyson. He didn't delude himself---Joseph had heard. "I'm being generous tonight. D'Loup has asked me to take his next two jobs while he is on *vacation*."

Vacation. It was a job, really. The thought sobered him a little.

He shook his head. "No, I don't think I want any more to drink...not booze, anyway."

His Sire didn't comment on this.

Tennyson reached to grasp his hand, where it lay on the bar next to his cigarettes. She was the soul of compassion. "Nicolai, if you need, I can..."

"No." Joseph interrupted, still smiling that strange smile. "That is not necessary, girl. Nicolai shall eat when we have left the bar. We can find something without troubling you; you've already given more tonight than you should."

He felt like the world was standing on its head; since when did Joseph get this damn chatty in public? What had really gone down between his Sire and Daniel D'Loup after he'd left the table?

Nicolai Valeska started looking for a way out from under his lover's hand. A glance towards the jukebox showed him where Rhys and Daniel were. Rhys had obviously picked the music to play, but now Daniel had the young tchatcha leaned against the finely-polished wooden wall. The two were having a quiet, private conversation; Daniel held Rhys by the shoulders and spoke softly---almost too soft to hear beneath the music that played, even for a drunk vampire.

But, he was able to hear what Daniel was saying. "You must apologize to her. I know that these are difficult times for you, garcon, but see this from her point of view. You have come to the club that you are the part-owner in and you flaunt yourself before Mattie as if you do not care how she might feel."

Rhys chuckled bitterly, closing his strangely slanted eyes as he rolled his head back onto the wall. "I'm not doing anything differently, Danny. I'm not flaunting anything and I don't think she gives a damn if I care. You saw her...she hates me as much as she ever did."

Daniel gave a sigh of exasperation, one gloved hand moving to cup Rhys' slender neck now. "You dance with whom you please, you fuck whom you please, and you do it where she can suspect every single move you make. She has made her choice, mon petite sauvage. You will not change her mind by showing your ass in public."

"What if I don't want to change her mind anymore?" Rhys gave a nasty smile, not opening his eyes. "What if I've decided to just be myself? I can fuck whomever I want, I can dance with whomever I want. That means she hasn't got the right to tell me what to do---and if I want to dance on the fucking bar, I can do it. I am part owner here, Danny, even if I'm the silent partner."

"She is the mama of your child, garcon." Daniel wasn't letting up. "Consider for a moment what this means. She goes home every morning to the son you gave her. Mattie does not hate you. She cannot hate you---you are part of the son she loves."

"No, Danny...you don't see or feel it the way I do. It's all in what you can't pick up. Mattie hates me. She thinks I'm a monster." Now, Rhys opened his eyes and the ugly, bitter smile was still there. The two malakh stood by the jukebox, in the dim shade, but he couldn't mistake the despair and pain in his friend's blue eyes. "You wanna know what the fucked-up part is, Danny? The worst part? She always felt that way about me, from the day I met her, back when I was still a messed-up kid. She's always looked at me and what goes through her head and her heart, it's about where I come from...what I am. I don't know why she took me as her---whatever I was. I don't know why. I don't know why because---even when we were fucking, she despised me. If I went see-through in bed, she---"

"Shh." Daniel put one leather-covered finger on Rhys' open mouth. "Shh. If you must open yourself to me in such a manner, we will talk at home. Do not shame yourself here, where others may see. Others may take these things as a sign of weakness and you will lose face. Can you be silent and show nothing until we have left the club?"

The benu malakh was upset; only a vampire could've seen the minute trembling. Daniel was so upset, he was actually glad that Rhys was staying quiet for a moment, even if he did want to hear the rest of this cruel confession. Seeing Daniel get upset made him think of Joseph being upset and somehow, he knew...if Daniel got upset enough, things would go badly before the night was finished.

"I don't know, Danny. I love her. I still love her." It was soft, a whisper; Rhys' cherry-lush mouth moved under Daniel's gloved finger. "Is that wrong? To love someone who hates me?"

"She does not hate you, garcon. She may fear you, but she does not hate you."

It was a terrible thing to hear---Daniel and Rhys. He didn't doubt it was true that Mattie feared Rhys. He didn't doubt it at all. But, he knew something that both Rhys and Daniel must surely be aware of.

Fear was simply a breath away from hate.

A new song came on and his gaze instantly jumped to the jukebox.

'Just around the corner, there's heartaches, down the street that losers use. If you can wade in through the teardrops, you'll find me at the home of the blues.'

The music was rockabilly and it made him wince with a mix of disgust and fascination. Rhys and his damn Johnny Cash music. But, there was something. The music made Rhys straighten up. It was a song from the soundtrack of a movie made about the country legend. The change was good for Rhys. The pain was gone, slid away out of sight behind the invisible mask that his tchatcha friend wore.

'I walk and cry while my heartbeat keeps time with the drag of my shoes. The sun never shines through this window of mine, it's dark in the home of the blues. Oh, but the place is filled with the sweetest memories. Memories so sweet that I cry. Dreams that I've had left me feeling so bad, I just want to give up and lay down and die.'

Within a few moments, Daniel was able to leave Rhys by the jukebox alone; the boy malakh stood there limp-limbed, eyes closed and head laid back on the wall, murmuring the words. The benu came to the bar, six or seven stools away, and ordered a bottle of bourbon.

'So, if you've just lost your sweetheart and it seems there's no good way to choose, come along with me, misery loves company, you're welcome at the home of the blues.'

It was Mattie who served him, bringing the bottle and a water glass. He couldn't help but notice that the bourbon was Jim Beam's Booker. 126 proof, aged eight years. Deep amber with the Old World labeling, he recognized the bottle with ease. He didn't care for bourbons or scotch himself, but he'd seen this ritual a few times in the last three years. Daniel drinking to deliberately get intoxicated, no small feat for a benu malakh, and he had expensive tastes.

'Just around the corner, there's heartaches, down the street that losers use. If you can wade in through the teardrops, you'll find me at the home of the blues. Yeah, you're gonna find me at the home of the blues.'

Odd habits, too. Daniel drank the fine sipping bourbon as if it was water.

The Johnny Cash sob-tune ended and was instantly followed by another song on the same soundtrack album. But, this one wasn't quite as light-weight and he felt like there could be a battle on its way. It was the rough country-blues confession of a man who'd shot his woman while flying on cocaine. He felt like kicking the jukebox into submissive silence. Why in the hell did Rhys have to have a hero like that?

"We went to see that movie, the one about Johnny Cash." Tennyson leaned in and told him in a quiet voice. "Me and Rhys. I think he went to see it every Friday afternoon that it was in the theater downtown." She gave a low chuckle and took a drink of her cocktail. "He probably saw it more than that and just hasn't confessed."

"I can't imagine why." He answered, dryly, looking again at the drunk-stoned tchatcha who seemed oblivious to the world. "Why in the hell would he want to see it so much?"

His hag shrugged her red silk shoulder and demurred. "I don't have a clue. The funny thing is...he likes the actor who played the part. He told me there, the day we went, that he's always thought there was a strange resemblance to Joe."

"Joseph doesn't look anything like Johnny Cash." He protested.

"Not Johnny Cash. The actor who played him. He's a lot younger." Tennyson corrected, giving a tipsy grin as she raised her glass once more and drained it. Her smooth, golden-brown face creased into dimples as she laughed under her breath. "Whatever his name is. I can't remember, right off-hand."

He could. He didn't say it out loud.

Rembrandt brought another cocktail to his hag and he shifted, trying to find Joseph. His Sire was nowhere to be seen. But, Dante had joined Daniel at the bar. The hacker-DJ was drinking a bottle of Bud Light and talking softly to the benu, who had put away nearly half the bourbon already.

Admirable. He wished he could drink as hard as the long-lived Swiss bastard.

Out of the corner of his eye, he spotted Joseph, now. Going to Rhys, carrying a glass for the tchatcha. A very large bloody mary---sans blood, of course, since his Sire wouldn't dream of asking any mortal to cut a vein just to feed Rhys' bloodlust. Joseph claimed that tchatchau didn't need blood to live, so Rhys should curb the habit. Something about controlling an addiction that could become cannibalism in the long run. Or whatever.

There, at Rhys' side, Joseph stood, offering the glass. Rhys was pretending that the ancient Undead wasn't close by, but the spicy tomato-vodka cocktail was welcome---Rhys took it from Joseph without even opening his eyes or saying thank you.

He decided to ignore it all.

It was nearly closing hour. People were leaving the club now, since Dante had cut the dance music off, going past the bar in twos and threes. The country music from the jukebox didn't end; Rhys was in one of his ugly moods, where he was nobody's friend. It was the kinda mood which had made Joseph mutter, in the past, that Rhys could be the Beast, the very monster of all monsters. But, then, Joseph claimed to have seen Rhys do things that Rhys would never have done in front of anybody from the club.

He wondered, briefly, if Rhys had known that Joseph watched.

Tennyson was tugging on his wrist, drunkenly whispering. "Hey, Nicolai?"

With a deliberate slowness---an attempt to retain his vampire grace in the fact of being intoxicated---he turned to smile at his hag. "Yeah, baby?"

She laid her warm-skinned brow against his naked forearm; the beads on her braids clicked metallic as Tennyson slid towards him a little, almost too close for a casual conversation. Her husky, Creole voice was drowsy and slurring. "I love you, Nicolai. I love you and I love Rhys. Nobody else. Too bad neither of you got a pussy I can fuck. I need to get laid...*god*..." The last of it was groaned in a terrible, guttural sigh; he couldn't see her mulatto face, but the burst of her breath was hot. "God...I need someone who can *fuck* and *fuck* and *fuck* and not see me for a minute. I don't want...I wanna be anonymous for a minute. D'you *understand*, Nicolai? Women want too much, they want to move in with you and they wanna get married. *Fuck that.* I just want some sex right now..."

Something in her confession made him horny. It wasn't the way she sounded---drunk and desperate for physical affection. No, it was the knowledge that this was Tennyson, his hag, a woman he actually cared about. And he couldn't touch it. He couldn't touch her. Joseph would skin him...literally. Worse, Joseph might do something to Tennyson, no matter how much his Sire liked the Creole girl.

Still. He was hard. So fucking hard. It felt like his leathers were creaking right over his hardness. Surely Joseph could smell him? Even if nobody else could here, among the malakh, Joseph must.

He needed to beg Joseph for this, someday...offer it as a sacrament to his Sire. He could imagine the argument he might give. *'Please, Master...let me fuck her in front of you, let you see me with a real woman, someone besides Misha, someone warm and hot and mortal and someone not a woman that we're not going to eat afterwards...let me be just a little more than your childe, your boy...'*

It was a dangerous thought.

Yet, he could imagine what it would be like, to taste Tennyson. What it would be like, to bend her double in front of Joseph...bend her hips to push his cock up her lush, caramel-hued ass. As round as it was...

Trying to banish the direction of his thoughts, Nicolai leaned over and kissed his hag on the top of her head, enjoying the feel of her braids as they slipped under his cheek and chin. He whispered. "Any man would be lucky to take you to their bed, baby. Any woman, too. But, if you don't stop, you're going to get me beat half to death. Joseph can't read my mind, but he sure as hell can smell the lust on me right now."

She looked up at him suddenly, a look of disbelief on her face. Tennyson hissed her words. "You want *me*? Oh, my god, Nicolai, that's...that's *twisted*."

"No shit." He grinned and shrugged. "But that's me. I told you, babydoll, after a couple hundred years, anybody gets a little mental. Just look around. The benu here, especially the one who is more than a century old, and then there's the vamps. Me and Joseph."

"You and Joseph and Daniel. The oldest guys here." She nodded, seeing what he was saying, even in her drunken stupor. "Crazy, mental, way past the expiration date."

Nicolai Valeska, who was born among the wagons of the caravan in a small forest village outside of Kiev and raised in Spain during the French Revolution before Napoleon's war, agreed in his most demurring fashion. "Joseph's mad as an Old Testament prophet, Daniel's drinking bourbon like it's water and looks like he's waiting for a gun at the back of his head, and I'm thinking about fucking you and Rhys both until you're screaming and raw and bloody even if it gets me dusted by my Sire...yeah, life is truly a crazy bitch for the immortal."

"I know you haven't made your mind up yet, but I would never do you wrong. I've known it from the moment we met. There's no doubt in my mind where you belong. I'd go hungry, I'd go black and blue...I'd go crawling down the avenue. There ain't nothing that I wouldn't do, to make you feel my love."

His partner was singing and the tremulous tune echoed in the bar, as it was emptying. It was closing time and Mattie was busy wiping up the spills and the detritus, her freckled face quiet and contemplative. Dante sat at one end of the long, cypress wood bar, a bottle of beer in front of him; his ex-partner's hacker step-son was nursing the cold brew and shredding a wet napkin. Now, at this hour, it was only 'family' and the last, remaining players who had not wandered out into the dark, early hours of the morning yet.

Rhys was sitting on the floor in the corner, by the jukebox, his head leaning against the black base of the machine. His garcon's eyes were closed and it was obvious, to any who looked, that the young malakh was entirely too stoned or drunk to care very much for what happened next. The voice that sang was one full of some sadness which had no cure and no discernable source, as if the song possessed a secret only Rhys could translate.

"Storms are raging on a rolling sea, down the highway of regret. The winds of change are blowing wild and free, yeah, but you ain't seen nothing like me yet. There ain't nothing that I wouldn't do, go to the ends of the earth for you. Make you happy, make your dreams come true, to make you feel my love..."

"Time to go." Mattie called out, to no one in particular.

Daniel turned his head to look at the others who remained. Joe Snowden and Valeska were putting on their coats, in preparation against the chilly air of a late New Orleans winter. With them was Tennyson Beaulieu, already snugged into her black suede coat---the fille looked as if she could be a player, her dark eyes searching every face in the bar with an overt ferocity that made him smile. She could be more than a greenhouse manager, he believed.

It was Joe's murmuring voice that now drew his attention, where he sat on the stool beside Dante. The massive vampire was now ready for the cold wet in scarf and gloves and a long, cashmere coat the color of cocoa. Joe Snowden spoke to Tennyson, his lack of accent a mere trick of how old the creature was. "Can you drive, girl?"

"She's too drunk to drive." Valeska answered for Tennyson, who was staring at Rhys, now, with a stern mien. "We can't let her."

"Very well." Joe allowed, a faint smile on his young-looking face. An ignorant human would never think this was an Undead thing. "Girl, give me your keys. We'll make sure you get home safely."

Daniel felt like rolling his eyes at Joe's courtly behavior. Knight of Templar, oui?

"Nah." Tennyson slurred it and he realized how very intoxicated the fille was. She was steady on her feet, but the alcohol and cannabis could be heard in how she worked to be coherent. "You can drive me home, but...but Rhys gets the keys." The way she said this came as a rhyme and the Creole fille giggled, losing the intensity of her expression.

Without warning, her hand came up and tossed something jingling in Rhys' direction. He watched as his tchatcha partner moved; Rhys' arm rose and his large-knuckled fingers opened and the keys were neatly captured without a word. Rhys had done this without opening his eyes and it made the skin on his back crawl, a sudden reminder of how different his tchatcha garcon was, even in the half-hidden world of malakh. Very few could do such things; it was a mark of what Lorraine had created, in Steven's child.

He met Mattie's gaze, then, as he turned to look at her, wondering what she must think of it. Her gray eyes had seen the toss and the catch and her mouth was tightened flat in some difficult emotion. These things always disturbed the Golden Wolf, even as they disturbed him.

Then, the expression changed in his ex-partner's face and she was business again, making a shooing motion with her wet towel. He could tell that Mattie had already imbibed more than one or two glasses of whiskey; the cultured tones of her accent faded into a Northern British dialect. Aberdeenshire. "All o'yas, get th' hell oot o' me bar. Whut th' fuck do ya think t'is is, mmm? A flop-hoose? Ga hame, ya daft gits."

In his corner by the now-silent jukebox, Rhys let the keys he held give a non-musical jangle as he offered a low, pleased chuckle and spoke loud enough to be heard. "I still love you, Goldie."

It was time to leave, perhaps.

He gave Dante's bared arm a squeeze as he slipped from the bar stool, enjoying the slight buzz he had won at the expense of a now-empty bourbon bottle. For benu to become intoxicated, a great deal of booze had to be taken in at a fairly quick pace. The hazel-eyed hacker smiled at him---Dante was not intoxicated and he knew, it would take more than a few beers to knock the husa-hekau malakh off track. Dante's size, alone, was a deterrent; the son of Rob Webster was built on a large, lanky scale and preferred cannabis to alcohol.

"Get the kid out of here before she loses her temper." Dante whispered into his ear, pulling him close by the hand. "Mattie's throwing off serious vibes and it's almost all daggers at *him*."

Him, of course, being Rhys.

Daniel nodded and tugged his own coat on, at the wall, before reaching down to offer his garcon a hand. Rhys accepted the help and grunted soft and fell against his chest, sprawling arms and laughing breath. He felt a rush of heat from the contact and made himself into stone, to ignore the manner in which the tchatcha affected his body.

As he walked Rhys to the door, the garcon called out to Mattie, who stood behind the bar still yet. "I'm coming by, this afternoon. To see my son. I was thinking...I could take Gabe to Neutral Ground for lunch. I'll be there about three or four, Goldie..."

Mattie made a face and shook her head, the long wheat-blonde braid swishing in time to her aggravated disbelief. But, as he turned at the door, to meet her gaze once again, he saw the bare offering of a smile. She still yet cared for Rhys, no matter how insane the young malakh might behave, and her affection was being tempered by time's distance from the dying affair.

He made a wish that his ex-partner would someday forgive him, forgive their garcon.

Outside, they walked down the flagstones and through the iron spike gates and onto the sidewalk beyond the fence. There, in the darkness that still covered the streets, he held Rhys close to his side and watched the vampires with their Creole fille. Valeska stood a house-length away from the club's gates, his lean body bristling in a protective manner. Something was upsetting to the Undead gypsy...and he became aware of its source when he spotted Joe.

Joe was walking in the street, headed for the other side. A new champagne Mercedes sat there, idling, and he could see a woman behind the wheel. Her hair was light brown, to the best of his guess, and he caught a glimpse of white skin and large, soft eyes. Who was this? Why would Joe approach without Valeska, unless this woman was a threat?

He considered getting involved and then brushed away the idea. It was not his concern. He did not care much for Joe Snowden and the disdain was mutual, non? Let Valeska care for Tennyson Beaulieu; the gypsy vampire was more than capable of such a simple task, and he had Rhys to watch over.

Daniel sighed, walking his tchatcha around the corner of the house, to the edge of the next street. His own car sat there, waiting, and he could feel the impending storm that hung overhead. There was more rain on the way; he would prefer to be safely at home when the downpour began.

When he awoke, from a few hours' sleep, he would begin the preparations for their new assignment.

He and Joseph finally managed to get Tennyson out the door. She was bundled up in her long black suede car coat and gloves and he was wishing she'd bothered to bring a muffler---it wasn't icy outside, but to someone drunk, the chilly wet air could do damage.

He wore his leather jacket and gloves against the weather, but Joseph was better prepared in a long, brown cashmere coat. It was the cream colored scarf and matching leather gloves that made him want to laugh at the absurdity of his Sire's tastes.   Joseph almost always looked like he'd just stepped off the slick pages of GQ. Like it mattered or something.

They were taking Tennyson home. She'd passed her car keys off to the morbidly drunk Rhys, but she could always collect them sometime later in the day. As he walked beside her down the gray flagstones, through the front garden, Nicolai looked at his square-faced stainless steel watch and then up at the leaden sky. It was almost four in the morning and the whole world seemed at relative peace.

Relative being the operative word.

Chapter Eight

Valeska and a girl of obviously mixed blood stepped out the front door of the two-story monstrosity that might've been called a family home and wasn't. She'd managed to track them to here, Magazine Street, and this house turned into a nightclub of all things.

She lifted her silver flask and took a sip of liqueur. It was sweet, burning its way down her throat as she studied her 'little brother'. Nicolai Valeska hadn't changed much in the time since she'd seen him last. But, that was to be expected. He was still the prancing sweetheart, it seemed. He grew his hair long, now; that was cute. Very different than he'd looked the last three times she'd seen him, in London and New York and Savannah. But, a century could change a lot, even for the world of the Undead.

So pretty, to be a boy. Of course, he could only be called a boy in this day and age, when maturity came with hardness that Nicolai lacked. In his mortal years, at the time of his death, he'd been considered a man. Most peasant and gypsy men, at twenty, had wives and children. At least, they had, in the early nineteenth century. She could remember him when he'd been warm-skinned and alive, rough and funny and sometimes brutal in his passion for her. They were of similar builds and such different coloring, she and Nicolai. Joseph's mad Russian lovers.

Did it bother her that their Sire had killed the lively gypsy boy out of lust and self-hate, creating another childe from their shared blood? Did it bother her that, before he was even a vampire, Nicolai had replaced her in Joseph's affections? Yes and *yes*. It was too much like being replaced by a second wife, alive or Undead.

Joseph had brought Nicolai to her as a slave, someone to play mortal protector and servant to them. But, it hadn't been very long at all before her Sire---their Sire---had put the dark gypsy boy into her bed, for the sheer spectacle of watching this swarthy manling fuck her, the rabbi's daughter. What delight Joseph had taken, playing audience and director to those scenes---Nicolai was to take the Master's bride and companion in any way the boy saw fit, as long as it was intriguing for the bored and vicious Master.

It was a serious bone of contention between herself and Joseph. She'd left him because of what she'd been able to see of his twisted, ugly desire. She had watched him falling in love with their mortal slave, the teenaged gypsy he'd brought with him from his adventures in Spain. She'd forgiven him for using Nicolai to humiliate her, sexually, for Nicolai himself was worth the humiliation. She had developed a philosophical attitude worthy of any Jewess---let Joseph enjoy the spectacle of Nicolai enjoying her body; as long as she found her own pleasure right under his nose and under his sanctions, what could she care?

She'd forgiven all of that. No, it was finally, after a few years of the charade, the sadistic hunger in his eyes when he watched Nicolai that had sickened her. She'd fought with Joseph and his sick lust and finally left in Rome, knowing that she was leaving Nicolai Valeska to death...for that was the only place Joseph would take the boy. She had figured Nicolai would be dead before the week was out---she'd assumed that Joseph would finally put their gypsy out of his misery in a rage over her departure.

It was a decade later, when she'd finally dared to try approaching her Sire again---in the hopes of a possible reconciliation---that she'd discovered just how rank and perverse Joseph's hungers might run. A decade out had seen Nicolai bedded, raped, killed and brought into the world of the Undead...and well on his way to being a bigger monster than even Joseph was capable of. Nicolai and his violin and the little children...the young girls, the babies, the pregnant mothers. Nicolai the Pied Piper with a bloodied mouth and a sharp, lethal smile.

She felt responsible for the whole sordid mess, didn't she?   If she hadn't left, she could've killed Nicolai and put him out of the play---saved his soul, at the very least.   If she hadn't left, she could've kept Joseph sane.   Well, as sane as Joseph might ever be.

Still.   She couldn't say that immortal unlife hadn't given Nicolai a beauty beyond the mortal one he'd possessed.   When Joseph had brought Nicolai to her, the gypsy was still really just a boy, in his mid-teens.   A few years with them, living a different existence, had seen his lean frame and muscles turn into something marvelous to behold.   Before death.   Before unlife.

He was handsome in his way, looking merely twenty.   He appealed.

The girl with him.   *Interesting.*   She was drunk, drunker than Nicolai.   But, the two acted as if they could be more than friends or acquaintances.   Was this the trick of the night?   The sex-meal that Nicolai had picked up?   The dark-fleshed girl was absolutely stunning, to her.   Yummy.   She wanted to roll down the window, to take a chance at picking up the black girl's scent.   Would she smell like sex and blood and salt?   Would she taste like the other girls?   Could she possibly taste like Emily?   With such luscious mulatto skin, perhaps she'd taste better?

Long black braids with gold beads.   Long black leather coat over ruby-blood silk and black leather pants.   Mmm.   The girl leaned on Nicolai's arm and shoulder, drunkenly.   Ah, well, she wondered...there was something masculine about the girl.   Bi-sexual or lesbian?   Could certainly explain why she was drunk and with Nicolai.   Valeska was just a little too masculine himself for the average lesbian, but if drunk...any girl could be talked into anything.   And with Valeska, anything could become sickening and painful and deadly.   He'd learned the art of bloody degradation from a master.

With another sip of her flask, she silenced that thought.   She wasn't going to go save the chick, that was for sure.   That wasn't why she was sitting outside this odd nightclub.   Maybe she'd follow and steal the girl away from Nicolai, but she wasn't going to play hero.   She would be the panther taking the prey from the alley cat, yes.

And, look...the creature she'd come looking for.   The Knight Templar himself.

Joseph certainly looked healthy, for a man dead nearly nine hundred years.

He'd been eating better, it seemed, than the last time she'd seen him and Nicolai.   But, then, when one didn't have to be uber-careful in a small city like Savannah, one did usually find food more easily.

Her Sire was wearing a long brown coat over a white undershirt and with worn blue jeans.   And boots.   Another interesting sight.   Joseph looked like something from a rock video, if rock stars went around cleanly shaven with hair cut almost Roman short.

The fog was rolling in; February in this damn town was colder than she'd imagined.   She'd been in New Orleans for two weeks now, trying to track them down.   The last time she'd seen her Sire and fellow childe, they were still vacationing in that god-awful mansion in Savannah, Georgia.   A lovely house, lovely town...but not enough crime and sin going on to disguise the feeding habits of two vampires, much less three.

She'd gone to them when Emily died, hoping for some reconciliation; she hadn't wanted to be alone anymore...and without Emily, she hadn't wanted to even *exist.*   She'd buried Emily in Cairo and started searching for her 'family'.   She'd searched in Moscow and St Petersburg, in Paris and London and Madrid and Seville.   She'd searched Rome twice.   Every large city where a vampire might hide like the tiger in the jungle, she had searched for her Sire and her sibling-in-death, Nicolai.

It was in America she had found them, once again, trusting her footsteps to a mere whisper of rumors.   In a relatively small city of the South.   Joseph claimed that he liked the town and was just vacationing for a few years.   All because of the damned house, of course.   Joseph owned a small plantation house five miles outside Savannah; a house with beautiful marble steps and painted wooden columns that looked just like columns in Rome or Athens.   On the backside of the house there was a sleeping porch, a huge balcony with rails and reed blinds that could be dropped to hide the sleepers from sunlight or rain.   Reed blinds and great linen sheets that billowed in the sweet breeze---Joseph loved the damned house because of the sleeping porch.

Joseph and Nicolai had traveled mainly between Savannah and London and Moscow and New York, their four home bases. Out of the four cities, she liked London best, but she knew that Nicolai preferred Moscow. He'd always preferred the Russias and the Slavic people.

Their people.

The last time she'd seen them was on the sleeping porch of the house in Savannah and they had fought with words, ugly words. That was in the year 1920. She'd come for reconciliation and found them rutting together in the darkness of a country night, on that damned sleeping porch. In her grief over Emily, she'd condemned them both. It wasn't that she *really* considered their actions a sin---they were Undead, there was no more sin of the flesh to be considered. It was jealousy and a need to be loved and she had ached to touch them both. Joseph and Nicolai. Who didn't need *her* at all, anymore.

The deal had been struck in New York in the mid-1860s; she would never show her face again in the same city or town. Joseph had reminded her of it, in Savannah. She was never to approach him or Nicolai again.

She had never intended to break that promise.

She opened her mind and whispered to her Sire, hoping he could still hear her when she spoke without voice. *'I need to talk with you, it's important...I come in peace.'*

Immediately, Joseph's dark-haired head jerked up from where he'd been working the latch on the black wrought-iron gate. His gray-green eyes found her car without trouble, with no hesitation.

She didn't need the ability to read his mind to hear what he must have told Nicolai with nothing more than a single glance at his other childe's back. Valeska had already started down the block, away from the nightclub house, the chocolate-skinned black girl in tow. Without a word, Joseph must have told Nicolai something important. For, with not so much as a look around, the little gypsy pushed the hot, round-bodied girl up against the fence and kissed her full-lipped mouth. The girl seemed non-plussed, but went with it, her flailing hands going first limp and then down to hold onto Nicolai's hips.

She smiled, amused at the sight. Nicolai was a notorious lady's man...or, had been, in life. Vampire unlife hadn't completely changed that; vampires had the sexual morals of a pack of dogs.

The kiss didn't last very long, but Nicolai stepped in front of the girl in what could only be called an extremely protective stance. Now, she became aware of what Joseph was doing. He was approaching the car she sat inside of, his face like stone with self-righteous ire.

Beyond Joseph, she spotted two other men. Well, a man and a boy, whose features were lost behind a long sheaf of light brown hair. Maybe it was a girl...at this distance, with the looming figure of her Sire closing in, she couldn't take the time to be sure. But, the man was handsome enough; burly without being hefty, long dark hair in a queue. He had his arm around the lithe boy---or girl. Moving quickly away, in the other direction, with only a few glances back in the direction of her impending vampire family drama.

'That's right, sir, keep moving...you don't want Joseph to notice you watching. He can be excruciatingly thorough with eavesdroppers. I would know better than any other creature on this hateful world.'

Joseph was on the sidewalk next to her passenger side, now, but her Sire didn't make a move to touch the new, champagne Mercedes. He wasn't even looking at her. Instead, she watched, holding her proverbial breath, and waited for him to give a sign that he was interested in actually speaking.

He was looking up the street, his handsome face lifted to the early morning darkness under a flickering streetlamp. As she studied him, Joseph began to walk away, headed up the sidewalk. She realized what he wanted her to do---follow, away from the club. With a last glance at Nicolai and his female mortal, she put the car in drive.

Along the street, she followed Joseph at a crawl. He turned the corner and continued walking. On and on. At last, her Sire reached a spot where no streetlamp interrupted the darkness and no house lights intruded. Here, he stopped walking and waited. She pulled up next to him and cut the engine off once more, touching the button which would unlock the passenger door.

He got in without a word and she was instantly aware of his size. How could she have forgotten how massive he seemed? He wasn't of a remarkable height or build, compared to many mortals she had known, but at certain moments, Joseph became a Goliath. It was intent, attitude...his spirit was enough to fill the car's interior.

Joseph stared ahead at the darkness on the street and she watched him. He wore no expression; he was not happy to see her, but he wasn't going to show his disapproval. His jaw was set, his mouth a narrow line of dark rose. His eyes showed nothing but their innate and shadowed intensity. In silence, they sat.

Finally, he spoke, and she felt herself thrown backwards in time to the night she had met him. In his voice, she felt the memory come alive; once more, she could smell the hay and manure of that inn's stable and could almost hear the low knickering of horses.

"I thought you were going to keep the promise you made to me."

She took a deep, unnecessary breath and nodded, forcing herself to focus on the moment. They weren't in her homeland and it was not 1351. They were sitting in an expensive car on a strangely unlit block of Gravier. "When I made that promise, when I renewed it almost a century ago, I intended to do everything in my power to ensure our paths never crossed again."

"Why are you here? This is my city. If you have kept a finger on what I do, you're aware of how I treat our kind here." Now, he turned and lowered his head, looking up at her from under his dark brows; his expression held no affection and no sympathy. His voice was like gravel. "It's a closed hunting ground."

Licking her lower lip, she pressed the edge of her fangs into the tip of her tongue and then whispered. "I need your help."

"I've no help for something like you, Mishenka." He used her real name, the name her scholarly, gentle father had written down in his family book at her mortal birth in the Russian city where she'd lived as a girl. Joseph, saying it, was not being kind. "You do not belong here...you don't belong with me."

Misha shook her head and negated his denial, clenching one hand into a fold of the white velveteen shirt she wore. She was passionate, now that the words flowed between them once more. "You're wrong. I do belong with you. You're mine as much as I'm yours. Isn't that a true thing? The night we married, you said something...and it's something true. It's something that can't be broken, no matter how you feel about us. I bet even Nicolai could parrot it back at you with as much ease as I can."

Joseph closed his eyes and turned away, his face becoming nothing more than angles and curves of pale olive, skin laid perfectly over the bones of his jaw and upper cheek, his brow. She felt a desire to touch the flat curls that lay against his temple; he wore his hair like a Roman, but it was not enough to destroy the expresso-colored waves he'd inherited from his Aramaic mother.

"Whatever I might've said, the night I made you my bride, I regret it now." His hoarse voice was a murmur. "If I had let you die---if I had dragged your skinny body out to the mob, the night we met, you would have died a martyr's death. You would've been killed by those who were convinced of the Jewish evils. I've wondered since, on many a night, if perhaps that was not what was destined to happen. Perhaps I thwarted destiny---perhaps you are simply my punishment."

"I'm your *wife*." She gave up clenching her shirt and folded her arms across the white velveteen and the fawn suede jacket which hung open at her breasts and torso. Defensively, she demanded his attention. "I'm your *wife*. I'm your wife and your childe and if I must live with that, *so must you*."

He could have hit her. He could have named her Lilit, as he once had. But, no.

"Misha." He used her pet name. His voice husked and he shifted in the seat to finally look at her once more; there was sorrow and pain and aggravated love in his expression.

"Misha, listen to me.   You promised you would stay away.   If you cannot forgive me for Nicolai, then you *must* stay away. Do not play with my fond memories of those early years, when I trusted you."

It made her angry, bitterly angry.   She flung the truth at him, cutting them off at each word's end.   "Now, when I passed by thee and looked upon thee, behold, thy time was the time of love.   I spread my coat over thee and covered thy nakedness.   Yes, I swore unto thee, and entered into a covenant with thee, and thou becamest mine."

These very words he had spoken on the night he had taken her as his wife.

Joseph had taken her in, saved her life...given her an education of the world, loved her for the human she was.   He had resisted his blood desires for her until impending death had given him no more choices.   It was either take her as a childe or lose her forever.   He had done what was necessary and these words had come in the bright darkness that night.   These words, which held such importance to her, to him. Perhaps to Nicolai, too.

"How dare you." He whispered it, his eyes turning hard.   "How dare you throw it in my face.   You walked away---"   Her Sire stopped and shook his head in denial.   It was obvious that she'd gotten under his skin with her reminder of the vow.   "No, I'm not going to remind you of it.   You know well enough what you did.   What I want to know now is---what the fuck are you doing in my town?"

"The girl is very pretty.   Is she for dinner?"   She gave a sweet smile, lifting her flask once more.   The strong peach booze warmed her throat and gut as very little else could. Inclining her head to the side, she let it rest on the window as she watched her Sire.   "I wouldn't mind talking over dinner.   It's been so long since we shared a meal...as *family*."

Joseph went very still for a very long moment.   He lowered his head and then gave a heavy sigh, searching his coat pocket for something.   Then, he came up with a packet of cigarettes.   Lighting one, his face glowed red and orange for a second and then was shadowed as he answered, his tone slow and condescending.

"I'm not interested in sharing a family meal with you.   But, I do have other engagements. I promised Nico some quality time, together...alone.   So, be quick and tell me what you want."   It was the way he said the words; he was telling the truth and being obnoxious at the same time.   Deliberately reminding her of the heinous way he had taken Nicolai Valeska as a lover and an heir.

She sighed, in mockery of him.

The girl meant something.   He was hiding that much, diverting the conversation when he could easily dangle the prey in front of her.   He could tease about the entertaining dinner he had planned, but he didn't bother.   Yes...the girl meant something.

And he knew that she knew.

She took another drink of the peach brandy from her filigree-engraved flask. Its strong odor swirled through her head and reminded her of the fireplace medicines her Mother had made when she was very young and mortal.   Her Mother had used fruited brandies in almost every elixir and every cordial---to ward off the bitterness of the other, more important herbs.

"It's simple, really."   She pushed the open flask down into the fork of her denim-covered thighs.   With a sniff, she licked at her fangs and then her lips, careful to keep both eyes on the creature who sat in her car.   "I've found a cure for vampirism."

Joseph flicked ashes into the floorboard between his knees; it was another thing to remember---he did not give a damn for money and he wanted to irk her.   His tone was dry and flat.   "Still seeking a way to escape your fate?"

Choosing to ignore his sarcasm, she began to tell him the story of how she'd discovered a possible way out of the hellish unlife she had to endure.

It had happened only a month ago, at the Museum where she worked in London. Photographs of several scrolls' contents had been delivered from a dig site in Egypt.   The photos had been taken by a scholar friend who was currently working on this said site. Remembering her talent for ancient languages, this friend had taken loads of digital pictures of each scroll and sent them by courier from Cairo's Museum.

Upon seeing the texts in the digital pictures, she'd started putting together the phrases and coming up with strange passages that could have been part of The Book of the Dead, but weren't. Not any Book of the Dead that she'd ever seen. They were more like a physician's lexicon. The scrolls had been found inside a stone sarcophagus. An empty stone sarcophagus, carved in such a way as to suggest it was meant for a great prince or priest.

But, then, she'd found the pictures of text for one scroll which pounded out an octave chord. It was only one scroll among many and she'd examined the other pictures, for the other scrolls, but it was only this one particular papyrus that struck her as important. Important to *her*.

"The Egyptologists think it's a unique, never discovered passage from The Book of the Dead or something, but I recognized the wording. It made me think of you, of course." She gave a wicked smile, turning her gaze so that she could look at him sideways, from the corners.

"Because you naturally think of me when it comes to a sarcophagus." Her Sire lifted the empty palm of his left hand and ground out his spent cigarette in it. She instantly could smell the charred flesh, the stolen blood, the stale smoke; it meant nothing to her. Joseph chuckled, his voice thickly acerbic as he dropped the cigarette butt into the darkened floorboard. "Yes, of course. Makes perfect sense. Do tell me more."

She looked away, studying the empty street in front of her car as she went on, explaining. "All the scrolls are full of a story concerning the ancient crud about children of angels and children of Lilit that you used to spout when you were drunk or feeling particularly suicidal. Some, I recognized from stories my Father told, stories out of his oldest texts. But, most...I knew you'd be able to help me piece together."

"What makes you think it's a cure for vampirism?" Joseph asked, tilting his head to the side as he cupped a hand against his jaw. It made him look regal, the expression of intense consideration. Maybe her Sire was going to take this seriously.

"It's a formula that talks about the Sang-rael." She rolled down her window a few inches and lit a cigarette of her own. The smoke swirled lazily in the car before seeking escape into the damp night air.

The silence swelled between them as she smoked, enjoying the taste of stale peach brandy in her mouth. Her Sire's expression became impossible to read; he went on, studying her with his intense eyes and his solemn mouth, but she could intuit nothing of his thoughts or feelings.

Finally, Joseph Snowden, her husband and Sire, the first love of her long existence both mortal and Undead, began to chuckle. He was thoroughly amused. Genuinely amused. His jade-colored eyes narrowed and she could almost see the tiny lines around their lids, the folds that showed something of his 'mortal' age. He was so young-looking, so handsome...and such a piece of work. Such an *asshole*.

He reached for the flask that sat between her thighs. His knuckles brushed her denim-covered skin and she fought the thrill it sent up and through every bone of her body. Joseph lifted the flask and toasted her before taking drink to punctuate his answer.

"Whoever told you the Sang-rael was a cure for vampirism is a fool and a liar."

She blew smoke rings at him, dryly arching a brow. "Well, that would be you...wouldn't it?"

Joseph scoffed, aiming the mouth of her silver flask in her direction as he shook his head. He still leaned against the door, the window; the curls of his hair seemed darker here, darker than sable or ebony. "Mishenka, I never told you the Sang-rael was a cure for vampirism."

"You said that when you found the Sang-rael, you'd be free." She blew more smoke at him. Somehow, she felt more relaxed...more like the old days, when they'd shared centuries together and argued philosophy from dusk until dawn.

"That doesn't mean it's a cure for the state of our existence." He frowned then at the flask he held, as if the liqueur was disgusting. "Where in the forbidden name of hell did you get this thing? It's so Victorian I feel like I've stepped back a century."

She didn't speak of it; the flask was none of Joseph's business. If he wanted to know, he could always ask Nicolai---Nicolai knew of the flask's origins. Nicolai knew of the girl who had given her the lovely, etched silver gift.

In the stifled decades of late Victorian England, she'd been among the first female students allowed to openly study in the ways that men and boys enjoyed. To keep a proper facade, she'd lived as a boarder in a house with a family who understood her nature and accepted it. The man of the family was a dean at Cambridge named James Whitman. Dean James Whitman was extremely educated in the ways of the ancient world and its half-forgotten creatures---which made him and his family extremely forgiving of her strange existence. They had known of blood-drinkers and the children of fallen angels---had known of these and were willing to take a chance with her, in the spirit of kindness and scholarly interest.

She had found Dean Whitman in 1889 while seeking to learn something of what the ancients may have known of her species, her breed. Dean Whitman had taught classes in Ancient History and Literature. These classes were, of course, necessary to the budding Egyptologist and Anthropologist, but her first encounter with him was a year before she ever attended the first lecture.

She had visited him in his home in the summer of 1889, asking for knowledge usually frowned upon when the student was a woman. Her apparent youth and unusually mature way of speaking had convinced Dean Whitman to help her find the information she sought. A tentative friendship had started. Over the course of the next year, the Dean and his family had become aware of some differences---she was not like them, she did not age and she might heal quickly from fatal wounds. She could not contract lethal illnesses.

The telling event had come with the influenza that struck the entire family in the winter of 1889 and 1890, taking one of the youngest sons. She had come to stay with them, to work as their healer---the family's physician could not be reached and no other physician would approach, as there was much sickness in the city. She stayed in their house and used those bare skills she had remembered, from her Mother's lessons. But, as he healed, Dean Whitman realized that she wasn't likely to become ill. She wasn't mortal.

In the end, by the early spring of 1890, he had asked her to stay, to consider being his house-guest. For the sake of gossip, she was called 'cousin'. She would consider them off-limits as prey, in the ancient tradition of hospitality. One could not harm one's hosts.

But, she'd fallen in love with the man's oldest daughter, Emily, who had loved her in return. Everywhere she had traveled, in her search for education, Emily had traveled at her side. There were few gentlemen callers for a blind girl, no matter how lovely or how witty she might be, and Dean Whitman had accepted the fact that Emily might never marry, even at the advanced age of twenty-three. So, in the spirit of fairness, Emily had been allowed to attend what university classes were possible. Emily had followed her into the world of Egyptology, much to Dean Whitman's unorthodox delight.

In London, Nicolai had found her and Emily, in the year 1892. It was there she'd sworn Nicolai Valeska to secrecy. He could never tell Joseph of her young English girl lover, for fear of what their Sire might do to the tender creature. To her knowledge, Nicolai had kept the secret. Emily had lived a good life and traveled with her to Egypt, to study further.

It was in Egypt where disaster had struck. In 1916, cholera had taken Emily Whitman's life and she had begged God to allow her to die, as well. She had promised Emily, at the end, that she would seek a cure for the 'disease' and 'mutation' which must surely keep them apart forever. For, if she could not die, then they would never meet again. God surely would not deny them their love, even in the face of her monstrous affliction, but for that re-union to occur, she must be able to die as a mortal.

The thought of sweetly blonde Emily made her straighten up, made her remember what she was...what she detested about her unlife. She pushed on, taking the flask away from her Sire, unsmiling now.

She capped the flask, putting it away into her jacket's inner pocket as she tossed the spent cigarette butt out the window. She kept her voice casual. "According to the inscriptions I deciphered, if certain elements are introduced to the Sang-rael, it has the power to cure any

84

disease. It can make snow in the desert...it can make the desert bloom forever. With the elixir within it, the Sang-rael has the power to change the world with only a few magical words."

"You got all *that* from a scroll?" Joseph still wore his serious, studious look as he watched her, his face lost in half-shadows. He sounded dubious, chiding. "As educated as you are, I would think you'd remember that coffin texts are usually figurative. Any word on whose grave your Egyptologist friends disturbed? Who did this sarcophagus belong to?"

It was simply a reminder to her that Joseph Snowden was not an uneducated fool; he'd been a student of the lost arcane long before her birth in Kiev. Her Sire had studied the ancient world in all its dark corners.

Misha pulled the papers out of her jacket pocket and began to slowly unfold them. "Some priest from Nubt and Dendara. A priest of Sekhmet who also worked as the personal royal scribe for Ramses the Second. Ramses the Great. The scroll sarcophagus was in his tomb, along with the one that actually held his body."

She was hoping that the reference to Sekhmet would pique his interest; he'd often told her, in the early days, that several ancient war gods were involved in blood sacrifice---but that only one goddess was ever said to actually drink blood. Knowing that it was a priest of Sekhmet who owned papers about the Sang-rael might make this whole thing a little more important to him, now.

"His name?" Joseph showed no hint of deep interest, but she knew it was a front. He wouldn't reveal himself too soon; for her Sire, talking with her had become a game of cat and mouse. Or perhaps a game of chess. She couldn't remember when this had started, the game, only that Nicolai must surely have seen it in its beginnings.

"I think, from what I was told, the scribe priest's name was Odion. Odion Bayhas." This much, she admitted freely. Anything more she knew of the long-dead priest, she would keep to herself.

"Bayhas. A Guardian name. Hmm." Sounding non-committal, Joseph lit another cigarette; the smoke filled her nose. "Tell me something about this mystery formula."

"The formula is imbedded in the text. I've got a biochemist working on the possibility, with me. He's written it out from my translation notes. The ancient ingredients all have modern-day counterparts, so they can be either created or distilled from herbs and minerals. Everything but the Sang-rael. It's the unknown element, but the most important."

In fact, she thought, the most telling thing about the Sang-rael, was how it seemed to be mostly made up of the same elements as blood. But, not human blood. Those elements could be re-created in a lab, too, but not the most important part of that bizarre chemical. There was something in the Sang-rael which wasn't blood and wasn't herb and wasn't mineral. Something...elemental. Like fire or air.

Perhaps this was the very part of its mystery, the essence of what made it holy and sacred and powerful. The words mentioned, in the texts, didn't have a translation in the modern world. That was what she was hoping Joseph could provide her with---some understanding of what to look for, in searching for an elusive element. But, more importantly---she hoped he would slip and give her the proof she was seeking.

That the Sang-rael was a living patron of Pandora's Box.

"Unknown element." He sounded even more doubtful. Her Sire flicked ashes into the floorboard again, his gaze leaving her. He left his head against the window but now his eyes moved, shifting to watch her hands and the papers. "Does not the coffin texts tell you of what the Sang-rael is---if it is the Sang-rael, in fact?"

She smiled, feeling a thrill of impending victory. Joseph was interested in the papers she held. She let them fall closed on her lap, fingers loosely sprawled over the white print-out. "Our translation calls it the vessel of the Protector. It talks about the cup of dark possibility and bright promise. It talks about the balance of ma'at which is achieved in this vessel. That within its depths can be found the most divine utterance. The Unspeakable Name. There was even an ancient formula on the papyrus. Something comprised almost wholly of this vessel. The vessel already contains its most important ingredient."

"Which is?" His tone was short; her Sire blew smoke from his nostrils lazily as he brought his gaze back to her face.

"Blood." She let her smile grow. "It contains blood."

"Blood." Joseph arched a brow at her which only added to his mocking smile.

The sarcasm was all the worse for his humor. He wasn't being the slightest big nasty, there was no snide cruelty. She could've handled that. No, he was genuinely bemused. As if he was surprised in a vague way at the antics of a pet. If she'd sat up and miaowed at him, he would've enjoyed it just the same. He wouldn't treat her so trivially if he knew that she'd figured out the Sang-rael's hidden nature.

She reached out to touch a finger to the car's CD player. The Tom Waits play list came up and a funky, super-real cello-bass beat began as she answered, turning her face into a mask of pleased understanding.

"You don't believe me." As if she really said *'You do grasp this---you of all people, I knew you would get the meaning of it all.'*

Joseph nodded, his tone placid. "I have my doubts as to your faith. You want to believe this is a cure. It's not the Holy Grail---it's a weapon."

"You seem really sure of that." She didn't give up the smile. Let Joseph hang himself; the more he defended his so-called secret truths, the more likely he was to slip and give away the identity of the world's most powerful creature. He must surely know---why else would he be a nightly customer at Pandora's Box?

Now, her Sire pulled his head from the window, straightening as he pinned her with a quick frown. "I was a Brother in the Temple, a student in the Scion. I was a scholar of those mysteries the Brotherhood was protecting." He stopped, now, his intense gaze turning implacable and complicated. "Why am I telling you any of this? You never wanted to know. Tell me why you think I must have something of use to you."

"Because I didn't *know* you might be holding the cure for this---" She stopped on a hard hiss, her throat suddenly tight with emotion. With a glance down, she saw that she'd crumpled the print-out. Her voice was a little hoarse, choked as she went on after a breath, softer and collected. "This page outlines everything. The formula written down here could be a cure for many diseases, if it's completed. The scroll spoke of the witch's and the priest's most important magic. Whoever possessed the Vessel could do *miracles*. The words---the scroll calls it the Vessel of Arakelba."

Looking back at him, she caught the glimpse of change.

Something flinched in his eyes, deep like a flash of light on the stones of a dark well. He whispered, his voice cracking in its bottom. "Is it so terrible that you'd wish to die just to be free?"

There. There, in his gaze. The horror and grief. It showed so clearly for an unspeakable moment, a single tick of an eternal metronome that revealed her Sire's secret self. His soul. His true heart, the man behind the monster.

It was a breathless, ephemeral second.

They stared at each other and she heard the words as if Joseph voiced the sentiment. *'I did this to you, Misha, and you hate me, and I've mourned for the loss of your humanity every night ever after.'*

She didn't have the power of breath to make her voice stronger, so she whispered still yet, her voice rising and falling into a murmur with the need to make Joseph believe. "It reminded me. Every word I translated. You and your damned books, the files, the scrolls. Every goddamned thing you told me, the things I didn't want to believe. You were my teacher and I remembered. It's real and it's out there."

She didn't have to say all the reasons for wanting the Sang-rael. They both knew.

Misha licked at her lips and leaned closer to him, inhaling the scent she remembered intimately. He'd always had a wonderful smell; not what anyone would imagine for a vampire. He used a rare spice for cologne. She pitched her voice lower, to make the plea obvious. "Please, Joseph, just give me some information on where to look. You've collected all the dusty papers from the secret places---I know, I was with you. You've got to have some idea where the Sang-rael is. I know you---you wouldn't give up."

"Why should I give you even a single clue?" He wasn't rising to the bait. His eyes narrowed into contemplative slits as he moved backwards, to rest the crown of his head on the glass once more. He'd put out the cigarette and was studying her, no emotion of any kind in his expression. His face could easy have been a solid, stone mask, for the heart he now showed.

Here it was. He was giving her a logical, unbiased place from which to argue her point. She could give her evidence, explain. "Because you know me, too. You know I wouldn't use the Vessel for the harm of mankind. I wouldn't use it for anything but a cure. The formula looks like a cure for almost every disease known to mankind. If we can't use it as vampires, maybe mortals can use it to save their children. When I'm done, I'll give it to you, Joseph. I'll bring it to you, locked safely in an ark of such grace this world's *never seen*. Joseph, it could make us mortal---it really could be the purpose to our existence, giving such a gift back to the world we've preyed on. Don't you *want* to live and die as a mortal? Don't you remember the things you dreamed about, when you were still human? Didn't you want children? Children born, not *made*?"

"I was a Brother Knight, Misha. I took an oath of celibacy, when I was human. I never gave a thought to marriage and children. They weren't on the schedule." Her Sire closed his eyes now, releasing her from the sharpness of scrutiny. She heard the breathless whisper that came from him, words she'd heard many times over the centuries when they had lived as lovers. "Verily I say unto you, there be some standing here, which shall not taste of death until they see the Son of man coming into his kingdom."

It was a quote, a verse from that book of Christian mythology he'd been taught to believe in when still just a child. He'd been taken from a faithful Jewish mother and given into a life of sacrifice and surrender and battle as the warrior of the Temple. She felt sorrow for him, the things he had believed for nearly nine hundred years, even in his most heathen and blasphemous years.

She couldn't imagine believing anything for so long---she didn't believe much of anything, but she did believe in his devotion to the cause of his existence. He'd come into the world of blood-drinkers and held tight to the faith of the prophesy for which he'd been hand-picked by the Knights. He was a special person, alive or Undead, and the Knights had taught him to believe.

After he'd become a vampire, Joseph's elders in the Scion had decided that he must be the Wandering Jew of legend---only, the Son of man mentioned in the prophesy wasn't the Messiah but a warrior for the world, the left hand of redemption. The one child of Israel born to endure until the day of some unfathomable reckoning. Perhaps he was, if such things were true. She couldn't know for sure; no one could.

"An ark of grace." Joseph cracked one eye to study her again, concerned curiosity making a knot of his brows that darkened him. "What do you mean by that? Why an *ark of grace?*"

"Why?" She shrugged, settling sideways in her leather seat, relaxed now. Her Sire was taking this serious and wasn't blatantly parrying every word she said. "Why's it important? It just came to me."

Ark of Grace. It was something Uly said; she wouldn't tell Joseph about Uly.

"It strikes me as poetic. I never imagined you would be a poet, Misha."

The paper she held onto was getting wet from the sweat she produced. Just being so close to Joseph, after so many decades apart, was having a strange reaction on her body. She wasn't aching to touch him, but the idea of spending a while in New Orleans wasn't exactly a repugnant thought. As long as she could spend her nights talking for hours and hours once more with the strong, intense creature who had showed a scared, ignorant Jewess from Kiev what beauty might exist in the world.

She made herself sound calm. "You once told me you knew things...that you had clues."

But, it was Joseph's turn to shake his head, smooth and easy inside the long chocolate brown wool coat he wore. He'd closed his eyes solidly, again. "I don't know where the

Sang-rael is.   But, I do know what it might be capable of.   It's no mere chalice you're seeking.   You're better off using a Petri dish and forget all the mysticism."

It made her suspicious.   He wouldn't meet her eye, now.   There was no fire in his argument.   Something in that made her hackles rise.   "What are you hiding?   You're hiding something.   You do know where it is, don't you?   *Joseph---*"

"I took an oath to protect the Sang-rael from the powers of darkness."   He interrupted.

Now, he looked at her, green-gray eyes darkened in the shadows as he sat upwards in the passenger seat and leaned forwards, getting close enough to touch.   His face showed nothing of the age in his voice, his gaze.

"Now I'm a power of darkness?"   She could hear it in her voice, the disbelieving pain.

She had to hurry this crap up, to get away from him.   The ancient asshole was really getting under her skin and that wasn't allowed anymore.   She could love Joseph Snowden all she wanted, but she had to stay on guard---he wasn't to be trusted, necessarily.   And there was Uly to consider.

"It means, Misha, I can't give away what I know about the Sang-rael.   Not to just anyone.   I have to know who I'm dealing with, what their true intentions are."   His eyes were solemn as they moved over her again; she was close enough to feel the exhale he gave---an unnecessary breath.   "I want you to meet someone.   His name's Dante.   When you've talked with him for a couple of hours, I'll give you the clues you want.   If you talk with Dante, I will help you.   But, then you'll take the papers and leave."

She nodded, in agreement.   Whatever he wanted, in the way of a promise, she'd willingly go along with.   "Okay.   When do you want me to meet him?"

"Tomorrow evening, after dusk.   Let's say sevenish, shall we?   You will find him seated at my table at Arnaud's.   That's an excellent restaurant...the address is 813 Bienville Street."   Joseph was tugging on the gloves he wore.   He was nearly finished and it showed in his slow movements as he straightened up, pulling back.   His smile was somber.   "You can't miss him, even among the other mortals there.   He's very tall and very handsome."

"That's not much to go on."   She scowled at the lack of information.

Joseph gave a heavy sigh, as if troubled by the need for more.   "Look for the brown-haired mortal who draws everyone's eye as if he is some great arch-angel made of flesh and blood.   You will understand when you see him.   He is the absolute image of what you might believe a pagan god should be, if one deigned to walk among us.   I will tell him to wear a blue tie."

"Fine."   She agreed.   "After I talk with your friend, I can have the papers.   When?"

"Give me a week to gather all the information."   Her Sire's smile was fake and too pleasant.   "I have to go through the files and scrolls once more and write the clues down for you."

"A week?"   It made her skin prickle, the incredulity.   "You're going to make me wait a week for something you can give me in two nights?   I know you don't need a week, Joseph.   You probably have those clues already lined up and written out."

"A week."   He insisted.   "You have your choice.   A week or nothing."

She gave a heavy sigh of her own, giving in.   "Fuck.   Okay.   Where do you want me to meet you, to receive this?"

"I will contact you."   His hand was on the door's slim handle, already.

"Right."   She reached for the console, intending to get a piece of scrap paper and a pen.   "You'll need my cell phone number---"

"It's cute, my dear, but don't worry.   I've never lost track of you.   How could I?"   He chuckled, his softness completely gone now.   His tone was harder, steely, and her eyes lifted to meet his as she stopped her movement.   Her Sire tilted his head to the side, revealing the high plane of his cheekbone and straight brow, the curls that laid flat.   "I don't have to tell you what'll happen if you follow me home, Misha.   I'm sure you learned your lesson the last time, like a good girl."

Then, he got out of her car and began to walk away, up the street they were parked on.   She was sure it was the wrong direction, but didn't dare to follow.   His last words were enough to remind her of what could happen when she tried to corner Joseph Snowden---a vampire known for his cruelty to other vampires.

She sat still, listening to Tom Waits grind and gravel his way through a strange blues song, and simply watched Joseph's disappearing shape as it moved up the uneven sidewalk. The brown coat flared at his knees and it looked nice. He always did, though. No, she wouldn't follow him, not even to try talking with Nicolai. The last time she'd disobeyed and followed him to his lair, she'd paid an ugly price.

It made the stolen blood chill in her veins, the memory.

It'd happened in the mid-nineteenth century, before she'd gone to London. She had tracked her Sire to New York and found him. After a heated argument, she'd followed him to his lair and been trapped. She'd ended up chained to a bed in the darkness of a ramshackle tenement on the bad side of that city. There, for two months, she'd been a prisoner. She would've starved if not for Nicolai---who had taken beatings from Joseph for his kindness to her.

Nicolai with his violin, luring the vagabond children...

Misha shuddered at the memory and decided that nothing would be worth another two months at Joseph's doubtful mercies. He was a quiet creature, but if she did disobey the command to leave him be, she would suffer.

Instead, she sat still and watched him turn a corner, a half-dozen blocks away.

No, it definitely wasn't worth the trouble, to double-cross Joseph Snowden.

Chapter Nine

She hadn't changed, his Misha. She hadn't changed much at all---he had not heard her voice since 1920, but he'd watched her from afar several times. Her tastes in clothing had evolved, as had his---she had grown with the century. Her voice was the same, her tone was even the same---his bride was still the little warrior, unwilling to back down and accede the battle.

Oh, her *scent*. So different, yet the same. Some new flavor lingered on her skin.

But, the things that passed her lips now were a new song. Something he'd never have believed in a full thousand years. In the early years of their association, he had told her a great deal of the mysteries he knew of. As Master to her mortal self. As Undead husband to a living bride. As Sire to childe. As friends and lovers and everything in the terrible spaces between. He'd given her what he knew, leaving only the very most important things a secret. She had never truly believed any of it. They'd argued many times in the quiet hours over these very same ideas, the stories he had told to her.

What use would Misha, in those centuries, have had for the deeper truth about the prophesy and the Sang-rael, the Holy Blood? She had scoffed more than once, the rabbi's daughter, educated by a father who had doted upon her shining face, her sweet smile, her quick eyes.

Now...oh, unholy night that he should see her again and that she should come asking for such! She'd found him and Nicolai and seen them with Tennyson, who was meant to be kept safe. She'd seen the girl he protected and he had lied, to say that this mortal piece of prey wasn't important in the slightest. How could things have gone so out of control so quickly? He'd never imagined Misha would come looking for him---not with such a question on her lips!

He stalked along the darkened streets, taking the longest way home. He had to get home, to his lair. To the condo he and Nicolai owned on Julia and Baronne, only a block from Carondelet's street car track. He had to get there and safeguard everything. But, would she follow? She had been punished for the transgression before, but with this obsession and this need---Misha might disobey and follow. She might track him to his home. She might already know where he slept, where his study was kept.

If so, he wouldn't be safe---Nico wouldn't be safe.

And Tennyson.

It wouldn't be wise to leave Tennyson alone for a while; the girl would simply have to stay with him and Nico tonight. If Nico had taken Tennyson home already, he would double back and retrieve the Creole child from her apartment on St Anne's. She might have to stay at his lair until he knew things were safe and Misha was gone from New Orleans.

Of course, the girl wouldn't agree to that and it would look highly suspicious. He would need to vouchsafe her. Later today, after a few hours, he would call Rhys Lorraine. Rhys might be a child of sin and darkness, but the boy understood vampires. Rhys could protect Tennyson when she was not in his sight. The tchatcha had a taste and a talent for killing the Undead. He himself had witnessed this. He had allowed Rhys to join in on his hunts; he did not have to like the malakh to recognize Tennyson's safety in its mortal form.

But, now, oh. He needed to call Dante, make the arrangements. Dante would have to check Misha carefully---find out the truths that his bride managed to conceal from him. Truths only a husa-hekau might be capable of seeing. With the right words, Dante could influence a mind to explain itself in silent empathy. Dante would be able to discern Misha's true intents.

His wife. His wife had found him and for what? She wanted the one secret he could never give. She was misled as to its nature and that was a plus, but how misled was she? She knew the Sang-rael was *filled with blood*. How long before her vampire mind put two and two together and came up with the correct answer? She was a very bright woman, his Misha. She would find out the truth on her own and then Tennyson would no longer be safe in his care without a fight.

And she'd spoken of the Ark of Grace. Could she have been nudging him---claiming it was simply words, nothing of import? The Ark of Grace itself was nearly as serious a matter as the Sang-rael. As terrible and wondrous as the Sang-rael al-Mahdi might be to contemplate, it was the Ark of Grace that remained a soft and sweet secret to all that studied its existence.

He had known of the Ark of Grace almost as long as he'd known of the Sang-rael.

The Ark of Grace was, according to the story and scrolls, a living creature who embodied every pure virtue and honor that was denied to the Sang-rael, as a warrior. They were counterparts, destined to work side by side. He had often believed, in knowing the dark nature of the soul that slept within the Sang-rael, that the Ark of Grace must surely be the light and love that the Destroyer-Protector could not possess. Two halves of the same soul, perhaps? Or perhaps the Ark of Grace was an avatar of the Lamb? He could not be sure--- the translations were spotty at best. He did know, of course, that the translations spoke of a child, but there was no hint of where the child came from or what the child might be. For all he knew, the child could *be* the Ark of Grace----a loving child who would lead the warrior Sang-rael back into the light of God's love after countless battles and horrendous wars.

Ha. That was no certainty. Pure speculation. He had nothing but the hints and rumors...and the name Ark of Grace. Well, that was the translation of the name. The name didn't have a literal translation; it came from a scrap of ancient Aramaic, which was traced to a Nubian glyph, which was traced even further back to a glyph of a language so old that there was only a small handful of preserved examples of its usage. The glyph, to the best of any linguist's guess, was a single word that meant Vessel of Thanks or Blessed Crucible.

If Misha could throw out the words *Ark of Grace*, then she might know more than he suspected.

Might he be forced to kill Misha? He didn't know if he possessed the strength to do so.

Perhaps, if it came to such a fight, Rhys Lorraine would oblige him in that, as well. He could strike a bargain with the tchatcha. Anything in the world he possessed in exchange for the death of his immortal, Undead bride, simply because he could not destroy her on his own by any means. All for the safety of Tennyson---Rhys would certainly agree that Tennyson was worth the danger of fighting a vampire of such age and cunning.

Damn, that he didn't know more warriors who were capable of tracking and killing vampires.

Dante. He needed to call Dante. Then, he needed to get himself home.

The cell phone he held was smooth and sleek. Motorola, black, state of the art. He put the headset on as he walked, mindless of the broken sidewalk and the tree roots which displaced the concrete. With a single button, he dialed and then clipped the phone to his jeans without a thought.

It rang twice and then a third time.

He felt the first drops of rain fall, striking his cheek and his hair. The early morning rain had come and he would be soaked to the skin by the time he reached his lair. Home. What would Nicolai say about Misha coming here? Nicolai cared a great deal for Misha---it was more than the Russian blood, the Russian mind. He had taught them to love one another and that bond survived.

Joseph frowned. Would the mad malakh answer already, for the sake of hell?

The rain was most assuredly falling; it soaked into his coat now, barely stopped by the fine herringbone wool. He tugged at his leather gloves, making them tighter on his fingers and palms. He was in the Central Business District now, walking towards Canal Street along

Dauphine. He was headed in the wrong direction, for the moment, but he intended to double back. He would reach Canal Street and walk up to Rampart. He would go back down Rampart until he reached Julia. Somewhere, along the way, he would find prey. He had to have blood; he didn't possess half the strength he might need in the coming days. With Misha in town, with so much at stake, he needed more strength and cunning and these things required that he sate himself on mortals.

At last, he heard the click in his earpiece. A slurring voice husked. "Yeah?"

He gave a sigh, barely audible. The wet was cold and he felt a shiver starting in his arms and hands. By the time he reached home, he would be half-frozen with the rain. And ahead, on Canal, he could see fog rising from the ground.

Stepping carefully over a patch of broken concrete, it was nothing to change the tone of his voice, to mask the emotions he felt as he spoke in a semi-teasing way to the hacker. "I just left your sight an hour ago, Webster. I can't imagine you're sleeping so quickly." It was no introduction, but he needed none. "I have a problem that needs your gifts, my malakh friend."

"Joe?" Dante's voice was sharper this time, clearer. "Wha---what's going on?"

He gave a wintry smile, studying the houses and businesses as he went past them; he had to find prey and soon. Quickly, he answered, his voice low and clipped. "I've just left the company of my exquisite wife. I'm quite sure, if Mathilda trusts you as thoroughly as I was led to believe, she will have informed you of such a person."

He had to hope that Mathilda had informed her step-son of something concerning his background. He knew, from previous talks with the hacker, that Mathilda was a secretive person; but, Dante was her most trusted confidant. If she would tell anyone of what to be careful for, it must surely be Dante Webster.

"Your wife. The---" There was a rustle on the other end of the phone-line. Dante's voice dropped and became hoarse, almost breathless. He heard a loud click---a door perhaps. "Mattie just said that if your wife ever came around, you'd make sure trouble didn't find the club."

He was almost to the corner of Canal Street now; he began to explain the possible danger. "My wife was waiting for me outside the club. She sat there in her car for an indeterminate length of time. No doubt, she saw many faces. She has come to ask a favor of me concerning some files I'm in possession of."

"Okay."

The fog was chilly; there must be some criminal or homeless person willing to follow him into a dark alley. He smiled at the thought of hot, spiced blood. "I need you to meet with her tonight just after seven for dinner at Arnaud's. The reservations aren't necessary. Just tell the gentleman that you want Snowden's table."

"Uh, Joe---"

Joseph pushed on, overriding the hacker's worried voice. "Talk with her, read her, glean whatever you can of her intentions with the gift of your angelic blood. It's very important I know what she truly intends before I give these papers to her."

"Whoa, hold on, Joe. You want me to meet a vampire for dinner and drinks and a scan?"

"This is of extreme importance, Webster." He picked up the scent of two humans close by, in the shadows afforded by a brick building and its balcony, the filthy alley that would be nearly invisible to mortal eyes. He went on walking, smiling, as he sent out the mental feelers that would help him 'see' his prey. "The longer she is in town, the greater the chance she will step into our office. We do not want my wife in the office. There are far too many innocents involved here. Meet her, talk of anything but Pandora's Box and its players---be especially careful to say nothing of the mortal innocents."

The two mortals were aware of him, now; they were curious and coming to the edge of the alley; he stopped walking, to give them time. He'd been correct; they were homeless and yet quite sane. Criminals, both. Partners, it would seem. They would be a perfect meal. Now, he only needed to let them decide upon their course of action and then he could go on walking, drawing these two away from the hazy streetlights.

Dante's voice was speculative. The hacker was going to do this work for him. "So, nothing about work or the kids that come in. Can I entertain her with a verbal tour of New Orleans' history, then?"

He wanted a cigarette, but didn't dare; it would dampen the scent of his prey. Who were watching him from the shadows. He turned his back on them and took a few steps towards the block of Rampart. To give the prey a reason to chase. "If you so desire. More to the point, steer the conversation to her work. She's a historian, a linguistic anthropologist for a museum in London. Delve into her work and its current projects. Find out why she's here, what she really intends."

"So, what she wants from you has something to do with her current project at work?"

"Yes, intimately so."

He could hear them clearly now, the prey. They were decidedly on his trail. Now, he began to move; he walked to the corner and turned down Rampart slowly. He knew how he looked; businessman out after hours in the edge of Vieux Carre. He would make good prey to thieves and killers, if he was mortal. The two followed him furtively, careful.

He ignored that and spoke, explaining what he did dare to explain. "She has come to me, asking for some papers of ancient text which I would loathe to see in the wrong hands. It's sentimental, Webster, you must see that. She's playing on our association to get this favor from me and I must know what she wants the papers for."

"You're trusting a lot in me, Joe. You sure you're okay with all this?"

As he reached the crossing of Tulane Avenue, he quickened his step to let the prey think he might escape. He thrust his gloved hands into the pockets of his coat and ignored the rain that soaked his hair. His only worry was that the headset would be ruined, drowned. Hopefully, he could get finished with Webster before he lost the reception.

He cast his voice carefully, to make it understood how important this matter was, to him. "Listen, Webster. Read her as deeply as you can go. Take a diverting and handsome friend with you, as witness. You want someone who can keep the conversation going without your help. This must be someone who is quick with a question, new angles, someone who can woo a lady with true intelligence. As your friend ask the questions, you will be able to go deeply into Misha's mind and find out the secret of what she needs these papers for."

The rain was letting up, already, but it was still a nuisance. He blinked against the drops that caught in his lashes. His hair was completely wet, now, and dribbles of water ran down the back of his coat and scarf and into the strap undershirt he wore. It only enhanced the cold tick-tick feeling he got when on the hunt, being pursued by the prey he pursued.

"Okay, I can take Jules." The Southern California accent was smooth.

Joseph closed his gloved hands into fists in his coat pockets, breathing through his mouth for a moment to catch the scent of his prey, the two men on his trail. It was damp, the scent was strong. He asked, frowning as he tried to picture the man with a name like Jules. "Do I know him?"

"He's Daniel D'Loup's son."

Yes, of course. Now, he had a picture. Short, stocky, very handsome, mulatto with a mane of long dark curls and hazel eyes. The face came to him; a face that was of similar age to D'Loup's but without the strange ageless quality of a benu malakh. Demi-malakh working in the professional world of white collar offices. D'Loup's son was a lawyer in a reputable law firm in New Orleans, if he wasn't mistaken. His mental image came with the singular thought of: suave, quick-witted, and silver-tongued. Very much D'Loup's son.

"Excellent. I believe I've met him, in fact." He nodded to himself, answering the suggestion. He was nearly to Gravier; he needed to slow down or he'd end up taking his prey too close to home. "He resembles his father greatly but possesses a skill in the art of conversation that Daniel woefully lacks. This man is your partner in more than friendship. Correct?"

"Um, yeah."

He'd slowed himself gradually; there was no point in dragging the prey so close to his lair.   If he reached Lafayette before he finished with the phone call, he'd have to go towards Lafayette Square, on the other side of the St Charles tracks.   Hmmm...that would afford him a good hiding spot for the left-overs, as well.

So, Alan Webster was bedding D'Loup's son.   That was certainly an intriguing piece of information, but it was good to know that his suspicions concerning Mathilda's step-son were correct.   It was the curse of malakh that they were, without much variation, bi-sexuals governed by malakh pheromone markers instead of by social morals and religious beliefs.

"This is good.   My wife is somewhat put off by relationships of that kind.   It sets her on edge, the sight and thought of two men in conjugal union.   She's more likely to reveal something of great importance if she is off balance."   Joseph smiled a little broader now, enjoying the taste of his prey's scent as he considered Misha's hypocrisy.   It was something he had reviled in his bride, her disgust for such choices when she was no saint of any calibre. Did she truly think he was unaware of her own preferences?

"What's she look like?"   Dante sounded genuinely curious.

"She's of average height for women now.   She is close to a height with Nicolai.   Her name is Mishenka, but I would recommend you call her Doctor Ben-Moshe.   She is slim and well-bodied and her hair is a pale brown that could nearly be called blonde."

He let his bride's maiden name roll off his tongue and felt a pang of pale grief for the death of a rabbi's family.   He wouldn't have been in Kiev if he hadn't wanted to talk with the local lord and with the local rabbi, for two very different reasons.   Between the two, he had liked Chaim Izrail Ben-Moshe far better.

His frown returned as he worked to keep his mind on the tasks at hand.   Now was not the time to dwell on the senseless violence he'd witnessed that last night, in Kiev, in 1349.   Later, when he had sent Misha back out of his town, he would give long consideration to her brutally murdered family.   He would light the yahrzeit candle and recite Kaddish for them, perhaps.   He would wait until he was alone, to do so.   Chas Veshalom that Nicolai might comment on it.

"Her eyes?"   Dante interrupted his secular thoughts.   It startled.

"Blue, blue and gray."   He walked a little slower still.   The rain was almost gone.   The thought of Misha's eyes, so clear and solemn at the tender age he'd taken her in as a mortal traveling companion, made him shiver.   How could she still have such an effect on him, after so many decades, so many centuries?

"Anything distinguishing about her?"

Joseph pictured Misha carefully as she had looked in the car.   "She will wear her hair pulled back from her face, perhaps in a bun or a knot.   She appears to be a girl in her late teens or early twenties, much like the children who come to our office, but this is not the way in which she deports herself.   She wears the clothes of a talented, educated woman and behaves as such.   In this day and age, you might call a woman of her appearance sophisticated or even mannish.   Don't be fooled, she is quite beautiful and is capable of using that beauty."

He had fallen in love with her so easily, hadn't he?   Witty and brave child, willing to go into the darkness of night with a kind-speaking stranger who offered escape from the mob of villagers who wanted to kill her and her family just because they were Jewish.   How could he not have loved her?   And, yet...when had he fallen out of love?

"Gotcha.   So, what happens once I got this info for you?"

The prey behind him were getting braver, moving just a little faster; soon, they would be within ten steps of him.   He was truly looking forward to the kill, now.   Something, anything to wipe away the memory of his mad love for Mishenka, his brazen shrew of a wife.

"I'll get my wife the hell out of Dodge, as you might be wont to say."   His voice came out droll as he smiled, lop-sidedly at how his thoughts of her could never reflect the physical allure she held.   She might be a shrew, but she was intensely beautiful to his eyes.

"Awesome, Joe.   Works for me.   As soon as I get finished, I'll give you a call."   The hacker sounded worried, as if he had more questions and did not dare to ask.

"Oh, and Dante?"   He raised his brows, quickly remembering something.

"Yeah?"

"Wear a blue tie." His footsteps echoed on the wet pavement as he crossed Poydras at a sedate pace, as if early mornings were a favorite time of day for him. Which wasn't too far from the truth, if he wished to examine the dark corners of his own psyche for its foibles. He loved early mornings and fog and rain. There was something wondrous about pre-dawn hours spent alone or with mortal prey.

"Recognition factor, right?"

"You would be correct." With a deep breath inward, Joseph tightened his mouth over the fangs which threatened to slide free as he let the hunger start working itself loose from the chains of self-control. "Another concern, Dante. Don't let her get you alone. Never forget, even for a second, that she's a vampire."

The street lamps looked unearthly in the fog as he quickened his pace by a heartbeat. Let them give chase; let them hear his footsteps become a rhythm of wanting. As he put the headset of his cell phone into the deep pocket of his coat, Joseph lifted a gloved hand to rake through his hair. It ruffled, wet and sleek.

Soon. Soon. Soon.

Now.

He headed down a brick alley. Here, blue dumpsters sat between two apartment buildings. Black trash bags claimed either side of the red brick path. Here, he would let his prey close in. In the shadows, he stopped and pulled out a piece of paper. It was the grocery list Tennyson had dropped from her own pocket in the bar as she was putting on her coat. Now, he studied it as if the words meant something to him, but his skin and his ears listened.

They were almost to the alley, their footsteps crunch-slapping on loose gravel.

Bread. Two percent milk. Mustard. Bologna. Roast Beef. Potatoes. Onions. Double A Batteries. Tampons. Sesame Seed Oil. Butter. Yogurt. Eggs. Advil Sinus Tablets. Kool-Aid. Coffee.

He drew his brows in with a frown at the thought of feminine hygiene. Had he lost track of the moon cycle, to forget Tennyson's menses? No...she'd just had it and the sweet smell of dead blood was no longer a perfume on her skin. So, she couldn't need new supplies so quickly. Perhaps the list was old.

"Hey---you okay?" The voice was pleasant, sounding genuinely concerned.

"Yeah." He shook his head, turning to look up from the list, still frowning as if bewildered. With a shrug, he gave a helplessly simple smile. "I'm looking for my sister's house, but I think I'm on the wrong street now. I just got into New Orleans last night."

He'd played this role before, for hundreds of years. The well-dressed and handsome gentleman stranger looking for his family and in need of help from whomever might stumble along...thief or innocent. From cut-purse to soft-faced matron to strong workman, he could be guaranteed a meal from this deception; who did not want to help the stranger who looked healthy and moneyed and completely at a loss?

"Maybe we can help ya." The other one spoke, his voice and accent giving him away as a native from the Algiers side of the river.

"Maybe you can." He smiled, shrugging with indecision as he studied them.

In the shadows, he could see perfectly well and it was obvious to his preternatural sight that they were well-fed. The need to rob him was not easy to guess at; they didn't appear to need anything basic. Their clothes were decent and they didn't seem to be starving and he could smell no drugs or alcohol on them. Perhaps they were only looking for trouble, something to liven up their blood.

He waited until they drew close enough, their smiles insincere. He went on, giving the idea of hopeless tourist with his every move. It was the same as a bird with a broken wing, wasn't it? The wrong kind of mortal responded to it with predatory interest, every time.

Out came the gun he was waiting for. The stubbled face went hard and brutally cold. "Okay, buddy. Your wallet, your watch, everything."

The other thief had a knife. He looked them over quickly and assessed the situation. Slowly, he put the grocery list back into his coat pocket and held out his hands.

"Wait, wait." He backed up a step, his long coat brushing a pile of garbage bags. "What're you doing? There's no need for trouble."

The two thieves moved forward on him, anticipating his fear. Joseph gave a low chuckle as he moved as fast as his inhuman muscles would allow; he ripped the gun away from the thief's hand and then took the knife from the other man, tossing both weapons into the closest dumpster, only three feet behind him.

"Of course, that doesn't mean there won't *be* trouble." He ground the words out, grinning wickedly. It showed all his teeth, including the predominant fangs. He felt the darkness on his features and knew that the mortals could see the red glint in his eyes, even in the shadows.

Both of his attackers knew, in that instant, that he wasn't human. That he was the wolf in a lamb's clothes. It showed in their shocked faces. He gave them no chance to run, no chance to shout. He slammed his fist into the chest of the gunman, knocking the mortal unconscious instantly. The other, he grabbed by the throat, uncaring of how the unconscious one would fall to the garbage-strewn alley. It was this one he wanted immediately, the one who spoke like a native of Algiers across the river.

His fangs slid forth with an ache that was bone-shivering as he dragged the frightened thief to his mouth. In a second, his mouth found its target and he crunch-slid his way through succulent male skin and stubble and salty sweat, loving the flavor of adrenaline and fear as it burst onto his tongue. The man moaned---it was like a sob vibrating against his cheek and his mouth---and he felt his manhood grow hard.

Gripping with his hands, he held the scruffy thief closer---they were pressed together from head to knees---one fist gripping lined flannel jacket and its buttons and the other clenched in lank, blonde hair. It was love, it was lust, it was adoration. It was a tango, a waltz, a Hora. The blood was like a hot, spicy wine and he let himself drown in its flood---in the wild thump of the prey's heart. On and on, he gulped, feeling it warm him from the inside out. The wet didn't matter, anymore. He grew dizzy with the intensity.

The flood slackened and the heartbeat began to drag---it was thready---and at last, he pulled his fangs free. The blood was a mere trickle on the bared throat he examined. He licked up the tiny spill and then released the hold he gripped onto the man's head. Quickly, without losing the unconscious body, he pushed aside his coat and reached for the spare butterfly knife he carried in his back jeans' pocket. He flipped the blade open. Without hesitation, he cut the thief's throat from ear to ear, obliterating the four fang holes with a jagged slash.

At last, he let the body drop. In only moments, the heart would stop and the prey would be dead. But, now...wildly gleeful with the hot blood that moved through him, he considered the other man. The one who'd pulled a gun on him. A more fitting end, perhaps? He picked up the unconscious thief's hand and pressed the knife into it. Then, gripping the hand and the knife, he pushed it into the dying man's throat. Blood slid over the still-living man's fingers and all the way onto his sleeve. If nothing else, this one would be seen as the possible murderer. If he wasn't mistaken, the local police would see it as an open and shut case---murder between street scum wasn't an uncommon event. Perhaps there wouldn't even be an inquiry.

Now, it was time to go home, to Nicolai.

He wiped his creamy leather gloves free of blood on a black handkerchief and then buried the worn cotton in a bag of garbage that sat on the ground beside the dumpster. Fed and warm, he set out walking in the fog, headed for the old, converted warehouse that served as his lair. As he walked, making his way quickly, he let himself think of Mishenka again.

Thinking of her brought a song to mind. He hummed it, melancholy at the bittersweet memory of how beautiful their existence had once been.

'Sunday is gloomy. My hours are slumberless. Dearest, the shadows, I live with are numberless. Little white flowers will never awaken you, not where the black coach of sorrow has taken you. Angels have no thoughts of ever returning you. Would they be angry if I thought of joining you? Gloomy Sunday.'

It was a good thing, having Dante meet with her; if there was a darker ulterior motive to what Misha requested, Dante would know of it. But, he could just as easily refuse without a second's thought; why was he choosing to give Misha something so valuable, something so precious?

He couldn't. No matter the outcome, he could not give the truth of the Sang-rael to Misha for any reason. There was nothing she could offer him that might change his mind on the matter---nothing.

'Gloomy is Sunday. With shadows I spend it all. My heart and I have decided to end it all. Soon there'll be candles and prayers that are said, I know. But let them not weep. Let them know that I'm glad to go. Death is no dream, for in death I'm caressing you. With the last breath of my soul, I'll be blessing you. Gloomy Sunday.'

She still possessed the flame in her eyes, the fire and intensity he had loved from the very start. It was heartaching, how they had grown apart. It was more---it was a sin. But, as they were not holy creatures or mortals with free will, there was no penalty to be paid in exchange for a cleansing.

They were damned and without hope for redemption, so what did it matter if his wife had abandoned him? Furthermore, what did it matter that he'd taken a mortal girl as his bride, the pure and ephemeral beauty to his Undead beast? What did it matter if he took a gypsy boy as his lover and childe? Did it matter if Misha took lovers? Did it matter that he beat and tortured Nico when the need for self-flagellation hissed and sobbed in his head? What could it possibly matter, in the scheme of things, if he had spent hundreds upon hundreds of years being exceptionally cruel to his food? Was there some way to repent of his unholy state?

No and *no*.

Raising his head to the chilly, quiet air, he smiled at the darkened sky. Beyond the evil he had done, he had wrought two somethings both beautiful and brilliant. He had taken two mortal children and given them the benefit of his education and his blood. They were unlike any other jewels and he had taken them from their native time and place and put them into settings of apt timelessness and perfect strength. They would never grow old and they would never die, his two loves. They were the epitome of their people, the Ukrainian---both gypsy Slav and Jew.

They were his masterpieces and proof that evil could create. No, that was not exactly accurate. He had taken God's creations and created them anew, both profane and divine.

Nicolai came to his inner eye and he chuckled, still tasting the blood in his mouth. Nicolai, the violin-playing gypsy with flashing dark eyes and a mane of coal-dark hair, a free and defiant spirit even in the face of slavery. He could, for a moment, feel his boy's touch--- there, on his cheek and his throat, the strong thumb that moved down and down and offered forgiveness without words.

How could he truly repent of Nicolai?

How could he repent of Mishenka?

She was there, in his mind, in all her glory. As he allowed himself to see, she was the mortal girl---his companion and his responsibility and then his bride. She of the high cheekbones chiseled sharp, she of slanted eyes the color of a pale autumn sky, she of a mouth cherry soft and ripe and full of smiling quirks, she of the skin like palest rose gold and milk.

For a brief moment, he felt her there, leaning close and over him. He felt the slide of her light brown hair as it caressed his hands and face and she offered a kiss he could not resist. The phantom did not leave but lingered, haunting him; when he reached the building where he made his home, he was aching and mournful again and she was still there, under his skin.

He and Nicolai had a studio-styled condo, half of the third floor of a converted warehouse on Baronne, just a block off Julia. The building was brick and concrete and glass, but on the third floor, the interior walls were sponge-painted the colors of sand and chocolate and a muted rose and the windows were covered by heavy curtains, to prevent sunlight.   It was a very nice condo, if one liked condos.   He didn't.   He was still partial to old tenements and houses built a century ago---like the houses in the Garden District.   Like a lot of houses in New Orleans.   But, the condo was good for them, nonetheless.

As he went up the stairs, he could hear and feel the mortals around him.   Sleeping, peaceful, quiet.   And then, in the last meters to his own door, he heard them.   Felt them.   Tennyson and Nico.

"But, who could she be?   Why?"

"I don't know why, baby.   He's taking care of some business.   He'll be back."

They were concerned for him; it was touching.

His mind flashed into the not-so-dim memory of a night when he'd come back to the lair to discover his young and mortal Jewess companion had prepared him a feast, complete with mulled wine and golden-lit lamps and spiced lamb with rice and yumara and freshly baked bread.   A feast that any mortal man would be thrilled to see, but which he'd found bemusing at best.   At the time, only a few days after coming into his company, Misha hadn't yet realized the whole truth of what he was.   She had created the feast in their rooms at an inn while in the guise of his tender nephew, directing the innkeeper's wife with crude sign language under the pretense of being mute.

He'd laughed that night.   As he had laughed many times, after, because of Misha's innocence.   In those early days, she'd known he was different from other men, Christian or not, and yet she had not grasped the whole truth of him yet.

He was smiling at the thought of it as he unlocked the door and entered.

Tennyson and Nico were sitting together; his childe looked distinctly worried and the relief was palpable, when Nicolai's dark eyes fell on him.   He shed his wet coat and gloves and scarf without a word, hanging everything up.

The Creole girl looked ill, as if she might be poisoned by the alcohol she'd imbibed.   Bleary-eyed and ashen despite her skin tone, Tennyson Beaulieu was laying on the fawn-colored leather, arms half out of her coat.   It appeared as if she'd stopped in the middle of taking the coat off and simply flopped down into a sprawl.   Nico, on the other hand, sat on the heavy ironwood coffee table among the magazines and books, half-bent over his leather-clad knees, his long wavy hair hanging like dark silk around his cheeks and throat.

"Give the girl some water, Nicolai."   He instructed, putting the last of his things away at the entryway.   "She could go into shock, with so much poison in her system."

His childe got up and began moving, headed for the kitchen, light and easy on his feet despite the alcohol he knew Nicolai had taken.   Nico's voice was full of concern, coming at him from across the main room.   "What did she want, Joseph?"

Misha.

"She wants what I can't give."   He sighed, rubbing a hand over his cheeks and brow as he moved to the middle of the rug, coming to stand before Tennyson and the couch.   "It would be better if our young friend stayed close for a while.   For a few hours at the very least, a few days if possible.   She noticed the girl with you, outside the club, and I have my suspicions as to what she'll do, to gain the upper hand this time."

Nico was coming back, carrying the water glass; his dark eyes were overcast with the same, growing concern.   Without using names, his childe got the point across admirably.   "Joseph, you don't think she'd try using our friends against us, do you?"

"I cannot be sure."   He began to move back and forth, pacing the large Moroccan rug, trying to think.   The blood in his throat and in his veins made it quicker, easier to think in a coherent manner.   "I have a suggestion.   When the girl's not with us, she should be with Lorraine.   For her own protection.   Lorraine has fought and killed our kind before---he'll know what needs to be done.   He'll instinctively sense if there are vampires near him.   This would be the safest course of action where the girl is involved."

"What the hell are you talking about?"   Tennyson slurred at him, holding the glass between her hands like a small child.   She'd managed to sit up on the couch, but her agate-hued eyes were unfocused and he couldn't be sure the Negro girl was seeing *just one* of him. "I don't need protection."

It was obvious that she had no idea what they were talking of. That was good.

He smiled and moved to squat down in front of her, his hands gentle as he stroked back the braids that fell over her shoulder and onto her throat. "You must go to bed, girl. You've things to do later today and that means you must get some rest. You'll stay."

This was the cue for Nicolai to take Tennyson out of the room and prepare her for bed. The girl would stay, would sleep in their bedroom and be safe. He knew that his childe would see the necessity of these things. And Nicolai did.

Tennyson didn't protest as Nicolai stripped her of the coat and walked her to the bedroom.

With a sigh, Joseph lit a cigarette and dropped his lighter on the large, dark coffee table and began to pace.

Now, alone...he had to think. He had to consider his options.

His thoughts drifted almost immediately to the past, the memories of days long past.

Five years after he'd taken Nicolai as a slave in Spain, Misha had left. At the time, Nico had reached the age of twenty and could be considered something of a man of worth since he was attached to a master who owned property. That had occurred in the first years of the nineteenth century, in Rome. He'd hunted for his wife in Italy for weeks and then months, during which time he'd initiated his mortal slave into the life as his catamite. But, Misha had disappeared and could not be found and upon killing Nicolai and discovering that he'd created another childe, his sense of shame had surfaced. He'd given up looking for Misha and left Rome.

Yet, everywhere they traveled, he sought his bride. In the end, she had found him.

Ten years after leaving, she trailed him to his lair in St Petersburg and discovered the situation. They'd fought bitterly; he had wanted her to come home to him and she had despised him for taking Nicolai as childe and catamite. Misha left only a few weeks later, not to re-appear until the mid-century, when she tracked him to New York and its slums. There, they'd argued again in the alleyways for a few nights before he decided he could take no more. He'd forbidden her to come back, demanded that she never approach him again. Eager to argue this point, she'd followed him to the lair in a filthy, overcrowded tenement; he'd punished her, to make Misha understand how very serious he was. Two months at his mercy, chained to a bed in a dark room, had made her very certain that she was finished with the argument.

He had kept tabs on her, of course; he'd always known where she was, through a series of carefully maintained contacts. He knew that she and Nicolai had talked extensively only a few decades later, in England. He didn't care; as long as she stayed away from him and did not bring more grief in her wake, Mishenka was welcome to speak with Nicolai. He knew of her girl-lover, in London---the girl she'd taken off to Egypt with.

It wasn't until the second decade of the twentieth century that she'd found her way back to him once more. In Savannah, at his plantation house, she'd come and her demeanor had spoken of a woman who was ready for the grave. She hadn't said much of the pain, but he'd innately known that his bride was mourning for a dead and lost love. For this pain, he'd forgiven her intrusion; who did not wish to go home when in anguish?

Her visit, then, was a mere two nights.

He'd marveled at the idea of her loving anyone beyond him and Nicolai.

Now, she'd come to him again, nearly a century later.

He knew of her travels and her homes---the modern day and its technology made the process of keeping tabs so much easier---he'd kept an eye on his wayward bride. He was astounded at the way she worked among mortal scientists and historians and anthropologists without arousing very much concern or suspicion. She was a master at the power of mesmerizing; the people she worked with either knew what she was or believed she was a miraculous genius, brilliant beyond her years. She had convinced several of her long-term co-workers that she was a benu malakh who preferred to work at night---those co-workers who knew of malakh, of course.

Others, who didn't believe in vampires or malakh, seemed to ignore what was obvious. Doctor Mishenka Ben-Moshe worked among the living and many didn't notice that she grew no older and yet had stayed in the same department of the British Museum for fifty years. Perhaps it was simply the punctilious mindset of the educated, old-school English; they may notice and say nothing for fear of offending or prying.

He couldn't give her Tennyson, he couldn't give her the truth about the legacy and the prophesy. If Misha knew what the Sang-rael was, she would find some way to use it---she was in earnest about the scrolls that had fallen into her grasp. The scrolls sounded like a missing link in the information he had gathered, the clue which would have taken him to recognize the Lion's bloodline much faster.

Giving the truth to Misha...that could and mostly likely would lead to Tennyson Beaulieu's death. But, he must give her something that would take her far away, on a wild-goose hunt. He had notebooks and files full of false clues and the information that had led him to believe those false clues. He could give her these, perhaps. But, to have Dante check Misha out...that was a good idea. He would find something more of his wife's intentions and let Misha believe that he was simply being cautious to an extreme because he intended to truly give over the trail to her.

He had to think on it, had to consider the angles. Always, consider the angles.

Chapter Ten

Misha became herself once she was sure no one was watching. She wiped at the tears that fell, that refused to stop as she got out of the car in the parking building. She didn't care that her fingers weren't very clean, now. She was tired and emotionally wiped out. She could feel dawn coming quickly and knew it was time to give in---find a well-shadowed room.

She'd driven back to the corner of Royal and St Peter, back to LaBranche House.

The night clerks knew her on sight, from the last fortnight's late sojourns. They were accustomed to seeing her come in at this hour. They welcomed her, wet fawn-suede trench coat and soaked, wet-rat draggling hair, without comment or curiosity. They were even discreet enough to not mention the tiny speckles of blood that just might be obvious on the collar of her white velvet blouse---nor the twin patches of mud on the knees of her jeans.

She smiled at them, straightening her shoulders; after all, she was a wealthy customer who kept odd hours but who brought no trouble to the hotel or the restaurant. She was a known historian and anthropologist from London, whose accent and origins were most definitely of the Jewish Ukraine. In her jeans and high heels and white velvet blouse and flowing buckskin colored coat, it didn't matter if her blondish-brown hair was straggling down from the bun she wore it in or not. To the night clerks, she was still the genteel lady, Doctor Mishenka Ben-Moshe, and she never forgot to tip them with extreme generosity.

And the tears? Only the rain. Of course.

Clicking across the parquet floor, she headed for the elevator.

After leaving the street where she'd sat and talked with Joseph, she'd headed back into the true French Quarter and down towards the waterfront. She had needed to eat---being around her Sire brought the hunger out in spades. It hadn't taken her long to find the prostitute she wanted. Petite and with hair like autumn leaves or flame, of some Gael-Celt or Viking descent, naturally, the young woman was perhaps legal with the shaded, blue eyes of an exhausted child.

She'd enticed the girl into her car and they had talked for a few minutes---she'd offered the whore a drink of her peach brandy. It hadn't taken her very long to decide that, yes, this was the one who wanted her the most. A baby grown old too fast; she had given herself over to the pale eyes of a child barely able to hide the flashing glimpses of an iron-harsh life and the cold ashes of broken dreams.

Together, they had left the waterfront and driven up towards Esplanade. She'd turned the car out onto the streets that led to Marigny, to find the whore's shotgun row cottage. There, she'd let the girl take her to the back garden---she had a fetish for feeding out of doors---and she had discovered how different this one was from the majority of whores she had eaten. The girl was clean---remarkably clean. She'd given into the need for a taste of more than blood. On her knees in a muddy patch of ground under a willow tree, by a beaten-down picket fence, she'd lifted the whore's skirt and used her tongue to lick at a wonderfully shaven vulva. She'd brought pleasure to the girl---something the whore had seemed shocked by.

Then, standing, she had embraced her victim in a long, gentle kiss---the girl had trembled at her tenderness and her honest affections. She'd asked for her prey's name and was rewarded with a shy whisper, the drawl of a voice cracking with unshed, embarrassed tears. 'Jayne.'

Something so simple. *Jayne.*

Her care and gentle behavior had unnerved and scared the whore. And it was a sad state of affairs that the girl hadn't struggled at all, when the kiss turned into sharp teeth and a growling purr. Jayne hadn't even tried to pull away. She'd guessed right, from the beginning---Jayne, the whore, had wanted death more than anything else except love. Except love, honest and genuine love.

Tenderness had frightened the girl. Death seemed to have reassured.

She'd cried all the way back to the hotel. In her mind, she could still see the girl---after draining her of blood, she had carefully hidden the evidence of her deed by doing what Joseph had always insisted she do, making the prey look like a human kill. Anyone who looked at only the surface would see a whore who'd probably met a vicious and deadly john and nothing more. Not so unusual.

Upstairs on the third floor, she unlocked the door of her suite and looked around at the darkened room as she closed it once more, smoothly sliding the deadbolt into place. The suite had two rooms and a water closet---very lovely. The sitting room was done in French Colonial, very attractively. It was dark; the lights were off, but this didn't deter her. She stood motionless, without so much as a single unneeded sigh of air, and listened for the sound of his incessant heartbeat---his breathing.

He was there. He was in the bed chamber. He was at rest.

Misha pulled off her suede trench coat and dropped it on the over-done gold brocade chair. Just as easily, she removed her brown leather high heels. Still, no overt sounds. As she began to pad across the darkened room, she pulled off her white velvet blouse, taking the pins in her hair with it. As the collar finally cleared her head, the wet waves fell slap against her cheeks and neck and shoulders. Free---having never worn a bra in her long existence--- and wearing only her jeans, she stopped at the door of the bed chamber.

There, she stood and watched him.

The room was pitch-black---he'd drawn the thick curtains and shades closed for her, already---and yet she could make out everything clearly. There was the tester bed with its tall, spindly posts that rose nearly to the ceiling and the seemingly impossible wooden cap that sat upon them. There were the walls done in Colonial French creams from the waist up and dark rose silk brocade from the waist down. There, not far from the bed, on the ceiling, swished the constant hum of an old wood-wicker fan. There were the long, carefully covered windows that took up most of the wall---they led out onto wrought-iron balcony that overlooked the busy street.

The breeze from the fan made the curtains rustle just the tiniest bit---something only the Undead could hear. The air was sweet with his scent, that impossible myrrh and frankincense. There was the King Louis XVI Berger chair, at the foot of the bed, cocked almost sideways in the space between the first and second windows, sitting on the red Persian rug. The chair was solid, made of mahogany and carved in acanthus flowers and leaves, its brocaded seat and back a watery pale gold and rose with a Florentine design. She really liked the chair more than anything else in the room.

With wolfish intuition, she listened and watched. He was here, in bed. She could see him under the creamy yellow-white duvet. He was like some statue of a god, so still and quite. His heart beat steadily, his breath came without a hitch. His black curly hair lay in whorls upon the pillow. He was laying on his back, his arms flung open and free, his feet completely relaxed and limp.

He was achingly beautiful. No small coincidence she was attracted to him, with his olive skin and strong features. He looked so Semetic, her Greek princeling. His arms and chest glowed in the darkness---he seemed to be asleep, but she couldn't tell for sure. He wasn't human and she couldn't gauge him by his heartbeat or his skin reactions or his hormone-laden sweat. She had found him to be mesmerizing from the very start, fifty years ago. He was sexy and possessive, but he didn't love her the way Joseph did. Yet, she couldn't bet on that, either---she had no way of knowing anything, for sure, with Uly.

So, she stood in silence and watched him, and wondered for the thousandth time why she'd aligned herself with someone she couldn't fathom. They'd known each other for just over fifty years, but the love affair had only started a mere two decades ago. They had never become exclusive and it was a silent agreement---there would be no eternal commitments, no marriage of any sort. She liked it that way and so did he.

He was benu, a malakh from ancient Greece. Their colleagues had slowly, over time, come to understand what they were---or, at least, they'd come to understand what Uly was and they believed she was the same kind of creature. Malakh could be accepted and forgiven, in the world of anthropology and archaeology, where malakh were a carefully hidden secret from the larger world---but an acknowledgement of the vampire would only confuse and upset the careful balance of the scientific world.

Because their colleagues accepted Ulysses Ithaca, they also accepted her.

The world of science and history was a strange plane of reality.

Did she love him? She did. As much as she'd loved Emily, her lost English girl. As much as she'd loved Nicolai. But, *never* as much as she'd loved Joseph. And that was acceptable. It was forgivable.

"He won't give you the Vessel." He sounded somewhat British, somewhat American. His voice was low, calm, his lips barely moving. It was a speculative statement. His pale eyes didn't open. He was awake, even if her preternatural senses said otherwise.

"Can you be sure of that?" She wasn't surprised, though, that he was awake in bed, looking like a statue of gilded flesh. "Joseph's still my Sire. He wants his unlife to be different, too, even if he won't admit that. He's still looking for the next coming of the Lion. He's not doing the same things he did fifty years ago."

"How do you know, Mishenka?" Her name was soft, like a flower's petal, coming from his mouth. "Just because he's working a steady job in the world of mortals? Just because he doesn't torture humans indiscriminately without care for being caught?"

Misha unbuttoned her jeans and slid them off. Naked, she moved to the bed's side. She sat down in the Berger chair and reached for the spindly table that sat beside it. There, she found the cigarettes and lighter and ashtray. She lit one before she answered, never taking her eyes off the shadowed, unmoving figure in her bed.

She couldn't tell Joseph about Uly. No more than she could've told him about Emily.

"No, I say he's different because I know him." She gave a crooked smile and brushed her thumb against the damp hair that fell over her cool forehead and into her eyes. "I know him better than anyone else, Uly. I know him better than Nicolai does. I know him better than he knows himself. Joseph's changed and he knows where the Vessel is---he knows and he's protecting it. He knows the Vessel can be found in that bar. He's careful to not reveal anything to me, of course, but---Uly, he's changed and I've got a feeling that it's because of the Vessel. The Vessel has changed him all the way to his bones. I want that."

He stayed quiet now, but she watched as his eyes opened and turned toward her. His gaze was heavy, like the stones of ancient temples and tombs. She didn't have to see them in the light to know what color they were, his eyes. They were a light brown. His tone never changed, was still yet low and calm. "Mishenka, why do you really hunt for the Vessel? Do you believe you'll be happier as a mortal? Do you think mortals know something about the world which escapes your grasp? I know why I seek it---I want to free my brethren from their tombs, I want to fight the rising dark, and this requires magic only the Vessel can produce, I want to protect and teach the al-Mahdi---but why do you want this cure of yours?"

She'd never told him of what the Sang-rael meant to her, to the unlife she'd led.

She had worked for nearly a century as a linguist historian and anthropologist, but it was nothing compared to Uly. Ulysses was a benu of rare and unusual talents---his age and intelligence alone was enough to ensure a place for him in the British Museums as archaeologist, anthropologist, historian, linguist.

He was four thousand years old, give or take a decade---even he wasn't too sure about the exact year of his birth as a mortal. He was old enough to remember the stories of the Midael and the Grigori---of the heroes and monsters and gods the angels had spawned among the humans. He was one of these---the son of a god. A god whose real nature was angelic and intemperate.

Until coming to this city, seeking Joseph and Nicolai, she'd made sure that no one could imagine a whisper of the truth about them. Who knew how far Joseph's eyes could see or how far his ears could hear? She hadn't wanted anyone to know that Uly was her lover. So, no one had.

He looked so young for the millennia he'd seen. She knew the stories---he was legend for the mortal world, a hero remembered for his cunning and his prowess. When mortals remembered him, it was his honor and his fidelity they recalled. It was his steadfast tenacity they lauded. One of the oldest stories in the world---one of the best known---was about him. And he was more than legend or hero. He wasn't perfect---he was benu malakh with all a benu malakh's foibles.

He was her playmate.

"I want the Vessel for the end of certain diseases. Vampires who want to be mortal again should have that option. Mortal children who are dying from cancer and HIV shouldn't have to die." She flicked ashes into the cream-white ceramic ashtray, licking at the curve of her lower lip, giving him the only answer she owned. "I want the Vessel because it's engrained in me to want it. Evil shouldn't be allowed to reign on earth---not human evil or demonic evil or even malakh evil. The only way to purify the world is to use the Vessel's magic. The legends say that one unspeakable, ineffable word, spoken within the blood the Vessel holds, is enough to cleanse and correct everything. All it takes is the Vessel and the intent to do right."

"What happens if evil claims the Vessel?" Uly's voice rumbled up from his deep chest and through the pipe of his throat. "Can evil claim it? If so, how will you know which has won, evil or good?"

She didn't want to go into the stories again---to tell Uly once more the tales Joseph had given her for hundreds of years, when they'd lived alone as Sire and childe, husband and wife. It was late and she was tired.

"Later, solodky lyubow." Misha stubbed out her cigarette and blew smoke into the darkness above her head. She ran a cooling hand through her long hair and stood, stretching her back. It was growing time for her to rest, to fall into sleep and let things go. A thought dawned on her as she pulled back the duvet and crawled in at Uly's side. He was fiery---his skin always felt entirely too warm at first, until the heat warmed her bones. She mumbled, laying her mouth against his shoulder, immediately comfortable as his arm closed around at her ribs. "I've got to go meet some guy Joseph works with. A dinner date at some fancy restaurant."

"Why?" He rolled her sideways until they were laying chest to chest, her face nestled against his shoulder and collarbone, wrapped up into his arms. His mouth rested at her forehead, his breath ruffling the drying strands of her hair in the front. The rest of her long blondish-brown hair was caught under his forearms and elbows, snug and protected. "Why would he want you to meet with a man he works with? What is the significance of it?"

Misha sighed, giving her head a little shake that rubbed her cheeks back and forth on his silky, hot skin. Growing drowsy, her voice husked. "Who knows? Maybe the guy is some kind of psychic---Joseph doesn't trust me, doesn't trust anyone. He gave this as a condition. I have to meet and talk with this guy before I can have the papers."

"Ah." It wasn't the tone that let her know...but, it was gut instinct which said she wasn't going to bed just yet. In his arms, she felt the change and the shift. Uly wanted her body's pleasure.

Perfect. She needed that, when she was willing to admit it. After the talk with Joseph, after seeing Nicolai for that brief moment...after the young prostitute she'd killed for blood...she needed honest, earthy affection.

When he lowered his mouth to her breasts, Uly looked up and found her with a mouth opened in want. She met his gaze boldly as he flicked at her small nipples with his teeth and lips, testing the pebbled hardness. He kissed her breasts slowly and she could feel his hardness pulsing against her thigh. She slipped her fingers up to touch his cheeks as he licked at her chilly skin with a tongue made of flames. Uly let his hand stroke, open-palmed and long-fingered, across a taut nipple as he gentle bit down around the other one, tasting the way it stretched out as he sucked the whole of it into his lips.

He whispered hoarsely, pressing his lips to her ear. "Love, you're a dark goddess, a queen worthy of tribute. Solomon himself would envy me. The kings of Greece of my youth would, if they might see you as I see you, willingly take their men to war for your perfection. Helen, lover to Paris of Troy, was a crack whore when compared to your ageless beauty."

That was too much and she laughed.

Under Uly's mouth, she tensed and screamed, but he stole the sound with his lips. It took all of her brain, all of her substance. Something broke within her, then. Not with a snap but with a sigh. Like an earthen dam breaking, washing away all the pain a cubic centimeter at a time.

It was Uly's affections that did this. It was part of his gift, part of the legacy he owned from his angelic ancestors. He was benu malakh, but he was more. He had the power to take away pain with the touch of his hand. He could also give pain with the mere brush of his fingers. It was, of course, all in his intentions. A casual touch did nothing; but, if the ancient Greek benu chose to make his feelings known, a single finger was enough.

With her, he never gave pain. He always strove to remove it. Something in him fed on the pain he drew out of her heart and her soul. He worked to pull it free of her very core unrelentingly, every time they came together in the flesh. And she had a lot of pain and grief to give---she was six hundred and fifty-eight years Undead now, and she'd played witness to the rise and fall of humanity a number of times.

He had her by the ribs and shoulders with one arm and her hips by the other. She couldn't go anywhere that he wouldn't allow. But, not true---with her vampire strength, she could do whatever she wanted. But, she loved the things she heard in his voice, in his body. He was jealous of Joseph and of Nicolai. He was demanding equal time, demanding that she give herself totally over to him---heart and soul. Uly wanted this---the idea of claiming her, of taking what he wanted. To Uly, she was everything and the world and he was nearly as immortal as her---so, they belonged together.

She didn't always agree---in fact, she was so very much her own person.

But, it was nice to let Uly think he owned her. Especially when he was feeling jealous.

She could feel his mouth at her ear, the tickle of his shoulder-length black hair as it brushed over her cheek. Her eyes rolled up under the lids as she lost herself to the animal her Greek lover had become. At this moment, she was only his creature and she had never belonged to Joseph at all. She wasn't Undead and she wasn't centuries old in her unlife. She was no one but Mishenka and she was Ulysses Ithaca's bitch.

He moaned a curse in his ancient language.

She knew where it came from---his fetish for her. He loved smooth, soft, chilly things like ice cream and milk and marble. It was the woman's sensual, earthy beauty that beckoned, mixed with the absolute inhuman strength and feel of her body. The world centered here, on how he needed her. He held her close, as if to meld their bodies into one, so she could never leave. Uly's long fingers dug harder into her hips and then slid up to grasp her shoulders, to lever her movements to his liking. They were her fingers, as much as his, and she loved them. Loved them with a knowledge that no one else could've understood. Only a killer could get it---the true measure of Uly's hands, of what beauty and cold strength was to be found in his fingers.

She knew---he wanted to make sure she wouldn't want to leave him, not even for Joseph and Nicolai. He wanted to take her completely away from the thoughts of them, her Undead family.

Memories blurred; her long, immortal unlife flickered and flashed.

Uly showed her what he saw of them---he didn't fear the vampire power she held. More than anything, he loved her and wanted her because of who she was, to him. She was a darkness he couldn't live without. He was where he wanted to be, the most. In this moment, no one existed but them.

The danger crackled between them---it shadowed everything they did, adding spice to the moment. His grip tightened on her throat and she wailed, vampire strength roaring from within her chest. The headboard creaked and her muscles rippled as the orgasm tore through her. The wood cracked, breaking under her hands and she felt it giving way, falling. She didn't care. She fell against the wall, fingers finding the panel and plaster underneath as Uly went with her, claiming what belonged to him now.

She laughed breathlessly, on the edge of hysteria as her insides clenched and she came again, muscles locked up. The clutch of it made Uly curse and shudder as he bit down onto her neck, his fingers tightening a little more. His voice was muffled, his lips pressed flat to her skin, but she could feel the promises he made as his cock jerked in the vice-grip of her body.

Uly swore it---he *wouldn't* let her choose Joseph, he *wouldn't* let her choose the Undead.

And she collapsed under him, in silent agreement.

What could the Undead offer that might compare with the fiery love of a malakh?

Chapter Eleven

Joseph paced up and down the Moroccan rug. The cigarette was spent, gone. Now, his Sire was chewing on one well-manicured thumbnail. And he stood, watching in bemusement. No one would ever believe him if he told these things. Of what a pissy drama queen Joseph could be.

Now, Joseph was worried over Misha and he wondered how much of it was concern over what Misha wanted this time and how much of it was guilty love and shameful hunger for the wife who'd walked out on them. That's how he saw it---Misha had walked out on them *both*.

"How dare she? How dare she show her face here?" Joseph muttered around his thumbnail, eyes shadowed by the downward angle of his head. It was hard to see his Master's expression.

"She's yours...just like me." He rubbed his shoulders back and forth on the hard doorframe, scratching his back as he answered an obviously rhetorical question. "Did you really think she'd never come back?"

"She hasn't come back." Joseph was growing agitated, his lean and muscular body showing the emotional strain. "She's here to *torment* me. She wants something---when she gets it, she'll go away again."

"Until she needs something, *again*." He wanted a cigarette. His own nerves were jangling, but he didn't feel like going after his pack---they were in his leather jacket. "Besides, Joseph---is it so bad, seeing her? I've missed Misha."

Now, his Sire stopped and turned to stare at him. The thumbnail was forgotten. Joseph looked upset. The skin around his eyes was reddened, his gaze fiery. Almost too much to bear, too much emotion within the pale green-gray eyes. His voice was a husky growl. "Whose side are you on, boy?"

Nicolai shrugged, folding his arms. "Yours...I'm always on yours. And that's what you think, too. You think it's wonderful to see her, but you wish she didn't hold a grudge. You don't wanna hate Misha, but she makes it impossible to love her."

"Two hundred and thirty-one years both mortal and Undead and already a philosopher." Joseph's words could've been a sneer, but his Sire didn't seem to have the energy to spare for real anger. He went back to pacing, one arm folded against his chest, and a thumbnail caught between his front teeth. That made his words slur. "She wants information I can't give her, Nico. If she had the information, she could destroy everything. I've worked too hard to keep this, I've come too far. I can't just hand Mishenka what she wants, now. But, if she stays..."

"If she sticks around, Joseph, she's gonna find out all the little chinks in your armor."

His Sire muttered it at him. "I have no chinks in my armor."

Nicolai sighed, rolling his eyes. "No, but there's the office. She could walk into Pandora's Box any time she likes and tell Mattie or Rembrandt that she's one of us and before we even know she's there, she could slaughter half the humans. What about Tennyson? If Misha finds out that we have any kind of real connection to Tennyson, she won't hesitate to turn that screw---not if she's really interested."

Joseph chuckled sourly, not glancing at him. The thumbnail was clicking against his Sire's top fangs, which had distended themselves. "What of Lorraine? You don't fear for your malakh boyfriend?"

It's a slur, poking and nasty.

He didn't deny or admit anything; in this kind of mood, Joseph might explode on him or might let any comment slide off like water. He lifted the corner of his mouth in a cruel grin, showing his own fangs on that side.   "If Misha goes after Rhys or anyone Rhys protects...well, my money's on Rhys.   I can only feel pity for her, if she fucks with Rhys Lorraine."

With a chuckle, Joseph nodded, still distracted. "Yes. He's a rare hunter."

He smelled fresh human blood. It was a gnawing reminder that he hadn't fed---really fed---in two nights. He couldn't count the taste of Rhys he got on the dance floor. That was like comparing a kiss to the act of intercourse itself. But, then, even draining Rhys would never satiate. He could never have enough of the tchatcha's blood. The last drop would be as sweetly spiced as the first gush and that would still only excite him to the flavor. The oceans---all of the water in the world---could be become Rhys' veins and it still would never be enough.

He was hungry---he could feel the hollow places in the arteries of his body. He did remember human hunger---hunger for bread and meat and milk---and it was nothing by comparison. The hollow places were aching worse than any shaky, weak, stomach pangs could.

His mortal hag was in his bed, naked and warm and and so very, very healthy with her own searing, thumping wellspring and all its gorgeous tributaries. And Joseph had fed. It was so unright. So damnably unright.

"She's still as lovely tonight as on the first night."

Nicolai dragged himself back to the moment, seeing and hearing Joseph anew.   So handsome, so predatory---feral. And full of some man's life. Some *other* man.

"I wish you had Mishenka stuffed up your ass." He muttered, pushing up away from the doorframe. He stalked around the room's perimeter, out of his Sire's reach, to rummage in his jacket pocket. Hunting up his smokes. But, Joseph didn't seem to hear or see him; his Sire was still pacing and gnawing at the one thumbnail.

Joseph's voice was speculative, quiet, growling---yet, so civilized and full of concern. "I smelled something on her tonight. She wore a strange perfume. Something I can't quite place, Nico. Myrrh and...frankincense? Yet, she also smelled like her usual perfume. Why would she use two scents? To smell like the church, the synagogue?"

He put away his cigarettes again and took a long drag on the smoke he'd lit. Pulling at the hem of the Lycra shirt he wore, he sat down on the coffee table's edge. With inhuman grace, he removed the constricting, slinky material and dropped it into the floor, a forgotten second skin. He didn't bother to answer his Master; there was no point---Joseph didn't need his input, now, to keep the ball of speculation on the roll.

In just his jeans, Joseph looked like sex on the prowl---and he smelled coolly damp, from the rain. And the scent of that human blood was intoxicating, as intoxicating as a dozen vampire martinis.   Now, as he talked, Joseph's voice took on the half-lost cadence of a creature born nearly a thousand years ago in Jerusalem. "Why---but, there was something else I can't understand. What about the look of her---she's changed and changed in some impossible way. She's changed in some way we shouldn't be able to change. The way she smiled---the look of her eyes. Something in how her fingers moved. Something big has happened to her, something I haven't seen or heard. It's been almost a century and she's---like a different woman."

It made his skin tingle, the sound of his lover's accent coming through. That was rare enough, the lilting tones of ancient Hebrew being mentally translated into English. Unnecessarily, to be honest, because he himself spoke several languages. Languages were easy for the gypsy---even the Ukrainian Rom. In the past, they'd talked in Ukrainian, in French, in English, in Spanish, and in Yiddish---the language of Misha's people.

With deft fingers, he rolled the fiery end of his filterless Camel cigarette along the edge of the Communion plate, watching the ashes fall away as he dared to finally voice his opinion. He wasn't quite able to erase all the sarcasm---a dangerous habit. "You spent over four hundred and fifty years with her and you think she's changed *now*? Joseph, we *do* evolve. If you didn't see any changes in four and a half centuries, it's because you were fooling yourself. Every time she comes around, she's changed. I see it, she sees it---maybe your eyes are finally open?"

His Sire stopped pacing and stood in the middle of the rug, looking caught. Almost dejected, almost lost. Joseph's voice was low, careless, almost too soft to hear. "Not like this, Nico. Not like this. You should've seen her as I did. Heard her, as I heard her." He could nearly swear that the elder vampire heaved a sigh of grief-laden breath. "It's as if a fire has crawled through every cell and every vein and every bone. She's not our Misha, now. It's as if something has come alive in her---the way she talked, it made me think of her as she was, mortal and living again."

With the cigarette hanging off his lower lip, he groaned in frustration and closed his eyes. He was already sick of this conversation. He didn't want to talk about Misha anymore; Misha didn't love them, didn't want to stay in the same town for more than a few weeks at the most.

He'd given up on his own mad adoration of her almost a century ago. Oh, he still loved her, but what was the point? She didn't want to be with them. That door was closed and if he was pushed to truly see Misha again, for more than a week, he'd find himself hoping she'd stay. Which she wouldn't.

There was a place in his brain---at the back, where the most primitive part of his spirit and nature kept immortal company---that sniffed out a strange hint of what might have changed in their Jewess. Joseph might've been blind to the little traces of evolution in them, his two Ukrainian childer, but he was aware of how Misha could change. The strange idea he caught scent of, in his back-brain, had to do with lovers and how a lover's body could leave effluvia in the after of a flood. A flood that came in sweat, blood, tears, and spunk. Even a vampire could smell like a mortal, in small ways, if the vampire lived with---and loved---a mortal.

Misha might have a new lover. She might have a *mortal* lover.

He'd smelled the little English woman on Misha. Hadn't he?

What had Joseph said, about the scent? Temple spices? Frankincense and myrrh. Purification spices---what mortal ever smelled like *that*?

He smoked and ignored Joseph's continued rant---until he realized that he was doing exactly the same thing as his Sire---expending too much thought and energy on Mishenka.

Nicolai stubbed out his cigarette into the golden plate's incised center and spoke, deliberately raising his voice to override his Sire's. "Would you stop thinking about her for five fucking minutes? Can you please fucking stop talking about her? What do I have to fucking do? Get on my fucking knees and fucking beg?"

It got the desired reaction. Joseph was stunned into furious silence. Damn. No one, not even Rhys, would ever believe what a prissy, pissy drama queen his Sire really was, behind closed doors and out of the public eye. Not in a full thousand years.

He could almost count the seconds, the angry tick of his Sire's internal gears.

Before he had the idea that he should get out of the way, Joseph was on him with a hiss of dark rage which contained words only a blood-sucker might understand. "Ah, but Nico, you little evil shit, are you *offering*? You're beautiful on your knees, like a fallen saint."

Nicolai fell across the littered ironwood table, under Joseph's foot. He strangled on his come-back, voice breaking under the impact. "You and your fucking *saints*---I hate to tell you, baby, but this is home. You can't play the abandoned husband with me, *Joe*. I know you---*remember*?"

There he lay, flat on his back, on the coffee table, among the scattered photograph books and knick-knacks, caught under Joseph's foot. His Sire was enraged, but it was a cold anger. The kind that would get him tortured. He let his head fall back over the empty space---his upper shoulders and neck and head weren't laying on anything at all. He felt his hair fall loose, whispering, as he stared up at his Master, his lover. There, beyond crushing foot and denim-covered knee and long, lean body, was Joseph.

Who looked like the Joseph who'd taken him out of Spain. Who looked like the Joseph who'd sat in a chair beside the luxurious bed, holding a whip of plaited willow, watching him and Misha between the sheets with cold eyes---the Joseph who'd given him the same simple order every night for more than a thousand nights. All he had to do was fuck his Master's wife while the Master watched. If he failed to do everything he could, to Misha, he would feel the sting of that willow whip...and he would feel it until he felt the blood dribbling, too. This was the Joseph who'd tied him across a wine barrel in the cellar, in Rome, and showed him how blood and spit could be used to keep skin from shredding.

This was the Joseph who'd raped and pillaged and tortured a broad swath through the underworld for centuries before he'd come into the picture as a enslaved Rom. Only...the rape and pillage and torture had gotten worse after his arrival; it had seemed that with both him and Misha there, watching, some fresh horror in their Sire broke free and howled at the night.

This was the Joseph who might drive wooden stakes through his wrists and tie him to the ceiling---all for the pleasure of fucking him on his tip-toes or even for just playing mumbly-peg. This was the Joseph who would use a knife to peel the skin off a pregnant woman's burgeoning belly, just to have a chance at licking the opened, bulging outer viscera of a womb.

He lay still under Joseph's foot and refused to back down; as childe, he wasn't supposed to challenge his Sire so openly. But, something perverse flared up in his Undead brain. He had to be difficult; he had to make Joseph wild with rage and lust. He had to be the one who peeked through the veils and wouldn't lie about what he could see.

With a one-sided twist of his mouth, Nicolai spoke again, wry sarcasm his natural state. "If she loved you, Joseph, she wouldn't have stayed away. I can see how she might've decided she could need a vacation, after those first five years with me around. Two's company, three's hardly a marriage. But, if she really, really loved you, Joseph, she would've come back after the first ten years and she would've stayed. She would've *stayed*."

Joseph's gray-green eyes were pinned to him---so silent, his Sire---and he used that to his advantage. Again, he spoke, using one of his hands to trace the shape of the foot planted on his neck. Two fingers, around and over the toes and the arch and the heel. Such lovely feet for a man who'd existed as a mortal at the beginning of the Second Crusade---a hard-working knight, of all things.

"If you love her, Joseph. If you love her more than you love me, then let me go and do something about it. She won't come back to you as long as I'm in the picture. Only, I'm certain she'd be really put out if you dusted my ass. So."

It was a bad game he'd played a few times, always with variations. He did love Joseph, but he couldn't help pushing the buttons that would set his Sire off like a fanatic roman candle. Every time he wanted to divert a problem with Joseph, all he had to do was start throwing out challenges.

This time, it was easier. Misha was a sore subject. Joseph growled at him, eyes narrowed. He could see the gleam of redness sparkle deep in their pupils. "You're not going anywhere, Nico. You *belong* to me. Misha, too."

"Keep telling yourself that. Denial's cute on you. Stupid, but cute." He gave a wicked smirk.

It was like being jerked up by a force of nature. Joseph pulled the hard foot away and then hoisted him into the air by his hair. It hurt---it made him want to shout in retaliation, but he gritted his teeth instead. Never let it show---never.

He dangled over the rug and the coffee table, his naked feet in empty space. He was surrounded by the buzzing rage that came off Joseph in waves and spikes, almost visible. Instead of struggling, he hung motionless and stared into the eyes of his Sire, now level with his own.

He whispered, forcing himself to keep smirking. "You can't prove it."

Joseph's eyes flashed with red in the depths, exciting and dangerous. The hand in his hair moved, shaking him with ease. "You're in trouble, boy. Your mouth has gone too far too fast, once more."

He didn't answer it. He didn't need to.

With a low growl, Joseph seized his mouth in a plundering, consuming kiss. He gave into it and felt himself being gathered closer---his feet still didn't touch the rug, but the hand that'd held him by the hair was now gripping the back of his neck. The other hand and arm held him at the waist and hips. He was being crushed, embraced wholly, held up off the floor in the grip of a vampire who wanted him. His Sire, his Master, his lover.

He slid his hands down Joseph's chest, touching the strange heart-shaped scar before he found a place to grasp at the waistband of Joseph's jeans. Hungry and wanting, he welcomed the tongue that ravaged the inside of his mouth. He pressed harder into the kiss, feverishly demanding. His cock throbbed hotly inside his pants, rubbing against Joseph's hardness---he could feel everything on his Sire's body, they were so tightly pulled together.

Then, Joseph shoved him backwards, dropping him. He fell against the ironwood coffee table and hit the rug on his ass. He didn't have time to protest---not even time enough to get off the floor. His Sire reached down and gathered his wrists in one big hand and pulled him along the rug and around the couch. A piece of him was growing even more excited---he loved it when Joseph played rough---and he was being dragged towards the kitchenette. There was fun to be had in the kitchenette.

But, out of the blue, at the last moment, Joseph changed course and he found himself scrambling along in the direction of the second bedroom, half off his feet. It was on the other side of the condo from the main bedroom---their bedroom. Tennyson was sleeping in there, the main bedroom, but Joseph was dragging him along to the other one, past the kitchenette and its dining table that he never needed. He was going to the bad room. The room that Tennyson was never allowed to see. The door was kept shut and locked; she probably thought it was just a closet.

He tried to gain his feet, tried to break his hands free of Joseph's fist. Nothing worked. He didn't dare shout---he'd wake Tennyson, he'd wake the neighbors, and then the cops might get called. How could it be explained?

'Oh, yes, officer, my Undead lover beats me, but I love him anyway. Every time he thinks I've overstepped his precious ideals, Joe strings me up and makes sure I remember to be afraid and happy all at the same time. Does that count as domestic abuse? No? Is that because we're gay or because we're vampires?'

In the little bedroom, he spared a glance for it.

The walls were lined in mattress and tapestries---Joseph's contribution to keeping the neighbors ignorant of what happened here. The mattresses were bolted into place along the wall-studs and worked wonderfully for sound-proofing. It wasn't really such a little bedroom; it was the same size as the main bedroom. He just thought of it as being the little bedroom because...well, what was he supposed to call it? The torture chamber? The dungeon? How about *Joseph's Office*?

Joseph's filing cabinet was there. With its locks. Joseph's weapons were there, too. The closet was full of weapons, well cleaned and honed and ready to do damage. Not that Joseph used them much---just when they went hunting vampires. After all, the humans they occasionally killed, as assassins in Pandora's Box, were most often killed in the most discreet manner. The old drain and turn and dust routine was one of Joseph's favorites.

But, to him, the most important part of the little bedroom were...the bed, of course, and the rack. And the wooden cabinet that held Joseph's toys. Joseph had to have his toys. The bed was shoved into the farthest corner, innocuous and almost silly in the knowledge of Joseph's rack. The bed was dressed in simple satin---a deep burgundy, cooling blood color. It had only two, simple pillows and they were dressed in black satin. Yet, he never cared what the bed looked like. The wooden toy cabinet wasn't even on his mind, much.

It was the rack that played hardest in his daydreams and nightmares.

It was the rack that Joseph dragged him to, now.

Within moments, he was hanging by his arms from steel chains strong enough to withstand vampiric strength. The black, cast-iron manacles weren't padded; they bit into his wrists as he worked to stay up on his tiptoes and the pads of his feet, where Joseph had put him.

His Sire's face was like stone, now, but there was nothing cold in Joseph's expression. Joseph was extremely angry and feeling the need to prove a point to him. He had a feeling that it would be a day when he woke up already in bed, having been put there by his Sire after he fell into the dark, helpless sleep of the Undead.

He didn't know whether to be excited or afraid.

The rack was made of railroad ties. It was solid, black, and the nails were railroad spikes. It smelled of death and pain and thick creosote and hobos and coal. The basic shape was that of a children's swing-set. The A-frame doubled with struts for support. But, the only thing swinging from the chains was him. There were two chains hanging from the A-frame sections that could be hooked to a missing piece---the missing piece was a split tie that served as a bar. The bar over which he might find himself bent double, if Joseph decided for it.

Joseph had built the rack with his own hands. Just like he'd built the massive wooden bed-frames, one for this room and one for the main bedroom. Beautiful bed-frames, carved with ivy and oak leaves and lovingly varnished in dark cherry. Joseph was a carpenter---and there was a sick irony to the knowledge that only he could truly appreciate. Joseph had built almost all the furniture in the condo over the last three years and it was a shame his Sire didn't turn such a talent towards a market full of potential wealth. Cause...Joseph built sturdy yet beautiful.

In just his leather pants, Nicolai hung and fought a bone-deep shiver that threatened to wrack his tendons. No matter what happened here, it was going to be terrible and lovely all at the same time and he was going to try not to scream. That was part of his perversity---he had to refuse Joseph the pleasure of hearing him repent.

Joseph was moving around behind him, at the cabinet now.

He knew what was coming. The vampire in him was pleased to think on the pain. There would be holy water, crosses, a rosary, a steel-barbed whip, Communion wine. There would be blood, spunk, tears, and sweat. He would probably fall to sleep while still in the manacles, while still under the lash and the knife. And he'd sleep well-sated, the rest of a beloved slave. How many times had he been through this and similar? He didn't care to count the nights, anymore.

He heard the splash of liquid. Was that the wine or the holy water? Did it matter?

Then, his Sire appeared before him. Oh, the old bastard was ready to play, that was for sure. Joseph still wore his faded blue jeans and now carried a shallow ceramic bowl. The bowl was put down on the rugs, just beside the foot of one railroad tie. Joseph reached for his leather trousers, stepping close enough to kiss. They brushed in all the right places. Shoulders, arms, chest, abdomen.

He fought another shiver---this one made wholly of lust.

His Sire was the hottest, most feral Undead creature to ever exist.

The leather trousers were undone and big, steady hands began to slide them off his hips and legs. He wouldn't be needing them now. He watched Joseph steadily---he never begged for mercy anymore. What was the point? It never got him out of this. He had a feeling, sometimes, that if he begged these days, he might only excite Joseph further. That might make it worth the degrading effort...to have Joseph go wild. Joseph never went bug-ass crazy for him, anymore.

He just couldn't quite muster the words.

Joseph was the hottest, most feral Undead creature to ever exist, but there was someone else that got under his skin. Rhys. And Joseph knew it. Rhys Lorraine was the hottest, most feral *living* creature in the world---not that Rhys was aware in the least, Rhys was oblivious---and Joseph knew it was a distinction, knew it was the reason he hungered for the tchatcha boy.

But, Rhys wasn't here. And he was glad. He couldn't imagine what Rhys would do, in this room. Would Rhys be indignant at how he was treated by Joseph? Or...would Rhys bribe Joseph to be given a chance at him, the chained vampire? Could Rhys keep pace with what Joseph might do? He felt his veins go just a little more hollow in psychological hunger...there was something *old* and *terrifying* inside Rhys.   Something nobody else ever seemed to notice.   But, he noticed it.   Oh, yes.

And he ached to touch that half-hidden, unrealized, ancient darkness just one more time.

Now, Joseph took his mind and gave it a good twist.   The trousers were gone and his Sire raised a wet hand to touch his throat...to trace the shape of his jaw.   The hand burned and itched and he began to shake harder.   Holy water.   True holy water---which was really hard to come by, these days.   It wouldn't kill him, but it could leave burns and blisters that took days and weeks to heal.

And Joseph was inventive with it.   Could make him sorry.

Joseph's hand moved in abstract designs across his chest and down over his ribs.   He was hairless, muscular, and lean.   That gave his Sire room to work with what could be done to him, physically.   His physical, immortal beauty also lent a certain air of destructibility which Joseph loved to exploit.   It was like handing the ancient Templar a marble statue, a chainsaw, and a Discman with Godsmack or Monster Magnet playing, for inspiration.

All the little things he'd said and done tonight that could've gotten on Joseph's nerves...they all came back to haunt him, now.   His Sire kept a mental tally-board for moments like this.

More wet and Joseph stepped closer, wrapping both hands around his hips.   The holy water burned his skin like boiling oil.   He whimpered against his will into the mouth that descended on him.   Joseph didn't seem to feel the holy water himself; something that always puzzled, but not enough to question.   Cause, there was no real explanation for some of the other things Joseph could do, either.   *Like stay awake most of the day without falling into Undead slumber.*

In just his jeans, Joseph kissed him and he felt his skin tingle and burn at the same time---lust and pain.   The holy water was rolling down his asscheeks, making him groan in delight as the scald crept into the crack and onwards.

Now, Joseph spoke, taunting him, lips buzzing against his.   "I could get the plant mister, Nico.   Pour it full of this...stand back and watch you bubble and crack and smoke.   How long do you think you'll last under a full spritz?"

He gave a muttering laugh into his lover's mouth.   "Tease.   You wanna see if the walls really are so sound-proof?   Tennyson's here."

"Yes."   Joseph licked his lips and then moved down to open a sharp mouth against his chin...his throat.   His Sire's voice was slightly muffled, there.   "You're right.   No reason to scare your young friend.   But, I will make you very, very sorry, Nico."

He barely managed the words---his throat refused to let him talk.   "Show me..."

Chapter Twelve

The light that managed to fight its way through the tree's branches came dappled and muted, green and gray and watery.   Daniel lay on his back and breathed in the scent of familiar ground.   This room was very much his own and possessed the mixed odors of sandalwood and myrrh and cannabis.   Closer still, the fever-skinned boy sleeping in his bed gave off the humid-sweet smell of an exotic lily and he inhaled deeply, wanting to soak up every drop.   He smiled to himself, happy.

Oui, *happy*.

While he lay on his back, Rhys slept curled in against him, naked arms and legs tucked close and possessive at his knees and chest.   He did not mind being his garcon's point of emotional comfort, if it meant he could enjoy such quiet moments.   One arm braced behind his head, the other held Rhys at the ribs.   All that lay between them were their shorts and the thin-strapped undershirt his tchatcha partner wore.

Their ritual; at least once a week, Rhys slipped into his bed and slept in this manner, needing the touch of another's skin in order to find rest.   He let it be a matter of pride, in his heart, that the young malakh sought him out, instead of going to any other.   If his garcon was cognizant of the erection it caused, Rhys pretended to not notice and, so, they continued in the platonic nature of their ritual.   He had become so accustomed to the fever-hot skin of the tchatcha, he often missed its presence when he awoke in the night and found himself alone.

This time, the ritual had changed in a subtle but definite way.   Instead of coming to him in the dead of night, after hours of restless dozing and eyes dull with sleep, Rhys had entered this room before he could get under the sheets.   Dressed in only a tank-top and boxer shorts, his partner had crawled into the bed drunk and bleary and on the edge of complete unconsciousness.   There, in his arms, chaste and tender, Rhys had told him of the plan for their new 'job'.   He could hardly disagree, when the garcon was using such uncanny logic for the weapon of choice.

Daniel shifted once more, attempting to ignore the twanging throb of his erection.   He could not allow Rhys to know that he felt such desire; his partner seemed impossible when it came to love and how could the garcon possess any sense of hunger for him, in return?   They were not family, in the sense of blood or genes, but under the skin, their natures were similar enough.   Rhys would look on him with pity, for did the tchatcha not love Mattie?   Asleep at last, drifting off before him---as always---Rhys had whispered a mewling sigh of pain, the name of a lost lover.   *Goldie.*   Mattie Curran still lived in some shadowed piece of his partner's mind, haunting the younger malakh even in his rest.   Was this not some part of why Rhys found his bed, aching for comfort?   Mattie had sliced Rhys' soul to ribbons and the garcon could not yet escape the sting of that wound.

He sighed, frowning; he dared not slide himself out from under Rhys' unconscious body.   He needed to take care of his urgent need and could not---to move his tchatcha's limbs would bring the garcon up from the deepest slumber.   It was Rhys' nature, being so trained to respond with quick action when alerted by a sudden difference in his environment.

Ah, dieu. He would go *mad*.

Daniel slipped his hand out from beneath the nape of his neck and let it glide down the length of his own body, being careful to not touch Rhys' leg or arm.   He was naked but for the shorts he wore and their buttons were no great challenge.   Soon, he had the problem in one sweat-dampened hand.   Tipping his head to the side, he studied the face of his partner, eyes at half-mast, as he indulged himself.   He could be silent; this was his nature, non?

As he rubbed his fingers and palm over the swollen flesh of his chinois, he indulged himself in another fashion. He let himself remember a time when he had nearly given into his desire for Rhys, while the garcon still lived as Mattie's kept lover. He had fantasized many times of the moments when he could have changed the tempo of their dangerous dance, the pull and thrust of a life lived on the razor's blade.

It was London, two years ago, and they had stayed together in a hotel overlooking Soho, doing their last assignment as part of a Company elite kite team. The job was simple enough; coerce a scientist into giving them the secret to a new medical procedure which could revolutionize neurosurgery. The American government wished to implement the procedure and the scientist behind the innovation did not wish to sell or trade the research involved.

After a particularly fruitful evening of mingling with scientists and doctors at the conference, they had retired to their hotel, slightly intoxicated and ready for the next phase of the job. All they had needed was a night's sleep and an early start; he could have taken the silent hunger in his bones to a new level and done the unthinkable with his half-drunken protégé, but he had refrained.

He wished, now, that he had followed his instincts.

The radio had been left on and it hit his ears as the door opened; a spicy Latino rhythm. Rhys, with a broad grin of tipsy glee, had sashayed across the carpeted floor to the sound of castanets, swaying his slim hips in the tailored suit he wore. He had watched the garcon's movements with appreciation, closing the door behind himself as Rhys danced a mambo, seeming unaware of the eyes that devoured the sight. The suit, a Brooks Brothers, was expensive and somehow did nothing more than make Rhys look like a criminally attractive schoolboy with ruffled hair.

He had stood at the door's frame, leaning one arm against it as he tugged at his tie, loosening the bedamned silk as Rhys swayed along the floor of their suite, humming and lost in the golden haze of being partially drunk. The music's richness had only heightened the intoxication, only heightened the beauty of Mattie's young lover. It was obvious, to his mind, that Rhys had failed to notice him; terrifyingly astute when on the prowl, the garcon had now let down every guard and every precaution, thrown care to the London night wind.

Pulling the black tie off, he had let it drop to the polished table that waited by the door, in delicious agony at the sight of Rhys. Exquisitely sensual when caught by music, the younger malakh made the room seem humid with just the twist of hip and arm and the hand which swept casually through the tchatcha's sienna-brown hair; while working for the CIA, Rhys' untamed waves had been kept relatively short, cut to brush at his collar and no more.

He had ended the night there, standing at the door as his young protégé---Mattie's lover---had danced off to sleep, falling half dressed into a queen-sized bed. He had moved from his post only after he was sure Rhys was lost to the waking world---pouring himself a bourbon, he had walked to the bedroom's doorway to study the garcon who unknowingly held his heart and soul in an invisible cage. His wolfish instincts had howled, begging him to do what his body demanded; he had refused, finally going to his own room for a few hours of tortured wrestling with his conscience and his blood.

Ah, but if he had done what his blood and his body had cried for?

Therein lay his fantasy.

It was a delight to watch Rhys, but he had even more delightful plans for tonight. Pacing into the room, he moved to stand behind the tchatcha; it was easy to catch Mattie's lover by the arm and twirl him around in mid-step, glimpsing the flushed, startled face as he swung Rhys into a dip, staying in tempo with the dance.

His voice was soft and murmuring as he asked. 'Enjoying yourself, garcon?'

Breathless, Rhys hung in his arms, bent over backwards, blue-hazel eyes wide. He had taken the garcon by surprise; his tchatcha malakh stared up into his gaze. He could feel the unlikely heat that came from Rhys' body, from under the lavish clothes and he felt too young, as if he had never been imprisoned or hurt by a lover...as if he had not lived centuries past his own first death.

    Rhys stammered, the word unsteady. *'Ou-ouais.'*

    The garcon was so delicate, so innocent, so fuckable. He was tempted to drop Rhys, just to see what Mattie's lover would do. He lifted and settled the younger malakh back on his feet, but he left his hands in place---on Rhys' arm and around Rhys' back. This kept them close enough to breathe the same air.

    'That is bon.' He smiled, curling his mouth in a deliberate smile. Keeping his voice soft and pleasant, he rubbed Rhys' arm through the suit's jacket sleeve; slow and with meaning. 'I want you to always enjoy music. It is what we are...non? Creatures of light and dark, of music and love?'

    Rhys' swallow was audible, visible, and awe-inspiring; the manner in which he had unnerved the garcon was worth any effort he might put forth. To make Rhys speechless was a miracle in itself; the younger malakh was rarely without wit. 'I...I like the music.'

    He went on smiling at the way Mattie's lover stuttered, at the nervousness in Rhys' voice. The garcon did not understand yet, but this would change. Raising a hand to brush at the tchatcha's soft and hairless cheek, he slid his other hand's fingers down Rhys' back, to find a place at the long, slim waist---right at the top of his hip. The brown-haired malakh quivered under his touch, staring up into his face with a trembling mouth that begged to be kissed.

    Speaking gently, he drew Rhys closer. 'You look worried, garcon.' Rubbing his thumb against the tchatcha's fervid cheek, he tightened his grip. 'You need not be. I will take care of you. Have I ever allowed you to be hurt?'

    Rhys opened his mouth, wordlessly, looking unsure. The garcon licked at and then bit at the cush of reddened lower lip, breathing shallow. It was too much, the way his young partner abused those lips. With a slow nod, Mattie's lover whispered. 'Oui, I know. I...I think I've always known. Um...' With a shudder, Rhys pulled back and blinked, as if waking up. 'Maybe I should...maybe I'll get some sleep. I've had too much to drink, Danny.'

    The nickname made him ache more. Rhys was the only person alive who called him Danny.

    Watching Rhys' mouth, he shook his head in question. 'You think so?'

    Their faces were so close, he could dare to kiss the garcon.

    Rhys nodded once more, lowering his gaze; the tchatcha's voice was a husky sound. 'I don't know. I don't really think I'm tired, but...'

    At last, he leaned in and captured that sweet bottom lip with his teeth. Mattie's lover tasted of champagne and something intangible that he could not put words to. When he pulled back, he breathed the words against his protégé's mouth. 'I think you have had just enough, mon jouet.'

    The scent of Rhys' flesh inflamed his blood as the garcon leaned up into his chest, pushing closer clumsily for a chance at more. Mattie's tchatcha lover, so talented with the sensual arts, seemed to forget what these movements meant. Rhys touched his arms, his shoulders, but with only butterfly fingertips; the caress was an opposite of this kiss---Rhys' mouth was firm, insistent, and eager.

    Keeping his smile, he took a step back, letting go of his protégé. The game must be played, the prey must be won over. 'Perhaps you are correct, mon ami. Perhaps you should sleep.'

    Rhys dropped his hands, fine-boned face turning crimson. The mix of the garcon's bloodlines could be seen, then; the high cheekbones, the smooth olive skin tone, the strong nose and brow that showed the Arabic Misrene influence. Mattie's lover could not look at him, could barely contain his trembling fear. Rhys went on, nodding for a moment, the full pout of his lower lip caught between strong, white teeth---a telltale sign of the younger malakh's inability to express certain emotions.

    Then, as he watched, Rhys turned away, his voice choked. 'Bon nuit, Danny.'

    'Bon nuit, Rhys. You are intoxicated. I should not take advantage of you in this state...'

It was a challenging taunt from his tongue, the words sly.

How could he play such a game with the tchatcha? It was cruelty.

Rhys moved away, face tipped down in submission. This was a beaten creature, one who was accustomed to taking second-best, accepting little or nothing in exchange for all that he gave---and Rhys gave one hundred percent. It was a knife in his heart, a jagged void that ached in his chest. He could not let the garcon go, tonight.

Before he could speak, Rhys stopped on the other side of the suite's lavish main room, only a meter from the bedroom door. His heart beat faster, watching the garcon. What would this malakh do? Hands by his sides, Mattie's young lover remained silent and did not move, as if attempting to ascertain what to say to him that might change the evening's outcome.

He wanted Rhys to move, to do something; would the garcon be brave enough?

'Mon ami...are you ill? Is everything fine?'

Mattie's tchatcha raised his head now, looking tousled and tense even from behind. The suit he wore did nothing to change this. Rhys slid both hands into the pockets of his trousers and shrugged, not shifting to meet his stare. His tone was tight, dangerous. 'Depends on your definition for fine.'

His young partner was of a height with him, but much smaller in build. If he wanted to be a complete bastard, he could take what he wanted, and Rhys would either break his neck or accept his desire. Would it be worth the risk?

He took one step and then two, the concern growing. 'Rhys...are you upset with me?'

Rhys turned fast and stared at him, blue-hazel eyes full of angry tears. He stopped moving and blinked at the sight of how it made the young tchatcha look; he had seen eyes like these before, non? Where had he seen this same expression in eyes like these? So often, in the last decade, he had asked the same question. Where did he know this face from---it was something more than the resemblance to Steven and Roan. Something in his memory far more---

Primal.

The garcon came at him as he stood in thought, his lust momentarily dampened by the wispy scraps of forgotten knowledge. Then, without warning, Rhys grabbed him by one wrist and he felt the bones grind together as it was held out and away from his body. His protégé attacked, mouth rough and graceless and like a wet fire. He was pushed backward, but did not care. He wanted this and pushed his tongue past the garcon's lips, tasting a hint of blood.

He was staggered by Rhys' determination; cupping his partner's head with his free hand, he devoured the bloodied lips in time to the tango that played on the radio as Mattie's young lover clutched at his shoulders, tugging him closer. Precious and sweetly earnest, Rhys was his.

Daniel squeezed at the flexible hardness of his erection, eyes drooping to slits as he watched the tchatcha who slept against his body with an unlikely ease. He could fantasize all he liked, non? It hurt no one if he longed for his partner's love. At his side, Rhys gave a noisy snuffle and mumbled restlessly. The sound brought a smile to him; the garcon was so comfortable in his bed as to disavow all barriers. Rhys was never so open when awake.

The tchatcha's hand moved over his collar, his throat, holding him tight to that feverish mouth. He was being pushed back, step by step, and he did not care, not even as he stumbled. The carpet muffled the sound of their shoes as Rhys became rough, shoving him down into the over-stuffed chair of their hotel suite's main room. He laughed at it as their lips parted, as he bounced on the cushion; he did not have long to chuckle---the ferocious *garcon fell on him, desperate for his kisses.*

His blood pumped fast with the violence of Rhys' attack even as he followed his instincts, giving in to the tongue that plundered him. He could taste the champagne and the odd trace of blood as it melted away. His partner was so pure and innocent, despite his decadent, knowing manners...despite the time spent in Golden Wolf's bed. He wanted to grind himself into the youth, mark this perfect skin with his colors.

Rhys' fingers stroked through his hair, tugging away the strap that held his pigtail in place. As if half-asleep, his young malakh protégé slid off his lap and into the floor, kneeling between his legs as the kisses went on and on, threatening to break his control. He trembled as if it was his first attempts at these sensual arts---as if he was, once more, a virgin---but, he had no moment to laugh at these realizations before the teenaged tchatcha gave a groan of frustration, working at the buttons of his shirt. Rhys was trembling; with a growl of ripened frustration made into annoyance, Mattie's lover jerked his shirt open, sending buttons to scatter in a haphazard spray.

The shirt was ruined, but he could not care. It would be replaced. Right now, he wanted the scented skin of this garcon spread out under him, writhing and sobbing in need. The feel of Rhys' touch on his chest, in his short curls, was the sensation of silken branding irons. He let go of the captured wavy hair, letting his fingers slide away and down to cup the rounded jaw and cleft chin; he lifted Rhys' face to his kiss as his other hand slipped down the tender garcon's back, into his trousers---he rubbed and squeezed at the tight, smooth flesh of Rhys' bottom. This was a truly fuckable creature, his tchatcha protégé.

Daniel rolled his eyes under the slit of his lids, using a wet thumb to torture the tender flesh under the distended foreskin of his chinois, and pushed the fantasy into a different arena. The feel of Rhys' sleeping breath on his skin, ticking the curls of shortly crisp hair, made his blood burn hotter. He felt as if he might spontaneously implode.

Running a naked arm under Rhys' neck, he gently brushed his lips against the exposed throat and ear of his garcon as he wrapped his other arm around the younger malakh's waist and hips, keeping him close. He craved this...the desire to stroke Rhys' dusky peach skin. He shifted up slightly and breathed at his lover's ear, uncaring for how the tchatcha pretended sleep. 'Do you have any ideas of how very much you have come to mean, in my heart?'

Rhys was awake and quietly aware. It was in how his breathing nearly stopped, upon hearing these words. His blue-hazel eyes stayed closed, though. He splayed a hand on the thin abdomen, laying claim, and stroked his fingertips along Rhys' skin, smiling tenderly as he looked down into the reticent face of his lover. The only lover he wanted.

He kissed at the garcon's ear, still smiling quietly.

'Danny...' Rhys whispered, his eyes still closed.

Daniel tightened his grip, planting another gentle kiss. His voice remained low as he demanded an explanation even in the budding of passion. 'Who are you, mon precieux? Why do you use this name and why do you say it this way?'

His garcon gave a murmur of pain and tried to draw away, his face darkening, eyes tightening shut. Rhys was unable to explain his reasons, giving the matter more weight than he had firstly ascertained. But, now, the garcon was retreating; he did not let it happen. With strong, sure hands, he kept his lover snuggled close to him, using his fingers to explore and touch and soothe. Rhys' hand was on his, following every move tentatively.

'Je desole, mon petit.' He kept his voice a rumbling murmur. 'I will not press you. What reasons you possess, keep them. This does not sully us. I will not allow you to be hurt. You are safe, with me. You belong to me, mon jouet, mon amour. You belong to me

as I belong to you.'

Rhys was squeezing his eyes shut as if to block these things out.

'You do not belong to Mattie, she cannot love you without making a slave of you. Do not go back to her bed, garcon, I insist. If I find you in her arms, I will kill Golden Wolf...do you see I cannot tolerate such? I will break her skull if you let Mattie chain you to her side.'

Rhys shuddered, giving a tiny, breathless moan. His lips quirked at the thought that the sleek, young tchatcha enjoyed his savagery. He traced the outline of his lover's mouth, the curves that beckoned, being careful. He chuckled low in his throat and gently pulled the teenaged garcon over and around, to face him.

He kissed at his lover's eyes and then his nose and cheekbones. Small, delicate kisses. Rhys opened up for him, pliant; despite being a lethal warrior, ruthlessly trained for the work of a soldier and an assassin, the sienna-haired malakh melted into his arms like a scared child.

He whispered, cradling Rhys close. 'You need never fear a return of what came before---there is no one left alive to trace you to this, no one left alive who can imprison you in the labs. Let yourself be mine.'

Rhys started to protest, his eyes opening now in the glow of light from an unseen source. He didn't allow the denial. He licked his way past the cupid's bow lips, tasting of the hot decadence inside. At last, the tchatcha stopped trying to speak and gave into the kiss. When he pulled back, it was with a sigh of desire. This made his lover's eyes widen, making him look like an innocent. He grinned, instinctively, at the expression and then lowered his eyes, pushing close for another kiss. A deep, soulful kiss.

There were no words to truly express what he felt, but he had tried. All he wanted was that Rhys might comprehend what their love meant to him. To know he was loved, too. It was heart-breakingly simple, so crystal-clear, this moment. He would not be the one who lost everything and then complained that he had never gotten the chance to say what must be said. Never again.

He was not offering excuses or a maybe...he was offering a forever.

His lover heated up, slim hands finding his face, holding him close, and all he needed was in the kiss Rhys gave. At last, they drew apart, breathing hard, and the wild, anxious look he saw in the garcon's blue-hazel eyes was terrifyingly real and honest and it made his heart beat faster.

'Come here...now.' He slid backwards, out of the bed, onto his knees. There, on the floor, he waited. Rhys hesitated, staring at him with a confused expression. He repeated it, holding out his hands. 'Come here.'

He was obeyed.

On the bed's side, Rhys sat naked and exposed for the frail-seeming angel he was. Daniel held up his hands, palms exposed in a primitive offering. Tentatively, the young malakh gave him those hands he loved. Gingerly, he held them, kissing at the backs of slender, strong fingers that offered him so much even when afraid of being betrayed...and it was the best hope he could dare to ask for, that he might be loved as much as he loved.

Over and over, he pressed his lips to Rhys' hands, turning them to touch his mouth to everything he could find. The palms were sensitive and when his lips met them, one by one, he heard the fast, tortured intake of breath. Tenderly, he flicked his tongue out, tasting the salt there. It burned, but only for a moment. But, then, unexpectedly, Rhys folded him close, into a hug. He sat on his knees, his arms around his lover, face burrowed into the hairless chest of a man who was still scared of being hurt by what love could do. It was in how Rhys' heart beat, in how his skin trembled so lightly...

He whispered, his breath hoarsely damp as he spoke, asking his god for some sign of acceptance. 'Am I yours, Rhys? Do you love me at all?'

'Oui...dieu, Danny...' Rhys' fingers touched his long, dark hair so gently, as if afraid he might break. His lover sniffled and then his voice cracked. 'I...'

'Shh.' He smiled, tears stinging his eyes behind their lids. 'Let me love you.'

He had only his heart and soul and body to give, after centuries of being abandoned by love; nothing else on earth belonged to him. And he might be damned if he would allow Mattie to keep this garcon. His body and heart and soul were his, no matter what the shadows shouted and hissed at him in the darkest hours, and he could give them to anyone he wished.

Rhys was the only god he recognized, now. He would sacrifice himself in the name of love.

And hope his offering was enough.

He wanted to build a wall of his own, someplace safe where he could put his gifts, to vouchsafe them for Rhys. So that Rhys would always know that, no matter, it was in his name and in his love that these things were done. If he could build a fortress, he would arm a thousand knights for the protecting. Would Rhys love him, when their love was at last consummated, or would the garcon lock him out in the same manner Rhys refused all others? He buried himself into the act of making love, to lose the gut-clenching, watery-kneed terror. He had to be brave. He had to be the knight who carried the flag.

This was about the shape of his heart, non?

Only a handful of times had there ever been a holy need to love the man he knelt for; Rhys meant as much to him as Henry had, in the second and third decade of the century...as much as Denis had, in the fifth and sixth decade. He understood why, naturally; this garcon was the son of his dead friends, the survivor of profane experimentation, a most precious treasure from L'Bon Dieu.

Anything that was Rhys, he would love, and he would be loved in return. No matter what his crimes. He was beyond fear or shame or guilt; he throbbed and ached with a heat that nearly hummed.

'Danny...'

Tears stung his eyes.

It was a moan and he glanced up with watery gaze to see the olive-toned tchatcha watching him with an expression of utter adoration. This made him want to cry harder; if Rhys knew how long he had wished to take the boy as his lover, well, he could not think about that yet. After long, golden minutes, he opened his eyes again slightly and glanced up once more. Rhys, still pushed up onto his elbows, smiled in that sexy, drowsy fashion. He leaned up for a chance to kiss at the garcon's mouth. Rhys anticipated the action and bent his neck to meet the advance. Their mouths met gingerly, lovingly, in a rare and delicate moment. A kiss from the lips of his flawed god.

Rhys eased back from devouring his tongue and smiled, weakly, looking tortured. An idea formed quickly; he stared at the smile on his lover's cherry-ripe mouth and then raised his fingers to touch the curve of Rhys' upper lip, tracing along its surface light as a feather. So sleep and kiss-swollen.

'I love you...mon chere.' He murmured, feeling satisfied.

By no means did he feel like the Casanova that Rhys often made him out to seem.

He touched his fingertip to Rhys' eyelashes, gentle, then slipped that same finger down, along the angular plane of unforgiving cheekbone. 'The hint of red in your lashes and the shape of your face, your jaw. This way the edge of your lips, they curve in and under, as if to claim they are shy. I see your papa and your mama when I look upon you, they gave you more than the malakh...ouais? You are most beautiful.'

Rhys' eyes were full of pain. A terrible, mournful pain.

He had often seen this expression in his protégé's stare, from the very earliest days. Rhys, even when pleased or sated, might find some grief to understand on occasion. It was not often, but he recognized this.

Daniel's voice faded and he let his hand drop to his lap, almost covering his own erection and the contact of his fingers on overly sensitive skin made him shiver as he looked at the bed beside his lover's sleek thigh. 'I apologize, garcon. These things are not important.'

It came as a whisper from the lovely mouth that often appeared feminine. 'I might destroy you. I might destroy anyone I love. You know that. It's the way he made me. I'm meant to be a weapon, a sword...I'm not meant for romance or the weakness that love can bring. Look at what I did to Goldie...I pushed her and she...and it could happen again, me wanting more than I should or keeping people pushed completely away. She was right to kick me out, Danny. She was right to say it was over---I'm not even the same as other people. I mean, think about it---'

He knew, he must stop the flood before it truly began.

His breath came in a rush as he growled, tugging Rhys to his mouth, to kiss away the despair and the words that could break everything like so much worthless glass. Pulling the garcon to his feet, holding his young face, he kissed at the mouth of his lover, his only love. At last, needing air, he drew back, but only to rasp his denial.

'You are mine. You have always belonged to me. I claim you, garcon. Understand? It changes nothing in how I feel, these things you say. We are written in stone and in flesh--- we are forever. For ever.'

Rhys sobbed into his lips, trembling hard, but as they kissed, his lover began to calm, to relax, to touch him with knowing and deft fingers. Little by little, the teenaged malakh worked over his face, cradling his cheeks and jaw, kissing at him. Rhys' hands held his backside, keeping him close in a tight embrace, as if he afraid he might try to escape. A new heat began as his garcon's lips found his throat, bending slightly to reach him. He was oiled and clean and fresh, ready to be loved, and Rhys was not going to let him go.

Daniel chuffed slowly through his nose, trying to not let it rasp as he cupped a trembling hand over the spill of his semen as it cooled in the curls of hair on his abdomen. At last, he let his eyes close, blinding him to the glorious malakh whose head lay against his naked shoulder. It was too much, the images playing in his brain; to think he might have seduced Rhys at any time and had yet to even make an overture. It could not be, was not to be, and he must convince his heart and body of such a truth. Yet, in the early morning light, the feel of his partner's skin brought these torments.

Could the garcon have heard him? Rhys did not sleep so deeply. Might his tchatcha have awoken and become aware of what he did, defiling the sanctuary he offered? It alarmed him, bringing a strange quiver to his insides---the knowledge that Rhys might lay so silent, hearing his painful and hurried release.

Wiping at himself with the folds of his sheet, he dared to look once more at Rhys. He must know, of course; he could not let it frighten him, the fact of what he did...of what he felt. He would confess, if he must. But, the garcon slept, long dark lashes unmoving. His tchatcha partner's bronzed face was pink at the cheeks---Rhys' pouty lips hung open as if prepared to sigh or whisper. He could not see the curve of cleft chin or rounded jaw: these were nestled into his shoulder.

With a slow, carefully drawn breath, Daniel closed his own eyes once more and let himself fall back into a stupor, the tides of sleep sifting his brain like sand being carried out to sea.

'He deals the cards as a meditation. And those he plays never suspect. He doesn't play for the money he wins. He doesn't play for the respect. He deals the cards to find the answer. The sacred geometry of chance. The hidden law of probable outcome. The numbers lead a dance.'

It came, unbidden, the words to a song by Sting that his Vivienne had introduced to his ears, a song that made him feel bereft and empty now, in the quiet minutes. It was not a song he associated with her, his dead Creole fleur. Non. In his heart, it came to him, its rhythms and melody bittersweet in endless minutes of listening to Rhys' body as it slept.

'And if I told you that I loved you, you'd maybe think there's something wrong. I'm not a man of too many faces---the mask I wear is one. Those who speak know nothing and find out to their cost. Like those who curse their luck in too many places. And those who fear are lost.'

He could live with what Rhys was willing to share; it was better to be the love that truly dared not speak its name than to own his partner's pity and disgust.

'I know that the spades are the swords of a soldier. I know that the clubs are weapons of war. I know that diamonds mean money for this art. But that's not the shape of my heart.'

Chapter Thirteen

I can't breathe; it's too damn stuffy and my body feels like someone in a large truck ran me over at some point, while I wasn't around to catch them. I open my eyes just enough to know that the room is dimmed---there's a glow coming from some distance and I know it's the bathroom door that's slanting a bar of artificial light across the wall at the foot of this bed and I am vaguely aware of where I'm laying. I just don't know what to do about it.

How the fuck did I get here? The last thing I remember was...

Joe and Valeska arguing about some woman and maybe that woman was me?

Fuck.

I try to shift position and can't. I'm caught under a heavy steel bar. I know that steel; it's Valeska's deadweight arm laying across my hip. Let's hear it for so-called necrophilia. Go, me. I've been in this sitch before. More than once, I've woken up like this, wedged under his cool-fleshed body like a teddy bear. At least, I can tell, this time, he doesn't have his face buried into my throat. That's always a scary moment, realizing that I'm sleeping in a vampire's lair, in the vampire's bed, and the said vampire might decide to sink his fangs into my skin while he's unconscious.

Rare, really, this point. I wonder, for a moment, what Joe thinks about it. Joe usually doesn't allow this kinda crap, from either of us. Of course, I also wonder...why didn't they drop me off at my own apartment?

Oh, yeah...there was something about the woman and about how it wasn't safe for me to be alone. In case something...something that could happen, something to force Joe's hand in some sitch. Valeska had insisted 'she' stay, sleep where it was definitely safe. Just 'til the sitch could be settled. So, they were protecting me?

I hold my breath for a second and listen.

I don't hear anything, but that's pretty normal here. Neither Joe or Valeska breathe when they're sleeping. They're corpses, right? Joe doesn't usually breathe at all, but Valeska still does. Not often, but yeah. More importantly, I don't feel anything. Nothing but Valeska. Where's Joe?

My head's pounding; I feel sick to my stomach. Let's all give a big cheer for hangovers. On second thought, let's not. I don't wanna throw up. I start the slow process of getting out from under my Rom protector. I wriggle sideways until he grunts and shifts, moving off. With a sigh of relief, I slide off the bed and out from the covers. It's always too warm in here, in this bedroom. Urgh.

I'm naked...no surprise. Valeska won't sleep with clothes on and the times I've passed out on him, he's stripped me for the sake of his own comfort. Not that he wants anything to do with my body, really; just comfort and cuddling. Yet, I recall him saying something about sex last night. We were talking sex and he said he wanted to fuck me and Rhys. Weird. Not what anyone could expect from a kept boy vampire like Nicolai. Not with the chance of Joe overhearing it.

I raise a brow at the thought as I gather my clothes in the dark and slip into the bathroom.

"Don't ask me what you know is true...don't have to tell you I love your precious heart. I...I was standing, you were there, two world collided, and they could never tear us apart. We...could live for a thousand years, but if I hurt you, I'd make wine from your tears."

Singing an old INXS song softly to myself, I wash up and study my wet face in the mirror. There are a few lines in my cheek where I was laying on the pillow. I notice the damage of booze in how my skin feels. I've got to stop drinking so hard so often.

"I told you that we could fly cause we all have wings...but some of us don't know why..."

I rummage in the medicine cabinet and find the painkillers. You wouldn't think vampires would have something like that, right? Well, they might be dead humans with a demonic-type animus that gives them superhuman abilities and a thirst for blood, but I've noticed a few things about them that's just like any other human. They can get drunk and they can have hangovers and they sometimes need Tylenol. Valeska likes to eat human food and smoke cigarettes. Joe smokes, too.

How's that for crazy? Bram Stoker had no fucking clue.

Joss Whedon, on the other hand, must know some *real* vampires.

Maybe he knows Joseph. Could be a reason the big guy likes those TV shows.

I shake a few out into my hand and swallow them, cupping cold water to my mouth as I swish out the last of an icky after-booze flavor. Did I throw up, earlier? I don't remember. As I tie back my braids with one of Valeska's leather straps, I think about the deal I made with Rhys. Egypt, huh? Well, I could certainly use a vacation and if my friend's right, it won't be a dangerous job. It'll put some real money in my pocket, too. Something I can use. I could open my own greenhouse, if I had some serious cash.

Rhys said he'd give me a fourth of the money from the job. He didn't say how much it was. But, I know how this stuff goes; Dante's told me that Rhys gets no less than ten thousand a job and, for the biggest jobs, he has gotten seventy-five thou before. And that's after he splits the money with Daniel. So...

I finish up my morning-after ritual and creep out of the bathroom. Standing beside the bed, I look at Valeska. Joe's not in the room at all and my Rom friend seems...so young and small. I'd never really thought about it. But, in his sleep, Valeska looks like a kid.

A solemnly *dead* kid.

On my way to the door, I spot the violin...it lays on the bureau, in its case. I've heard Valeska play a lot. I hope I get a chance to hear him play again, soon. Something in my gut tells me that this job with Rhys and Daniel isn't gonna be so cut and dried as Rhys makes it sound.

It's in the living room I find my boots. And my coat. And Joe.

The large vampire is sitting in a recliner, reading. I can tell, by looking at the bound file, that it's something important. A case or assignment? Joe doesn't even glance up at me as he speaks, his deep voice soft.

"There's coffee in the kitchen, girl."

Joe seems like a bloodthirsty asshole, but...the whole knight thing is still there.

Silent, I nod and look at my watch. Good god. It's one in the afternoon. Wasn't I supposed to be somewhere today? Oh, yeah. Hell. I have a meeting with the chair of the Sociology department at the college to discuss the thesis I'm writing---correction, the thesis that I'm half-assing. The meeting is in less than two hours. I've got to get my ass in gear.

On top of all this, I have to tell my boss at the greenhouse that I'm taking a leave of absence---two weeks of personal time. He's really not gonna like that. Then, I remember that my car is at Pandora's Box and Rhys has my keys. *Dammit.* Looks like I'll be taking the streetcar to Tulane and hope I can get to the right corner before it passes.

And here it was, I thought I'd be doing better this year. It's the same crap, just a different day.

The stranger arrived in the midst of a storm which brought great drifts of snow and the bitter cold of a wind blowing from the north. It was unusual for the town to get such a freeze---winter was not such a terrible thing for Kyiv, there on the banks of the Dnieper.

Until the winter of 1350 and 1351.

The stranger was boarding at the Gentile inn at the end of a frozen-mud wasteland that served as a village square on their end of town. When she went there to deliver her mama's medicines to the innkeeper, she'd seen him in the inn's main hall, where the Gentile men gathered to share a drink and to talk of their businesses and of the local farms. She'd seen him speaking with the priests who presided at Archangel Michael's Cathedral. She had seen him far more than she should have since her mama had forbidden her to go out of the house unescorted because of her age and her sex. All because of her betrothal to the farm-boy from the south shtetl just outside of their city.

She hadn't wanted the betrothal, but the matchmaker had scoured all of Kyiv and the surrounding areas for a boy with the proper background and the proper nature for her---the youngest daughter and the most difficult child of a rabbi. Her papa had accepted the farmer's son and traveled from the city to the countryside to talk with the man who owned such rich farmland and who was more than pleased at the idea of a rabbi's daughter marrying his daydreaming, worthless son. Apparently, the son wasn't cut out for farming and had spent most of his life in school, studying the texts and books of their ancestry and their faith. He might become a student of the rabbi, if the rabbi approved.

And the rabbi, her papa, did approve.

She, on the other hand, did not.

The betrothal had been spoken of, to her, but what could she say in protest? She had protested and her older sisters and her mama had given her a stern talking-to, suggesting that she be happy her lot was so pleasant. The boy was good to look at and he was intelligent and he didn't, if the matchmaker was to be believed, seem inclined to be anything but a scholar. Scholars rarely lost their temper with their wives, so she was blessed.

She didn't feel blessed. She felt like God was deliberately ignoring her pleas.

That was His right, of course, and He was busy. Why would He listen to the pleas of a youngest daughter of a rabbi whose synagogue was barely visible on the human horizon? Her papa was not a great and important rabbi, so why would God listen to his youngest child's tortured prayer? Especially when she sounded so ungrateful.

So. Since the betrothal, six months ago, she had been forbidden to go out of the house unescorted. She could only go out with her parents or with Tolya, her twin brother. She had to shield herself from the eyes of men, now, because she was considered a bride--- untouchable and not to be spoken to, anymore, even by her boy cousins. Her papa had been very careful to explain the rules to her---she was promised to the farmer's son and that meant she was to be considered a precious jewel that the family must guard and protect until the time of the wedding. Which would come at the time of Purim in the month of Adar.

The wedding had to wait because her papa had insisted that the farmer's son be of the same age as the bride. She wasn't sure if that was important or just more of her papa's oddness---he believed in the balance of all things, in God's creations and in nature and in man and in man's creations. They would both be fourteen, which was a good number, as it was a double of seven, which was a holy number. Together, they would be twenty-eight--- and that was lucky.

Her papa had come to her, privately, and talked of what her own covenant with God was meant to become. She was smarter than any of the other of his children, except maybe Tolya---she had loved the books---and she was quick and she would make a good wife for the farmer's son. The farmer's son was full of grand ideas and the holy books and was something of a poet. He needed a strong, stable home and a good wife who knew how to be a helpmeet to such a man.

Her papa had smiled and told her, rubbing two fingers through his bushy, graying beard, that boys like the farmer's son grow up to be men like him---Papa---and he would admit that men like him often needed a sharp-tongued and smart wife, to ensure the every-day chores of life were accomplished. A rabbi might sit all day and argue the books and talk and think, but his wife would run the house and be an irreplaceable treasure---for she would bring the rabbi's mind back to earth, where the daily world and its troubles waited.

That was a strange thing for a rabbi to say, but her papa was odd now and then.

So. She would be standing under the canopy with the farmer's son a day after the boy's birthday. And she had made a habit of sneaking from the house without an escort in the early mornings before breakfast and the twilight dusk, after supper, for weeks now...so that she could watch the stranger as he moved around town. He seemed to stay up all night and sleep during the day and she was shirking her chores to watch him, as much as possible. It always led to scoldings and even punishments at home, but she felt it was worth that much, at the very least. He was fascinating---

The stranger had been among them for three weeks now---three Sabbaths had come and gone---and he had finally come to visit her papa at the time of Tu B'Shvat.

Papa said the stranger wasn't normal. Papa said that there was something very, very wrong with the man. The stranger was from Jerusalem and claimed to be a Hebrew scholar---but the stranger visited the churches and cathedrals of the Christians, too. Papa said the man asked terrible questions---questions about lost truths. The stranger asked too many questions---and he came to Papa to ask about the time in their history, as a people, that was forgotten---and forgotten for the best reasons of all. And if anyone would know what a good question was, it was her papa---her papa was a teacher and a rabbi.

And that was why the stranger came to their house one cold evening, after supper, to talk with her papa. When he arrived, she was outside milking the cow in the stock shed. Tolya, her twin brother, was fighting the wooden pitchfork to clean the byre. She knew something was odd because the animals grew quiet. Their cow and the yearling calf and their chickens and the ducks---even their dog---went silent and nervous. As if some darkness had descended unannounced. When she came into the house with the bucket and headed for the cool room, to put the milk up for cream and butter, she caught a glimpse of her stranger sitting in the front room, at the table, with her papa.

She'd stopped and stared, until mama spoke sharply and told her to mind her chores. Then, the stranger had turned and met her gaze with deep green eyes and a blank expression that slowly became a smile. A smile that turned only one side of his mouth up. His eyes had stayed cold and that---that---had made the smile frightening.

Of course, she'd obeyed her mama and went on, with the chores. But, she'd kept her ear open. And she'd heard the moment her papa made a painful, hoarse noise in his throat at something the stranger said. The stranger had spoken in a low, calm voice and at the second he must have revealed some terrible truth, for her papa had made this sound...the sound of a wounded animal. Within minutes, the stranger had left, promising to return for the information he needed...the information which had led him to the rabbi.

Helpless, she had watched her mama and papa talk about this stranger who came to their home, asking questions no one with any shred of sanity should ask. The handsome stranger with eyes the color of moss and a smile that could freeze someone to the very spot where a God-fearing person stood. She and Tolya had moved, being quiet---almost mouse-like. As if being silent and furtive could remove the threat. The worst part being that they had no idea what it was about the stranger which frightened their papa. What had the stranger said to make their wise and funny papa scared?

Being the boy and being a few hours older than her and a student to papa, Tolya was the first one to approach the subject with their parents. The results had amazed her---instead of drawing in and shushing them and suggesting that they not be concerned about this, their papa and mama began to talk of dark things. Of creatures who might wear the face of mankind, but who could not be human. Creatures whose hearts did not beat as a human heart did. Creatures who did not go into good sunlight but only came to visit at night. Creatures with no love of God, no love for humans but the love a lion must have for its prey.

They were told a great many things, but the truth remained. This man was going to return and he would want the information he'd sought papa out for. The stranger knew that papa possessed such knowledge, for papa kept arcane and ancient scrolls. The stranger had tracked papa's scrolls and books all the way from Egypt and Jerusalem, these places where the stranger claimed to have studied.

It was during these years that whispers against the Jews began to reach even her young ears---but, it was in the month of the stranger when things began to reach a fever point noticeable to even a scholar like Tolya. Every day, when he went out to walk in the city after spending endless hours with the holy books, Tolya came home with news of what was being said about Kyiv and the world beyond its gates.

In these days, the talk was of Plague and about Jews being chased from their towns and shtetls, accused of creating the death that was sweeping away life in every large city. The talk was of the Jews who were not chased away but murdered. The whispers were becoming increasingly hostile, fearful. For, naturally, these matters made the Gentiles of Kyiv wonder about what was to come. Would the Plague come there? Would it be started by one of the Kyiv Jews? This was, as Tolya said, the way many Gentiles thought of the situation at this moment.

What no one in their little Jewish quarter could have imagined was how quickly the world could turn itself upside down, inside out. They'd flourished in Kyiv for hundreds and hundreds of years. It was a story told, in the city---the princes may have founded and named the city of Kyiv, but it was the Jews who built its first walls and its first streets. The Gentiles came to them for a great deal of things; many different goods, including the services of physicians and scribes and even teachers for the Gentile children.

And yet it took nothing for the poorest Gentiles, whose hate and suspicion was always the greatest, to rip up Jewish Kyiv by the roots when the bad day came at last. All it took was a strange illness to make itself known in the weeks while the stranger walked among them. An illness that could be linked, through ignorance, to Plague.

The symptoms were not the same---these people, ill, did not burn with fever or develop the dark spots or cough or do anything that could be proven as Plague symptoms. Instead, they were pale, chilly, and wanted to sleep more than anything else. They were unmarked...papa had commented on that himself, having been called to look at a young Gentile boy who was showing these unusual symptoms. Papa had commented on the knowledge that this was not an unheard of illness, only rare...and that the strangest part of all was the lack of marks or spots. Also rare, but...not unheard of.

Papa seemed to know what this illness was and he conferred with a few of the learned men of the synagogue before approaching the Gentile men and the priests of their Churches to suggest a cure. The disease was created by evil, he'd said, and evil was walking among them at night in this dark winter. Evil was sitting among the Gentiles and they could not see, for they did not believe anymore.

The Gentiles seemed to take this the wrong way.

Then...the Plague came.

Papa was called to the bedside of a city official---one of the important Gentiles. He and the physicians of the Jewish streets. They were called upon by a Gentile physician, who had much respect for men of education and skill despite religion. Together, these men conferred and came to the same conclusion. Plague had arrived and its first, noticed victim was a minor nobleman whose business function in the city of Kyiv was important enough to warrant trouble with the man incapacitated.

Then...the city official died.

It began as rumor, the stories of people dying on the other side of Kyiv. The law and the order began to disappear like smoke before a foul wind. Rumor became truth as the stories became more real---it was no longer hearsay, but recognized as first-hand account. People she had known all her young life had seen the dead bodies of men and women and children who were dying in the narrow, dirty streets of the poorest quarter in Kyiv. It was not just these unfortunates---the rich and well-fed died, too, but not all at once.

Her papa came up with a plan to stop the Plague in the week before Purim Katan. He went to the city's important men. They listened to him and agreed that he might be right on how to stop this pestilence. But, once he was gone, they agreed upon something else.

For...was it not the same in every city? The Jews were said to start the Plague.

It was the Gentile physician who respected the Jews that came to warn them.

Papa and the other rabbis disagreed on how to handle the coming storm. Papa said that the best way to avoid a massacre was for the Jews to leave the city for a time---go into the country and live in one of the small shtetls until the Plague had worn itself out. The other rabbis said that the Jews should lock themselves into their streets and their homes and pray---to not give into the hate of the Gentiles.

Papa and mama made the choice for the entire family; all of her sisters and her brothers and their wives and husbands and their children would go to the countryside and live in the shtetl---the one where her betrothed's family lived. This was to be safe. By the time papa and mama had started the arrangements, it was too late.

The houses were on fire and the people were screaming. She hurried to gather her clothing into a bundle. She was following Tolya, carrying his bundle while he rushed to prepare their mule. The mule would carry the bundles for the whole house. Tolya was praying as he worked, tying the bundles that mama and papa had given them to secure on the mule. A crash from within the house caught their attention. Then, without any further warning, she heard mama scream. Papa shouted.

Then, the house was on fire.

She smelled the burning wood and cloth. She smelled blood.

Tolya, trying very hard to keep his head, urged her to sneak out through the back streets and hurry to get away---she should go and he would follow. He had one more bundle, papa's books, and then he would be ready. He would bring mama and papa with him. She argued with her twin, insisting that their parents must be dead now. Then, as they stood arguing about what to do in this terrible night, the Gentile physician appeared in the open doorway that led to the back street. He urged them to come, he would get them to safety---he'd already seen what was in the front streets and, yes, the house was on fire and their parents were dead.

Still carrying Tolya's bundle---hers had been strapped to the mule---she followed her brother and the Gentile physician as they hurried down the back streets. The physician, with his brown hair and brown eyes, promised to get them to the farm where her betrothed's family lived. There, outside the city, they would be safe. There was no guarantee that any of their brothers and sisters would survive.

It was once they reached the Gentile section of the city that this plan showed its futility. There would be no escape. A battle ensued between the Gentile physician who helped them and two angry men who now knew what the doctor was attempting to do. Tolya told her to run. She hesitated, unwilling to leave her twin. But, Tolya pulled two large, ugly knives from the inside of his woolen shirt and coat and, under the brim of his hat, she saw the anger of a Jewish man who has finally reached the end of his flowing piety. He would protect her with his life and he might take life and it would all be for the sanctity of her life.

Tolya gave her one of the knives and she brandished it in front of herself, barely able to keep a grip on it for how hard she trembled. None of the angry Gentiles could get past her twin and the physician, so she didn't need to try using the weapon. She wasn't sure she could.

Her hair was straggling out of the kerchief on her head and her legs felt cold beneath her long skirts despite the legging-trousers she wore. Her leather shoes weren't perfect and the cold seeped through the icy street and into her toes and then into her legs. Tolya put himself between the murderous Gentiles and her, as she stood, motionlessly clutching his bundle of clothes and a scary knife.

It was twilight---the sun was going down and the knives caught the glare of the sunset and turned red and gold and she felt her blood grow icy---colder than the ice and colder than the hate in the eyes of their attackers. The whole Jewish section was aflame. The fire and the fading sunlight mingled and became part of her enemy. The shadows were safer----her heart sang it out in a terrible melody that was so very different from the chanting, undulating prayers she knew by rote.

Everywhere on the streets behind them, there were dead bodies. They stood in the street that ran from the Gentiles to the Jews. And the Gentiles didn't want to let them live. Tolya and the Gentile physician were fighting with the angry men and it was all done to protect her. Why did she stand there, doing nothing?

'Mishenka---run!' Tolya shouted, his voice made deeper with rage and fear. 'Run!'

She ran. She ran and she didn't look back.

Clutching her knife and ducking into the shadows and the back streets, she managed to stay out of sight for the better part of an hour. At least, she believed it was close to an hour. Things moved too fast and she couldn't breathe normally---she whimpered even when she breathed.

At last, she found a section of cobbled street that wasn't being flooded by enraged, bloodthirsty Gentiles. There, she saw the open and welcoming door of a stable---attached to an inn---but it would serve her as a hiding place until she could gather her wits and decide upon a plan.

There, in the farthest, darkest corner, behind the horses and mules, she drew her shawls and coats closer for warmth. The stable was cozy---cozier than it had a right to be, on such a terrifying night. The animals made it warm and there was a lantern hanging from the roof beams that lent a golden glow to everything.

The bundle of her brother's clothes inside a quilt lay on the dirtied straw in front of her as she leaned against the wooden wall of the stable and studied the knife in her hands. She held it with both, unable to stop the shaking of her bones. It wasn't glowing red and gold now; it was a plain, sturdy blade. It was steel and had a shine that made her think of the silver candlesticks that papa and mama kept for the holy days. The hilt was solid and wrapped around with filthy leather---filthy with sweat and use. Someone had used this knife regularly...and it made her wonder where Tolya had gotten the two knives. And why.

Trembling, she listened to the sound of a pogrom being committed in the distance.

She became aware of someone entering the stable when the animals went completely silent and edgy. She froze in place and hoped that the straw was high enough in her hiding place to keep her from being seen or heard. The man entered the edge of her sight when he came to the horses. It was the stranger who had visited her father. She hadn't seen him in a week, since she'd been practically locked in the house due to the Plague's presence, but there was no mistaking that face and that form. He was one of the most handsome men she'd ever laid eyes on---and so obviously of Hebrew blood, with his strong features and with how he carried himself.

But, she was sure he couldn't see her in the darkness of the stable's farthest corner.

She was mistaken.

'I can hear you, little woman.' His voice was low; he sounded amused as he stood on the other side of a large, muscular bay mare. 'I can hear you, I can smell you. You are a woman already and you bleed. I smell the fear and the wet in your clothes. I smell the clean under the dirt. You are a Jewess...a little Jewess.'

Silently, she held her breath and prayed.

'Come out, little woman. I am not of the mob who kill your world tonight.'

She could barely see him, on the other side of the horse. He was putting a blanket on the bay's back and then lifting a plain, leather saddle---the kind used by soldiers. She didn't dare move; he must be lying, Jew or not. Papa had said the stranger was evil, not to be trusted, something inhuman...a monster.

The stranger spoke to her as if they were acquaintances, as if a girl would be allowed to be alone with a stranger, someone not of her own family. He spoke to her as if they had known each other every day of her life. 'I'm leaving tonight, little woman. Kyiv has worn out its welcome with me.'

She didn't answer, but instead listened and watched him as closely as she could. If she acted like a mouse, perhaps he would forget that she was in the stables where she didn't belong. Perhaps he would be a good monster and go away---he said he was leaving.

The stranger talked on, as if he didn't mind that she was only a girl and a Jewess. As if it wasn't forbidden for a man to talk with a girl not of his own family without a guardian present. 'I can understand hostility between the followers of Jesus and the Chosen People, as the Christians cannot fathom anyone who is able to exist without the light of the Son---they are a fanatical people, the Christians. But, I cannot understand how they would blame the Chosen People for a plague that is caused by filth and vermin. I cannot understand how they can kill the Chosen People tonight when they have so much to gain by allowing the rabbis and the learned men to teach them of how to rid Kyiv of this sickness.'

He was cinching the saddle into place. He gave a low, muttering laugh. 'I don't suppose you brought your father's books and scrolls with you? That would be a great stroke of luck. No, you must have left them behind. No girl would dare to handle the holy texts...'

Her eyes went large with surprise and shock. Did he know who she was? Did he know that he was talking at the daughter of a certain rabbi? Did he know that she recognized him? She bit her lower lip and clutched the knife harder to still the tremble of her arms and hands. She couldn't let him get closer; who knew what he would do? She huddled even closer in on herself, to stay small and unseen.

It did no good. He knew where she was, he knew who she was.

Now, he came across the stable and picked her up before she could prepare herself. She barely realized in time that he was moving, he was so quiet and fast. She dangled by her scarves and coat in his grip---he was very strong, though not so large as papa, and only a little taller than her. She struggled, whimpering, but refused to cry. At his feet lay the bundle of her twin's clothes and she swiped at him with the knife she held, trying to get free. The stranger, handsome and well-dressed, laughed at her with his soft, calm voice.

'Little woman, you must stop this. If you give me an injury, who will get you out of this city alive?'

'Put me down---it is forbidden that you lay hands on me!' She growled at him, struggling harder. 'I am betrothed to be married and my papa is a holy man---'

'If you are here alone, your father is dead.' The stranger said with such precise logic and such a precise, clipped tone. His green eyes were quiet and chilly and thoughtful as he held her up to his eye-level, to study better what he'd caught. 'Where are the books that your father kept secret? I need them. If your father is dead and your brothers are dead, they will not need these books any longer. I will take them as payment for getting you to your husband's house.'

This silenced her and she hung, half-strangled, staring at him. She lowered the knife, her hands gone numb. She whispered in the quiet, growing terrified. 'You would do this? Take me to my husband's father's farm? You want the books as a payment to do this?'

Dark-haired, green-eyed, the stranger smiled now and nodded. He was dressed in dark clothes with a traveling robe pinned at his throat with a strangely shaped bronze clasp. The clasp was a raised circle-shield carved with a sigil she'd seen in some distant memory...it was familiar and yet so odd. It had nine points, three triangles laid at angles upon each other, much like the Magen David but with one more triangle. Within the circle of these was a stylized eye.

She laughed, her voice choking bitterly, as she mocked him, answering. 'Then, it's just as well that I don't want to go to my betrothed's house, for I cannot give you the books. My brother had them on the mule when we were attacked in the street. They are maybe lost, the books you came here to find---my brother is lost with them, I think. What will you do now, with me?'

The stranger didn't stop smiling as his eyes moved over her with the slowness of a predator. His tone was still amused, quiet. 'Perhaps you might serve a different purpose, little woman. You will come with me.'

'What if I don't want to do this?'

'Is there much of a future for you here, in Kyiv? Do you have men who have lived this night, who can take you into their homes? No, I think you must come with me. I will keep you safe and you will live and that is more than these heathens desire---yes? We will thwart them, you and I. You will survive to carry the truth about this night and I will commit vengeance in the name of your family---a very old, holy family of a very old, holy bloodline. I will commit vengeance in the name of your father and in your name.'

A fury born of pain and fear raised its head in her heart. She nodded, feeling bloodthirsty now at the idea of getting revenge on the Gentiles who had killed her family and razed her home. She nodded once more and whispered at the stranger who was a monster and yet who did understand what she felt.

'I can take you to where I left Tolya. Tolya's my twin. Maybe the books are still there. Maybe we can find them. If you will keep me alive tonight.' She tried a smile of her own and it trembled as badly as her bones. Her kerchief was fallen away from her face, exposing the long hair that was considered a prize in womanhood. It fell around her narrow face, nearly blinding her as she blinked against the pale brown strands. 'If you help me, your name will be written in the book of life...even if I must wrestle the angels to accomplish it.'

Now, the stranger lowered her to the straw and he gave a laugh as bitter as her own. His eyes were tilted upwards in bemusement as he shook his head. 'Little woman, if you had the power to accomplish such a thing, you would be considered a meshiach...and we all know that the meshiach can be no little woman from Kyiv. No mere mortal can offer me a cleansing for such horrors and sins as I have committed---only a meshiach or a chosen warrior of God has the tongue for arguing my salvation.'

So, he was a monster, as papa had said.

She agreed with him, nonetheless.

'First, we must make it safe for you to walk in the streets tonight.' The stranger stood back from her, the thoughtful look in his eyes once more. The hood of his cloak-robe was flung back and she could study him now with impunity---they had struck a bargain, she had the right. He was more than simply handsome. He was beautiful, monster or not, with dark brown hair that touched his shoulders in its length. 'What did you bring in that bundle, little woman?'

'Those are my brother's clothes---we were fleeing the city.' She dared to speak up; a new strength ran in her veins. She could count this stranger as a tentative ally. What other did she have, now? Her papa was most likely dead---her mama, too.

'Then, as I get a horse ready for you, little woman, you must become your brother.' The stranger turned away and began moving among the horses again. 'I will cut your hair and help you make yourself into a different sort of mortal.'

'I do not understand.' She shook her head at him. 'Become my brother? How is that possible?'

'Go into the shadows again and get rid of your clothes, little woman. Put on the trousers and shirts you find in your brother's bundle. Put on the cap and the jacket. When you are done, I will cut your hair. You must become a boy, to keep you safe.' The dark stranger was preparing another horse, as if these things happened every night.

This was unheard of. No self-respecting woman would do such a thing. She stared at his back in new shock. She had put her life in the hands of a monster and what fresh horror did he want to commit? 'I can't. I can't do such a thing---it's unholy. What if I'm seen?'

'What if you're seen dressed as a Jewess? Do you think the Christians will take mercy on a little woman? Go. Move. We must get started, if we're going to do this.' He did not brook an argument.

She trembled harder as she did as he bid. She kept an eye on him as he worked among the horses, as she slid out of the clothes she wore. In her brother's bundle, she found the trousers and shirts she must use. She even found a farmer's cap. Something neither Jewish nor Gentile. The sight of it was a surprise. Had her brother intended to hide himself among the peasants of the shtetl in such a way, perhaps pretending to be not-Jewish?

Soon, she wore Tolya's clothes. When she stepped out of the corner, she was almost a boy.

The stranger was finished with the two horses. One, a giant bay, and the other a dappled gray. He had attached bundles of his own onto them and was ready to go. Now, she went to stand before him, holding the knife again. Did she dare to really trust the stranger? The trousers felt odd, without the heavy swish of her skirts. The cap felt odd, too.

She stared into his face. Expecting something she wasn't sure of.

'Put the knife in your belt, little woman, and take this cap off.' He instructed.

She obeyed. In a few moments, he had pulled her long hair back and up to the crown of her head and he stood behind her, his own knife in his hand. She held herself still, breathless and afraid. The sawing of the knife he held as it moved through the thickness of her hair made a sound that vibrated through her skull and her skin. It did not hurt but it was enough to bring tears to her eyes.

'My crowning glory...' She whisper-breathed the words.

'No.' The stranger said, still cutting with his sharp knife. 'Your hair can grow again. Your crowning glory is your life and how you live it. This, if taken, cannot be replaced. You must let the past die tonight, little woman, and now be my brother...my brother from Kyiv. Do not speak unless I give you leave to speak...not tonight. We do not want the Christians to know you are female and Jewish. You speak Yiddish, but I think you may not speak any other languages. You must stay at my side and stay silent, for the sake of your life.'

She agreed without words. It wasn't true---she spoke the common language of the Gentiles here in Kyiv and some Hebrew, but perhaps silence would be best. For the moment.

When the stranger finished, he came around to stand before her once more and he held the long tail of her hair in his large hand. None of it had escaped him. She ran her hands over the remainder, what stayed on her head. It was heartbreakingly short and much like her brother's. She imagined she must look like Tolya now, Tolya who could be dead. It brought tears to her eyes, the idea of being so utterly alone. She'd never spent a day without Tolya.

'Do not cry for this, little woman.' The dark stranger shook the tail of her pale brown hair in his fist. 'Again, I say...it is nothing. It will grow back.'

'My brother must be dead.' She said and her voice cracked. 'My family, all of them, must be dead. What does it matter if my hair grows? What does it matter if I'm a boy, now, to save my life? I have no life. It has been taken.'

'No, it has not. You still live.' The stranger put her hair in a leather pouch and buried it among the saddlebags and bundles, for safety. Apparently, he did follow the rules of how to treat the body. 'Now, put your cap on and come. We have work to do.'

The cap fit right over her short hair and hid anything that might make her look like a girl. The stranger helped her into the saddle of the gray mare. Once settled, she watched as he did the same, swinging up onto the bay. They were almost too high for the doorway of the stable.

Now, the stranger cocked his head to the side and smiled at her, his eyes warmer than before. It was as if they were going to be friends. 'I cannot keep calling you little woman, for you are not a little one and you cannot be a woman, even if you are niddah, as all women are. You are nearly my height and in those clothes, you are a handsome boy---my little brother. What name would you answer to?'

'Misha.' She managed, though it was nearly soundless; it was still a terrible mystery of how he knew she was niddah at this time---what man knew when a woman was bleeding unless he was informed?. 'My name is Mishenka ha-Rav Ben-Moshe, but my papa called me Misha. My brothers always said Misha was a boy's name. A Gentile boy's name.'

'Yes, but it is a good name. It is a name for the greatest of God's warrior angels, Miechel. Miechel is the same as Mikhail, here, in Kyiv, so you were named after the city's patron angel.' It was then, as he spoke with that same warm smile, that she realized something. The stranger meant to keep her safe, meant to do exactly what he'd promised to do. 'My name is Joseph Snowden and you must call me Joseph. Like you, I was born of the Chosen People. I became a bar mitzvah at eleven. My name, then, was Yusef Bar-Ya'el.'

It was startling, frightening to have the trust of a man who might be a monster. She studied him from under the short brim of her cap and then asked. 'And when was this, that you were born and given such a holy name?'

Joseph, the stranger, mused for a long moment and then answered her with a shrug. 'In the Christian calendars, it was the year 1122 Anno Domini. To the synagogue and the elders in Jerusalem, where I lived, it was the year 4882. A long time ago.'

The mere thought of that stopped her heart for a moment. He wasn't human.

Why would he tell her such a thing? Did he not realize that such truth brought power?

'Come. It's time...we should go see if we can find the books and scrolls that your brother has likely given his life to defend.' With that, Joseph Snowden hup-hupped to the horse he rode and ducked the ledge of the stable door as he went out.

She followed.

In the streets, it was night. Where they rode, in the cobbled streets, the noise was audible but not overwhelming. That was to change, she knew, if they went back into the section of the city where her family had lived. She followed Joseph, keeping her face half-covered by the long, knitted scarf she'd found in her brother's bundle. They rode down the streets and towards the smoke and screams that she felt so disjointed from. Was this what she'd come out of, tonight? Was this what she'd fled? It couldn't touch her anymore...

It was dark; the street lamps had not had their candles and oil lit yet. Perhaps they would not be lit tonight. What did that matter? She knew her way and she wondered why she'd felt a need to watch the stranger these last weeks. Why had she felt a need to break her papa's rules and frighten her mama by sneaking out during chores to find this strange man from another time and another world? For, that was what he had turned into. He wasn't of her people, no matter what he'd been in his youth. He looked so young, only in his early years of being a man, yes, but he wasn't. He wasn't human.

Was it fate that she should follow him, so intrigued? Was it fate that he should come to her papa, looking for the arcane knowledge? Was it fate that she should find him, when she had fled from the massacre on this night?

Soon, on horseback, they found their way to the streets where she'd grown up.

The fires burned in nearly every house. There were bodies everywhere on the cobbles and in the dirt. They lay across the doorstep, their blood splattered all the way up the wooden frame to the mezuzahs. They lay in the direct middle of the narrow streets. Men, women, children. The well-fed and well-dressed among the ragged, hungry. Death owned no discrimination of wealth and wisdom, no bias for position and caste. She could not look away. Her heart was numb.

Joseph pulled two wrapped torches from one of his bundles and leaned out from the bay's saddle to light them with fire from a burning thatch. He passed one to her, to give them some more light to see better by. As if she needed a torch, when so many flames were eating away the life she'd once lived.

Then, they came to the place where she'd fled from Tolya's side. The mule lay there, dead and nearly blocking the way. Even in death, the obstinate animal was aggravating and difficult. The bundles were there, too...most of them. They looked as if they'd been picked through. Her clothes lay scattered all over the muddy cobbles. But, there, in the darkness, she saw something that made her heart jerk in new fear. Blood. A huge puddle of blood seeping into the stones. Blood that didn't stop at a puddle. It went off into a trail that led away from the mule and the bundles. A trail that led away and up the street, up the sloping street...and out of sight. Neither Tolya nor the Gentile physician were there to be seen---but, there were bodies. The bodies of their attackers. The men who had tried to stop them.

'Blood.' Joseph's voice sounded strange and she glanced up fast, her lower face nearly rising completely from the scarf as she stared after him. He wasn't looking in her direction. He was stating the obvious, with the blood, but it was something in his tone. He sounded grim and yet...expectant. 'Two people went off in that direction, bleeding. Only a little while ago.'

She didn't want to know how he knew. It was enough that he did know.

She took the lead now, pushing past him on her mount. She managed to get the gray to move around the dead mule's head. What kind of animal were these, that they didn't go crazy with fear at the scent of death and blood? They were his, obviously, but...

Without thought, she raised her torch and began to follow the trail of blood.

Up the slope of the road, she followed the trail. It didn't get any smaller, but it didn't get any bigger either. It was as if someone was dragging a corpse. It wasn't footsteps, the blood...it was a swath. Something dragged, soaked in blood. Her instincts told her that it was a bundle, not a body. Around them, people fled with their own tears and their own families---or what was left of them. The attackers were behind, fumbling and drunken. It was a testament to the mentality of the ones who could do something like this...they had to be drunk to bolster their enthusiasm and desire for the death of their neighbors. And who had started this? Whose voice had caused the emotional conflagration?

She would love to see that one hanging from the city's walls, at the end of a rope. A very evil desire.

Then, as they entered a Gentile area, she saw it. The body lay crumpled against the stones of a building, folded up as if in agony or sleep. This was where the largest trail of blood ended, yet some small trail continued onwards into the darkness in drips and drabbles. And her heart shattered, when she realized that the pale strip she could see at the back of the body's coat was his tallit and the tzitzit tassels at the end on either side. It was her twin, her Tolya. Tolya, the youngest son of the rabbi Moshe, was dead...and she'd never seen a day without him. How could God expect her to go on, living? Wasn't there a mitzah of the halakhah, which forbid her to exist without her twin?

Instinctively, she howled in anguish and reached to rip at her bosom in thoughtless keriyah. She nearly dropped the torch in her rush to get off the horse. It was so much higher than the mule and she stumbled, getting away. She fell to her knees and grabbed at her brother's body and turned it to face her, in the light of the torch. His face was bloodied, but it was obvious to her sight immediately that the wound came from his throat. The fatal one. There was a huge puddle of blood under him, soaking his clothes. His throat gaped like a second mouth smiling at her.

She retched and began to sob, touching his bloodied cheek. He was still warm. He was only just dead. There were more wounds that showed themselves among his clothes. Nothing lethal. And the fingers of his right had been broken. Bent and wrenched and broken. He'd been carrying something, something that had been ripped from his arms by force. A cold voice in the back of her head whispered, pointing out the logic.

The holy books. The bundle with the texts. He'd taken it with him this way and maybe it'd been covered in blood. Maybe he'd had to drag it---the bundle was more than a wounded man could carry, maybe. And he'd been robbed. Someone had slit his throat and broken his hand just to take the bundle. He'd fought them, most likely. Tolya was a rabbi's son and he knew that the books were worth more than his life...they were the books of their history and their people. If one lost the books, the truth was lost. No rabbi would allow such a thing.

And the son of a rabbi, learning the same profession, would have died to protect the books.

'Tolya...' She whispered, weeping for him. 'I'm sorry. I shouldn't have run and left you alone...'

'Misha.' Joseph remembered the name easily and said it as if very familiar with her. 'Misha, he is dead, but the one who killed him is not. The trail goes on. Let us go and see if we can find the one who has murdered your brother.'

It was so hard to get up and move away from his body. She forced herself to do so, sniffling. Handing Joseph the torch, she hoisted herself back into the saddle. Once settled again, she accepted the flaming brand once more and turned to explain to the stranger who had helped her so far. 'He was carrying something. It was stolen. I think...I think it was the books. They were heavy in the blanket and they weren't back with the mule and...' Her voice gave out, then.

'Then, we are seeking not only a murderer but a thief.' Joseph said, frowning. She could see something in his face. Something that was half-hidden in the torch-light. Something ominous and inhuman. The flames flickered on the cloak-brooch at his throat, throwing dazzles of color outwards. His voice went deeper, full of some ugly fury that he kept in his chest. 'We will find this one and I will make sure he gives up his life for what he's done tonight.'

In the darkest corner of her heart, she agreed.

The coat she wore was of stronger stuff than the dresses she'd worn and she hadn't managed to rip the cloth over her heart. Her grief would have to wait. It would have to wait just a little longer. Tightening her grip on the torch and on the reins of the gray she rode, she pushed onwards, now following Joseph. Joseph, who seemed uncannily aware of the blood's trail.

It seemed that they rode a mile, the hooves clopping steadily. At last, Joseph stopped, reining in his bay. The silence here was crazy, after the screams and terror and fire she'd come out of. They'd reached into the heart of Gentile Kyiv, a part where the houses were very fine and showed the money of their owners. There were trees on either side of the street and the street itself was much broader.

Joseph swung down from the soldier's saddle and threw her the reins. The torch was dropped to the cobbles as if unnecessary, now. Without a word, the strange man began to walk past the houses ahead. The trail of blood had petered out some distance back, but her newfound protector had insisted that he could still see it.

She stayed put, waiting, holding her torch and the reins of both horses.

But, as she watched, Joseph did something unexpected.

Satisfied that he had the right house, Joseph gave a mocking laugh and strode up to the front door. Without any warning, her protector raised his left boot and kicked it. The lock broke and the wood cracked. The door flew back and in, giving way before him. Dark cloak swirling behind his legs, Joseph entered without a care for the inhabitants. She felt like weeping again...or turning tail to run. Sane people didn't break the doors of houses. Sane people knocked, gave the owners time to receive them.

In only a few moments, Joseph came back out, pulling a man along behind him by the hair of the head. It was the brown-eyed Gentile physician who had helped her and Tolya. She leaned over the horse's neck and protested at Joseph as he tossed the man onto the cobblestones before her. 'This---this is the doctor who helped us, Joseph---he must've been wounded, he must have tried to save Tolya---'

'Don't let a handsome human face deceive you, Misha.' Joseph smirked, not bothering to look up in her direction. He gave the fallen physician a hard kick in the ribs. 'He is the thief. The books and scrolls are in the house, stacked up in pretty rows on a table in the very first room. He killed your brother and he stole the sacred texts.' With another ferocious kick, Joseph continued. 'And he's not your friend, be sure of that. He's no friend to mortals.'

There was blood on the Gentile's hair and face and collar. Blood everywhere. But, most of all, on his hands. They were coated in drying blood. Dully, as she stared at him, she thought--- 'The blood will stain. It'll take lots of washing to get the stain out of his skin. And he wouldn't be alive long enough to worry about the blood on his clothes or his face. Joseph's going to kill him. If I don't do it, first.'

'He's not even human, Misha.' Joseph's voice broke in on her thoughts.

'Not human?' She leaned even more out of the saddle, staring at the Gentile. 'Of course he's human. What could he be, but human? Doesn't matter how old you are, you're human, too. At least, you once were. You were born of the Chosen People, you said so yourself. You became bar mitzvah. You had a human name, a holy name.'

'Not human anymore.' Joseph's eyes gleamed with some strange light that had nothing to do with the torches---not the one in her hand nor the one on the cobbles. He gave her a flat, chilly smile and his gaze stayed cold like deep water. 'But, I was, once. Unlike our friend here. He's a demon. He's never been human. He's been searching for those books for a long time, I imagine. Longer than I've been searching for them, perhaps. I haven't killed anyone for the truths I seek---only someone who intends to use the truth for dark purposes would dare to sully those scrolls and books with the blood of their keeper.'

It dawned on her...perhaps Joseph wasn't the only one papa had feared. Perhaps papa had known how important and dangerous these texts were...perhaps papa had known about demons who might want to steal the arcane truths from the one whose family had carried and protected them for so many centuries.

'Do you want to kill him or shall I?' Asked Joseph, cocking his head to the side as he looked up at her.

She stared at the man who lay on the ground, moaning in pain. Joseph shrugged and hauled the Gentile up off the cobbles, dragging him away and back to the house's open door. She didn't dare to protest. Let Joseph take care of it. As long as her brother's killer was dead, what could it matter? The law of the ancients demanded a life for a life, particularly when it was a young teacher whose life had been taken first.

Nervous and scared, she waited.

It was a wait of only minutes before Joseph reappeared. He was carrying a bundle over his shoulder. The texts and scrolls, probably, wrapped up in some clean cloth. When he reached her side, she realized that his cheeks were pinked. Despite the chill of the night air and the torch's amber, crackling glow, her protector was flushed and warm-seeming. He hadn't, before...not so much.

He was smiling. He tied the bundle onto the bay's back and then pulled himself into the saddle. Now, she dared to ask---just to be sure. 'My papa's books? The sacred texts?'

'Yes.' He answered and pulled the bay's reins around, to keep going through the Gentile section they'd come to. His smile scared her. He'd done as he promised---he'd avenged her brother. What would he do now? Would he keep the rest of the promises? To avenge her family? To protect her?

Joseph was silent as they rode and her fear only grew.

It was hours later---but time wasn't relevant now---that her protector finally reined in for a stop. They'd passed over a bridge and through a small gate left unlocked and open. Now, they were on a long, dark road in front of a cottar's shack. She followed his example, getting down off the gray. There was no sign of life here. The shack looked abandoned. Had he known that it would be so or had he ridden this long to find such a place? The shack's front looked dilapidated, the ground around it appeared stripped of grass and hard with rocky soil.

'Where are we?'

'We are outside the walls of Kyiv. You're safe.' Joseph answered, pulling the bundles and saddle off his horse without looking around at her. 'If you would continue being safe, get off the mare and help me.'

Ah. A threat of danger?

She slid off the gray and followed his example, pulling the saddle free. Padding silently in her brother's boots, she moved towards the shack. It did seem completely abandoned. Was this where they would rest, out of the city? Misha pushed the door open and found the place musty and full of darkness. In the deep shadows, she could see a table and a hearth and very little else. She hesitated to enter. Instinctively, she looked for the mezuzah and there it was, nailed in place just at her eye level. This had been a kosher home. Where were the owners? Why had they left and not taken the prayers with them? Had they been killed and...?

Joseph spoke, very close at her back, and she jumped with fear. 'We will stay here in the day and travel again, once the sun has gone down. I've hidden the horses behind the house. There is grass and water. They will be fine, I think.'

He moved past her, briefly raising his fingers to touch the mezuzah with unspoken reverence. So, he was observant of the mitzvahs. That boded well. She once more followed his example, kissing the fingers of her right hand and briefly murmuring a prayer as she held her fingers only a hair's breadth from the prayer case.

She watched as Joseph worked. He went back and forth, through the door, bringing their bundles in. He had three of his own, plus the texts that he'd rescued for her. In a little while, an oil lamp burned on the table and revealed how terrible the house was. It was dirty with animal traces. It must have happened since the humans had left---animals coming and going, using the house as their roost. Another little while and Joseph had a fire burning in the hearth with wood he'd brought in.

'Are you sure that's a good thing---won't we be caught, if the smoke is seen?' She was anxious, watching him move around the single room. Her green-eyed protector was pulling down a curtain that hung in the corner, revealing a large pallet bed.

Joseph began beating the curtain, to get the dust and insects out of its cloth, moving with quiet efficiency. He chuckled, shaking his head, and didn't look up at her as he worked. 'I wouldn't think anyone's searching for us. Tonight will make work for many, when the sun rises again. A pogrom? Oh, yes...every official in Kyiv will have their hands full in the daylight, when explanations and excuses must be found for the murder that has been done. I doubt, Misha, that anyone will realize that a young Jewess escaped the slaughter, and if by chance someone thinks on the missing body of a rabbi's daughter, they won't think on it long. Too much else to be concerned with.'

He was right, of course. Her body was calming, now, and it was starting to be warm inside the little shack. She gave a big yawn, stifling it with the sleeve of her coat. Now that the terror was leaving, she felt exhausted. As if she'd worked hard all night long. Slowly, she began to look over the bundles that Joseph had brought in. His cloak was thrown over the table where they lay. The lamp sat there, revealing in its amber glow the shadowy shapes.

The books, the scrolls. The sudden realization that she would never see her family again hadn't really slapped home yet. She studied the bundle which held papa's books. The cloth was velvet of some kind. Deep and rich and purple. A fine color for the holy texts.

Her belly growled and she flushed in embarrassment, glancing at her protector.

He had finished with the curtain and was searching the pallet to see how safe it was, how clean. Now, at the sound of her body's noise, he looked around with raised brows. Really, he was a handsome man, and he was amused by her again. 'I think you did not eat this night. Was your father in such a hurry that he failed to make sure his children were fed?'

She flushed harder, becoming upset. 'He had more important things on his mind. We ate a piece of bread with butter. There was no time for cooking.' Her belly growled again, in protest, at a thought of the bread. It shamed her to say anything of hunger. 'I don't suppose you brought food?'

'I didn't.' Joseph had turned fully to face her now, his face speculative as he answered. 'I didn't give it thought, bread or meat. But...there are a few hours before the sun comes up. I believe I can remedy the complaint. Wait here.'

He left the shack, closing the door behind him. Misha felt worry and then curiosity. And then, she began to search the place they'd come to. She lost track of time, doing that. The shack was almost bare, but she'd never seen a place so deserted before. Yet, there were the bundles. She didn't dare to touch Joseph's bundles---that was the height of rudeness. But, papa's books---that was another matter, altogether.

Papa had encouraged her to read, to learn how to think beyond what other girls might think. It was considered not-right, the teaching of Hebrew to a girl. But, papa had done this, showing her the way to daven. Perhaps, because she was his youngest child, he had doted on her mind more. She understood almost as much as Tolya, about the books and the faith and the laws.

The sudden remembrance caught her unaware and she trembled, touching the purple velvet cloth. Her twin was gone, dead. Her parents were dead. Perhaps her older brothers and sisters were dead, too, with their own families. She couldn't bear the thought of it---even the babies, dead. She began to weep again, gripping the velvet in her hand. She raised her face to the ceiling, aiming her words at the God who could allow such a horror.

'Why? Are we not your Chosen People? Were we not good enough? Did we do something to make You angry, Lord? I know...I shouldn't question Your ways, but...why? Why? Why?' The word came out of her, louder and louder each time as she sobbed. It seemed so unfair, so not-right. Did the slaughter come because the Jews hadn't shown any signs of the Plague? Why did the Gentiles crave the death of her people?

She let go of the cloth and sank to her knees at the hearth, pulling the cap off her head. She felt almost naked without her long hair and she was in a strange house with a man who wasn't of her blood. He might be of her people and then, again, he might not, and there was no other place on earth where she could go. She was lost. There, on the side of the hearth, she leaned against the stones, losing herself in the flickering crackle of the flames, and let the grief come. She lost track of time, weeping and wringing Tolya's cap between her dirty hands.

'Things might've been worse.' His voice came from nowhere and everywhere and yet didn't startle her, she was so far into her own head. 'You might've died in Kyiv tonight at the hands of the same demon who killed your brother. You might've died at the hands of those who killed your mother and your father. You live, so...your people live.'

'I'm alone.' She whispered it, unblinking as she went on, staring at the fire. 'You've saved my life and I'm alone. I can't stay here with you. It's improper, it's impossible. I can't stay, not with you and not alone. You're not my kinsman and I'm to be married to Itzik in only...'

Joseph moved in the corner of her sight and reached for the iron pole that was slung over the fire. He made noises while fiddling with the pole and didn't answer. At last, though, the pole was slid back into place on the stones. A dead, skinned rabbit hung from it, impaled on the iron. She wrinkled her nose as the bloody meat began to sear in the flames, dripping life into the coals. The rabbit was beheaded and skinned and looked disgusting, unappealing, yet, her belly began to growl and complain at the smell of burning blood.

'I've brought you water, as well; I found a bucket and a dug-out spring just beyond what must surely have been the garden. There's a bottle of strong wine in my things. You need a drink and some food, Misha. You will feel much better when you've gotten through the shock of this. You will be able to grieve properly, then.' He was making more noise now. Finally, he sat down at her side, directly on the hearth, and offered her a cup. It smelled of fermented fruit. 'Here, drink. I watered the wine, but it is still excellent.'

Numb, she accepted the cup; it was clay and glazed brown and fit perfectly into her hand. She didn't want anything at all, but Joseph was insisting. And his words sounded like things her mama might have said to her. Such concern in his voice and him a stranger. A strange stranger.

Staring into the contents, she whispered a prayer to thank God for the shelter of the roof and the warm fire and the food that was cooking and the wine in the cup. She thanked God for the protector who'd come to help her survive. With a sip, she realized that it was a good wine.

She glanced at Joseph and saw that he was drinking from a second clay cup that was painted in an intricate pattern of blues and yellows. He hadn't watered his wine down---she could smell it and the scent was sweet. That was worrisome---men could do monstrous things when intoxicated and she was alone with him. This was wrong in itself, but to be alone with a drunken stranger was worse.

Her instincts for the passing of time were fairly accurate---she could feel the change in the air that heralded the early hours of dawn Joseph got up, without comment, and used the heavy curtain that lay on the pallet to cover the one window of the shack. Now, they were in a cocoon that was growing warmer. Back and forth, Joseph went outside into the cold, bringing wood. Soon, they had enough to be safe and warm for the day. He stayed quiet, for the most part, taking care of their needs without any help. A small piece of her heart felt sick with a guilt over it, but she couldn't care. She had nothing inside her that could care.

At last, the rabbit was cooked. Several times, Joseph had removed the iron rod with the meat speared on it from the flames and rubbed it with the brush that he dipped into a small wooden pot that he'd taken out of a bundle. The smell of the herbs was delicious. When he deemed the meat finished, Joseph tore the rabbit into shreds off the bone and gave the food to her in a wooden bowl. He didn't take any for himself.

'You must eat, too.' She insisted, offering him the bowl in an effort to be as kind as he'd been to her.

'No.' Joseph waved the bowl away, giving her another of his odd smiles. 'I'm not hungry. I don't think I could eat. But, you should eat as much as you can, Misha.'

She began to eat. The meat was wild and full of the flavor of wildness, but the herbs made it very tasty. In silence, she ate the rabbit and drank watered wine. Soon, she began to relax and grow calm inside. Warm and fed, she leaned up against the stones of the hearth once more and prayed inside her heart and her mind.

'You should sleep.' Joseph broke her concentration with a whisper. His face was somber and thoughtful. The curve of his mouth and the slant of his eyes were growing lax with drowsiness. 'We both should sleep. Misha, do you want to go away from here when the sun goes down? Do you want to go back into Kyiv, to find your family...for what must be done?'

For what must be done. Her papa and her mama and her twin, her family...they should be given the proper burial, the cleansing. She'd left them without doing what was necessary. But, she was just a woman, a girl. She could not do these thing without help, without the people...and her people were gone or going.

'Will it be safe? Will you help me?' She whispered back at him, her short hair falling to tickle her ear. She brushed at it, scratching her neck. 'Do you think they'll kill the ones who try to mourn?'

'I don't know, Misha.' Joseph took a drink of wine and gave a heavy sigh, making a face of disgust. 'Each time this happens, it is the same and yet it's different. I've seen it happen so often, but I can't predict what the results must be. You must believe that your loved ones will be accepted and forgiven by God even if they are not properly buried. Consider this...if we go, it may not be necessary and we might be in danger from the ones who lived, Jew and Gentile both. The ones who are still there, they will probably take care of these things. Your father was a rabbi.'

'I want to sleep.' She yawned and lifted her cup to drain it dry. Licking her lower lip, she blinked at her protector. 'This is wrong. Us being here, like this. We're alone and you're not my kinsman and you're not my husband.'

'Do you have a living kinsman I can take you to?' Joseph pointed out. 'Can you consider me your friend and know that I offer my protection as a promise I made?'

She nodded and gave in. She was too tired to argue, too tired to be worried. Crawling to her feet, she moved to the pallet and laid down, pulling at the cloth to make a blanket for herself. She didn't know what Joseph would do---lay down beside her or lay on the hearth---

And for this moment, she didn't care.

Chapter Fourteen

She opened her eyes and gasped. The sudden inhale was a shock to her dead lungs, to the stolen blood in her veins. She stiffened, her instincts now working overtime to tell her brain about the details of the environment.

Uly wasn't in the bed. The room was warm. The curtains and bamboo wood shades were drawn. She could see the dappling glimmer of sunlight that didn't touch her skin. There was coffee and food nearby---eggs and bread and ham and sweet rolls. The sound of a knife and fork could be heard; as could the whisper of paper pages turning---slick pages, perhaps a magazine. He was up and he was in the main room of the suite, having breakfast. And the sun was beyond the shades and this was good.

Her internal clock said noon or nearly so. She had hours more to sleep, if she wanted. Nonetheless, she couldn't go out of the building or into rooms where the sun came through the windows. So. She relaxed and pulled at the creamy duvet, tugging it up around her shoulders and neck. There, curled into a ball on her side, she closed her eyes once more and began to tremble with memory that brought tears. She cried, remembering.

Joseph. Joseph, who had loved her for so long, until Nicolai had come into the picture.

For two years after the pogrom in Kyiv, she'd lived solely as a boy. As Joseph's brother and companion. She'd watched over him as he slept and he'd helped her survive the deaths that had taken her from home. They'd traveled all over Europe and even into Africa. They'd gone to the East, to India and then to China, later---all much, much later. But, those first two years, they'd stayed in Europe. Searching for more holy books and texts saved by the rabbis of many villages and cities. They'd witnessed the heartbreaking murders of many Jews, as Gentiles attempted time and time again to wipe out the Chosen People.

For two years, she'd lived with Joseph and she'd learned about the demons and the malakh and the Undead, the peoples beyond the human equation. She'd learned that the Gentile physician who had killed Tolya, and was killed in turn by Joseph, was more than demon---he was actually a malakh of surprising age, a benu. Joseph had educated her to his search, the things which he believed. She'd learned of his childhood in Jerusalem and the life he'd had as a warrior. She had learned, gradually, over time, of what made his body different from hers. She'd gone from pity to horror to fascination and back many times.

At last, one night, in Berlin, she had woken to the sound of Joseph drunkenly singing as he came back to their rooms in the small, plain hotel. He'd gone out hours before, as soon as the sun was gone, and she had decided to sleep---then, of course, to wake when he returned. Her protector had staggered in, falling against the walls and the table as he sung to himself. She'd said nothing, letting the matter go, until he had made the room too hot by stoking up the fire. In the middle of the summer, no less.

He'd told her then and there, in the slurring tones of the inebriated, that he must either send her away or take her life, for he was in love. His affections were becoming dangerous to them both, they were such a distraction and such a fever. She had finally grown into womanhood and Joseph found it unbearable to exist in close quarters with a woman he desired, having existed for so long in a state of sexual purity. Joseph, like her, had come into their relationship a virgin and had remained so, even after death.

Saddened at being pushed aside out of Joseph's sense of nobility---the fear of what may happen, through his passion---she'd moved around their rooms in abject silence, doing as he bid---preparing to leave him. He'd watched, slouching in a chair with his head between his hands, just as silent. But, when she reached for the door, intending to go---sick at heart with the idea of what might happen to her, away from him---Joseph had moved with inhuman speed. Slamming the door shut, he'd thrown her bodily against it and claimed what had belonged to him from the very first night, in Kyiv.

They had married---somehow, Joseph had found a rabbi who was willing to do the job without a discussion of the matter with her family or with his. One evening, just after the sun went down, they'd met under a canopy in the rabbi's presence and were given the blessings. Monster and mortal together, bound by law and love.

For, by then, she'd forgiven him for what he was.

But, it wasn't meant to last. Joseph had said, from the start of their marriage, that he couldn't bear the sight of her growing old as he stayed young eternally. Already, she'd gone from gangly girl to woman and then to his wife. He'd taken spells of melancholy over that very issue. They traveled, as man and wife, for three years...until the day in France when she'd been wounded in a fight with some would-be robbers.

She'd begged him for death. She'd begged him for mercy---if she could not give him a son and he could not give her a daughter, they couldn't follow the imperative of a real marriage, according to Jewish law. She'd begged him for understanding. She was in pain and couldn't live long, with her belly ripped open, spilling poison into her blood and her blood out onto the sheets of their bed. If he couldn't live in the sun with her, she wanted death forevermore. At nineteen and three years married in 1356, she hadn't realized how very *mad* Joseph could be, where love was concerned.

Until that moment, he'd never used his fangs on her. It was an understanding of their marriage. Her blood would not feed him and she would protect the dark creature God had given her to love. Laying in their bed, locked behind the door of a room they'd rented, she'd asked Joseph for leniency and mercy. She'd begged God to make it easier, to take the pain. Two days of pain as her body had suffered with fever and wracking chills---bleeding to death would have been pleasant compared to the slow torture of a wound infection. And all the while, Joseph had sat beside her, head in his hands, and watched with a look of abject misery in his face.

At last, he'd left. While she was dozing fitfully, in a fever. When she'd woken, her first thought was...he'd abandoned her to die alone, unable to watch any longer and unable to do the merciful thing of ending it quickly. But, that hadn't been the case. Joseph had returned, freshly fed and pinked with mortal life in his veins. And he'd committed an atrocity on her, against her will. She'd clawed him in her weak way, hysterically trying to stop it. Yet, when it was over...she was changed and dead and nothing could fix it.

Vulnerable yet granite. Joseph.

It came into her head, unbidden---unwished for.

'Let me go, I can't---'

'You will not die. I won't let you leave like this. Misha, please---'

'We're wrong, we're wrong, wrong, wrong. I'm not like you. I can't give you a son. You can't give me a daughter. I can't give you life---'

'But, I can give you forever, Misha, please---'

She'd forgiven him for it, after a few months of arguing and weeping. Forgiven him as much as she was able to. Bound in marriage and then in blood as Sire and childe, they'd stayed together for the next four hundred and forty years---or nearly so. For, over time, Joseph had developed a streak of cruelty towards her---based in his own self-hatred---and it had driven a wedge between them in the last years of the French Revolution. He'd created a business for himself, a mercantile of luxury items and spices, going back and forth between the countries. She'd traveled with him a great deal of the time, but not always...not always, for she did need moments away from his cold anger.

Joseph had never laid a hand on her in anger, but his mental cruelty was worse than any slap or punch. And, then, in 1797, when she was in Rome and he was traveling to and from Spain, Nicolai had come into the picture. At four hundred and sixty years old, she'd been shocked at the idea---Joseph had come back to their villa in Rome with this Russian gypsy boy in tow, taken as a slave in Spain.

She'd had no idea, then, but quickly learned how dark and twisted her husband was.

"Instant psychopath, just add a violin-playing gypsy with the face of a fallen angel." She whispered at the dimness of the tester bed's wooden top where it loomed above her. She managed a weak smile and tucked her head back down against the pillow, quivering with anguish.

How could Joseph have been such a monster when he was capable of such goodness? And how could she have loved him so much? How could she still love him, with almost everything of her soul?

It was something she had never found an answer for, in all the years she'd existed.

He woke to the sound of the violin. Nico's violin.

He'd fallen asleep in the recliner after Tennyson Beaulieu left. He remembered her leaving, the words he'd said about coffee, his slide into dark sleep. It was easy to do, falling into oblivion with the files and books; he had done it many times over the centuries. Licking his dry lips, he considered the girl who had left the condo in a rush.

He'd prayed as he listened to the sound of her rushing down the hall and down the stairs. He'd prayed that she wouldn't be seen by anyone who might wish her harm, anyone who might wish to use her against him...and against Nicolai. Nicolai, who made the violin weep so sweetly now.

Joseph pushed the recliner into an upright position. He put his files on the floor to the side; he still needed to decide which clues could be given to Misha without risking a true path to the Sang-rael, that Chosen child who'd slept in his bed this morning. And it was now afternoon, his usual time to do the business with a living world. Even if he couldn't leave the condo. But, his heart wasn't into doing business. There wasn't anything that really needed to be done, to be honest. And the violin was the beckoning finger of his concubine, his childe.

He recognized the piece as being a re-working of Bach's Toccata and Fugue as performed by Vanessa Mae. Classical, almost holy and yet passionate.

Wearing his jeans and a button-up, he followed the music through the darkened rooms.

When he reached the bedroom, he found his prodigy. Nicolai, hair hanging loose and free against his narrow shoulders, stood wet from the shower in only a royal blue towel. His childe's back was to him; Nicolai swayed with the music, the sweep of the bow. He stood, quiet, and watched, remembering the early morning hours and what he'd done, in lust.

The windows here were open, the heavy curtains swirling up and away from the window in a hard breeze. The sunlight, of course, was beyond this, and wouldn't threaten---it was too late in the day, on this side of the building, for sudden bursts of sun. It was as if his childe was serenading the daylight which was forever beyond his reach. He could hear the raindrops pattering outside on the iron fire escape; it was drizzling and this seemed to only add a deeper sense of melancholy and power to the music.

Nico had bounced back fast, despite having had no meal of his own, and looked to be completely healed from what he'd done to his childe's body. But, then, he'd tried to not take blood from his gypsy. Instead, he'd shared what surged through his own veins, feeding his boy. His body remembered it better than his mind, now reacting to the sight of Nicolai mostly naked with the tawny violin in hand.

It gave him pause and he stood motionless and simply watched. Nico, now, in this moment...

This was the boy he'd fallen in love with. Not the little hellion who defied all convention.

The bare skin of his lover's upper torso stood out against the dark curtains that fluttered and waved in the breeze. Nicolai's head was tilted to the side as if embracing the violin he held, the instrument that he caressed. The long strands of his wet hair were enticing and almost begged to be threaded through the fingers of a lover. Him, maybe. Yet, he could easily imagine Nicolai spread out beneath Rhys Lorraine and it brought a twinge of jealousy. Yes, he was jealous of the tchatcha bastard who could bring out the very best, most hedonistic side of Nico.

At the angle where he stood, he could see Nicolai in profile. His boy's eyes were closed in concentration and enjoyment of the song that soared from the strings. It was as if Nico made love to the violin, forever caught in his youth.

When the music ended, he held himself very still inside. Nicolai lowered the bow and the sweet-voiced violin and spoke to him quietly, speculative. Honestly. "Did you want something, Joseph?"

Did he want something? Oh, yes. He wanted the boy who could create beauty from nothing. He wanted the boy he'd stolen from the gypsies. He wanted the gypsy man he'd kept, despite his marriage to Misha and despite the part of his brain which said that men should not love other men so utterly. He wanted Nicolai to love him. He wanted Nico to lay him down in their bed and take away his concerns, his worries for what Misha's presence threatened. He wanted Nico to be his man. It was shameful, in his heart. A part of him was very aware of how hypocritical he was---he could fuck Nicolai every night for a hundred years or more and that was perfectly okay, but yet he felt such fear at the thought of giving himself to his boy.

He nodded. If his heart could beat, it would be lurching crazily.

Nicolai took the need for words away. Laying the violin and its bow on the bureau, his gypsy came to him, the gentlemanly seducer. The one who took great pleasure in pleasing his lover, sparing no emotional or physical expense.

Joseph gave himself up for lost.

His lover's mouth curved in an insolent smirk.

Maddening boy. He hissed the words, beyond pride. "Fuck me."

With a low growl, Nico seized his mouth in a plundering, consuming kiss; the difference in their size was forgotten. Her slid his hands down his lover's naked, wet chest, to find the towel at Nicolai's hips. He pushed himself forward, grinding their pelvises together. Hungry and wanting, he welcomed the tongue that ravaged the inside of his mouth.

Anything for this, in this moment. He took a deep, unnecessary breath; it rasped in his throat as his body shook. Such shame, so desire. Nicolai would never tell anyone about this---never---for to do so would mean the eternal death and his childe was in love with two mortals and had no intention of leaving them yet.

He had a strange mental flash of when Nico was still mortal---of watching his gypsy slave take Misha to bed. He had loved to watch them together, his two Ukrainian beauties. Nicolai, mortal and young and so generous---a boy whose idea of sexual domination had more resembled the mauling from an overeager puppy. There was no trace of that, now.

"Mine!" Nicolai whispered at him. His childe's soft voice was the sound of vengeance, the howl of retribution. "God damn you, *mine!*"

He knew why. He knew why his childe would punish him with the word '*mine*', reminding him of the evil they both existed within. Nico laid claim to him, refused to allow any back-sliding. Nico used the word '*mine*' as a reminder---a reminder for many things. Nico laid claim to him, adamantly refusing to allow any claim from Misha. Misha had left, Nico had stayed---this gave Nico the right of ownership, if such a thing could exist. Nico's life had been taken through force, by inches, and the word '*mine*' fit there, too. It was Nico's life he'd destroyed, crushed, raped. If anyone had the right to punish him, it was Nicolai Valeska, and so he craved it---he wanted this, wanted to tighten the bond between them.

For, if Nico would do these things in retaliation, then Nico could stay.

And that, really, was all he wanted. He couldn't bear to be alone. Not now.

Chapter Fifteen

It was three hours later, when she was on her way to Daniel D'Loup's house over on the edge of the Quarter, that it came back---Joe Snowden, awake at one in the afternoon.

That was odd, all by itself. Vampires usually slept in the day. Certain ones could stay up and function...but their extrasensory abilities were null and void. She knew it was possible for them to stay conscious in the day, but she'd never seen Valeska or Joe awake in the sunlight hours. What was going on? She didn't have much time to give it consideration. She had to talk with Daniel, per Rhys' suggestion, and get some things in order. Like her passport and the leave of absence and packing. Rhys had told her Daniel could help with all of it.

She wondered if he'd be there...Rhys. She could remember him saying something last night about spending the day with Gabe. The thought was laced with fuzziness left over from the booze.

As she opened the tall, black iron gate of Daniel's house and let it close behind her, Tennyson realized her stomach was fluttering. It came with a start, like a jerking of some hidden string. Nerves. She was nervous. Sheesh, what was there to be nervous about? She didn't have any reason to be afraid of Daniel, not really. The man had never done anything to hurt her.

She was careful, gingerly walking along the winding, tree-shaded brick path that led up to a fading white porch which wrapped around three sides of the sprawling house. One good twist of her ankle and she'd be laying on the ground in agony and then what? When she came to the porch, she pushed through the vines that threatened to overtake the wooden banisters and rails in pursuit of a few peeled, creaking boards.

She'd been here a few times, but not often. Every time, she came to the same conclusion: Daniel was letting the exterior go to hell on purpose and it was probably for security purposes, because the inside looked nothing like this.

Ringing the doorbell, she stepped back in reflex and hugged herself against the chill of the air. It was just the air and had nothing to do with the sudden worry she felt. What if Rhys hadn't talked things over with Daniel about her part in the job? What if Daniel vetoed the whole idea?

Before she could make up her mind to leave, the inner door opened.

Her heart jumped and began to beat crazy at the immediate sight of the assassin who stood on the other side of the screen. Daniel looked serious and...wore only a pair of jeans. His broad, hairy chest was exposed, revealing the muscles that she'd never seen bare. God, he was big through the shoulders and arms and...his long hair was hanging loose, looking flyaway and almost animalistic and kinda frizzed at the ends.

She swallowed and tried to speak; her voice caught and bubbled in her throat.

Daniel raised his brows, waiting.

Did he enjoy her discomfort?

"You must be cold." Daniel murmured, at last, after studying her in bemusement for thirty seconds that felt more like a half-century. He pushed the screen door open with his large hand, stepping back to make room. "T'plait. Come in, fille. I have been expecting you."

So---Rhys had told Daniel. That was good. She didn't wanna explain herself.

The foyer looked the same as it always did; classical French and subdued. She followed Daniel through the house in silence, not sure what she should say. Did he expect her to talk about the job, about the reason she was in his house? She hoped not; she didn't understand her decision, even now. *Why had she said yes to her friend?* What had possessed her to say yes to such an insane plan?

She followed Daniel to the kitchen and then to the sunroom, beyond it; the sunroom was the kitchen porch, closed in by glass and fixed up as a small greenhouse. Daniel's personal garden and she was kinda envious; she could only wish for something like it. Well, if the job went right, she'd have a chance at buying a greenhouse of her own.

Staying silent, she watched as the half-naked man picked up a watering bottle and began to move along the various pots and bowls full of hothouse vegetation. He seemed to be waiting for her to speak and she licked nervously at her lips, wondering where to begin. After a few minutes, he stopped the torture while plucking dead leaves from a lush Belgian ivy's underside.

"My partner has explained to me of how he spoke with you last night in the office. He asked you to accompany us on a job." Daniel never glanced at her, dumping the dead leaves into a twelve-inch terra cotta pot that sat on the end of a low wooden counter by the sunroom's door. The malakh's long brown-black hair curled wild against the sides of his unshaven throat. "Has he said to you anything of what this job entails?"

She nodded and then managed to croak. "Yeah. I have to play the decoy."

The malakh assassin raised his brows again, scrubbing at his stubbly cheek before continuing with the plants, his accented voice neutral. "You have the time to work, today? We will need to prepare your entry into Egypt quickly. This means, you must have the necessary papers and a passport that cannot be refuted, if scrutinized by the authorities."

"Yeah, I got some time." Tennyson began to gnaw on the corner of her lower lip.

"Bon." Daniel flicked his gaze toward her now with the reward of a genuine smile on his curving lips. "I suspect my partner has done something to convince you, in this matter, but I will make it my personal duty to ensure your safety. No matter what l'garcon has planned, your life shall be my responsibility."

She nodded, fighting the shiver that tried to crawl under her skin.

"Now." The dark ex-operative put his watering bottle down and nodded at the door. "Let us get coffee. We have much work to do and, before we finish, shall need the help of a hacker. I have arranged for Dante Webster to join us..."

Dante Webster has a way about him that encourages women to fall in love.

Oh, believe me, it's never on purpose. Dante likes women, but he prefers men. When I say he likes women, I guess I mean...he worships women and loves the heck out of them, but he's told me that he's only bedded two in his whole life. And, considering all the women who would do anything---including murder and theft---for a chance at Dante? It's a heartbreak.

Me, I could care less. If he fucks his cute little college twinks or the hot and hung business professionals, it doesn't matter to me. As long as he always loves me. Cause...when Dante loves you, it's like the damn sun shines over your head all the time. At least, it shines when he's in the room with you.

You ever seen the surfers from southern California and the Baja? The hot ones with perpetual tans and gorgeous hair and whacked ideas about real life? The ones who wear hemp jewelry and retro clothes and sandals? Yeah, the ones with a degree or two under their non-existent belt and a taste for pot.

Dante's one of them. He just lives in New Orleans right now; he has a big serious thing about his family and most of his living family is in New Orleans. The women around here find him irresistible because he's exotic to their senses. It's the malakh scent that comes off his skin and the SoCal accent and the total hippy aura. He's smart and funny as hell and he used to work for the government, as a hacker.

He's Mattie's step-son, by her dead husband. Dante's mother is some socialite. Rumor has it---I've never heard Dante say if it's true or not---that his mom is related to the Kennedys. You know, the ones from up north. Like a cousin or something. He's practically American royalty, but to watch him, you'd never know. He hasn't seen his mom in years and doesn't care---she abandoned him when he was a baby cruising around in diapers.

To look at him, in a work sitch, you think clean-cut and Ivy League. He has that look; think Monty from that movie 'With Honors'. That's the kinda guy Dante is, on the surface. When he worked for the government, he probably dressed like that, too. But, when you know him, you get the feeling that he would be right at home on the beach or in some beatnik poetry coffeehouse.

Dante, physically---I've heard---is the spitting image of his dead father. Six and a half feet with auburn hair and hazel eyes and glasses, he's got a load in his pants that would choke the most expert cock-sucker. Better yet, his favorite place, sexually, is on his knees. He loves to give head. Basically, a dream come true, if you're a gay man that Dante finds attractive and let's be honest here---okay?---I've seen Dante so trashed that he was hot to fuck the crazy shape shifting ex-Company asetau who usually sits off in the corner by himself.

Remember him? Javier Clay? I pointed him out to you---the cute guy sitting at the bar last night. Yeah, the one I told you about, worked with Mattie and Daniel and Rhys---he was Rhys' partner for about two years. And let me tell you something---if you'll take Javi home, then you got balls. Javi's awesome to look at, but damn---imagine it. You're with this guy and you don't even know if what you're seeing is the real him. What if he changes faces on you, in the middle of everything?

Motherfucker, please.

The story goes that Mattie raised Dante from the time he was about eight months old until his Dad died---then, he went to live with his grandmother. He's told me that Mattie's the first person he can clearly remember and, to him, she was Mommy. When he was seventeen, he went to work for the government and got himself divorced from her, legally. He'd been living in her custody for about a year at the time and someone above the elite corp teams decided that Mattie's step-son would best serve his country if he put those awesome talents to use in a way that Uncle Sam ordained. All that raw talent and skill for math and computer programming, reined in for the government's CIA and FBI. And the elite corp teams, too.

He's thirty, now, and basically retired from government service. Basically. You never really retire from stuff like that unless you die. Speaking of which...ask Dante sometime what it's like to have your Mommy shoot you in the gut, on assignment. Trust me, he's brilliant when it comes to the computer and world communication networks, but the man's got serious family-emotional issues and Mattie Curran's at the core of them.

Oh, did you know that Daniel D'Loup's got a real yen for his partner? Yeah. Rhys doesn't seem to know---I mean, you'd think he'd notice some crazy shit like this, right? Him being malakh and so naturally seduction-aware.

It's me and Daniel and Rhys with Dante, at the table in the kitchen. Rhys isn't really at the table; he's playing in the floor with his son, Gabe. We've managed to get a lot of work done, considering the limit on time. When he came in with Gabe, Rhys said that Mattie was gonna pick up their son in a little while and then he told us about the coffeehouse and the band they heard play. Normally, Rhys isn't a talkative person---it takes something big to get Rhys into a talky mood---but when it comes to Gabe, Perseus Shadow's old rules no longer apply.

How did I know about Daniel? Well, I know the look of real, painful love and...I know they're not lovers. At least, I believe that's one of the things Rhys wouldn't keep silent. Besides, he's never said anything about any kinda attraction to Daniel, so I have to believe that Daniel's keeping it to himself---this big, dark secret love.

Poor guy.

Dante Webster, whose real first name was Alan---Dante's his middle name, his dad was a fan of Alighieri---sat at the old wooden trestle table with a cup of lukewarm coffee at one elbow and an ashtray at the other.   A lit cigarette hung from his sexy-soft bottom lip, streaming wispy bluish smoke in what could almost be a voudoun pattern of prayer, as he rattled away on his laptop's keyboard.

The hacker's hair, she noticed, had gotten a trim sometime today, while she was out running like crazy. He had the look of a fifties movie star. Clipped short in the back and on the sides and kinda longish on the top, showing the little waves as the front fell out of place and onto Dante's forehead. Right at the top of his glasses. He had one eye squinted half-shut, against the smoke, as he blew foggy poison into the air from his nostrils.

In a snug tee-shirt and baggy jeans and hiking boots, her friend looked like any freshman college kid she'd ever seen, except...he was a decade too old to be doing college in the fresh way. But, the whole thing just reminded her all over again of what she'd thought, the first time they'd met. He was one of the best guys she knew---one of the most honorable. And he was awesome, to watch, when in gear for cyberwork.

Tennyson lifted a spoonful of pie to her open mouth and savored the taste of crumbling cinnamon-sugar as it melted into the gooey-crisp apple. She wasn't sure who'd made the pie, but damn. It was like something out of a fine restaurant. Better than all that? Daniel had dribbled Southern Comfort over the ice-cream, to give it a bourbon glaze. As she enjoyed the treat, she watched and listened. Dante and Daniel were discussing the wherefores of her papers, the necessary elements for her trip out of the country.

"And you're sure you don't have a middle name?" It was directed at her; Dante was looking up over the edge of his wire-framed Ben Franklin glasses. His hazel eyes were full of serious thought. "Most people have one. Anybody who checks your passport might think it's kinda odd if you don't. They'll look closer."

She shook her head, wiping a thumb over her lower lip before gasping around a bite of the pie. "No, my mom didn't give me a middle name. Just Tennyson Beaulieu. I mean, if I gotta have one, I use..." Could she tell them about Ashwin? It seemed so private, the hidden connection to her father. "Well, it's a word I saw written down, when I was a kid. I don't know where it came from, just a name." Deep breath. "Ashwin. Tennyson Ashwin Beaulieu."

It was Daniel who reacted; the malakh's dark eyes swelled and then went narrow with an odd expression of thought. As if he was trying to read her mind and couldn't get through the bone. But, that was ridiculous---Daniel wasn't the kinda malakh who could do things like that. Was he? He seemed suddenly very interested in her; he leaned closer, over the table's end.

"Ashwin, chere? Where did you read this name?"

She startled, almost drawing back from him as Daniel reached out to touch her wrist with his huge hand.   Before she could answer, a shriek of laughter from the floor caused everyone's focus to shift and swing over to the pair of malakh who wrestled on the rag-woven rugs. Rhys gave a growl and Gabe giggled, tackling the knobby-slender man who opened both arms to the fierce little toddler. Together, father and son tumbled back; Rhys had the little boy wrapped up snug in his grasp---her friend wore a delicious grin, obviously enjoying this chance to make his son happy.

The hand on her wrist tightened and she jerked her attention back to the dark-haired Suisse malakh who was demanding an answer. Daniel's dark eyes were unflinching and almost cold---and she had a feeling, in that moment, that he could kill anyone---even his own kids---if he was contracted for it. Her heart lurched several moments before she got a grip on it and leveled a returning fire of cool appraisal for the youthful assassin.

With her brows raised in askance, she was soft-spoken, showing just what she'd learned from Rhys and Valeska both. "Why do you want to know, Sword of Death?"

Daniel's face changed quickly and the malakh laughed, roaring with pleasure. The grip on her wrist slipped down to caress her fingers, as if they were more than just semi-friends. He sounded highly bemused. "These things are not important, ma petit. As you know, curiosity killed the cat."

"Yeah, but for a while, I was a suspect." Rhys' voice, coming from below the table, was sleek and drowsy, as if he was sated.

She glanced at him, peeking under the edge of the weathered table. Rhys was laying flat on his back, on the rugs, Gabe in his arms. The toddler was splayed out, arms and legs wrapped around the long, slender body of her malakh friend. They looked comfy together, father and son. Rhys with his light brown hair and blue eyes and olive-toned skin and high cheekbones, and sturdily built Gabe with his strawberry-blonde curls and nutmeg freckles and softly pale eyes---a mix of tan and gray with blue---and cupid's bow lips the color of ripe cherries.

Of course, anyone who knew Rhys' reputation as Perseus Shadow would never believe the guy could be so in love with a little kid---so devoted to a baby---but then they wouldn't have a clue as to why the malakh had wanted this boy to be born in the first place. She knew, though. Rhys had a deep-seated need for family that he kept hidden most of the time---it was something that had developed in the ten years since he started to work with Daniel. She'd heard some of the story, anyway, but she wasn't sure of how much to believe.

Rhys' eyes moved to the side and he studied her in the quiet---the only sound was Dante's keyboard clicking away. Then, her friend's lids slid closed and he smiled, showing a hint of his white teeth. His large-knuckled, skinny hands seemed to hug Gabe even tighter, as if he feared some unknown element would snatch his son away.

As if Rhys *could* show fear.

When she finally met Daniel's gaze, she realized...the questions raised by her so-called middle name were still very much on the Suisse malakh's mind, but he wasn't gonna pry and ask about it. Not when Dante and Rhys were listening. But, she knew...the sitch wasn't finished. She'd have to answer him, eventually. It was there, in the small, dangerous smile he now gave her.

"Okay...you have the proper auths." Dante sat back and lifted his cup of coffee for a drink, pausing to take the cigarette from his mouth. He looked pleased with himself. "All of this'll pass inspection by any agency in the world. According to your papers, you've had a passport for the last two years and you've got all the necessary shots and medical exams for travel in any country."

"But---" She frowned, focusing on him as she set the fork down on her saucer. "I don't have the shots or the medical. What if I get some whacked-out disease---"

"You'll have the right shots for travel in Egypt...for anywhere in the Middle East." Rhys cut in, interrupting; he sat up, now, still holding Gabe on his lap. "As soon as Mattie gets here. She's supposed to be bringing the stuff for both of us."

"What about Daniel?" Tennyson asked, still serious, looking from one man to another.

"Oh, Cookie, don't you be worrying about the big guy." Dante grinned, poking the tip of his tongue out with a crooked grin. "The benu don't need immunizations. That's just for us, the ones who can die from malaria and dysentery and cholera and SARS and AIDS."

"Tchatchau, sakau, saihu, sa-hekau, hekau, husa-hekau, asetau..." Rhys whispered to Gabe, naming several of the different, mortal malakh breeds. "And don't forget the humans."

From under her brows, she shifted her gaze to study the brawny malakh who sat at the end of the table with his eyes closed, a study in contemplative silence. Daniel's jaw was stubbled, sable-dark hair tugged smoothly back into a knot at his nape; he was the closest thing to a living immortal that she'd ever met.

And her safety was in his hands, in the hands of a malakh she wasn't so sure about.

She tried to smile and it came out lopsided.

Chapter Sixteen

The air was chilled, but the dusk felt right. The slowly rising fog was a promise.
Nicolai Valeska stepped out onto the sidewalk and slid his shades on, smiling to himself.
He was a god tonight, a pagan idol.

He'd chosen to wear his favorite jacket, leather with zippers and silver fobs over a skin-snug Lycra shirt the color of cooling blood. Leather trousers hugged his hips and protected his legs. Black Timberlands offered the same definitive protection for his feet. He had hours before he needed to show up at Pandora's Box. Joseph was going to gather files for Misha and that could take some time. Time *he* needed, to be the hunter.

He hummed a Los Lobos tune to himself, running a finger down the concrete and steel wall of the building. *'Someday. I will go home. Someday. I will go home. And I'll find peace in the house of my heavenly father. And I will feel pain no more. I...I know. Down in my heart. I know. It won't be long. Til I shall see the face of my savior. And I will feel...I will feel...I will feel pain no more.'*

Nicolai set off up the street, headed towards the Quarter. He needed to hunt. He needed to find sweet-skinned mortals drunk and stoned and insensible to the danger of human-faced predators. The town was his, thanks to how meticulously Joseph cleaned up. Only a very few vampires dared to step foot in New Orleans, thanks to his Sire, and they didn't come down to the Vieux Carre.

To do so meant true death.

If other Undead knew the truth about Snowden---a legend among the bloodsuckers of the world---they probably wouldn't fear him nearly as much. And that would just mean more hunts for his lover. Joseph was a pussy queen, a bottom pretending to be a top---or maybe it was the other way around. He wasn't always so sure.

'Someday. I will go home. Someday. I will go home. And I shall take the hand of my savior. I will feel...I will feel...I will feel pain no more. I...I will feel...I will feel...pain no more. Coming home, come home, ah, coming home.'

He needed to hunt. Only, he'd love to have his tchatcha friend with him. But, Rhys Lorraine had told him on the phone that he had things to take care of---that they'd see each other at the club later tonight. A damn shame. He'd wanted to hunt with Rhys as his witness. Something in hunting humans always felt more exciting when he was being watched by the blue-eyed malakh assassin.

Once he reached Canal Street, he opened his vampire instincts. It was still the Mardi Gras season and the tourists filled every street of the Quarter all hours of the day. It was never hard to find prey, in such circumstances. Booze or drugs or lust always led the willing to him. And with so many possibilities, he didn't have to drink too much from one. He could space them out, take a little from here and a little from there. Hit every walk of life, so to speak.

He started down Bourbon, carefully watching the roving crowds. College kids, clubs on vacation, fraternities and sororities on a different sort of hunt. Old, young, middle-ground. Very few children...but, of course, this was the evening and children would put a damper on celebrations. One couldn't drag children into bars and saloons anymore. There were laws against such things. Such a shame. He craved children's blood, with its pure adrenaline and its promise of love and hope. And he was always careful to not kill them these days. Children were beautiful and holy.

He found a lone blues singer underneath a balcony's canopy on the edge of Toulouse.

He stopped to listen with a crowd of warm-blooded humans. One man with guitar and a blue Maxwell Coffee can. White-haired, pale enough to be a vampire. An albino. Clean-cut and handsome, the man's voice was rough and sweet at the same time. He was bouncing both feet on the brick sidewalk in time with his playing, providing some percussion. The guitar was an acoustic instrument that had been turned into an electric---the amp sat off to the left. On the amp sat a big Styrofoam cup full of beer.

He wanted this one---the albino. He loved the taste of music in blood.

"I tied my bandana took my pack from the floor. You were still sleeping as I stood at the door. Once more I was headin' to God only knows where. That's when it hit me I was already there."

The music had slid into a bluesy country song by Waylon Jennings and he smiled to himself, not moving among the humans who murmured and whispered about the talented guitarist. Someone muttered that the albino was blind and he studied the blues singer hard, considering it with his head tilted to the side. Yes, the albino was blind---or mostly so---and had lovely, pale honey-brown eyes.

"I could ramble a thousand miles or more. Never find the light I've seen in your eyes before. You gave me the freedom to go on my way. But you gave me much more, you gave me the freedom to stay."

Black dress shirt and tight jeans and black boots. And a black leather drover's hat on his short, white hair. The man was handsome and more---he was sexy in the way only a soulful boy could be. What would it take to draw the guitarist away from this corner and the balcony's black-striped canopy? What would it take to get the albino down a dark alley and into his arms? Something told him---scent or instinct or both---that the bluesman wasn't homo. This one had a wife and kids, probably----he had a wedding band on his left side, third finger. Plain gold, gleaming softly in the streetlight's halogen glare.

"Why keep on runnin' just to wish on a star. Searching for Heaven when I know where you are. Life is just empty when you're walking alone. So wherever we're going girl, Lord, it's good to be at home."

But, still. Could he do this? Use music as the aphrodisiac that might snare the albino for him? He wouldn't kill this one. No, just a drink---just a mug's full. Enough to make him gleam inside with life and heat and music. Enough to make the prey dizzy and high with blood loss.

"I could ramble a thousand miles or more. Never find the light I've seen in your eyes before. You gave me the freedom to go on my way. But you gave me much more, you gave me the freedom to stay."

Patiently, he stood and waited. The crowd departed, one by one, and were replaced, one by one, by others. The blues was replaced by country classics, such as Johnny Cash and Willie Nelson and, yes, Waylon Jennings. The songs went from *'City of New Orleans'* to *'Blue Eyes Crying in the Rain'*. The beer in the Styrofoam cup disappeared in between tunes and he steadily stayed and watched, enjoying the chance to see and hear a virtuoso. The albino was a real talent.

Then, a young woman stepped up behind the albino; she was about the same height as Tennyson Beaulieu, but with a white scarf tied snugly over her head. She wore baggy carpenter jeans and an oversized men's white dress shirt unbuttoned over a dark blue wifebeater.

She was skinny---the kind of skinny that spoke of illness---with dark circles under her eyes. He'd seen healthier corpses. On her feet were sandals---brave against the chilly weather. She had lovely eyes, dark brown, almost hidden behind wire framed glasses, and she owned a gentle smile for the albino. They were friends, obviously. She used a pitcher to refill the cup. It was in between songs and the guitarist grabbed her hand, speaking softly in a true, southern way. Tennessee or Kentucky, perhaps.

"Stay and sing, Alvie---" The albino grinned, addressing the small crowd with his country-fried voice. "We're gonna do two more songs and then take a break. But, we'll be back. This is Alvie. She's gonna sing with me."

It wasn't much of an introduction and the young woman blushed. She put the pitcher down on the amp and smoothed a hand over her cotton flour-sack scarf. She had the same look about her features as Misha---the straight brows and high cheekbones, strong jaw and lush mouth. Her teeth were even and white and pretty when she smiled nervously.

The guitar started again and the crowd stirred. It was a Johnny Cash and June Carter number. Nicolai grimaced mildly. He wasn't a fan and, time spent listening to music with Rhys, had educated him to this. But, he was determined to get the albino alone---more determined than before.

The two sang together wonderfully, though. The young woman named Alvie had a rough-edged bluesy voice that suited the song well. The people gathered on the sidewalk clapped in time to the music that spangled its way through the guitar and out of the amp. The song was a classic country piece that even he could recognize---especially since his tchatcha friend had played it often on the stereo.

One song went into another and he waited. At last, the two duets were over and the albino put the guitar down, sliding it into a black hard-side case. It wouldn't be messed with here, not with the woman watching over it. The crowd was dispersing and soon, he was the only one left standing before the microphone and the amp. The skinny, young woman named Alvie sat down in the chair her albino friend had vacated, taking a sip of beer.

She spoke softly to the albino. "The can's almost full, Jay. You want me to cash it out at the bar?"

"Yeah, that'd be fine." The albino sounded distracted, packing things up with slow movements. The mark of a blind guitarist. "Is there someone---"

Alvie looked up and met his gaze, her lovely brown eyes solemn as she studied him over the rim of her glasses. She nodded, answering Jay. "Yeah. Not the usual."

They were odd, as if they'd stepped out of their own time and place. He had the feeling, the way this woman watched him, that she knew what he was. That she had some idea of what lurked in the world outside the gaze of ordinary mortals.

"I'm a musician. Too." He dared, stepping closer. He drew his cigarettes out, lighting one. "I was passing by and heard the music. You're very talented...both of you."

Alvie nodded, tilting her head to the side as she studied him from behind her spectacles. She was freckled and yet tawny, as if her ancestors might include a Native American bloodline. So Appalachian, both of them, the albino and his under-weighted female friend. Her voice was hoarse and husky, very contra-alto, like Tennyson's. "What do you play? Music-wise."

"Violin and piano." He admitted, taking a deep drag of his cigarette. He pulled his shades off, pushing them into his hair and out of the way.

"Me, too. Violin. And cello. And just a little guitar. But I won't shame myself by opening the case in front of Jay---my voice is instrument enough, with him." Alvie gave him a wanly crooked smile, shifting in the straight-back chair to glance at her guitarist. "Jay, if you want, I'll take this stuff into the bar. I think we got someone to talk with for a minute. Let's go get a little Beam and another pitcher."

"My treat." Nicolai offered, giving the two musicians one of his most seductive smiles. "I would love to talk with you. Music has been the biggest part of my life. It's fantastic when I find talent in the Quarter."

He helped them carry the equipment into the dimly lit bar. It was a tiny honky-tonk and he quickly discerned that they were sharing the apartment above its smoky interior. In fact, the balcony they'd been singing under was part of said apartment. After a few shots of Jim Beam, Alvie told him it wasn't easy, finding a life in New Orleans. She and Jay had come down from 'up-north', found the apartment and day-jobs, and then needed to make money on the side. They performed in a couple of local clubs, but made almost as much by performing on the street.

The albino was straight and separated from his wife and son. Alvie was divorced and had left her own children with her mother back home. But, she wasn't exactly straight. It was in her voice, in her mannerisms---she was bi-sexual or maybe a complete lesbian. But disdainful of labels.

"I am what I am. Nothing more, nothing less. Jay's my closest friend and...I guess he's more. He does IT work and I do construction. We make good money, but most of it goes home to our families. Gotta feed our kids. You know?"

It was nearly a half hour before he got his chance at one of them. Alvie went to the WC and he followed, excusing himself from their table as the jukebox started playing again, this time a bluesy-boozy N'awlins folk song. He eased his way into the narrow, cinnamon-scented room---so like a coffin in its wood-paneled closeness. There, he smiled at the skinny woman in her white flour-sack scarf, who sang along softly with the music floating through the air.

"Yesterday, I had a dream I could fly through the sky. Then I woke up in a sweat, not dead yet, but on the ground. I'm up in Johnson City, Tennessee, looking for the we in me. Lord, fly me over Pontchartrain, back to the land of sugar cane and summer rain. Nevermore shall we part. Nevermore shall we part."

She was taking down her trousers and didn't seem the bit surprised to see him.

"Kinda wondered how long we'd get to last here before something found us." She gave him a wry, knowing smile. "Thought it was odd that I hadn't seen any yet."

"Any what, sweetheart?" He leaned on the WC door and folded his arms against the front of his motorcycle jacket, smiling back in his most charming manner.

"Demons, vamps..." Alvie had managed the button of her trousers and now let them drop to the floor as she straddled the toilet. She didn't seem the least put-out about urinating in front of him. "I bet you spotted Jay and automatically just homed in on him. You didn't think he was protected, so you thought...easy meal. Maybe not the whole death feast, but enough to fill your belly and your veins. Enough to give you a taste of the good stuff that runs in him. The music."

That startled him. The realization that this little, sickly-looking woman realized what he was and wasn't the least bit shocked or scared. He pulled his head up from the door a few inches and sneered, defensively. "Yeah? Well, it'd have to be your pale boyfriend, wouldn't it? You're not exactly the most appetizing thing I've seen tonight, bitch. You look like death barely warmed over."

Alvie was pissing and she gave a low, murmuring chuckle as she reached for the thin toilet paper on its spindle. Her tone didn't change, didn't become anything but the bemusement she'd shown him so far. "From what I've been told about my kind, from the time I was just a little shit at my grandma's knee...our blood could poison you, if it's taken without our consent. It would be like drinking quicksilver. And I'm telling you, Mister Valeska, you don't want none of Jay neither."

"Why not?"

"Because, if you lay a hand on what's mine, I'll send you home in a coffee can." She wiped herself and dropped the paper in the toilet, straightening up. She started doing the button of her trousers again. He noticed, off-hand, that she didn't wear any under things. And something in her tone, in her nonchalant attitude, made him think of Rhys Lorraine.

"You're mortal." He made his hands, under his arms, into fists, and studied her closer as she whispered a line of the song that was still playing outside in the bar.

"And she cried cause her gold was gone and she cried cause she was all along and I'm hunting with a lonely heart, crying nevermore shall we part...shall we part."

Could she be more than mortal? Malakh, perhaps?

"So? I'm a witch. From a long line of witches. The kind that do serious hoodoo." Alvie was still smiling at him, her brown eyes crinkled into slits of genuine amusement as she approached him. There was no fear of him; she either believed she had an ace up her sleeve or could manipulate the way her body reacted outwardly. "I'm not a vicious woman by nature. I prefer to let things live in peace. But, I'm telling you now. You lay a hand on even so much as one white hair of my boy's head, and I'll make sure your last thought on earth is about just how damn sorry you are. They'll be hearing your screams from one side of this town to the other."

She stood directly in front of him, still wearing that damnable smile and within reach of his hand. If he dared to touch her. Something prickled in his spine---in his skin---warning him that it wouldn't be a good idea to try. She was sickly, but she was made of more than flesh and bone and blood.

Her hands were lax, pushed into the pockets of her carpenter pants. The front of her scarf had slipped a little, revealing that she was bald under the snowy white flour-sack. He hadn't noticed that before. It looked freshly shaven or naturally bald. Cancer, maybe? The contrast of dark blue wifebeater and white dress shirt drew his attention. And then he focused on her face with its odd, ancient-seeming wisdom.

'And all those words I never said gently bled from my mouth, and I am ready to embrace this place where I belong. I am afraid I need to love. If I don't, I'm gonna flood. And I'm calling to you in the dark, just a hunter with a lonely heart. A lonely heart.'

She looked older than her physical appearance had let on, before. She was maybe thirty years old, but there was something in her eyes, in her smile. She wasn't benu malakh---she didn't have the scent. She wasn't completely human, though. Something in her smell gave it away, now that she was sweating.

And she was...sweating. A fine perspiration lay against her flat, seamless brow and the puckered curve of her upper lip. The scent made him think of unripe olives and black iron and deep waters---waters so deep and so icy and treacherous. It brought an image of a stone-lined well covered in moss and lichen and offering sweetness with a single taste. That was what she seemed to be---a well old and eternal and full of coldness. She could offer such sustenance with the water of her soul, but to fall into the dark was a drowning even benu malakh wouldn't survive.

She made him think of someone...someone besides Tennyson or Rhys.

Someone with true, brutal self-control.

Someone capable of real and calculated evil, yet with such love and devotion to offer.

Staring into her dark chocolate brown eyes with their dark lashes, it came to him.

Mattie Curran. Mathilda the Golden Wolf.

"I'm hungry." He began, taking a deep and unneeded breath. He unfolded his arms, loosened his fists. Reaching out gently, he touched the curve of her cheekbone---the bones were chiseled and sharp, like Mattie's. She didn't pull back from the touch. And he felt a strange zing of electricity between them---static shock and yet more, like a live current. "I love the music I sense in you. In your friend. It's what drew me. I wouldn't kill either of you. I want your music to go on. Why would I kill music? When it's such a part of me? When I was alive, music was my life. I lived to dance and sing and play my violin. All I want is a taste of that music. Something to keep me warm tonight, while I go hunting for something more worthy of death."

"So...you hunt the evil ones, mortal and demon." She breathed the words, her smile relaxing into something more pleasant and forgiving. "You've had a good teacher, then. I feel that in you, in the way your mind works. You're telling the truth. And, so, if that's the way of your hunt, maybe I can help you. Let's make a deal."

"Anything. Oh, god, anything for a chance to worship the music in your veins." More than the albino, he wanted this one. She had such power in her blood and he could feel it in the zing. She offered knowledge that no immortal could possess. She was a warrior who truly understood the battle and didn't own any fear, only determination. She knew death and sickness and the real expense of survival. That was where her music came from. "Name your price, woman...if it's mine to give you, to help you, then I'll give you the things you want most."

Alvie let him pull away her scarf. Under it, her head gleamed under the dim lights of the WC. She seemed so vulnerable, so naked. So fragile, even with the glittering spectacles she wore. She was dying and it was there, between them in the silence. She didn't fear death, but to fall in battle was more than her strong spirit could bear. This woman possessed too much heart to simply die; for her, the battle was what she loved.

She whispered, her smile grown soft. "I think you know what I need most."

He did. He knew. And it was unforgivably delicious.

As he sorted the false clues into their appropriate piles on the Moroccan rug, kneeling among them like the supplicant he truly was, Joseph let himself drift back to the year he'd brought Nicolai into his world---driving the first real wedge between himself and Misha.

The world was in an uproar, but still Spain and Italy were relatively quiet...if one stayed out of the way of the conflicting governments. The years blended together for him as he traveled back and forth, making money. Madrid and then Morocco and then Cairo, then back to Rome for six months. All points in between were in his travel diary. He had taken boats to England and Scotland, too. But, in these years, he stayed out of France; revolution was a messy business and he wasn't lusting after Madame Guillotine.

History was being made around him, in all quarters, and he was only concerned for his own business and the money he gathered as protection against the mortals and against poverty. Never again would he and Misha have to worry about hunger or existing without a home where they could lay their head. In the world before an acceptance of science, the Church had ruled and superstition could get a blood-drinker killed. Science disproved their existence; they were made safe and became more capable of walking among their prey without fear of discovery.

He had imported and exported, carrying items from the West to the East and from the East to the West. There was good money to be made in caravans and merchantdom. Money padded his world, made it safer to exist Undead. Made easier his studies and his search. If he killed the wrong person in his need for sustenance, money solved the danger...for the most part. If he was a little too eager in his pursuit for entertainment and allowed some small smidge of darkness to show---how he loved to take his prey apart before feeding!---money could smooth ruffled feathers.

True to his nature, having existed so long, he was a master of disguising himself. He moved through the world as a merchant in the robes and burqa of the desert-dwellers, an Israelite trader. He owned a herd of horses and camels and donkeys to carry his goods, including his quiet trade in slaves. He had a reputation for his slaves---only the best and strongest and most talented. Misha disapproved, but she stayed in Rome half the year, continuing their bookish search for the chosen one. The Lion, the Guardian of the Living, the Protector. al-Mahdi.

When he took Nicolai Valeska into slavery, things changed. He had thought to simply buy the gypsy and take him to Cairo, where he could surely find a buyer for such a talented musician. Leaving Spain, his caravan had crossed the waters to Morocco and then started the long desert trip through the north of Africa. He'd had no choice but to chain the Russian-born Rom, for it was a given fact that gypsies couldn't be allowed to roam free in slavery. Yet, he'd been careful to treat the boy good; a prize such as Nicolai Valeska could fetch a hefty price.

In Cairo, he'd dressed the gypsy boy in silks from the Orient and jasper, to offset Nicolai's dark beauty. But, in waiting for his effluent buyers to arrive, he'd watched the expensively appointed Rom slave and made a decision that changed the course of his unlife. He had decided that he must keep Nicolai Valeska for himself. He'd never purchased a slave, had never considered a need for one. Mortals were not to be trusted, where the safety of his unlife was concerned. Could he dare to trust a mortal with Misha's safety?

He took Nicolai home to his villa in Rome as a gift to his wife. This was meant as something more corporeal than the books she'd asked him to buy. Misha had, at the time, a great love of deep-thinking poets and philosophers and had discovered the works of William Blake. She had managed to purchase copies of that man's every book in the very year it was put out for sale in the market stalls.

When he presented Nicolai Valeska to her, the gypsy was carrying the vellum-wrapped copies of *'Visions of the Daughters of Albion'* and *'America a Prophecy'*, and *'For Children:*

The Gates of Paradise', all published within that year. A marvelous gift, he believed.

Misha hadn't seen the situation in quite the same way.

'Your faith was strong but you needed proof. You saw her bathing on the roof. Her beauty and the moonlight overthrew you. She tied you to a kitchen chair. She broke your throne, and she cut your hair. And from your lips she drew the Hallelujah.'

He smiled to himself as he hummed along with the Rufus Wainwright music coming from the stereo; a Leonard Cohen song, bittersweet and dark. No, Misha hadn't appreciated his gift. The fighting had led to him committing a great sin against her---to enforce his will upon the situation, he declared that he would not touch his wife again until she had learned to love the gypsy boy he'd given to her.

'Love is not a victory march...it's a cold and it's a broken hallelujah.'

To push the matter along---it was not amusement he was seeking---he'd ordered them to bed down together. He'd watched as Nicolai pleasured his bride, the seeds of a hot and vile hate taking root in his spirit and his mind. He had forced himself to continue watching; as long as Misha could hold out stubborn, he would shame them both.

Now, looking back on it, perhaps he should have explained the situation to her. Slavery, to his mind, was not what more modern minds would make of it. True, he had sold people into slavery where only death awaited them, but he was not responsible for the ends those unfortunates found. In the time and place of his youth, his breathing life, slaves could own property and often did.

Had he not been the born slave of some Knight before being sent to the Temple's stables?

'And it's not a cry you can hear at night. It's not somebody whose seen the light. It's a cold and it's a broken hallelujah.'

His wife had not seen the matter with such understanding. She had believed he would treat Nicolai, sooner or later, with the same indifference and disdain that often found slaves. Then, as time wore on, through five years, she'd realized the truth. He could never treat the gypsy with indifference---for he had fallen in love. Obsessive, mad love.

He could still hear her argument. The argument they'd had, the first night.

'What in the name of all that is holy possessed you to take a slave? Did you think we needed one?'

'It's his music, Misha. Music like his, you don't find but once in a century---if that often.'

'What? You want to---'

'No, of course not! And he won't be a true slave. He'll have a place here with us. A member of our house and hold. A part of our world. Of course, he won't be able to wander away---'

'How do you think to stop him? Joseph, he's a gypsy. You can't put gypsy boys in a pen and treat them like pets. It would be cruel, to say nothing of impossible.'

'You're being foolish, Misha. He's mortal. You've eaten a thousand like him.'

It was his own fault, falling in love with the gypsy boy.

Joseph sat down flat on the rug now, studying the pile of papers he'd assembled. He lit a cigarette and pulled the communion plate to his side, lost in thought as he leafed through the false clues. These were all angles he'd followed and discovered to be untrue, but only in the last two centuries. Only since Misha had left, in Rome. He could give her *nothing* that she might have already seen, among his scrolls and books.

Nothing that they'd already searched, together.

How odd...he wanted to believe Mishenka was right, that she could find a cure for vampirism in the dusty scrolls found in some sarcophagus. Yet, he could never hand over the Sang-rael...not for anything in the world. Not even if Tennyson Beaulieu's blood possessed a magic component that could fix any disease. How could he care so much for a mortal? Even one such as the Lion, returning?

After so many centuries, *how*...?

Leaning back on his elbows, relaxed on the rug among his files and scrolls and books, Joseph let the smoke curl lazily from his nose as he now whispered along with the stereo, the music echoing his heart. "Love is not a victory march, it's a cold and it's a broken hallelujah..."

Chapter Seventeen

'In the lonely night, in the stardust of a pale moonlight, I think of you in black and white. When we were made of dreams. I walked alone through the shaky streets, listening to my heart beat in the record-breaking heat. When we were born in time.'

The blues music was a remake by Eric Clapton as they followed the matre'd through the restaurant on Rue Bienville and Bourbon. Apparently, Joseph wanted only the best and had arranged a private area for this meeting. Every room they passed through or glimpsed was incongruously lovely and sanitary and decadent all at the same time.

She had chosen a different approach to the evening's meeting.

'Just when I thought you were gone, you came back. Just when I was ready to receive you. You were smooth, you were rough, you were more than enough. Ah babe, why did I ever leave you...or believe you? In the rising curve, where the ways of nature will test every nerve, I took you close and got what I deserve. When we were born in time.'

She knew Joseph well enough to recognize the disadvantage; she knew nothing of this man she was here to meet and yet he, the stranger, would naturally have been *carefully* informed of her. So, she had chosen to change some of the rules of their game. She could very well imagine what Joseph might have told the stranger about her---the ins and outs of her behavior and dress and mannerisms. He thought of her as a high-toned wallflower.

'In the hills of mystery, in the foggy web of destiny, you're still so deep inside of me. When we were born in time.'

The first rule to change---she couldn't dress as if going to work at the Museum or to a research conference dinner. This was America and, sadly enough, stereotypical American men were dazzled by European women who dressed like mysterious bombshells. She'd decided on a dark crimson sheath dress with no straps and barely enough stretching chenille to cover her womanly curves. It cut low at her breasts and fit seamlessly over every curve of her body all the way to its end mid-thigh. In the middle of the back, a few inches from the top, the material gave way to a perfect circle that covered nearly all of her lower back, including the very uppermost swell and dip of her backside.

With this, she'd chosen to wear a gold torc collar and wrist cuffs in the ancient Greek style, along with a band on her upper arm. They were a gift from Uly. They offset the color of her skin after she'd fed. The wrist cuffs were carved and formed to resemble Ionic temple column edging---as was the band on her upper right arm. The torc on her throat was a plain gold band with carved oak leaf and acorn end caps.

She had carefully wrapped her hair up and away from her head in the ancient Greek style, tying it with braids and pieces of tiny gold chain, leaving loose only a few strands at her ears and throat. But, instead of going with sandals, she'd worn four inch heels in black--- which matched the wrap she wore. The wrap was velvet and black wolf fur and it flowed around her body in a gorgeous contrast to the slinky sheath.

As she walked through the restaurant, she felt the eyes on her. Men and women alike were admiring, both openly and covert. Both jealous and simply pleased. She held her head high and kept pace behind the matre'd with the light step of a runway model that she'd trained herself to use. Here, she couldn't be the scholar or the green-thumb homebody; she had to carry off elegance at the *first* glance. And she'd made sure that Uly Ithaca followed suit, to compliment her as escort and companion.

And he did. He was a very tall, lean man with powerful shoulders and raven-dark hair. She knew that he must have cut a *terrible*, lovely figure in his youth---when his name had first gained attention. But, tonight, he looked like a runway model, too---hot stud straight off the pages of GQ.

He wore Prada and wore it well. No tie, but with his long hair hanging loose upon his shoulders and his careless stubble, it only made him look more ruggedly beautiful. And he was. In the way that only a prince could. His London Fog overcoat only made it more so, with the regal connotations that piece of clothing could confer.

He moved behind, deferring to her as if it was *she* born of ancient royalty. His hand was never very far from her elbow and she appreciated his subtle concerns. This was more than a meeting, despite the lack of information to its center---this was, in fact, a form of battle. With Joseph. The man they were here to meet would carry back all the truths and hints of what could be gleaned from appearance and behavior and decorum and conversation.

She had wanted to come to this meeting alone, to keep Joseph from getting even a whisper of Uly's presence. But, Uly saw it in a different way. He was growing weary of shadows and subterfuge. He had told her very plainly---he did not care if Joseph was her husband and had been so for nearly all of her existence. Joseph had chosen to throw her to the side for a heathen catamite---if he himself chose to love her, to stand as her consort, then it was most certainly *none* of Joseph Snowden's business. A marriage broken was a marriage broken and none of them could be held to the morals and rituals of mortal life. Uly himself had been married, of course, and he'd loved his wife, but Pene was dead---had been dead for thousands of years. There was no point in holding onto the dead, he claimed, for they most certainly didn't hold onto the living.

The matre'd led them to a quiet grotto room where the curtains were burgundy and revealed a table set for four. It was obviously big enough for eight. Four white pillar candles sat in the center on brass holders, cornered by eight clear shallow glass bowls which held floating gardenias. The chairs were upholstered and comfortable-looking and there was a painting on the back wall---a painting of Bacchus, god of the grape. It was *more* than suitable, she believed, looking at the private room.

The matre'd pulled back a chair for her and she sat, graciously, and allowed him to push her closer to the table. Uly faced the man, near the curtain, and spoke, his tone casual and easy. "If you please, we will have the wine list."

This was obeyed and soon, they sat together, sipping at wine and discussing the departments they worked within, at the Museum. This led to a mutual amusement concerning certain members of the staff who knew of malakh and who were aware of them---Doctor Ithaca and Doctor Ben-Moshe. None had ever been disabused of the notion that Misha was the same kind of creature as Uly, but that honestly didn't matter. The amusement came from a situation which had happened two months previously, when a few of the most junior staff members finally became aware of malakh...and the knowledge of 'proof' in two senior staff members they admired.

It always happened---the intrigue eventually conquered even the most staid professors and doctors. Someone would let it slip to the junior staff and then she might find herself being watched by wide-eyed innocents who were unwilling to voice their surprise and curiosity. It was the same for Uly. In this case, a young trio of junior professors had started watching Uly, after being informed of the myth-turned-reality. All of this was kept secret, of course; no member of the staff would ever break the oath of silent protection that came with knowledge of malakh. Who in the wide world beyond anthropology and esoteric history would believe such creatures existed?

"Do you think they're sexually curious, as well?" She asked her lover, sipping at the softly dry chardonnay.

"Naturally." He chuckled, holding his own wine glass by its tender stem. His dark eyes were lit up with humor. "Their scents, every time they come into the room where I work, changes. Both of the boys are caught wriggling like fish between wonder and resentment. And why not? If they've been told the truth, they are aware of the differences between humans and demi-god. The girl, she is much more honest with her interests. I admire that honesty."

"You're going to fuck her, aren't you?" She didn't mind; there was no point in being jealous, at her age, over a man who had seen a few epochs come and go. "If so...I may want to watch."

"You wouldn't join us?" Uly's brows lifted at the laughingly voiced idea.

"Mmm." She mused, giving it very little real thought. "I must think on that. But not tonight, I think."

She became aware of the changing atmosphere before the two men appeared, at the back of the matre'd. Uly did, too; she saw it in his suddenly sharp expression. Scent didn't describe it---two malakh had just entered their personal zone of fifteen feet. Two malakh of differing bloodlines, differing natures. But, it was more than scent. Something with great and frightening power was approaching---something with the nature of a tornado. Something with *killing* power. They grew silent, listening and focusing, their eyes on the open doorway and its curtains.

The scents had changed. Two scents. One, a light temple odor...incense and lilac flowers mixed together. The other, much stronger, was hyacinth laced with green grass...a much more natural, earthy scent, but one that threatened to seduce.

The only sound came from Uly, whose breathing had grown ragged, who now whispered. "There are two of them. It's a demi-benu and...also a husa-hekau, the one whose mind can set reality on its ear with mere thoughts. This one, he is dangerous...he can kill with the storm in his mind. Misha, we are in *danger*..."

"Shh." She murmured, unwilling to panic. In her lap, one hand became a claw. Was this Joseph's game? Did he feel so threatened by her request for information that he was willing to kill her, to protect the secrets of Sang-rael?

The matre'd stepped into view and then...the two, strange malakh were visible to her preternatural gaze.

One, whose temple incense odor was that of a demi-benu malakh, turned out to be a short man with shoulder-length dark hair and dark eyes. His hair was wavy and caught back at the nape of his neck in a simple knot. His coloring was nearly a match for Uly's. He wore Hugo Boss, but it did nothing to hide the odd impression of ethereality. This was the descendant of angels---and he was almost too beautiful to be real. His olive, mulatto skin was clear, his features strong and masculine. He was of mixed races---but, the mix only made him more attractive. He wore a welcoming smile that revealed even, white teeth, and his quick eyes held a wolfish intelligence.

But, it was the other. This, the source of terrible power.

She blinked in surprise at his appearance.

Uly stood up to welcome the two, but, out of shock, she could do no such thing.

The husa-hekau was very tall---as tall as Uly---with a muscular, powerful build. He was auburn-haired, the browns and golds and reds all mingling. His eyes were a pale hazel, green and brown together, and, behind the little square spectacles he wore, they held honesty in the manner of a portrait. Whoever he might be, this stranger was forthright and honest. He was smiling broadly, showing fresh-faced boyish charm with ease. His hair was clipped short in an acceptable fashion, short in the back and longish at both top and sides. He had unusually large hands, which drew her gaze.

He wore a gold earring in his left ear and a navy Brooks Brothers suit.

And a cerulean blue tie.

This was the one she was meant to meet.

"Good evening, gentlemen." Forever the natural diplomat, Uly held out his hand to them both, indicating that they should be at ease. "Strangers met, but well-met...I do hope."

"My name is Doctor Alan Webster." The tall husa-hekau had a West-Coast accent; his voice was musical, in the manner of most malakh. He stepped forward and offered his hand to Uly while nodding to the demi-malakh. "I hope you don't mind, but I had to bring a guest. This is my partner. Julien D'Angelin D'Loup."

"I am Doctor Ulysses Ithaca, sir, and this is Doctor Mishenka Ben-Moshe." Uly took care of the introductions. "Please, do join us. This is perhaps a meeting, but we need not stand on ceremony."

The matre'd untied the burgundy curtains and let them drop, to close the room.

"I feel distinctly out-classed." Taking the seat directly across from her, the dark-haired demi-malakh joked with a cleanly genteel Creole accent. "Here I am, a mere lawyer among doctors who must be all masters of their fields."

A lawyer? Joseph had sent a lawyer to her? Whatever for?

"You're never out-classed, Jules." Doctor Alan Webster gave a wry grin, patting his companion on the arm as they all settled in at the table. "Though I do feel a lot of awe, now that I've had a chance to meet you---both of you." This was aimed at them and the husa-hekau explained without needing the question. "I've read your papers. The ones published, anyway. And I think I agree with the theories you've presented, on the place of malakh in anthropology and history. If you don't mind me saying so, I'm something of a fan."

He'd heard of them...

And wasn't afraid to say so, wasn't afraid to say the world malakh in public.

That was an eye-opener, all by itself.

"Doctor Alan Webster." Uly said the name as if tasting it, his slanted eyes thoughtful as he studied the husa-hekau. "I think I've read something of yours, as well. You are a mathematician. And, if I'm not mistaken, something of a symbologist. You worked for the American government, didn't you? As a code-breaker and computer analyst."

"That would be me." Doctor Webster didn't seem phased; he wasn't arrogant about the notoriety, but didn't seem displeased, either. He was simply *honest*. "I work in the private sector, now. I was very surprised to discover that we have a friend in common, in Joseph Snowden. When he asked me to meet with you, Doctor Ben-Moshe, I wasn't sure what we would have to talk about..."

That made two of them, apparently.

"But, you're a complete surprise altogether." The hazel-eyed malakh continued, solely addressing Uly. "Joe didn't say anything about knowing someone of *your* background. I'm pleased to find you in the company of such a lovely...woman. I've been of the opinion, for some time now, that there must be a way for the two extremes to meet on common ground, malakh and vampire."

It hung there, between the four of them, the truth only half-unspoken. The husa-hekau was aware of what Uly was and had some suspicion as to Uly's true age. He was also very aware of her nature and the only question he had, about it, concerned how she could stay so close to a benu and not feel repelled by the inherent force of life that seeped out of such a malakh.

Neither of these mortals were the least bit surprised by them.

"He's really thrilled to see the two extreme poles in such a pleasant, cordial setting." The short, stocky French-Creole lawyer explained, directing his comment at her in particular. "Don't let him fool you."

"But, why should we not be so cordial?" Uly asked, his tone revealing a hint of darkness that his expression didn't show. "We are what we are. If any should understand my existence, it would be someone such as Misha." He used her nickname casually, showing more of their relationship's truth. "Do you not know any others who can mingle without the bias of life and death?"

"Not really, no." Doctor Webster gave a grin, lifting the wine to help himself, filling two glasses---one for him and one for the lawyer. "We don't know many vampires. Only Joe and Nicolai. And while I like them---they're employed by the same company I work for---the average malakh seems to be unnerved by their presence."

"Average malakh." She said it softly, lifting her glass in a mocking toast. "Now, that is a paradox in terms that I can appreciate. There are entirely too few malakh living in this world and I find them all, the ones I've met, to be distinctly unique as they move along the mortal coil. They are like flashing points of light in a sea of night, to eyes such as mine."

"Poetry." The lawyer grew solemn, impressed as he met her gaze, holding up his own glass. "I think even my papa would fall in love with you, despite your state of being

Undead...and that, madam, is a true compliment, for my papa is a very discerning and prejudiced benu of nearly four centuries."

It really was pleasant, being so open and yet so courtly.

"He must fall to love's blade and adore a mummified crone, then." She demurred, letting the edge of her mouth curl up in a sharp smile. "For I am six hundred and fifty years in my grave."

Doctor Webster caught the riposte and arched a single brow over his spectacles, his expression only made more delightful by the sheaf of auburn hair that lay against his forehead and the cocky smirk he gave. "Ah, so, when this evening is over, I must remember to go by the office and give my compliments to that sullen artist who so easily stopped time's ravages on your corpse."

It was humid, despite the coolness of the early evening breeze. The rain, drizzling down on the busy streets, had brought the fog and the fog caused dew to form in her hair, on her knee-length black suede coat.

Under it, she wore men's herringbone trousers in an oversized charcoal, a men's white dress shirt with the cuffs undone, old leather suspenders to keep everything on her body. The boots she wore had a good tread on them---that was a necessity in a town where the sidewalks went from perfect to nothing but gravel and grass within only a few blocks.

She could smell the food that cooked in nearby shops, could see the artists and their paintings under the halogen street lights, the crowds that flocked to this place---one of the most famous party towns in the world---for a glimpse at the infamous Vieux Carre in the Mardi Gras season. It felt like she'd get crushed---so many people.

'I started as an altar boy working at the church, learning all my holy moves, doing some research. Which led me to a cash box labeled Children's Fund. I'd leave the change and tuck the bills inside my cummerbund.' Tennyson shook her head and adjusted the scarf at her throat and turned a corner, keeping close to the black fence as she quietly hummed a Warren Zevon song. *'I got a part-time job at my father's carpet store. Laying tackless stripping and housewives by the score. I loaded up their furniture and took it to Spokane. Auctioned off every last naugahyde divan. I'm very well acquainted with the seven deadly sins. I keep a busy schedule trying to fit them in. I'm proud to be a glutton and I don't have time for sloth. I'm greedy and I'm angry and I don't care who I cross.'*

She was on Decatur and headed for Madison, passing along the backside of Jackson Square. Jackson Square was to the left of her now, full of paths and trees. It was world-famous, but right now, it was a half-hidden paradise, closed off to the public after dark. With the fog hanging low on the damp ground and the tall black iron fence, it looked like something straight out of a Gothic romance. And...it was probably dangerous, even more dangerous than walking the Quarter after dark. There could be muggers and rapists, which was why the Square was locked at twilight every day.

'Then on to Monte Carlo to play chemin de fer. I threw away the fortune I made transplanting hair. I put my last few francs down on a prostitute who took me up to her room to perform the flag salute. Whereupon I stole her passport and her wig and headed for the airport and the midnight flight, you dig? Fourteen hours later I was down in Adelaide looking through the want ads sipping Foster's in the shade.'

She smiled to herself. She was worrying too much. Walking down the sidewalk in the rising fog, she watched the fence. Her sharp eyes narrowed as she searched the street, watchful for observers; no one was paying any attention---it was Mardi Gras season, nobody cared. She needed to hurry, reach the wild area just ahead, get off the sidewalk, roam down by the river. There was something about getting to walk in the grass, smelling the wet...it was too good.

She watched the fence to her left and the boats visible to her right, where the Mississippi sloshed and slupped against the pylons and the reinforced bank. At last, she stepped off the sidewalk.   Into the fog she walked, her hiking boots making no sound on the wet grass in Woldenberg Park.

It was the riverside blocks south of Jackson Square.   At seven of the evening, there was a quickening veil of dusk in the chilly, damp air.   Why was the caramel-skinned fille here and at this hour?   He had tailed her from the house after the immunizations Golden Wolf had administered.   Tennyson Beaulieu claimed she had things to take care of and he had followed covertly, leaving Rhys to deal with Mattie and Gabe.   By this time, Dante had retreated, as well, claiming he had a date and still needed to get ready.

This fille was utterly breathtaking to watch; in the fog, she moved like a cat, sinewy and lush and with the same natural poise that he had often observed in the old-family Creoles from the Quarter for decades.   The regal grace Tennyson Beaulieu possessed was one he knew by heart; she could turn mundane actions into magic.

Why would she say the name *Ashwin*?   What was that name to her?

It worried at him.

Here, in the south side of the Quarter, behind the cathedral, in a moist and verdantly glorious Eden, they were the only two people on earth---as far as he was concerned.   Despite the season and their location and the passing boats, it was quiet.   To be fair, it was sweetly right to enjoy the fille from a distance; quite often, the mark was leery of being seen in its true shape and Tennyson's true self was revealed through her every action this evening.   She was not the pleasantly smiling human, now---now, in this moment, she was showing him something new, something he had not looked at, before.   Tennyson moved as if she was born to power.

Ashwin.   He wondered if it was *possible* that fate could drop such a thing in his lap.

'The velocity of time turns her voice into sugar water.   I'm on a concrete way.   The wind is blowing to the north-northwest.   It smells like sands of the southern island.   When a black cat crosses my path.   A woman in the moon is singing to the earth.   A woman in the moon is singing to the earth.'

Daniel smiled, staying motionless behind a patch of trees as he watched the fille crouch in her knee-length leather coat and run gloved fingers on the untouched dew.   Here, she left her scent, her mark, a proof that she had passed this way.   She moved on through the fog towards a white-graveled patch, her beaded plaits clicking with a low rhythm; once he knew for certain she would hear nothing of his movements, he silently walked to her left, dozens of yards behind the svelte, voluptuous form of Tennyson Beaulieu.

He kept his eyes on the fille who moved in a panther-slow way through the park towards a new tree line and he wondered what secrets her body carried, in its genes.   Pierre Lorraine and Steven Rose could have discovered the secrets---Pierre, damn him, had possessed Steven's malakh gene charts and no one knew where they had disappeared to, after the project was disbanded---together, they could have told him what this fille was.   Together, they could have told him if she was of malakh blood.

As he narrowed his eyes in consideration, Tennyson gave a laugh...low and murmuring, but he heard the natural charisma in that sound.   She had a sexy laugh; he could not resist another smile as he stepped behind a piece of machinery left upon the concrete dock.

Josiah Rhys Lorraine walked along the sidewalk, thinking about Tennyson.

About the mark on her body.

Elegant black lines forming an impossible sigil on chocolate skin.   Nine points, three triangles, the single dot in the center.   It had bothered him for the last three years, since he saw it first on the lovely mulatto girl's naked shoulder.   She was someone important and he understood that in an innate, unspoken way.   He just couldn't sort out the whispers, figure out what it meant. Something about her, about the mark...it drew him like a starving child to a warm bowl of soup.

He liked her a lot. More than he should. She was someone he actually trusted---and he couldn't trust many. But, he didn't *love* her. Not in a way that could hinder his sense of judgment. Yet...it would be *easy* to let the beautiful seraph become a paladin in which to hide his weakness; in this moment, as he thought about her, he felt the earth shifting ever so slowly under his feet as if he could feel the music of long-lost spheres. Was it possible that the world held its breath for this profoundly sacred minute?

Once, he had felt this way all the time, abiding and constant. The chords that had once played in the marrow of his bones had quickly faded and deserted him, before he was old enough to explain to his Papa...before he was old enough to ask intelligent questions in his sterile childhood world. It was a half-forgotten faith that made him want to touch this second's breath. He could make the world stop here and go on giving him the peace he felt now. He could bottle it, carry it as a shield against the coldness, this magnum opus.

The things he loved, he protected jealously.

He was at Wilk Row. Something at a Decatur Street store window caught his attention and he slowed down, coming to a stop, to look closer at the merchandise. Twilight wasn't a reason to stop work and close down for the day---not around here. It was a very old bookstore---on the bricks, in front of the big windows, there was a set of shallow bins with discontinued stock.

Hmm.

Rhys leaned over a bin and examined the contents, gloved hands in the pockets of his coat. Most of it was paperbacks, but...in the second bin, he found the old stuff. Old novels and texts like the ones Papa had read to him when he was a kid. And...the antique books, in French. Oh, nice. He picked up one and opened it, looking at the sharp typeface and the yellowed fly page. It had belonged to a couple of other people, but was marked with a small ink stamp that claimed the book was a re-sale to the store. Secondhand. Cool.

It had that gorgeous scent...thick pages going yellow and faded with time. The copyright date claimed it was just over a century old. The cover was heavy cardboard and paper, but the spine was in fairly decent condition and he could make out the gilt title of the story. 'Candide' by Voltaire.

He grinned, now, crookedly. Daniel would love it.

He'd heard about this book, in the first year after leaving his Papa. Daniel had told him the story of 'Candide' one late night, in Neuchatel, just after he'd gone there. Of course, Daniel had read this one when it was first considered an immoral novel. Only a few years after it was published in 1759. Daniel had quoted at him, from memory, right? Daniel, the unlikely optimist.

Rhys smiled and closed his eyes, holding the book. He could smell the fried fish from the next shop, but in his head, he could still hear Daniel reading 'Candide' to him...the benu voice a dark, warm, velvet blanket rumbling through that muscular chest.

Then, as he relaxed, remembering Daniel's voice from years before, he felt it...the awareness of familiar minds as his empathy opened like a moonflower in his head. There...the subconscious thoughts of people he knew, close by. Opening his eyes, he turned to look at the street and the sidewalk. It was like being able to smell certain scents and perfumes. He could submerge himself in a crowd and be okay, focusing on just one or two or maybe none. But, certain minds left emotional fingerprints that he could memorize. Fingerprints he knew better than most, only marked in emotions instead. Daniel was close by...and so was Tennyson. And...someone else. Someone even easier to pick up on with the talent that Papa had made him hone in secret.

A vampire was nearby...one he knew. Nick was close, maybe only a street or two away.

He put the book back in the bin and began following his instincts, thinking.

Mattie had left the house less than an hour ago with Gabe. They'd had a talk about how much he was drinking these days---about how drunk he'd gotten last night. About how he let Nick bite him all the time. Mattie wasn't happy. She was talking about leaving New

Orleans for England. She might want to take their son out of the country...out of the possible dangers that came with running Pandora's Box. She was willing to sign her half of the business over to him and to Dante, just to be rid of the whole mess. And since he didn't legally exist as Josiah Rhys Lorraine *or* as Josiah Rhys Rose, thanks to his Papa, he couldn't really fight her on it...not *legally*.

He didn't want her to leave. This was home, now, wasn't it?

And he *really* didn't want her to take Gabe out of his life.

He didn't have memories of his family---nothing but Papa, anyway. Daniel had told him about the family he came from. About his real Mama and his real Papa, about who they'd been in life. Daniel had told him, in detail, about the betrayals that'd led up to the way he was taken into the labs as a small child, how Daniel and Mattie had thought he was dead all of his first eleven years. He didn't know what to feel about it, if he should feel anything at all.

His childhood was all he'd known---even if Daniel said it wasn't a good one.

Gabe was the only thing he had, of real flesh and blood family. He didn't want to lose his son. There was so much to learn from a child, especially one of his own DNA. He wasn't always sure of what to feel when it came to the idea of fatherly responsibility, but he *tried*. He wasn't meant to have become a father this way, he was sure of that. Papa had told him, once, of the paths that a boy took on the road to being a man. Of the lessons he'd have to learn before he could consider reproducing.

His senses were taking him down to the river, off the beaten track. Hmm.

He began studying the fog and the figures that moved in the distance, near the water, off the sidewalks. It was not very long before he picked them out, the three. Now, that was *crazy*. Nick stood on a ramp near the pylons of the dock on the river between Woldenberg Park and the Aquarium of the Americas, Tennyson was approaching the vampire, and Daniel was just standing behind a forklift a good distance behind Tennyson.

What the hell was going on?

Chapter Eighteen

Valeska was a marble god under the streetlamp, in the fog, on the concrete platform.

He wore a leather motorcycle jacket and leather pants and a maroon, long-sleeved Lycra shirt that felt like heavy silk when she hugged him, sliding her face against his collar. With his sunglasses on the top of his head, holding back coarse, black hair from the pale angles of his face, Valeska looked like a supermodel on vacation. Even in the dark, illuminated by only a streetlamp, her friend was unearthly, inhuman.

They stood together for a few moments, being silent, and then she shuffled her booted feet and broke the quiet, brushing a gloved hand over her damp braids. "I'm leaving the country day after tomorrow. I took a job with Lorraine and D'Loup."

Usually difficult to read, Valeska's face opened enough to show his surprise. His dark, gypsy eyes widened as he spoke in a low tone, taking her arm at the elbow. "Are you sure that's a good choice? Once you start as a player, it's a difficult thing to get out of. Can you trust them?"

Strange...coming from Valeska, who did the same kind of work at Pandora's Box.

He was Rhys' friend.

Tennyson squeezed the hand that held her forearm and elbow, the leather not enough of a shield from the cold flesh. It was a reminder---he was a vampire and he'd once tried to feed on her in the ugly washroom of a sleazy diner. He was a hell of a lot stronger than her and if he wanted to change his mind about their friendship, there wasn't anything she could do to stop him---shit, she'd be lucky to notice a betrayal before it happened.

And yet...he wasn't wrong.

She liked Rhys, but...neither he nor Daniel were human. They'd never been human.

In fact, Rhys was so far from human that she wasn't sure of how to begin cataloguing the differences between them. He was supposedly the only one of his kind in the whole world and he'd skipped the whole normal childhood thing and went straight into working under the table for the Company while still in puberty. She wasn't even sure if her tchatcha friend *had* normal feelings, much less possessed any real ability to understand them.

"I don't think Lorraine'll hurt me." She shrugged and let him turn her in the direction of the cathedral. Together, they walked along the ramp, arm in arm. It was snug, despite the drizzle and the noisy crowd only a half-block back up into the Quarter. For the moment, it was easy to forget that anyone one else existed---Valeska had that ability, just like Rhys. It was something she adored in them both. She bit her lower lip and thought about the job, about the people involved. "I don't think either of them will. D'Loup's determined to protect me, make sure I come out okay. I believe him. Lorraine..."

"I think *Lorraine* twisted your arm." He used the name as if it was the title of an enemy instead of someone they both adored. Valeska tightened his grip, peering down into her face from a tilted angle, his long black hair brushing at the pale curve of his jaw and cheekbone. "You've got a weakness where he's concerned, Tennyson. He's tasted your blood too often. Joseph's right about that. It means a connection between you, something hard to break."

Okay, so it was jealousy. Uh-huh. A vampire jealousy. She called him on it.

"You gotta prob with him cause of that, the blood issue. Cause you aren't the only one." Tennyson frowned, sucking at the corner of her lip, where she'd gnawed. "Doesn't mean he'll let me get hurt. Lorraine needs my help and I *wanna* help."

Valeska didn't answer, but it was pretty obvious that he was upset. His somber gaze moved away from her, now, as he studied the overcast evening sky. She pushed on, remembering what had bothered her last night, what she could pull out of her hazy memory.

"Besides...I gotta ask. Who was that woman? In the car? You acted wiggy and Joe just..." She could remember how Joseph Snowden had acted, how the massive vampire had gone all possessive and odd. How he'd walked away from them, at the club's gate. "Joe doesn't act that way about me, but he did...and what was up with that?"

"She's no one." Her vampire friend scowled with a shake of his head; a sheaf of his dark hair fell out from under the sunglasses that held it off his face, giving him a softer appearance. "Just some woman Joseph's doing research for."

Tennyson dragged him to a stop, putting her weight against his undead strength. "No, that was no woman. She's one of you. I'm sure of it. So, what was going on? What is it about her that got Joe's fur in a ruffle?"

Standing still, looking down at her with his wide, slanted gypsy eyes, Valeska made a face of disgust and sighed heavily---vampires didn't normally breathe, but it was something her friend did on a fairly regular basis for some unknown reason. His voice, now, as he answered, grew hoarse with emotion---he didn't want to talk about this. "That woman belongs to Joseph. The way I belong. Only, she doesn't let Joseph keep her. She and Joseph fight every time they're in the same room...just over a century and a half ago, they made a pact, to keep the peace. She said she wouldn't come into his territory without an invite and Joseph said he intended to hold her to the promise."

Instantly, she knew who the woman was. The light blonde-brownish hair, the bright eyes, the white skin...it had to be Misha. Who, in life, had been a Jewish girl named Mishenka.

She whispered it. "What the fuck is she doing here? Why'd she break the rules?"

She knew, because of stories told to her by the players at Pandora's Box, that Joe Snowden hunted his own kind. To keep the vampire population in New Orleans down to a minimum. Joe didn't have any qualms about killing bloodsuckers who strayed into his territory, especially if they didn't follow the rules. He seemed to style himself as the vampire version of a sheriff or marshal. And she was cool with that. It meant the streets were safer. A little, anyway.

Misha had come to find Joe---it was obvious. Sitting outside the club at closing time? Not an accident. Joe Snowden had obviously given an unheard order to Valeska---protect the human---and then walked off to deal with Misha by himself, taking the possible danger away from the club's entrance. Away from *them*.

Valeska reached into his motorcycle jacket's pocket and pulled out cigarettes. Lighting one, her vampire friend blew smoke in the north-west direction of the cathedral and then gave one of his half-assed shrugs. "Who the fuck knows? She came looking for info. Templar stuff that only Joseph would know. He's gonna give her the info and then she's getting the hell out of Dodge. That's all she wrote."

She nodded, accepting it; she had loads of questions about the female vampire, but she didn't get a chance to ask the first one---Valeska's attitude was skittish, he didn't wanna talk about Misha.

"You know you were followed, don't you?" He asked, raising a brow as he smirked. "It's like some kinda parade out here, baby. D'Loup is standing almost within sight, just past that parked forklift, and Lorraine's *deliberately* letting me know he's at the fence line, downwind, and headed straight for us."

Followed? Dammit.

She turned and glared out into the gloom at the two unseen assassins.

"Don't worry." Valeska hugged her before stepping away, smoke curling around his head like an unholy aura. "I think they're just worried about your safety." He smiled, then, showing his fangs. "You're gonna have to excuse me, Tennyson. I got something to take care of and I still have to make my appearance at the club. See you there?"

Tennyson watched her vampire friend walk away, heading back in the direction of Saint Louis' Cathedral and Jackson Square. Standing still, she waited. After what felt like five or six minutes, Rhys appeared at her side; he was wearing his long chocolate brown corduroy coat and looked like he was pleased.

"Daniel's already gone." He gave her a wicked grin, winking. "He just wanted to see if you were okay. It's not cool to walk around here after dark, Tenny. All kinds of boogiemen lurking in the shadows."

She couldn't help it; she snarked at him. "Yeah, well, I was just in the same one-block radius with three killers and I'm just *peachy*." Rolling her eyes, she changed the subject. "Mattie gone with Gabe?"

Rhys nodded, his brown hair sleek in its ponytail. He started walking along the gravel, heading back up the slope and towards the sidewalk. She followed, working to keep up with his long stride. He looked so serious, being silent. And she had a feeling that he was worried, even though he acted like everything was fine.

She decided she had to know. Pushing herself to keep up, breathing harder in the chilled, humid air, she dared. "Something's going on. What's wrong? You're upset."

He didn't say anything, just kept moving.

"Where're we going?"

"I'm walking you home." Rhys glanced at her, his eyes softening a little. She could see the hazel clearly in the blue as they passed under a streetlamp's gleam. "After that, you're gonna get a good night's sleep, booze-free, and I'm gonna go take care of some business."

"What kinda business?"

"The kind that means we'll have a pipeline of info and equipment in Egypt. In case we need something we can't carry with us." He walked with his hands in his coat's pockets and she became aware that he was dressed up. Dressed up for Rhys, anyway. Dress shirt, kinda like hers, but with a tie. And his trousers were tailored. The shoes were Doc Martins, brown leather. Almost the same color as the corduroy coat. "Mattie supplied me with some names, network people who can help us, no questions asked...if we run into a sitch we can't field alone."

It made her head reel, made her dizzy. She was really in the middle of something new. She'd never had to think about crap like this...suppliers and weapons and networkers and pipelines and...assassins and thieves.

"Hey, not a big deal. I'll take care of it. If you think too hard about this, you'll freak out and then what? You won't be there, with me." Rhys was taking her hand, then, and she realized he'd stripped off his gloves. And she did the same, leaving her skin vulnerable to the cold. But, not for long. The malakh's fingers were holding hers and they were like a different kinda glove, humid skin full of toasty-hot coals. His over-active heating system was perfect for the chilly weather.

They hit Madison Street at the corner of the Jackson Square fence. She hadn't come so far from her apartment, really, but it was still six long blocks away, on Saint Anne's, just before the corner of Burgundy. She admitted her fears. "I just don't know if I can do this, Rhys. I've never done a job before and what if I do something that gets us in trouble? What if..."

"No what-ifs." Rhys tugged her hand in close to his side, where it was warmer still in the fold of brown corduroy and malakh skin. He was chiding her, in his teasing way, with a crooked smile that showed his innate sarcasm. "All you have to do is look beautiful and woo the gentleman...you do that every time you're in the club. You're gonna be great."

And she believed; something in her responded to the tone of his voice, the honesty he shared.

On the corner where they stood, at Bourbon and Saint Anne's, waiting for the light to change, the rain made colorful puddles on the asphalt. The cold air on her face caused her flesh to feel so much more than usual. Inside her shirt and the bra she wore, her tight, sore nipples chafed at the material. Were they visible, through the clothes and the coat? She hoped not.

Rhys tightened his grip on her fingers, continuing in his softly husking way. "Have you called your mama recently? She must worry about you."

She shook her head and made a decision to do that, call her mom tomorrow.

In the quiet that followed, she listened to the music of a band that was huddled under the eaves of a balcony behind them. A snare drum, a trombone, and a cello were playing. The music was waltz-y, going on and on like a lament against the rain that changed the night into a new beast.

'Your mama never told you how you were s'posed to treat a girl. Your papa never told you and now you're all alone out in the world. Sirens are streaming inside the winding sheets are pale. Devils are dreaming, dreaming of the blue angel.'

Then, a fresh breeze picked up and made the air even colder.

It was a holy moment; his hand holding hers on the crook of his arm, his much-warmer body a shelter between her and the growing wind that threatened to make her teeth chatter while she breathed the swirling scents of human, animal, spices, smoke, and the richly dark odor of the malakh at her side.

'Now I lay me down to sleep. But troubled dreams are all I find. Pray the lord my soul to keep. Pray so I won't lose my mind. Sirens are screaming on wings tonight, I'll soon set sail. Devils are dreaming, dreaming of a blue angel.'

The drum kept a slow heart's beat...the trombone slid languidly like a lover's hand over familiar, perfumed flesh...the cello became lips that whispered and moaned and tasted and teased...and there was a new sound among the others and that was a hum.

A voice...wordlessly singing...Rhys was humming.

The streetlight was forgotten, ignored, turning the rainy street below from liquid rubies to emeralds as she found herself slipping into the spaces between one heartbeat and another, between inhale and exhale. There were hundreds of people around, possible danger always, and the man who kept her close was both a protector and a friend. A deadly friend. A cry *rose* and *throbbed* in the air like a throaty call that each might hear and obey; the sweet, distinct words of the violin's song were impossible to escape. Like blood in her veins that ran through her body, which was no longer wholly hers.

'Your mama's going to take it hard. You always were your mama's boy. You're laying in the graveyard. Now you're not your mama's joy. Streetlights come streaming, I'll bat an eye and cast my spell. Devils are dreaming, dreaming of a blue angel.'

Tennyson felt the fingers that moved over her braids, tucking a fragrantly wet plait away with a deft touch that never hesitated. She turned to look up at Rhys, who was watching her with a quiet smile. Instinctively, she smiled in response, not needing words for what she knew. His hand went on, gentle to catch each braid despite the obvious strength of his naked fingertips.

Exposed, her ear was now examined with a delicate, careful touch. She didn't pull away, but let him trace each curve even when his thumb moved downward and along the side of her throat and then her shoulder. The thumb paused, heating up the flesh that covered the tight hollow of her collarbone. When he bent close, closing the distance separating their faces, she took a sudden breath and knew that he did the same.

Rhys' nose touched at her cheekbone and his eyes were darkened with sleepy emotion as they closed and she didn't see anymore, her eyelids dropping as his lower lip slipped along the space between the slackening of hers.

The music was the humid, tidal flux of blood that swelled and ached in hidden riverbanks, the hint of sensual offering as he was exquisitely careful and tasted the curved pucker but went no further, gentle to not destroy the chaste moment.

At their backs, the violin began to *wolf* a rough, broken cry.

She opened her eyes at the hoarse sob of music.

Against her cheek, Rhys murmured in an undertone, his lips too hot. "Tenny..."

Every muscle in her body changed in some subtle, new way. Tight and then weak. It frightened her and she hitched a breath and smiled with the gasp that came. The music had become a sassy, brazen march, was no longer the magical waltz. Rhys straightened up, his eyes soft and hazy but beginning to focus. The young malakh cleared his throat and smiled a real contentment she understood completely.

His words were quiet, only for her ears as she stared up at him in amazement. "Let's cross the street before we call more attention to ourselves, princess."

She didn't need to respond at all. His hand drew hers over the curve of his arm again as the light turned red, signaling pedestrians to move. Tennyson dropped her eyes to the ground and watched the slick, rainbow-oiled asphalt as her boots clicked along, following the unspoken command to walk.

The streetlamps shone on them as they walked along in happy tranquility, content to just enjoy the smell of flowers and rain, to look at the darkened houses with their evergreen veils of bougainvillea and kudzu, the finger traces of morning glory, honeysuckle, and the victorious trumpet vine.

When he knocked on the door, he wasn't really sure what he'd find. The honky-tonk downstairs was a live-wire---even the mechanical bull was going crazy. He'd seen Jay on stage there, playing music with a country blues band; in passing, he'd smiled at the nearly-blind albino. Who, of course, could see him better in the dark.

But, he'd come up here, to the apartment above, to find the girl.

He'd hung back, before, as Alvie got Jay set up for the evening---using the excuse that she had to take care of some things. Then, he'd followed her up here. Following his instincts, he had done something he'd never tried before. But, he'd made sure she knew the rules beforehand; she had to wait here for him, if she woke before he made it back. And for the last hour, he'd wondered if she *could* keep that in her head, for the *after*. He'd heard that not everyone could remember themselves, when waking up. Yet, he believed Alvie would. She wasn't like others---*period*.

If she'd left, without a leash, it would be only a matter of nights before Joseph found her.

It made his chest tighten with a strange emotion---the idea of losing this girl, so fast.

His choice to be so impetuous was already weighing on his Undead heart.

He now knew the eighth deadly sin. Regret.

He'd never sired a childe before; he wasn't even really sure why he'd wanted to do it, now. Only that, faced with Alvie and the illness that was robbing her of life---robbing the world of her music and her magic---he had followed his gut instinct. He'd come to the apartment with her and, together, they'd laid in the bed and he had done his best to recreate the accident of his own death and re-birth. Minus the rape, of course.

Now, he wondered what the fuck he'd do. If she survived the change and came back a vampire, what would he do with her? He couldn't exactly take her to Joseph. And...what if she didn't wake up a vampire? What if she didn't survive the change? She'd be a dead body in the bed of this place and Jay wouldn't have anyone to look after him, anymore. He would be guilty of her murder, only...he had a feeling Alvie wouldn't have seen it that way. She would've seen it as a mercy killing, despite her hardcore warrior nature.

Even now, he could still taste her blood. She'd been right---her blood had a strange flavor. Not malakh and not demon. Mortal and human but with an added element. The magic, perhaps. Silver and so easy...it was like moonlight on his tongue and in his teeth.

He raised his fist and knocked again, then dropping both hands to push into the pockets of his leather jacket. No answer. Well, only one thing to do. He would do what every other thief did and get past the lock without a key. Kneeling, he realized that it would be easier than he thought. The lock was in the doorknob and it wasn't a great one.

Pushing his sunglasses up to the top of his head to hold his hair back, Nicolai Valeska rifled his jacket pockets and came up with the paper-clip he needed. Unbending it, he broke the fragile metal in two. Now, straightening the two pieces, he had the lock-pick he needed. He went to work on the simple tumblers inside the door's knob. In only a few moments, he was able to push the door open, having tripped the lock.

The apartment looked just the same. One room with the bathroom attached like an after-thought. Darkened and quiet and clean, despite the under-scent of squalor. He closed the door behind him and reached for the lamp he could see in the dimness.

'We got somethin', we both know it. We don't talk too much about it. Yeah, it ain't no real big secret all the same. Somehow we get around it. Listen, it don't really matter to me baby. You believe what you want to believe. You see, you don't have to live like a refugee.'

Clothes hanging on hangers around the walls, for lack of a closet. A couch and two orange crates with a piece of ply-wood that created a make-shift coffee-table. A beat-up stove and refrigerator, both in avocado green and bearing rust along the edges where the paint enamel had come off with wear and tear. A single-bowl sink that looked like it would be more at home in a restaurant or a deli. The tall floor lamp with a crooked, battered cream-colored shade that cast its nicotine-yellow gleam in desperation. The full-sized bedsprings and mattress sitting fully on the floor, sheets and blankets draggling off the sides. A chipped glass ashtray there, on the floor by the window. Windows with blanket curtains, showing nothing of New Orleans now. A dismal room for two hungry souls who sent all their money home, to their kids---and used the remainder to pay for doctor's visits.

She was still on the bed, flat on her back, where he'd left her.

'Somewhere, somehow, somebody must have kicked you around some. Tell me why you wanna lay there and revel in your abandon. Honey, it don't make no difference to me, everybody's had to fight to be free. You see, you don't have to live like a refugee. Now, baby, you don't have to live like a refugee.'

Oh, he'd been so careful, ticking off a mental check-list of what needed to be attended to, before he left her alone to go through the changes. After draining Alvie, he'd fed her his own blood---as much as she could drink. He'd had to repeatedly open the vein, to keep it flowing. Then, as her body slid into the unconscious place, he'd gone to work on the situation. Plastic garbage bags under her body, stripped out of clothes. He'd even gone so far as to pull off the white flour sack kerchief and lay it to the side. Not for any particular reason. Only that he liked her better without it. Naked and so pale in her baldness, so fragile in her beauty, but with such strength in her slackened features.

Yes, she was Undead...sleeping, still, but most definitely *Undead*. There was that crazy glow under her skin that he recognized. And he didn't care about the smell---her bowels and bladder had released after he'd gone back to the street, just like he'd predicted. He could take care of that now. But, he stood motionless for a little longer, studying the childe he'd created.

'Somewhere, somehow, somebody, must have kicked you around some. Who knows, maybe you were kidnapped, tied up, taken away, and held for ransom. Honey, it don't really matter to me. Everybody's had to fight to be free. You see, you don't have to live like a refugee. I said you don't have to live like a refugee.'

Alvie. Alvie was going to be bald forever and she would always have the look of a refugee. But, he loved it. And there was a part of him---the music in his spirit---that found her loveable. Yes, he could love Alvie. The question remained to be answered, though, of what kind of vampire she'd be. Would she be smart and retain her human personality? Would she be a ravenous animal-demon who needed to be staked right away? Would she regret what she'd agreed to?

With a sigh, Nicolai rolled her sideways and pulled the nasty garbage bags off the bed with care, to keep from spilling the wastes. He discarded of them in the trash and then returned with a bowl of warm water and a dishtowel he found on the stove's oven handle. He began to clean his childe gently, studying her. The marks he'd given, in taking her blood, were faded out to just the palest of shadows. She had such beautiful fingers---the tapered fingers of a musician. She had a large, splinter-shaped freckle on the palm of her right hand. And the gypsy in him remembered it to be the mark of a witch.

Oh, yes, she was more than Undead...she was a witch. Something new.

He cleaned her up and then got rid of the water, wringing out the dish towel.

Then, he sat down to keep her body company until she found a way back.

On the elevator of her building, Rhys closed the oak-leaf lace iron gates and she punched the button for the third floor. The ancient motor started humming and moved with a lurch that inspired vertigo.

Catching her balance, she shifted to the back of the box, to examine their reflections. Three walls of the elevator were antique, faded-silver mirrors that ran from ceiling to floor. From the very first, she'd loved them. It didn't matter that she really couldn't stand to study herself in the glass...now, she had someone else to examine from three angles.

Rhys had said he'd walk her home and then, along the way, said he needed a glass of water.

She knew it had to do with his adrenaline levels---his endocrine system was different from hers, different from everyone's. And it meant he needed more water than other people, sometimes. Just to keep producing sweat, just to keep himself from dehydrating. It was the sweat that made him capable of going invisible...he'd explained that, once, early in their friendship.

The elevator was horribly slow. It would always be faster to walk the stairs, but she loved the dual knowledge she understood of the old monster. It had been installed with the turn of the century and needed constant repair to keep its old, greasy motor running, but it was beautiful to her. And the danger involved was part of the treat. There was always the chance the motor would stall and she'd get stuck. Or that the motor would completely fail and she'd find herself riding the small box to the wet, moldy basement very fast. It was a death-defying act to take the elevator---something she had to dare herself into, every time.

Rhys stepped up behind her, his face quiet and thoughtful. She could see them clearly now, in the mirrors. Her raw-boned friend looked bigger in the corduroy coat---as if he was more than a skinny guy who could dance like nobody's business. And why hadn't she ever noticed how odd it was, the contrast of his hair and eyes and skin?

His ponytailed hair was a light brown with some red in it...his skin was olive-bronze, almost a mulatto cafe latte...his eyes were wide and slanted and such a wild color. She'd seen people with blue eyes before; she'd also seen people whose eyes weren't entirely blue...eyes with a mix of green or gray in them. But, with Rhys, the hazel was like a pale tan and the blue was muted, muddied. Odd, yet...natural. It seemed right for him.

At his side, she looked so...ordinary and so very Creole. She was curvy and curvy wasn't considered attractive *these* days---Halle Berry was attractive, not a size sixteen Aunt Jemima.

The elevator was dragging worse than usual.

He leaned close, his oven-hot body brushing hers, as she stared at him in the warped, spotty mirror. His cheek touched the side of her head, causing a tingle in her hair and skin. His eyes moved, looking at her in the reflection...and she couldn't help but do the same. He was a few inches taller than her...and seemed larger, now. She liked how they looked, together, in the mirror. They looked just right.

He whispered, his silken mouth close to her ear. "I wanna make love to you, Tenny."

Her breath caught hard in her throat and chest; she'd folded her arms against her chest, but now her hands dropped to hang by her sides, revealing the open front of her suede coat, the lesbo-boy clothes she wore. Rhys' eyes were visible still yet as he pressed his lips to her ear; he was watching their reflections, too. His large-knuckled hands slid up and around her ribs, holding her close against his body from behind, and she felt the way everything tightened and then went weak again. Just like with the kiss.

She could smell him; the scent of his skin was delicious. Something between hot metal and exotic lilies. A mouth-watering musk. His smoothed hair was an invitation to her fingers. The offering smile was bright in his eyes, could be felt as he kissed her ear lightly, brushing back the braid that lingered on her cheek.

His strong fingers tightened on her ribs, massaging gently, rubbing at her skin through the cotton and leather. Her breath started coming in uneven measure as she let her eyes drift almost shut in pleasure at the way he held her close. In the mirror, she could see everything he did and there was no way she could escape the sight of the hands that looked so...

"Rhys..." She breathed, letting her head fall backwards to rest on his chest as he pushed the edges of her coat further to the side and exposed the taut lines of where her shirt and trousers revealed the softened curve of her rounded belly and hips.

"You are beautiful." Rhys murmured, his lips buzzing against her ear. He inhaled cool breath on her skin and she could hear the awe in his low, velvety voice. "You can't be anything but the living proof that the Universe is ruled by a goddess. Only a goddess would be so cruel...putting such a woman on the earth and setting her out of the reach of men."

Tennyson moaned, watching with growing desire as his fingertips found the edge of her shirt, the suspenders that lay on either side of her breasts. She pushed back, anxious to feel more of him through the clothes they wore---he was like a furnace and she would swear he was drying her coat with just his body heat. His mirrored eyes went on, searching every inch as he kissed his way down from her ear to her throat, firm lips open and wet and worshipping.

She was in shock. The only times Rhys had ever kissed her, had ever caressed her skin, things hadn't gotten so far...and they'd both been stoned or drunk. She didn't want to go all the way, under the influence; it was enough to be touching. They were sober now and the malakh was touching her in ways all the others, the women, never had. When was the last time she'd been handled *this* way, with such *hunger*?

Without warning, his hands jerked in opposite directions and wrenched her shirt open; the buttons went everywhere, scattering with the explosion. They clattered to the black and white tiled floor and pinged off the old, faded mirrors and she gave a harsh gasp at the coolness of the air, at the animalistic force he used.

"Oh, god." She whimpered at the way her nipples ached inside the white demi-cups she wore. Her arms didn't matter anymore and her legs felt like jelly and the craving she felt was so big that her skin seemed to hum with it. "Oh, god."

Rhys' fingers pulled at her shirt and revealed the high-yellow of her belly and chest, broken only by the waist of her dark pants and the snowy bra. She felt so tiny in his grasp and it scared her. She couldn't stop the tremble that made her teeth chatter, that threatened to crack the tendons and bones.

"A thousand kisses for you, goddess. You are heaven." He whispered senseless, poetic words into her skin, his normally-sharp gaze going fuzzy and she felt the wet fire he urged into the place where her throat and shoulder joined. Here, his face was half-hidden by the plaits of her hair, but the need she saw matched hers.

Now, his careful and sensitive hands smoothed down from her ribs to the top of her hips and then slid back up, to hold her breasts. He pushed up on them, making the flesh surge out of her bra. Fingers spread, he rolled their weight effortlessly in his palms, his thumb nails finding the tight stone of her nipples. Since when did a guy know how to *touch*?

"Tenny...goddess." Her name was some new delicacy on his tongue.

She moaned again, leaning into his arms, losing herself easily in the slippery heat that throbbed between her legs, the shivers that his corduroy-covered arms caused as they rubbed at her belly, the tenderly possessive squeeze of his hands on her breasts. He was hard; at her spine, even through the clothes, she could feel the length of his erection. He pushed his pelvis at her back in a hungry, seeking grind.

It didn't matter what she looked like...she wasn't cold anymore.

The elevator came to a lurching stop, having struggled for and reached the third floor.

Rhys' wet mouth traced along the line of her bared throat, finding her ear once more. His voice was darkly offering, ferociously commanding as he pulled her against his body with a sexy growl. "I'm gonna devour you, goddess."

She didn't need to say yes or no. The choice was made.

"My...apartment?" She whispered, stumbling over the words.

Both large hands slid down her body to claim her thighs with the spread of his fingers. He was holding her closer as he opened his teeth on the hollow of her throat, chuckling quietly.

"Give me your keys." Rhys murmured against the flesh he tormented. Then, he bit into the skin of her neck, working his tongue in a slow caress on the overly jumpy nerves.

Her fingers didn't want to do anything, but she managed to fumble her keys up and out of the coat pocket she'd stashed them in. They jingled in the quiet---loud enough to override the noise of cloth on skin, their breathing, and the pound of her heart. He caught them with his hand and she sucked a breath in as he turned her, bodily, in one arm. It was dizzying, how fast he moved.

And before she could steady herself, Rhys' arms settled around her hips and lifted, his fingers clenching at her ass. She wrapped her legs around him, holding on, her arms bringing his face down as she tipped her mouth to kiss at the curves of his face. It made him laugh, his lips opened in a gasp as her fingers clutched the back of his head, fisting at the neat ponytail knotted on his collar.

He turned, thrusting the iron gate of the elevator to the side with the slap of a momentarily freed hand. She kissed him, licking at the sharp, almost bitter taste and the silk-shaven flesh of his jaw as he walked down the twilight-darkened hallway and caused, with each step, her clit to rub the satin of her panties, under both pants-inseam and dangling coat.

"Apartment?" He asked and his breath was roughened; she could feel the hard, thick cock that chafed and nudged at her inner thigh.

"Ah, god, ah, ah...six, end of the hall." Tennyson tilted her head back, letting the kisses go as she stared at him from under her lashes and the beaded plaits that fell and tickled her face.

He was going to show her what was under the gentlemanly control, the teasing malakh hedonism.

His olive-tan cheeks were flushed, his cruelly delicate mouth reddened and slightly swollen, and his eyes were full of heat as he stared down at her. His movements faltered, paused, as he pressed his lips onto hers for a sliding taste, fast and careless and full of a wide smile.

At her apartment, Rhys braced her between his hip and the doorframe as he worked on the lock, his lips caressing hers harder, licking past them into the places he had only taunted before. With a low whine, she opened for his kiss, holding his face tightly to hers.

In the apartment, the lamps were on, and he set her down as he re-locked the door behind them and dropped the keys to the rugs where they bounced, jangled, and then were respectfully quiet. She shucked off her coat and slipped away the leather suspender straps with a simple shrug. Her destroyed shirt was next and she watched her new lover as he removed his long coat. On the divan, it was flung haphazardly. Each move was masterful, casual and yet deliberate.

As she turned and kicked off her boots, yanking her socks away, he caught her arms and pulled her close again. His eyes were slits of drowsy, unfocused lust.

"Mmmm..." He held her up on her toes, fingers twining with hers on either side of his shoulders, making her stretch and squirm at the clothes he wore. He buried his face into her braids and breathed, his words an accented groan. "You're killing me..."

She slipped a hand free of his grip and tugged at the shirt and tie he wore. His breathy sigh, in her ear, urged her on, and she moved backwards, drawing him across the room. She hadn't thought she'd really want a man---she had always preferred woman---but Rhys was, as far as she could remember, the only man who had ever made her wet without so much as a word. It felt right, going this far now.

He let go of her fingers to slide the palm of his hand over and through her hair as she blindly guided their steps, quickly finding what was under the shirt he wore. A tucked-in wife-beater. She easily forced it up and out of her way as she searched for his sweaty skin, agonizing for a single taste of his flesh.

In the bedroom, she didn't bother with the lamps; leaving the door open, there was plenty of light for her to see how gorgeous he was, in this moment. His eyes were deep and full of a different, animal desire as he gazed down at her, meeting her stare. The flush of his cheeks and the glaze of sweat that accentuated his angelic features...it was all delicious.

At the foot of her four-poster bed, on the nubby gray rug, Rhys went down to his knees, his eyes still focused on hers. She tentatively touched the hair that had fallen free of the ponytail, moving her fingers through the damp strands of brown. The strangely holy moment was made perfect when he jerked his wife-beater off in one fluid motion, ruffling his hair even more. The leather hair tie was next and waves of doeskin-sorrel messily slithered to veil the malakh's cheeks and brow and jaw line and throat as he looked up at her, a regal supplicant.

She'd never seen him with all his chest and back exposed. He looked so young, offering, with no hair and his tiny, cinnamon-coin nipples. The muscles were slim, stream-lined, showing the strength of a runner...a dancer. His shoulders rolled gracefully, smooth skin stretching as he lifted his arms and found the button of her pants with the fingers of one hand while he tugged at the waistband with the other. The light shone on his face from the doorway and showed the subtle, wondrous way his eyes dilated as the pants came down and she was exposed.

Now, she was glad she'd trimmed and shaved yesterday.

"You're a priceless creature, Tennyson." He smiled, there on his knees, and his fingers slid over the white satin that covered her hips, finding the curve of both pelvis and the hollow where hip met thigh.

She was shaking from the want that made her ache so much as she unsnapped her bra and let it fall to the rug under her feet. She'd felt this ache before, but there was a newness to what happened here. Nobody else---not even any of her ex-girlfriends---had ever made her so desperate. Was it the exquisitely forbidden nature of it or the tender way he acted, so gentle when she had an idea of how dangerous he could be?

'If I could have just a moment of you, would I be wanting more? If I could have just a taste of you, would I be addicted? If I could have just a touch of you, could I tear myself away? I would pray to be the rain that runs over and in your skin. With no consequence. To be the liquid in your glass that falls around your lips and mouth. Swallow me.'

She sagged into his arms. Hot tears instantly sprang to her eyes as her chest and throat ached sharply and she began to sob harder, horrified and overwhelmed by what was happening.

She couldn't stop it, the crying. It seemed to come from nowhere.

Rhys was licking her, carefully cleaning the slick flesh, and every touch sent spasms of electric pleasure through her spine and belly. She managed to turn loose of his hair and swiped at her cheeks, at the tears that rolled down from her eyes as she squeezed them shut over and over out of embarrassment, to get rid of the bleary wetness.

She clawed long strands of plaited hair back away from her face, finding sweat on both that dampened everything. With a deep, quivering breath, she straightened up and rubbed harder at the tears that wouldn't stop. Every muscle and nerve end in her body was twinging. Each breath she took made her breasts bounce.

His eyes were quietly happy as he looked up at her, his mouth resting at the round curve of her belly. It didn't completely muffle the word. "Better?"

Tennyson nodded, her throat hitching a hissed sob in response. She did...she felt a lot better. She felt like she could melt all over again. Still, she couldn't get a grip on the crazed way her heart and brain were shut down, too full of everything she'd been feeling.

"Good. I've been dying to taste you, it couldn't wait. But..." Rhys' lips vibrated and tickled her skin. He kissed the curved dimple of her bellybutton and grinned, his expression only half-seen where he hid against her belly. "I'm not finished."

Nicolai Valeska wasn't a patient vampire, but, tonight, he didn't have much choice.

He'd removed his motorcycle jacket and laid it over the sway-backed couch's dingy brown velveteen and then pulled one of the orange crates over and sat down on it, his knees spread. There he'd waited, his hands cupped before him as he leaned over his bent legs, his hair sheltering his wrists and making a hidey-hole for his face. He'd sat there for an hour and studied the scuffed hardwood floor beneath him, by the bed, and thought about the sin of regret.

He'd killed Alvie and didn't even know her whole name---she was going to wake up a vampire and he didn't have a clue as to what his childe might be. Was Alvie her first name or a middle name or just a nickname? What was her surname? Would she still work hard to send money home, to feed her children, or would she abandon them? Would she want to take care of Jay, anymore? He couldn't be sure of anything except that he'd created a new creature tonight on the spur of a moment...without any real thought.

Joseph would skin him for it. And he didn't believe he could hide this. Joseph was too smart for things like that. This was his responsibility---his childe. That meant he would have to either keep constant track of her, checking in every night---to teach her what she'd need to know---or he would have to turn her loose to fend completely for herself. And he didn't know which one would happen, yet. He wasn't Master material---he didn't have the psychological strength that Joseph possessed, crazy as hell or not. Whatever Alvie chose to do, he'd have to go along with---he wouldn't be able to stop her without a stake and chains.

He smoked a cigarette in the ticking quiet---only vaguely aware of the thumping country music from downstairs---and thought about it, forming a basic plan with contingencies. All of it hinged on what Alvie proved herself to be, of course, but he had to have some idea of what might need to be done. Flicking ashes into the floor, he took another drag and bent his forehead to his wrists once more and contemplated it.

If she was okay---mentally sound and emotionally balanced---then, he'd offer Alvie the chance to choose for herself. Stay here with her albino friend and go on, taking care of her responsibilities. True, she couldn't work a construction job, now---no daylight jobs for vampires. But, if she was okay, then he would be more than happy to help her find something comparable. As a witch, she would probably still have some of her abilities. And that would mean she could get money with just wishing for it, in the presence of the right people---using witch power and vampire power combined. He would let her get acclimated to the unlife she'd come into and then, when she was strong and a good hunter, he would take his childe to meet Joseph.

If she was *not* okay---crazy and savage---he'd have to get help and fast. He was under no mad delusions---he didn't have the ability to stop a crazed vampire on the rampage. He'd have to simply track her the best he could and then get Rhys to help him finish it off before Joseph got wind of his fuck-up. Tonight, if possible. It was always easier to do on the first night.

If she did have all her old witch powers, then they might need to get *Dante* involved. Someone who could kill with mere thought and emotion. They would corner her and do what was needed. If it was needed. He didn't know if Dante could kill a vampire with a mesmer, but he did know---from personal experience---that the wild hacker malakh was able to confuse the Undead. So, if needed, Dante could confuse the newborn vampire and then Rhys could do what Rhys did best. *Kill.*

Was there any way in hell that Joseph could see this whole mess as a good thing?

If Alvie was okay, then---he could come check on her every night and help. She would need to learn the right ways to hunt and all the protocols that Joseph had made him learn. They did seem like good protocols, after all. Protocols to keep a vampire safe---if the vampire was sane and smart. With her music and her gift for intelligence, Alvie would surely win Joseph's Undead heart. And Joseph would have to see why he did it. Why he'd created a childe of his own. He wanted this young, wounded woman to live forever. She was a creature who needed to exist.

He'd followed his gut instincts, this time, and all he could do was hope that he was right.

The skin on his back prickled, then, and he looked up, feeling a strange sense of alarm. Something was with him---and when he saw the newborn's eyes open, he dropped his cigarette to the floor and ground it out with one scuffed boot, putting himself on the defense. He'd never seen a newborn wake up, not this close, but he clearly remembered what it had felt like, from *his* side of things. He'd come up in Joseph's bed, wide open and ready to scream, fighting his own Undead skin.

Alvie's brown eyes opened slowly and went wide. Her mouth opened on no sound, moving like a fish jerked up from the water. The white of her skin gleamed like marble and he watched, holding himself very still, as her hands clenched and then unclenched in the sheets. Her lips closed and she swallowed---it was so rough, the sound audible to him. She stared at the water-stained ceiling and then her wide gaze moved to find him, sleepy and uneven.

The moment of realization. He would know, *now*, what he'd created. *Uncreated.*

Recognition was sluggish. Her full-lipped mouth, so deeply pink, moved without sound again, and then her brows knit together as if she was trying to figure things out. She whispered, the hinge of her voice unoiled. Creaky. "I...you're the guy...from..."

He didn't answer, didn't move. Oh, she was lovely. Oh, she was perfect. She had human thought. He didn't know what to do, what to hope for. He offered her a small, weak smile, silently and fervently praying to a god who had never deigned to show him any mercy. Let his childe be as quick and real and human as he'd been, upon waking Undead.

Naked and skinny, Alvie pushed up to her elbows too fast and the alarm in her face was nearly comical. Now, her voice was stronger, hoarse, as she leaned towards him. "It worked---I *remember* you, I *remember* what you---what you *did*. I remember the taste---"

Nicolai, realizing, let go of a breath he was unaware he'd been holding. Unnecessary breath, but there nonetheless. Strands of his dark hair had fallen into his sight, momentarily blinding him---he didn't care. He reached out to touch the high, chiseled cheekbone of the witch childe, managing to speak---his voice staccato and spastic with relief. "Do you remember who you are? Do you remember Jay and your children---the reason you're in New Orleans? Do you remember why you asked me---"

She gave a fast, brutal laugh; her face opened up like the sky after a thunderstorm, showing the sun. She was thrilled and he sat back to give her room. Alvie swung her bare legs up and over the edge of the bed, her pale eyes sparkling as she studied herself---as much as she could see, hands and feet and arms. Within the deep well of her gaze he could see the tiny red pinpoints---the vampire nature. And her fangs slid free, into view, like razor-sharp pearls, as she gave him a wide, toothy grin.

"Yeah---I remember." Alvie's voice was even more musical than before, possessing some new depth that life, by itself, had denied her. She caught his arms at the elbow and gripped them tightly, her laughter returning. Bald and naked and so fragile-seeming, his newborn childe was wild with glee. "Oh, wow---everything looks so *different*, everything feels so *different*!"

The sin of regret forgotten, Nicolai let the excitement catch fire in his chest and brain. He nodded, realizing the extent of what needed to be done, now. He had a responsibility that would never end---the world itself could fall, its cities turned to dust, but as long as he existed and as long as Alvie existed, he would always own *this*. The anchor of that simple idea gave him a new and real sense of purpose.

This was something Joseph couldn't deny him---something Tennyson and Rhys couldn't fathom.

For the first time in all the years of his unlife, he was *necessary*.

He grasped his childe's face between his trembling hands and pushed close, to kiss at her eyelids---one at a time. She was so precious, her skin so thin. He whispered, his voice catching into a husk in his throat. "Welcome to the adventure, babydoll."

Chapter Nineteen

It was real, it was happening; she *wanted* him.

Pushing back on his knees, Rhys didn't get a chance to rise.

Tennyson grabbed him by the shoulders, dragging him to his feet as she pulled him tightly to her, cool and wet mouth urging him to open for her kiss. He gave a sigh of delight and closed his eyes, feeling the slide of her fingers on his skin. So soft, so soft...Tennyson felt like rose petals and smelled like gardenias. She dragged him back along and around the floor until she finally sat down on the bed's side and he went to his knees once more, between her thighs.

In a few moments, he broke away from her kiss, gasping roughly. He stared down into her lovely, smooth-skinned face; she was flushed, it was visible, and he could see the passion that matched his own. How long had it been for her? She smelled like she was in heat.

Licking at his lower lip, he gave a lop-sided grin and breathed, intending to ask her if she had a condom. But, his voice stopped working and, anyway, it was a silly question---she didn't have sex with guys, so *why* would she have a condom? Tennyson was working on him, her mouth tracing the path from his chin to his jaw to one collarbone. She was destroying his sense of reason; he needed a condom, needed to know if she could handle it if he accidentally went invisible and a hundred-oh-six degrees while...or that she might be okay with the whole of his sexual ability, the crazy gender part of his real self...

He reached blind fingers to find her waist and hips; caressing upwards, he cupped her round, firm breasts. They were larger than he'd imagined, even having seen her mostly nude once or twice before. They were delicious looking and he could smell the heat coming off her skin. She was a voluptuous, nubile creature. He needed to be held, to be touched...it hurt inside, the feeling of emptiness he couldn't explain or fend off. It felt like he was perpetually falling these days, this last year.

Rhys gave up and let it go.

She gave a whisper of shock, reacting to his exposed body. "My god, it's..."

With a smile tugging at his lips, he moved back up to her breasts, squeezing the fleshy form of them in each hand, lightly pinching her stiff nipples between forefingers and thumbs. There, he bit into a nipple and she squeaked at the sensation as he began rolling the heavy undersides in his hands.

She was abso-fucking-lutely glorious. He could feel the ripples of emotion coming off Tennyson, through every inch of her luscious skin. It was surrounding him, dragging him into her. She wanted him, she needed to be touched, couldn't believe the reality of him and of what he was, under his clothes. She couldn't believe a *white boy* could be so sexy, even if he didn't really qualify as really white...she couldn't believe a *man* could be so sexy. Period.

She'd dreamed of this a few times, dreamed of him...but, not always in a sexual light. She loved his long hair and his hands, especially how broad his palms were and how long the fingers...he wasn't a big guy, but he had big guy hands and she loved it. She loved how he was kinda girlish in the face, how he wasn't hairy or rough under her fingers. She loved his eyes, she loved his smile, she loved the smell of his skin---the incense odor and then the sharp, ozone-like under-scent.

Whoa. She could smell the under-scent. Malakh tendencies? Yes, malakh tendencies.

Had to be why he was on the edge of pledging his soul to her. Had to explain why he was trembling with hunger. He didn't ever feel that way with the average human---only malakh.

He'd never had a woman with a body like this; the ones he'd indulged himself with were always too slender, fragile-seeming with boy frames, but not Tennyson. Tennyson had a body built for ritual worshipping dance and hot, filthy sex where anything might happen...and she was his to hold for now. That was enough; if she wished for more, tomorrow, he'd give it up with every ounce of energy he could find. Once crossing the threshold and changing the nature of their friendship, he would be hers until he was no longer needed. And he would fight to keep what he ached for.

"Fuck me." Her whisper was ragged, almost without sound.

Rhys kissed at her lips, biting into them as he murmured, fighting the shiver that was rolling through his skin, igniting his own rampant appetite. "Ma reine, as you wish."

His arms were tight around her, holding her head and neck and shoulders, cuddling her as their bodies moved together, the fire building into something she could feel in every cell of her skin. Even in her bones. She'd never had such a continuous, rolling orgasm...not one that lasted from beginning to end, rising and falling like the river's tides. And something else was happening...she could feel it.

She'd only had real, complete sex with one guy before now. And it had been nothing like this. Nothing. Rhys made love like a woman, only with a cock to add into the picture. She'd even had lovers who liked to use strap-ons and none of them could even begin to compare. Rhys knew how to fuck like nobody's business. But, then, he was…not like a woman or a man.

And she knew the truth about him, now.

He was both and neither.

And something was changing, building...like a hurricane on the rise. She could feel electricity under Rhys' skin. And when it came, it was different. It burst over her like the clouds opening up on the biggest storm of her life. An orgasm of a different kind. And, now, she opened her eyes and found Rhys' gaze. They were nose to nose and she gasped as he rolled his hips left to right, finding the deepest, most hidden places of her.

The electricity crackled between them, like static, but bigger. Rhys' eyes filled with tears, his face was flushed. His gaze was wide and full of tormented devotion, his soft mouth open with words that couldn't escape. She felt it, the ripples...ripples she'd heard about and never experienced. Certain empathy-malakh were capable of it, sharing what they called an apogee. A sexual joining so ferocious and real, it made two into one on the spiritual level.

Rhys looked like a boy caught between life and death and who hadn't decided which way to go. He was ethereally beautiful in the light that came from the bathroom door; beautiful in the way that foggy mornings were beautiful. Beautiful in the way that only a descendant of angels could be beautiful.

Somewhere, in that electricity, she heard his real name...she saw his childhood, the truth of what he'd been raised to become. It was too much to endure, the knowledge of why he existed...he'd been trained, taught to be the assassin and the government's soldier. Only through Daniel and Mattie had that been allowed to change. Yet, something in Rhys still thought of that sterile lab as home...and he knew such pain, such dark and dismal loneliness.

His mouth worked silently and she held her breath, cresting the orgasm on a soundless cry. Her eyes went wide with the shocking ripples that suddenly raced through them both, starting in Rhys and swelling outwards to engulf her.

He was all of her world, all she wanted to see, breathe, taste, and know.

He was absolutely Rhys and she knew him, on every level and in every cell.

Her eyes watered with the intensity of what it made her feel, that throbbing ache under her skin. She could feel something changing in her head, turning like a set of well-oiled gears, throwing arcs of thought and images and emotions and love...like lightening. Like a thunderstorm in her body.

She cried out with it, digging her short nails into his skin, at his ribs. Rhys was arching his pelvis down into her upward-lifted hips, his arms braced and his head lowered, eyes locked with hers as they both came, lost utterly within the nihilistic second.

Her breath hitched with a wordless noise and he caught her mouth then, thrusting his face to hers, anxious to stop her cry. His eyelashes brushed hers, his long hair slid over her cheeks and forehead. She abandoned herself in him, was suddenly aware the universe was holding its breath in a song that needed no words and was made only of their bodies and their minds and their hearts beating...separated only by the flesh that didn't seem important anymore.

The strange tingling in her blood was like champagne bubbles and it came from Rhys. He cried, she cried...mouths trembling together as his tears slid into hers, on her cheeks, and it became one perfect minute of comprehending love.

She was in him, he was in her, and the world outside didn't even exist.

When he caught his breath, blinked, and more of the tears ran off his face and fell onto her skin...then and only then, she shuddered and became Tennyson Beaulieu again. In her own awareness and not in his, not completely.

She began to cry harder, tensing up, realizing the depths of what she'd seen in that moment of apogee. It was like being a little girl again and being told to catch and count every grain of sand that fell from a broken hourglass in hands too small for the task.

"Shh, it's okay, Tenny, it's okay..." He buried his nose into her cheek and sobbed, gasping for breath. His body held hers down, still thrust deep into her. "It's okay. I didn't hurt you, did I? God...I, ouais..."

She clutched at the back of his neck, her fingers tangled in the thick hair, keeping him close as she wept brokenly for what she'd seen in his soul. And that was what she'd seen...she'd been in Rhys' soul, she'd shared his biggest truths. And he'd shared hers.

There was a new depth to her brain and in her skin and she could feel it...it was nothing like the heat that ran from her blood, from the fire of his flesh. And somehow, she knew...she would always possess a way to know what Rhys needed, wanted. She'd heard about it: certain empathy-malakh could do that---bond like twins, in moments like this. It was always the sakau, the ones with empathy...and Rhys had shown her his life in flashes, things she had never imagined.

He was indescribably beautiful, inside. So perfect in all his darkness and all his light.

"I'm okay...it's...oh, god." She pushed her face into his harder as he moaned her name. She stroked at his forehead, where it was touching hers, rubbing his cheek and his chin. She felt each ripple as something new even as the initial shockwaves faded. It was new...something alien and frightful and stunningly perfect.

"Stay...just stay..." She breathed the words, her voice cracking. "Just stay..."

"I'm here." Rhys closed his eyes then and she felt the race of the world come to an end. She wasn't sure, but it felt like she'd found a different world altogether in him, something she had never suspected could exist. He drew a shaky breath against her ear and gave a low, tremulous chuckle. "I'm not going anywhere, ma chere...ma Tenny."

It was thrilling, to watch Alvie on the hunt.

They moved side by side, as equals, despite the fact that he was her Sire. He couldn't quite think of her as a subordinate---she was too smart, too earthy for that. She made him think of several women all rolled up into one. Tennyson, Mattie, Misha...his own long-dead mother. He wanted to show her off to Rhys, to his hag, to all the denizens of Pandora's Box. She was so absolutely *perfect*.

Together, they'd left the apartment and left info with the bartender---to let Jay know that Alvie was going out for the night. His childe no longer needed her spectacles and had dressed herself in oversized clothing---carpenter pants, a white undershirt, and a thread-bare flannel done in blue and gray and green tartan. She wore nothing on her head---no kerchief or bandana. And as they moved through the crowds that still clogged the French Quarter, he made a decision about Alvie's well-being.

'She cries. Children often do when they're cold, and hungry, too. Come closer. Look deeply in her eyes. So delicate...quite unlike her smile. Life clinging backward, in the fall of dread confusion. Still this silence gnaws upon your fingertips. Cold yielding flesh, for instant isolation. Far more sinister than the price of doubt.'

First things first, tomorrow night, he was going to get her some proper clothes. She needed clothes that fit lethally snug on her skinny body and looked like a million bucks. She needed kohl, to dramatize the beauty of her naked eyes. She needed things that showed off the loveliness of her face and head. With feeding and some personal care, the terrible ravages of her disease would fade and reveal the luscious creature in all her glory.

He was thoroughly enjoying the whole experience, being with Alvie on her first hunt. Together, they'd meandered through the warm-blooded mortals in the chilly night and he'd gotten a chance to see what the world looked like, to the eyes and mind of his childe...whose face was so wildly expressive. She was a natural, when it came to the hunt. She instinctively *knew* how to behave, Undead. And she'd chosen the best victim, though he wasn't sure how she could be so sure so soon...it had taken him decades to perfect his ability to intuit humans.

'Yet you remain...still you remain...and she says...pray for daylight, pray for morning. Pray for an end to our deception. Pray for daylight, pray for morning. Pray for an end to our deception.'

So, now he stood in a darkened alley, smoking a cigarette, and kept an eye out for interlopers while Alvie fed. She'd chosen a hefty, intoxicated man who had clumsily come onto her as they were walking down the sidewalk in front of a long string of bars and taverns. The guy was fascinated by Alvie's bald head and waifishly wan looks and for that crime, he was now dying. He'd watched as his witch childe teased and taunted the man down the alley and into the shadows---as easily as if she'd been doing it for a century. She moved like a seductress of the first class, her lean body nearly lost in the oversized clothes she wore. But, it wasn't the clothes which had thrown the guy for a loop, right?

No, it was Alvie's wise and ancient smile that drew the asshole.

In the alley, he'd stood in awe and with excitement making his skin crawl as Alvie let the big guy lean her up against the wall for a kiss on her slender, vulnerable neck. The kiss went from neck to jaw to that lush, overly ripe-looking mouth. Then, Alvie changed the rules of the game. A sexy interlude became a gently done bloodbath.

She wasn't very clean with the feeding, but...it *was* her first one.

'Life clinging backward, in the fall of dread confusion. Still this silence gnaws upon your fingertips. Cold yielding flesh, for instant isolation. Far more sinister than the price of doubt.'

At last, she turned loose of the guy's windbreaker and he crumpled like so much dead meat. Which...well, he was dead meat. Alvie turned to look at him from across the alley, her face rising slowly so that he could see every shadow of her features, the shape of her brown eyes as she gazed up at him from under the angled line of her brow. Her mouth and chin and throat were covered in blood and it was glorious. He stomped out his cigarette with a laugh, hurrying to gather his childe up into his arms. She let him and stood in his embrace, giggling, as he kissed at her face, licking away the dark crimson smears.

'Life clinging backward, in the fall of dread confusion. Still this silence gnaws upon your fingertips. Cold yielding flesh, for instant isolation. Far more sinister than the price of doubt.'

She melted into his grasp, murmuring through her happy laughter. "Good god, Daddy..."

That made his guts clench and his Undead heart soar. It was strange and verged on the incestuous. But, he knew Alvie didn't mean it that way. She called Jay 'Daddy', too. It was nothing but a term of affection for her. A sexy, bluesy term of affection. Janis Joplin, Christine McVie, women of real-guts music. And wasn't that what she was, too? Only, she wouldn't age and she wouldn't die and she would always own the music that made him bubble and sing in the veins.

He was so wrapped up in licking the blood away, laughing with her, enjoying the witchery scent of her Undead skin, that he didn't notice they'd gained an observer...someone who watched from the mouth of the alley. He didn't notice a thing until the voice, dry and acerbic, broke in on his red-tinged daydreams.

"If I hadn't seen this with my own eyes, I would've denied it was even possible."

Nicolai let go of his childe and shifted fast, turning, and went into a defensive position before his senses had time to adjust. All he knew was...it was another vampire, it was female, and it was dangerous. Immediately, his eyes found the lanky figure that was leaning on the bricks of the alley's building wall.

One shoulder braced on the red-brown bricks, one foot caught over the other, arms folded...she was dressed to kill in the one of the classiest fashions he'd ever seen her wear. She was beautiful, the goddess. Almost behind him, just in his peripheral sight, Alvie was wiping at the blood on her face and throat, silently tense, and he made sure he was positioned between his childe and the elder who had been a partner in the fall of his innocence.

"*Misha...*" He whispered it, his voice choking at the sight of Joseph's wife.

Only then did he catch the mental whiff of her unique being.

She wore a dress in dark crimson---the color of fallen rose petals and blood. It looked soft, curvy. It showed a lot of her upper chest, including the swell of her bosom. It only covered her legs to the mid-thigh. Over the dress, she wore a black wrap that looked like velvet and fur. Her four inch heels were the same color. At her throat was a stylized gold collar. It was plain enough, but open a mere half-inch at the front. It had carved end-caps. Two oak leafs and an acorn, each side.

He could see that she'd done her hair differently, too. It was like something from a statue or a painting of Greece's Golden Age. It was complex, with braids and gold chains, and yet it affected a careless manner---a deliberately created negligence.

She didn't move from her post, but arched a brow at him in askance; her tone was pure and complete in its scathing bemusement. "Does Joseph know what you're doing, little man?"

This was a real threat and it was more than he wanted to face---she could tell Joseph on him before he was ready to present Alvie. She could fuck everything up---Joseph still believed in Misha, even after all the time they'd been squabbling and feuding. But, before he could panic and attack her, out of the need to protect himself and his childe, he suddenly realized why he hadn't smelled her out before this moment. She'd snuck up on him...and it was a dark cancer in his brain, the sneaky knowledge of why.

She smelled like a benu malakh, like sunshine and quick-healing skin and temples built out of the natural stone. Very much so. Didn't smell like any benu malakh he knew personally, but there was something in the benu that carried from individual to individual...a race marker. Hadn't Joseph said something about the way she smelled? That she didn't smell the same...?

He gave her an ugly smile, not shifting a muscle from where he stood protectively in front of Alvie. He practically purred in response. "More importantly, I think, Madame Snowden, is the question of...does Joseph know what *you're* doing? I smell malakh on you. Looks like neither of us are winning any prizes for loyalty to our Master tonight. I think he'd *love* your idea of wifely troth."

"As much as he'd love your pretty little newborn."

His childe gave a low, muttering chuckle, and spoke up at last. Her tone was flat and calm and lethal. His body reacted to the inherent music. "You know...I got this nasty tendency ya'll should maybe know about. I take genuine offense to being treated like a deaf retard."

Misha's smile grew a little more hungry. She answered, never taking her slanted eyes

181

off him. "Yes, darling girl, but you're no longer in charge of your own destiny. You're Nicolai Valeska's personal bitch. The smart thing to do? Get used to it quickly, so that you can move on to the more important things. Like the big, crazy bastard who will set you to fire as soon as he knows you exist."

The tense movements of his childe as she eased closer to his side reminded him of how fragile she might still yet be. She moved into his line of sight just enough for him to see the red points of demonic nature as they flared deep in her blue-gray eyes. She whispered his name, questioning. "Nicolai?"

"Joseph knows about her, Misha. My childe's not something you'll be able to use as your weapon here." He lied, brazen, as he moved to wrap his arm around Alvie from the side. He answered his childe without taking his focus off the elder who stood at the end of the alley. "Alvie, this is Misha. Once upon a time, she was my mistress."

"Your *mistress*?" His witch childe asked, her voice still soft.

Misha's eyes narrowed in distaste at the term.

It was then that he realized...Misha and Alvie were both chiseled beauties with a strong sense of self. He hadn't meant to create a childe who might be like Misha in nature, but...it snuck into his heart. *Fear*. Had he created a childe who could easily overwhelm him, outstrip him? If she was like Misha, she must eventually crush his heart and spirit and not give it a second thought.

Instead of letting the fear take him by the throat, he chose to answer his childe. But, he never looked at Alvie now, but kept his gaze on Misha. "I was a slave, babydoll. Misha and her husband, Joseph, owned me for the last five years of my mortal life. Then, when she left, Joseph took me as his lover. He made me a *vampire*. Just like the both of them." He smiled graciously at his Sire's estranged wife. "Misha, this is Alvie."

Misha shook her head in disbelief. "I can't believe you'd do something like this. After how you were treated."

He kept his tone light, his smile in place. "That's none of your business. What're you doing here, in New Orleans? Who's the big malakh I smell on you?"

Misha was carefully genteel, her tone just as casual. "It's between Joseph and myself, little man."

"I'm sure it is."

His childe snorted through her nose and he glanced at her in curiosity. She was eyeing him with unadulterated scorn, her words meant for them both. "You're crazy. That's not talking. That's just a lot of spoiled brat growling. Back and forth, back and forth. Don't you have anything better to do? If not, immortality must be really fucking boring."

Silence fell and lasted for a long moment as he studied his childe and she studied him. Then, Misha interrupted, laughing. "I like her, Nicolai. She's not a china doll. I believe you may have found someone worthy of you. Bravo."

She reached out to touch Alvie's jaw, studying his newborn's face with thought. All humor was evaporating. He realized that Misha had let down her shields, to give Alvie this kind of attention and consideration. And, if Misha admired his choice, then he'd created a childe worth noticing.

She spoke softly to Alvie and he realized that the accent he remembered had blended and become quite British in the long years since they'd seen each other last. "I don't scare you at all, do I? Oh, yes...your instincts tell you how old I might be. How dangerous I might be. But, you don't fear me. Has Nicolai told you of our master...Joseph? Joseph is a monster. A beautiful, psychopathic monster. You are absolutely perfect in your imperfection, darling girl, but Joseph will still make dust of you."

Alvie answered, speaking just as softly, and he was reminded---the two women were very perceptive, very smart. "Why would he kill me?"

"Joseph *has* to kill you." Misha said it in a matter-of-fact way, stating a well-known truth about their Sire. "He hates our kind. He kills vampires for fun. He kills blood-drinkers to clean up his territory. He'll see you as a *threat*, darling girl, something he must eliminate. But, not only for your nature. No. You are a threat to Joseph because of Nicolai. Nicolai must love you and Joseph won't abide that. If you love Nicolai, you must die...but, the threat is doubled if Nicolai loves you in return. So...Nicolai has killed you in more than one way. He's consigned you to a very short existence and an ugly ending."

His frail-seeming childe ducked her egg-bald head in acceptance, her words still little more than a whisper. "Death doesn't scare me. Nothing does. Dead is dead. Even if I survive only tonight, I'll have gotten a chance to feel truly alive once more. A chance to feel as if I've got some power over my destiny. Anything else is just icing on the cake."

He could see that Misha was digesting this with her usual aplomb. She seemed to get it, the real strength of his childe's heart and spirit. Alvie had the potential to become an elder--- the witch in her understood the real depths of what life and death could mean, but she'd already transcended the horror and desperation that disease brought. Alvie was a warrior and he believed her when she said that even just tonight would be better than nothing.

Misha looked at him, her eyes piercingly sharp; she was still touching Alvie's jaw and throat. "Do you intend to leave him, little man? Is that why you've made yourself a playmate?"

He hadn't considered that. He hadn't thought of leaving Joseph at all.

"No..." He licked at his lower lip, hesitating; he tightened his grip on Alvie's hip. "I'm not leaving him. I re-created Alvie because I wanted to. She's like me. She has the gift of music in her blood. She shouldn't have to die of cancer. Not with a spirit like hers."

He saw it without looking directly at his childe---she was impressed with his sense of intuition.

Misha finally smiled more honestly---as if they were still the best of friends. She cocked her head to the side and a few strands of her complicated chignon danced just over the delicate curve of her ear. She leaned closer to murmur at his newborn. "Nicolai's always had a soft spot for beautiful girls. It's hard to believe he gives himself to our Master in every possible way."

But, his childe wasn't buying it. Alvie's brown eyes were cold and hard as she answered without any hint of warmth. "He might have a soft spot for beautiful girls, but I'm not a *girl*. I became a woman when I gave birth the first time. I don't think beauty is a defining factor here, since...I was never beautiful and I'm even less so now. Maybe you were chosen for your beauty, but don't go assuming you know me just based on the strength of your age. We're not the same. We're not even close."

It made an impact; Misha stepped back, turning loose of Alvie's face. The chill rose in her gaze, belying the opened wound he saw there. She hated to be reminded of her age, of the fact she had never given Joseph any children. There was a hint of pain in her nasty smile. "You wanted to know why I'm here, Nicolai? I think Joseph's probably told you why already. I'm here to get some information on the Sang-rael and I'm not leaving until I've gotten it. I'm tired of playing his games. Tell him that."

"You tell him." He challenged her, stepping back from Alvie as he pulled his cigarettes out once more. He offered one to his childe and then lit one for himself. He contemplated his Sire's moon-cold wife, exhaling smoke from his nose. If he could get Misha to tell him what she was up to, maybe he could use the information to soften the blow with Joseph---he could use it to protect Alvie. "You gotta give to get, Misha. I can get you the stuff you want. You know I can. But, I want something in exchange."

Misha nodded, agreeing. "Fine. What do you want?"

With a thumb, Nicolai brushed at his straying forelock as it tickled his eyelids and cheekbones; he held his cigarette between his teeth as he answered, managing a cocky grin. "I wanna know what you already know about the mythical Sang-rael. You must have *some* idea of what you're looking for. So, what do you think you're gonna find in Joseph's papers that you don't already know?"

"I'm searching for the cure to vampirism." Misha had lit her own cigarette with a small silver-plated lighter, which disappeared into an unseen pocket in the wrap she wore. "I want to be mortal again. Human. The Sang-rael is supposed to hold the cure for our affliction, along with the cure to every mortal disease that has ever plagued humanity. Cancer, AIDS...I could cure it all, with the Sang-rael. What I do know for certain, I got from all those centuries with Joseph. But, I've gotten my hands on a very interesting piece of data, thanks to a fellow member of staff at the museum where I work."

"Yeah?" He took a deep drag, watching as Alvie slid down the wall to crouch near the ground; his childe's gaze was on the dead man they'd left half-hidden behind a pile of black garbage bags. He wondered, briefly, if his fragile childe was okay with that---being so close to her first kill, now outside the blood-lust.

"The Sang-rael is mortal. It's a living creature and it's in New Orleans. Within its *blood* are the secrets of the Universe and of God. The very name of God lies in its heart's darkest shadow." Misha said it in a strangely reverent way that made him glance at her in surprise. She hadn't changed so very much, behavior or attitude, since the days when he'd lived in Rome with her and Joseph. If he wanted to be honest, he could say that he genuinely hoped she never changed---he still loved her, no matter if she'd left him and Joseph or not.

But, then, it sunk into his brain---what she'd said.

"Bullshit. That's *crazy*, Misha." He scowled at her, flicking ashes roughly. "How could it be in New Orleans? If anyone would know, it'd be Joseph!"

Yet, he wasn't so sure of that.

"It's here." She insisted, her tone still reverent; her smile became wickedly crooked. "I tracked it here. The malakh I'm with, he can feel things like that. He's been tracking the Sang-rael for thousands of years, just like Joseph. He's tracked the Sang-rael to New Orleans...to the club where you and Joseph hang out. It's a mortal that you see almost every night, if my malakh is correct."

Nicolai couldn't fathom that. He looked from Misha to Alvie, who still crouched at his side. He tried to imagine which of the college kids it could be. A kid who could've eluded Joseph's notice. But, that wasn't necessarily the truth. Maybe Joseph knew...maybe Joseph knew and *that* was why they were working at Pandora's Box. Maybe that was why Joseph put up with the shit that went down around them. All because...Joseph could know who the Sang-rael was and hadn't breathed a word to him about it.

Misha was leaving. She turned, flicking her cigarette to the side, her mouth curled still yet in an insufferable smirk. "If Joseph refuses to give me what I'm looking for...I'll just find it on my own. Only, I won't be so kind about my methods, if I have to break my promise to our Master. Tell him *that*, Nicolai. Tell him I'm serious. Terminally so."

Then, she was gone---disappearing around the corner and back onto the street.

He dropped his own cigarette to the littered ground and crushed it out, cursing. "Fuck. Fuck, fuck, fuckity fuck."

He'd almost forgotten that his childe was there with him until Alvie whispered. The sibilant noise startled him. "She's telling you the truth. I got that. She knows something else about this creature. Something that could help her narrow down the search."

He dropped to a squat in front of Alvie; she was biting her lower lip with a strangely pleased expression lingering in her eyes. "What does she know? Did you get that, too, with your magic, babydoll?"

Alvie nodded, her expression sliding from pleased to studious. She turned her head to look down the alley, as if searching for Misha once more. "Yeah. This creature, it's a...both male and female. Not quite hermaphrodite, but something like that. It has wings. Big, black wings. It was raised in a doctor's office." She stopped there, sounding slightly unsure of herself. She blinked her brown eyes. "She knows someone who discovered some info about this creature, maybe twenty years ago. I got the feeling of sterility. Like a doctor's office."

Nicolai started thinking, pushing the gears in his Undead mind to work faster as he gave the idea chase. Hermaphrodite with big, black wings, raised in a doctor's office. Seemed like...that would be pretty damn hard to hide. Wouldn't it?

Then, it hit him. He *knew*.

The stolen blood in his veins began to burn as the horror swept up his spine and into his brain. He banged his head on the bricks behind them several times, in disgust at himself, as he pieced it together. His choices were narrowed down, weren't they? He'd have to go see his Sire tonight after all...and he'd have to take Alvie as evidence. All he could hope for was that Alvie's gifts would make her useful, in Joseph's eyes.

The confession came out of his mouth fast, incomplete, clipped short, as he clambered to his feet, beckoning his childe to follow suit. "I think I know who she's talking about, babydoll. Oh, shit. We gotta go find Joseph. If I'm right, a good friend of mine is neck-deep in big-ass trouble."

Chapter Twenty

He was in the wooded glades behind the compound.

He was outside the fence and its razor wire, away from the lazy sentries whose only job was to make sure no outsiders stumbled across this four-acre training ground with its buildings. It was autumn; his nose and his skin told him so. He could taste the chill with every breath, the tang of crisp leaves. Light was streaming down, dappled, from the trees above his head. Old trees, an old forest.

Looking down, he took notice; he was wearing the pale gray scrubs, but where were his shoes? He was barefooted, here in the woods, and that was unheard of. He felt a constant, dull pain in the back of his neck. Raising his hand, he felt the bandage...scratchy, stiff. Right at the base of his skull, in the sensitive dip of tendons. Surgery. He'd had micro-surgery on his medulla, his brain stem and his cerebellum. The pain wasn't enough to make him wince. But, then, he didn't have any human way to quantify pain. It wasn't something he understood; his mind was sharp, but primitive in certain areas of thought.

As he looked up into the sky and at the golden-orange-brown-red trees, he became aware of a whispering sound that seemed to come from everywhere and nowhere. Something moved in his peripheral vision and he went relaxed, focusing on it. Ready for action, if action was necessary.

A strange butterfly. Blood red and velvet black. It danced on the breeze, coming towards him. He cocked his head to the side and watched as the insect began to circle him in the golden sunlight. He lifted his left hand and it gently landed; he felt nothing of its tiny legs or the brush of its large, beautifully bizarre wings.

He whispered, reciting the strange little poem that circled in his head---he couldn't remember a time in his life when he hadn't known the poem, but he didn't remember where it came from. 'Mine is a heart of carnelian, crimson as murder on a holy day. Mine is a heart of cornel, the gnarled roots of a dogwood and the bursting of flowers. I am the broken wax seal on my lover's letters. I am the phoenix, the fiery sun, consuming and resuming myself. I pace the halls of the underworld. I knock on the doors of death. I wander into the fields to stare at the sun and lie in the grass, ripe as a fig. The souls of the gods are with me. They hum like flies in my ears. I will what I will. Mine is a heart of carnelian, blood red as the crest of a phoenix.'

The butterfly moved, flexing the wings he watched, and he saw the pattern shift. Black with red, the red shaped like odd eyes...as if it was studying him in return. He smiled at the vague thought and became aware that the whispering had grown louder while he watched the butterfly on his skin.

He looked up to see more butterflies coming from the trees, from the depths of the wooded area. Dozens upon dozens upon dozens, red and black and each one that came to him seemed to have larger wings than the last. Their wings made the whispering sound and he could smell it, a scent like some rare spice he remembered but couldn't pinpoint in his memory.

The stitches in his nape hurt, under the bandage. The pain grew and grew until he finally went to his knees, dislodging the butterfly from his hand. It came to his mind, to think: 'Papa will want to know why my trousers are dirty and I'll have to tell him that I fell from the pain and that means more paperwork and testing, to explain why I gave into the pain.'

The thought didn't stay; he opened his mouth to scream from the lancing agony that spread along his spine and into his skull. There was no sound in his voice and the butterflies began to swarm him. With each beat of their murder-red, black-sin wings, he was stabbed with flashes of light, brighter and brighter, like a strobe, until at last...

Darkness.

When he opened his eyes again, it was too bright to see. At first, he could feel nothing and it was as if he had gone numb and blind from the pain. But, as the light began to fade and recede, he heard music. A long, drawn-out note...a cello-like resonance that made him think of the low sound he heard when his wings flexed under the skin or tried to slide through to the surface.

Then, he could see again and it was something he knew...something he recognized.

He remembered.

The word had quickly spread down the double line of Legionnaires: the Colonel was going to ride ahead on the 'road' and he wanted his scouts and two of the new recruits. It hadn't taken the message long to reach his ears, he was only four camels back from the head of the column. Henry Alexander Ashwin, newly promoted to Corporal with the two green stripes it came with, swung out away from the line. His white-tan camel gave a huffing snort and responded without more than a nudge from his heels and a tug on the halter.

It was February, 1928, and the garrison was marching---riding---the twelve hundred kilometer journey towards the Quartier Vienot in Sidi-Bel-Abbes. There was a Legion inspection of all Algerian troops in a week; leaving behind twenty-five men and Commander Ahlstrom to stand guard at the Algeria-Libya border fort in Ghadamis, Colonel Augustine was leading the six-day trek to the Legion's Headquarters with less than a full garrison.

Usually, the Generals came to the forts for inspection, but this time, there was some big-wig involved who didn't want to travel all over the Sahara hinterlands. Henry was of the opinion that it was a waste of time; the inspection, the ride, everything they were doing this week. The only good part was how it got him away from the border and the fort, let him enjoy the interesting sights of the Algerian countryside.

Not that there was much to see. After the first day, he'd noticed...everything looked the same. Same little villages, same dogs and camels, same Berbers in their blue and black linen wraps, same sand. They'd been traveling for two days and were currently on the third day of sun, sand, and...more sand. Since leaving the fort in Ghadamis, he hadn't really gotten a chance to talk with the big guy in charge. And it was making him a tad nervous.

Not getting even a moment alone with his friend and lover, the Colonel, made him wonder what was going through Willem's sharp mind. It was almost like Willem was ignoring him...and that just made him more nervous.

Riding a fine white Arabian gelding, the Colonel hadn't even looked back as he left his second in command, Lieutenant-colonel Saint-Jean, in charge of the moving garrison and their struggle over the road towards Sidi-Bel-Abbes. That was just the way Willem did things. He trusted his scouts, knew they'd obey, trusted stickler Saint-Jean to push the garrison on to the next oasis where they would meet up again.

He was one of ten scouts that Colonel Willem D. Augustine had called upon. At his side trotted a camel whose mood was as evil as the look of the new recruit that rode her. He didn't have much to say to this guy, even though he knew Gergely wanted to catch him alone and talk. In the month since the recruit's arrival, he'd watched the guy long enough to figure out that Janos Gergely was one of the many who joined the Legion to escape the police in his own native Hungary.

Unfortunately, thin and weasely Gergely was assigned to the bunk-room that he'd recently been put in charge of, which meant he usually stood very close in general assembly and even insinuated himself into Henry's private time.

He was really starting to not like the little guy's persistence. Narrow of shoulder, narrow of chest, with dark, slanted eyes in his pasty, thin face, Janos Gergely was a nuisance. He was resourceful, though, and had already proven himself useful.

Private First Class Janos Gergely was one of the new recruits who rode ahead with the scouts.

They were silent, riding in the afternoon sun, side by side. And Henry was thinking about his relationship with the Colonel, who rode about ten meters ahead of them. The Colonel was also riding quietly, to the right and among the other scouts for the last half-day, since they'd set out ahead of the traveling garrison. Willem was relaxed despite his straight-backed stance in the saddle.

It hadn't taken long on the road like this, today, before his handsome friend had taken off the uniform jacket he wore and slung it across the pommel, out of the way---the five gold collar stripes of rank could be seen from Henry's vantage point. Willem's dark curls gleamed like red-tinted ebony in the sunlight; he knew, without seeing the Frenchman's face, that there was a shadow of beard. Willem hadn't shaved since they'd left the fort; none of them had. They were on the move and ordered to not waste the extra water that could be, as the Colonel had put it, given to the horses and camels.

He had to wonder what else he'd see in his lover's face, if Willem Augustine turned around.

He and Willem had gotten very close; their behind-closed-doors relationship had started just four and a half months ago. But, things had changed at Christmas. Willem, dark and regal and strong, had confessed to loving him...had started letting Henry in on his more secretive nature. This had opened the door to something he hadn't expected; his lover had a soft side that no one else was allowed to see. Willem was a private man who didn't share much of his personal history; that was normal in the Legion, where a man's past was considered unimportant. But, slowly, he was getting to know his lover-friend's more intimate habits and secrets.

For example, he knew why Willem Augustine would want to scout ahead on a well-traveled road, on a route the Legion had built and constantly maintained. Willem couldn't stand Lieutenant-colonel Saint-Jean and would probably rather shoot the man than to keep looking at him. It was a mute disdain, kept unspoken and private.

Willem wasn't a true Frenchman, according to Saint-Jean, who was convinced that their Colonel came from Gypsies. There was, also the fact that Willem was able to deal with the native Berbers and Tuaregs in their own languages. And the simple knowledge that most of the men in the fort would willingly follow Willem Augustine anywhere and wouldn't deign to spit on Saint-Jean if he wasn't second in command. His orders were followed, but only because they were orders.

As for Willem's end of the hate? Well, that was different. His lover would say nothing against Saint-Jean in the sight or hearing of any other man in the garrison...not another of the Legionnaires knew about the particulars. Most of them probably didn't even know Willem did hate Saint-Jean. But, he did. And he knew why.

It had started just after Willem was promoted over Saint-Jean, when they were in their second year. 4e Regiment Etranger de Cavalerie. Willem, in the heat of a battle with some tribal types in the hills to the southwest of Algeria, saved the entire group and brought the battle to a victory after four days of heated fighting.

While Saint-Jean was rallying the flag, trying to hold the men together by brute mean force, Willem had crawled into enemy territory dressed as a Berber and convinced the tribe's leaders---who were women---that their families and tribe would be best served by meeting with the Legion in peace. After all, the Legion might take the land and enforce some order, always willing to kill and be killed for that mission, but they were also bringing trade and safety to those who sided with them. Instead of continuing to fight a bloody, death-ridden battle against the men of the tribe, Willem went to the women and got them to call the war off.

The big-wigs at Headquarters, they found two things in this. Saint-Jean acted like a true Legionnaire, but Willem acted like a man with brains and balls who wanted to save lives on both sides.

Willem got the promotion, going from Corporal to Commander instantly, since so many of the ranking officers had died in the battle before it was brought to a screeching halt by the appearance of white flags and a cease-fire from the Berber warriors.

Saint-Jean had never gotten over it...and Willem's complaint, only spoken of to him in the dead of night and in private quarters, was that Saint-Jean had tried to have him drummed out of the Legion for the same actions which the big-wigs had honored. What the big-wigs saw as honorable courage, Saint-Jean saw as cowardice.

Plus, there was the little problem of how Saint-Jean claimed Willem didn't deserve the command because he wasn't a true Frenchman. As Willem had explained to him, solemn despite his obvious dislike of the subject, the Legion had started with over three quarters of its men coming from the country now known as Switzerland. The Swiss Army was the original core of the Legion, being where the rules and codes had been adopted, and Willem was Swiss-born.

He knew better than anyone else in the garrison that Colonel Augustine prided honor and courage and intelligent action above everything else and had a habit of rewarding those who showed all three, even when it brought personal detriment or pain.

It was why he'd made Corporal two weeks ago.

And he'd never tell anyone about Willem's breach of etiquette. Not about how Willem had told him the story behind the horrible crime that had led---through a convoluted path from imprisoned innocent to solitary soldier---to the Legion and never a whisper about how the Colonel liked his personal 'recreation'.

The road they were on, it had been built by the Legion; by Willem's regiment, in fact, a few years ago. Before he'd even dreamed he would ever end up in a place like Algeria. It was a trade route from Sidi-Bel-Abbes to Ghadamis, going through every major oasis in Algeria's middle-land. And they were riding ahead of the garrison not because of possible danger but because Willem probably couldn't take the sound of Saint-Jean's voice any more and had decided that it was either kill the bastard or run a half-day ahead on the road.

Still. Even knowing they were on familiar ground, no one was completely relaxed. Every eye was on the horizon, watchful. Even Janos Gergely was paying attention to the hills and desert they rode through.

Henry watched his lover with a steady eye, ignoring the little coughing sounds that Gergely made; Janos wanted to talk at him and he didn't feel up to that. So, with his gaze on the Colonel, he studied the figure of his friend in the saddle several meters ahead and memorized it.

In his shirt sleeves, suspenders slung low at his hips, Willem was dusty; he could see that, even from where he rode on his camel. But, he knew...it didn't detract from the graceful, muscular power that was their commanding officer. Among his scouts and among the regular men, Willem was...just one of the grunts. Yet, there was something in him that Henry recognized. Willem had been born to lead.

Not because of any noticeable leadership trait but because of how it was obvious to anyone with eyes...Willem knew how to lead because Willem knew what it was like to be on the bottom. He was the underdog who'd come out on top, now looking after the other underdogs.

Bare-headed, the Colonel could've been anyone...short, dark curls and unshaven face and rugged hands that drew attention away from the soft leonine slant of his cheekbones and strangely dark blue eyes, the almost effete shape of his mouth, the sound of a voice made for singing instead of shouting orders. His friend looked too young to be in command; Willem looked just twenty-one, maybe twenty-two. And how was it possible that this was Willem's second stint in the Legion?

He knew, if Willem turned around...his friend and lover would be wearing the smile of a cat who was unbothered by the heat or the dust or anything else. Willem looked too damned comfortable in the desert, as if the man had never seen snow much less lived north of the Swiss Alps, farming in the shadows of the mountains that separated France from Switzerland.

He found himself wishing, again, that he dared to ride ahead...move faster. To reach Willem. Better to ride in silence at the Colonel's side than to keep listening to the sound of Janos Gergely coughing in that deliberately annoying way.

Then, three of the French scouts began to sing together; it was a song they were taught

189

in drills, something he still stumbled through.   He knew French, having attended school in one of the finest institutions for education in his native land of England, but the French slang occasionally eluded him.   And he couldn't help but grin to himself when Willem's voice picked up the tune one line into the words, making it a round.

'Y a des cailloux sur toutes les routes. Sur toutes les routes y a des chagrins. Mais pour guérir le moral en déroute.   Il y a des filles sur tous les chemins...'

He lost the grin as Janos rode closer, almost bumping their camels at the shoulder, and spoke in a tone meant to be low but which fell short by several inches.

'I hear he was a Gypsy before he came to the ranks of lost men. Do you think, Ashwin, this could be true?   You know him better than I, you must know something of his life before...'

'Nobody talks about their past in the Legion, Janos. We leave it behind the first time we put on the uniform.'   He lifted the edge of his mouth in a smirk, never taking his eyes off Willem. He could follow the line of muscles in his lover's back, from shoulder to waist. And with only a little stretch of the imagination, he had the Colonel naked in his mind; naked and dozing off, his nether region barely hidden by a sheet too thin to do anything but tantalize.

He knew where Janos Gergely had gotten most of his information.   It was a new recruit's hassle.   He'd been through it, too.   For the first weeks after the new recruits arrived, they were subjected to loads of fairy-tale stories about Legion life meant to scare the pants off them.   But, at Ghadamis, it wasn't just the Legion which was made larger than life, it was the fierce-looking Colonel Willem Augustine, who---in his very first assembly address to new recruits---explained, in no uncertain terms, the rules.   And explained them in a way that could turn the bravest man's guts into water.

After that first assembly address, the new recruits were given time to get used to how things ran.   And their first night in general quarters was always given over to the old salts who told the horror stories...most of them about the current commander.   Who was already becoming something of a tyrant-king in the eyes of those new recruits who'd just been informed, by Colonel Augustine himself, that their lives were his...they would learn to trust and obey him quickly or they would die, perhaps by being staked out in the desert sun.

He'd been shaken, of course, when he'd heard the stories.   Who wouldn't? Not that he would ever admit to it.   But, he'd also seen something his first day which kept him from looking for the first chance to escape his wild decision to join up for adventure.   He'd met Willem, mostly naked in a vulnerable state and with an oddly appealing smile, before he'd been stood out in assembly and scared senseless by the coldest, cruelest Colonel who had ever lived.   He still had a difficult time believing, on a gut-deep level, that it was the same man---wickedly droll Willem and the fierce, lethal Colonel.

Janos Gergely, though...chances were good that Janos knew the stories were mostly exaggeration.   But, just as likely, Janos also knew...those stories were based in some tiny grain of truth.   And the Hungarian obviously wanted to know the base, unvarnished truth about what he knew of their commanding officer.   Who seemed to spend a great deal of his time among the men, who respected and admired him.   Their commanding officer, who seemed to have some kind of friendship with him, the son of a British lord.

New recruit stories.   And Janos's head was still full of them.

Damn.

'You are his friend, Ashwin.   I have seen you with him.' Janos wheedled.   'You were just promoted.   What did you do to deserve that honor?   You receive no more food than any other man and you work the same.   The Colonel, he shows you no extra favor, but you are his friend.   What do you know of him?   How did he really become the commanding officer of a whole fort when he must be younger than me?'

'No idea, Janos.'   He shrugged, scratching at the stubble on his throat; he still hadn't turned to look at the little weasel.   'Why don't you ask him?   Willem's not the bad guy everyone makes him out to be.'

'Sure.'   Janos complained quietly, his whining voice harsh in Henry's ears.   'Not a bad guy. The Colonel is a cream puff who likes to have his men beaten at breakfast, but he isn't a bad guy.'

'You deserved it.' Henry pulled at the kerchief on his neck, to wipe at the stubborn
sticky patch of half-dried sweat lingering just below his opened collar. 'You stole bread
from the kitchen. You know the rules, you follow the rules. You knew better.'

'I was hungry.' Janos complained. 'He starves us and works us like horses. No, I take
that back. He treats the horses better than he treats us, the men.'

'Did you know the Legion's wasn't a nursery when you signed up?' He shifted enough to
glance at the Hungarian riding beside him, causing his camel to huff and adjust with his
weight's new balance. He shook his head in disbelief at Janos. 'You're not a regular guy
anymore. You're one of us. That means you work harder and stay ready for trouble. If you
don't like it, you can always run away.'

'And let him catch me? I'm no fool, Henry Ashwin, but you sound like you believe the
trash they tell us. Are you the Legion's man to the bones, now? I was in the fort already two
days when he hung the men who had deserted and been caught. What did they do wrong but
run away? He hung them with his own hands and we watched. No, I think I won't run from
your friend, the Colonel. Not until I know I have some real chance of escaping the noose.'

He sighed and shook his head again, turning himself so that he could watch the horizon
and the men ahead. No, he wasn't the Legion's man. He didn't believe in the trash they'd
been given to read and think about. He didn't believe the garbage every green kid was told
by the recruiters. He didn't follow the Legion, not even because of the adventure he'd
thought he was signing up for. He followed Colonel Augustine, who had proven to him what
a real man could be like...what a real friend could be like. Colonel Augustine, who was
everything the Legion sought for in their best soldiers.

Willem, on his white gelding, cut a uniquely dashing figure...how often had he seen this,
on patrol? On long marches? To watch Willem, it was hard to not believe in the Legion.
After all, Willem was smart and handsome and obviously educated and he was loyal, right?

'How do you think he got the command?' Janos demanded, pushing close on his camel
once more. 'Maybe the stories are true. Some say he killed his way to the top. Do you think
it might be true? Maybe he did kill officers to get where he sits now. Maybe it was more.
Maybe he did favors of the other kind.'

'What other kind?' Henry asked, tiredly. He'd heard all the rumors; murder and
mayhem and whoring. None of it was new to him anymore, not where the stories were
concerned. The best he could hope for was that someone was telling new stories, something
more original. And he wasn't really hoping for all that much.

'It's said the Colonel gained his commission so quickly by the skin of his arse.' Janos
murmured it, as if the other scouts didn't need to hear what passed between them. As if they
hadn't heard the same rumors at some point. 'It's said he was a whore in an Arab country,
given to some house of whores when only a child.'

'Did they tell you where that house of ill repute was located?' He kept his voice flat, not
looking away from Willem's back.

'What does it matter where this house was?' Janos rushed the words with that voice
which grated like a yapping dog's bark. 'If it is true, he could have bought his way to the
position he now holds.'

'It matters, Janos.' Henry smiled to himself, sarcastic. 'In Arabic countries, boys who
are put in harems are castrated at a young age. They're usually so pretty you'd think they
were real girls, beautiful girls. Colonel Augustine doesn't strike me as the sort. He's not
pretty enough to fool anyone into thinking he's a girl.'

He didn't bother to explain that...boys weren't always castrated in the harems. That
sometimes, they were pampered and treated good and kept whole for the bath houses because
that's how the owner liked them. He didn't bother to explain how he knew about that
because of the stories Willem Augustine had told him.

Willem had never lived as a kept boy in a harem or bath house...but his friend had visited
places like that.

He mused on how little Janos knew about their commanding officer.

'He uses some fancy French perfumed oil, like a woman. He puts it in his bath water.' Janos Gergely went on, trying to beat the idea behind those rumors into his head.

Henry couldn't help but smile again. The scent might be perfumed oil or it might be Willem's natural smell. Didn't matter either way. It just seemed right on his lover; so what if Willem Augustine smelled kind of like church incense and flowers? It beat the bloody hell out of how the other men stunk.

'I think you could be wrong, my friend.' Janos pushed some more. 'Maybe he is a eunuch. He is softer than any real man I have ever seen. He is like the altar boys in the synagogues and cathedrals I visited in Budapest. Maybe he is less than whole.'

He ignored it; he knew what Willem looked like. Besides, anyone with an education in Arabic history or literature knew that eunuchs had girl voices and didn't grow beards or body hair. Willem had plenty of hair and his voice was a healthy baritone. The truth was...despite how young his friend was, there wasn't a man in the garrison who could out work their Colonel. And that was the point; Willem worked hard and went the distance that any good Legionnaire could. Willem was far from soft.

'Do you think it could be true?' Janos was trying his utmost best to get killed. 'Could he have used his mouth and ass to climb the ranks so quickly, Ashwin?'

Fisting his hands over the reins of his beige-white camel, Henry stared hard at Willem and wondered it for himself for a moment. Sure, he believed it wasn't true. But, was it true? Willem was brutal when he needed to be and sly when possible. He had the silver tongue of a devil and the voice of an angel. Could his friend have climbed the ranks from bed to bed, to reach 'Colonel' so young?

Oh, he didn't want to think about that. It made him angry enough to punch holes in people and that was entirely too uncivilized, even for a Legionnaire. To the annoying recruit riding at his side, he answered in an even, calm tone, keeping his eyes focused on the horizon now. On the road ahead. 'Colonel Augustine might do a lot of things. He might be anyone. He left his family and his life behind when he joined the Legion, just like we did. What I do know, Janos, is this. He knows what he's doing. Brains and guts got him where he's at. That's what I believe.'

'But, what do you---' Janos started.

Henry swiveled in his saddle and stared at the Bulgarian, narrowing his eyes. He cut the next line of questioning off before it could get started. 'Not to put too vulgar a point on this, but if you don't shut the hell up, sir, I'm going to hand you over to the first Bedouin slave caravan we find.'

In the quiet, he watched their commanding officer joke and laugh with a few of the other scouts, their voices rising and falling as they spoke in French and he wondered. Were the rumors true? He didn't feel that. But, he'd been wrong before. He often believed he might have been wrong to turn his father down, five years ago, on the offer of coming into the family business in Cairo and Karnak. If the rumors about Willem were true...did he care? Willem had been good to him.

But, Willem hadn't exactly spent the last half-day riding beside him. He knew Willem was cautious, to give no one the idea of their real friendship...but, was there more to it than that?

Did he care?

He tried to picture his lover in the silks and henna that he'd heard stories of---had seen pictures of---about harems, bath houses, and the more private casbahs. He tried to picture Willem dressed like a sweet-smelling dancer and the idea of it was so ludicrous, he started laughing abruptly.

His camel snorted, mocking him.

And there, ahead of him by several meters, Willem Augustine turned in the saddle to look in his direction, obviously reacting to his laughter. The Colonel's dark eyes found him quickly and as he watched, still chuckling, Willem's own smile rose and changed his stern appearance. Colonel Augustine went from being his commanding officer to a beautiful, regal friend who was happy to see him...just one of the men.

Almost too beautiful to be real.

Maybe he was being foolish, to worry.

Later, he rested at a fire with Janos Gergely and two other of the scouts, their tents circled around the stones they sat on. The oasis of El-Bayadh was lush and verdant, the home of a Berber tribe who were pleased to barter with Legionnaires.

They'd made camp, bartered, and were now waiting on the food to finish cooking. There were three fires; twelve tents, four to a fire. They'd bolstered their rations with fresh goat meat and cous-cous and yams from the Berbers. Tonight, as the sun was going down, they would eat good.

It was better than cold, half-stale bread and jerked dry meat any day.

El-Bayadh was the half-way point to Sidi-Bel-Abbes; they would head out in the morning, leaving word for the garrison that followed. As of yet, he hadn't spoken to their commanding officer in private. Willem's tent was at one of the other fires. He wondered if his lover was keeping the distance to quell those rumors which...well, there was no way Willem didn't know how the men sometimes talked about him.

But, he couldn't see Willem anywhere at either of the other two fires. Maybe Willem was in his tent? Well, after he'd eaten, he could go look. He'd think of some excuse.

The roasting meat made his belly growl. When it was finished---or close enough---the four of them dug in, talking over their bowls about the fort and wondering out loud what the remaining Legionnaires must be doing at this time. Commander Ahlstrom was notoriously harsh with the drills.

Going to Sidi-Bel-Abbes was almost like a vacation, the more he thought about it.

The sun was slow to slip below the horizon; it turned everything to copper and gold. When he'd rushed through his food, he wiped the bowl clean and stashed it in his pack and stretched, enjoying the fullness of his stomach. Sometimes, life in the Legion wasn't so bad.

And without a word, as casual as the breeze, Henry Ashwin moved away from the tent he sat in front of...and circled the other two fires, seeking some sign of his lover. Willem was no where to be seen...and the other scouts were eating their food. If Willem was in his tent, wouldn't he have come out to dinner?

Though, the way he prowled...someone was bound to ask him what he was up to. And he had already devised a tale for his use. He was just looking for entertainment. A card game, maybe.

But, no one asked. And Willem wasn't anywhere to be found.

Squaring his shoulders, Henry ventured out into the gathering twilight towards the Berber tents. He'd probably get himself into trouble this way, annoying the natives, but the more he thought about it...the more he became convinced Willem was avoiding him.

As he walked along behind the tent camp of the Berbers, he tried to rationalize things.

Willem must have heard what Janos had said, on the road. Janos Gergely had kept his voice low, but Colonel Augustine was known for an uncanny sense of hearing. Or maybe it was just knowing how the men talked; Willem had to know what the men said behind his back. Maybe Willem thought he believed it...

Maybe that was why Willem was avoiding him.

At last, he came to an opening between two black goat-hair tents and saw his lover.

Willem stood, his back to Henry, in shirt sleeves, with a bundle of cloth under his arm. The brawny Colonel had bowed his dark head to speak softly to the robed Berber before him. The other man was much smaller than Willem, in size. And it was obvious, from the muffled sound of their voices, going back and forth in the native's language, that Willem was haggling...bartering for something.

When the haggling was finished, Willem bowed low and offered something small in his hand to the Berber, who accepted it with a bow of his own...and an offering of something wrapped in leaves or cloth. A round, flat something. Willem put the object in his trouser pocket, big hand moving smoothly, and then bid the Berber farewell with the familiar words that he recognized from spending half his childhood in Cairo.

'Shukran, ma'sadikie. Ma'Salaama, y'allah.'

Because of his father's ideas concerning a proper education, he also knew Arabic.

Henry watched in silence, half-hidden from sight between the tents...and saw that Willem wasn't headed back to the Legionnaire tents. Instead, Willem was headed towards the wilder side of the oasis, where the trees and bushes grew untouched, a natural windbreak for the Berbers.

He followed, out of curiosity about what Willem had bartered for in private...and because he wanted to know why his friend seemed to be avoiding him.

The moon was just rising above the trees, the sun was finally setting. In the golden sunset's rays, he fell deeper in love. Willem was remarkable to watch; the officer was humming to himself, walking along a well-trod path through the trees towards the water's edge.

Then, Willem disappeared from his sight; even in the shadows, it wasn't hard to keep track of where his lover went, but the other man slipped between two tall bushes and suddenly wasn't there anymore.

He tried to be silent as he followed, creeping to the bushes to watch.

There, on the other side, at the shore, Willem was sitting on a flat rock, unwrapping his bundle, his gun belt already laid to the side. Henry never looked away as his dark-haired friend laid out both the almost-flat metal bowl, the straight-razor, a chunk of soap, and a small mirror designed to fit in the palm of one hand. He knew both these objects...he'd seen them in Willem's quarters, at the fort.

Then came the wooden pipe he also knew...that he'd seen in use, before. The bartered flat of wrapped 'something' now made sense. Hashish. Kif. He smiled to himself as he watched Willem crumble a small piece of the herbal 'remedy' and light its pungent fire in the pipe. Smoking, Willem Augustine stared up at the desert sky, his profile visible from Henry's position.

There was definitely something almost soft about Willem. He wouldn't go telling anyone about it, though. He had more respect for his commanding officer than that.

When the pipe went out, the last of its small pinch of hashish smoked, Willem put these things away and got up, walking to the water's edge to fill the little metal bowl with water. Back on the rock, the quiet Colonel washed his face and lathered with the soap; holding the mirror in one hand, the razor was applied...and Willem shaved.

So careful, so delicate, almost as if moving in his sleep.

When the shaving was done, Willem got up and emptied the bowl of soapy water on the sand and then laid it to the side. Henry held his breath, in awe of what he could see. Willem's bath-times were private; it was something no one interrupted unless the fort itself was in danger.

Muscles moved enticingly under the rumpled, dusty shirt...it was shucked away and dropped to the sand. This was followed by the boots and trousers. Then, his lover stood in only his knee-length underpants, which rode low on broad, muscular hips, held up by only the draw-strings.

Willem took his clothes to the water's edge and, with the soap, washed them.

Every inch of visible skin was dusky with the twilight, almost mesmerizing. The hair on Willem's arms and chest and belly was dark and curled, the reminder that his Colonel was obviously a man. Henry breathed shallowly, feeling his body respond with a tightening at the view. He was seeing something that had been fairly forbidden to him, before.

Willem acting like the everyday man, washing his clothes...preparing to bathe.

And he looked so much younger, now...exposed this way.

Wringing out the shirt and trousers, Colonel Augustine carried them back to the bushes. And there, only a meter from Henry's position, the clothes were laid out across the leaves and branches. He realized that Willem was still humming softly, in a breathy tone. A French love song...he recognized it, from other times he'd been alone with his friend.

On the sand beside the water that reflected the rising moon, Willem stretched in the gray-white underpants that nearly fell off his arse and gave a low chuckle, murmuring to himself...the words were lost in the meters that separated them, but Henry held his breath

194

again, unable to feel anything but how his heart pounded as his dark, curly-headed Valentino untied the draw-strings and let the last piece of clothing fall off his body.

There, in the moonlight, on the sand, Willem stood naked. Compact, muscular, and built like a boxer who could go ten rounds with the best prize-fighter ever born. He drank in the sight, amazed; he'd seen Willem naked so many times and never realized how vulnerable his lover could look, even while still seeming stronger and harder than other men.

Soap in hand, Willem began to wade into the water, his skin dappled in the moonlight that reflected from the oasis pool's swirling surface. His commanding officer waded until he'd reached waist-deep and then began to wash himself with the soap, repeatedly diving under the water to soak his skin and short hair.

Finally, he decided...he'd had enough of watching.

Emerging from the bushes, he smiled cockily. 'You know, old son, it wouldn't be that hard for some joker to slip out here and grab a Colonel's clothes while he cleaned up.' He reached for the wet shirt and plucked at it just enough to make the bushes rustle.

In the water, shadowed by the night, Willem turned around, obviously not surprised to see him. One large hand wiped soap over the man's neck and down his bare chest, slicking bubbles into the fur there. His lover's voice was droll, his answering smile sly and intoxicating. 'Some joker might find himself being summarily shot, non?'

The soap was used to rub at the skin Henry found himself wanting to kiss. Shoulders, arms, chest and throat. He strolled to the flat rock where Willem had left his unwrapped bundle. There, he nudged the gun-belt with the toe of his boot. 'It might be difficult for that Colonel to shoot said joker with his gun so far out of reach.'

His commanding officer was more like the smiling friend he'd come to rely on, now, practically flirting. Running a wet hand over his wet curls, Willem laughed. 'How far do you think this joker can run before the Colonel catches him? I might enjoy a light wager on the outcome of such a race.'

He laughed with Willem, sitting down to take off his own boots. 'This joker might think it was worth the trouble, just to get the Colonel's attention.' His voice was casual, but he heard the difference in himself...he could feel it. Time alone with the commanding officer of his garrison always made him feel like playing around.

Rubbing soap thickly over his tight belly, Willem's fingers stroked through the dark curls and towards the places lapped at by the water...just out of sight. He was eyeing Henry speculatively, his smile growing by a hair. 'Why would this joker want the attention of the Colonel?'

Stripping out of his own clothes and gun-belt, Henry Ashwin shrugged, watching Willem from under a sheaf of brown hair that fell over his eyes. 'Maybe the joker missed talking with his friend and was starting to think the Colonel was avoiding him like he had cholera.'

Willem's smile spread, became a broad, sparkling grin. With a flat hand, the other man splashed water in his direction, soapy from head to belly. 'Perhaps this joker needs to bathe. Perhaps his friend, the Colonel, does not enjoy the smell of camels or other, stinking men.'

Without hesitation, he waded into the cool water, sighing with appreciation as he moved towards Willem without hurrying. 'Disgusting, smelly beasts. Makes me, heaven help us, miss the smell of car exhaust.'

There was no warning as Willem tossed him the chunk of soap and slid under the water's surface, rinsing away the dirt and lather. Bubbles swished and whirled on the darkened ripples and he slapped at it with his own hand, pushing the frothy scum away.

Rising from the water again, his lover slung wet curls from wide, dark blue eyes. And laughed, blushing with happiness. He loved this, to see Willem happy. Swiping at the drops that ran down his broad, high cheekbones, Willem shrugged. 'I would not know much of automobiles. There have never been many here in Algeria.'

And that didn't help with the question he had about how old Willem was. He knew the guy was somewhere between twenty and thirty, but...the only thing his lover had ever admitted was...people in his family tended to look younger than their real age. They were probably close to the same age, even with how Willem looked younger. After all, this was

Willem's second five-year stint...they couldn't possibly have taken him into the Legion as anything younger than maybe fourteen.

And cars really were rare in Algeria, even in the cities. Even now.

He wiped at his own face, sputtering at the water Willem had shook on him. 'Well, at least you got a horse to ride.'

Willem splashed him again, wetting his chest this time. 'Oui. He is a very big horse. I think sometimes my horse does nothing but eat and work.'

He grinned, bending his knees to duck his head. Wet from hair to toes now, he began soaping himself. 'Sounds like the perfect horse for a soldier.'

The Frenchman moved a step back in the water, hands disappearing from sight in an obvious way. With a grin that made him as handsome as any movie star from Hollywood, Willem shook more water from his curls. 'Mon ami, we are in perfect agreement. But, what of when I am no longer a soldier?'

This was turning out to be one of their better games into foreplay.

He moved closer, squishing sand under his toes as the water moved around his belly and hips. Soaping at his chest, at his arms, he tilted his head to the side, suggesting in a low, teasing voice. 'Then, you'll have to teach your horse a few new tricks.'

Willem's eyes lowered in a sleepy, lust-filled way. With a sigh, his lover reached out to touch his hips under the water. Big, strong hands that felt warm in the cool water. And he felt his manhood stir at the gentle grasp on his waist, at the sound of Willem's accented voice. 'Perhaps my horse might become a farmer's horse, learn the farmer's life. It is a hard life, but no worse than a soldier's. If the soldier decides to be a farmer once more.'

'Then...' He gave a smile of his own, stepping into the arms that beckoned. The soap didn't matter suddenly. 'The farmer would need someone with a strong back at his side. Just like the soldier needs someone to watch his back for him.'

Willem's hands slid over his hips and down onto his backside, squeezing his skin. It was a tease, his lover's face flushed with intoxication and desire and happiness. 'The soldier may never return to the farm. He might decide, when he is no longer a soldier, that he wants to be a vagabond. Oui? See Italy and Spain, perhaps...maybe he will even go to America.'

The country's name sounded like music on Willem's tongue.

He drew Willem closer, letting the soap go so that he could touch his lover's muscles at arms and then at ribs and waist. They were almost nose to nose, their breath mingling as he looked down at the shorter man. 'Haven't seen terribly much of Italy or Spain or America, but I imagine I might be persuaded to show you some of the more attractive spots in England.'

Willem looked up at him, head tilted to the side. There was a hint of sensual promise to the smile now. 'What of the horse, mon ami? Do you think maybe the vagabond might sell his horse for a handful of money that could take him to America?'

He rubbed his soapy hands up and down his lover's shoulders. His words came soft, husky. 'Maybe, or send the horse out to his family's farm to wait there until the vagabond is ready to settle down with that strong back and strong arms to tend the land once more.'

There was a sudden blackness he could see in the Colonel's eyes, a tenseness in his clean-shaven face. The flush of desire was waning and he didn't understand why. Then, Willem's hands slid away from his arse, almost like his friend intended to pull out of his arms. 'Would the horse expect the vagabond's promise to do this, return to the farm? Might the horse not get tired of waiting for so long?'

He had the distinct feeling they were talking about two separate horses and two different vagabonds. Staring frankly into Willem's eyes, he pressed his forehead down against the wet curls on his lover's brow. 'If the horse loved the vagabond as much as the vagabond loved the horse, then the horse would wait for eternity...if given that chance.'

Willem's eyes were full of dark heat. They breathed in the quiet, touching from head to chest; he could feel the brushing tease of his lover's manhood move along his thigh.

Willem finally lifted the corner of his curled mouth in an acerbic half-smile, murmuring. 'It is a good thing then, mon ami, that we are neither vagabond nor horse. We need never *concern ourselves with such.'*

'Yes.' He felt his blood heating up in response to the Colonel's voice; coyly, he pulled Willem's hips to his, pushing close so that their manhoods met in a rush of water and lust. 'An excellent thing we're just two soldiers with more muscle than good sense.'

And Willem held him again, fingers moving back into place on his arse. Opening his mouth against Henry's jaw, the commander gave a soft whisper and seemed to melt into his arms even while standing up. 'I do love you, I would never make you wait an eternity.'

That made his heart feel four times bigger, swelling over-full in his ribs. He smiled again, kissing at his lover's ear. 'We're never going to be forced to find out if we have to wait for each other, Valentino. I'm not leaving your side...I don't have the patience of Job."

Later, the lovers sat on the flat rock, watching the moon and the stars as they filled the sky.

It was a peaceful moment, clean and pure. Something to cherish. Henry sat with the dark, noble Colonel between his thighs; he held Willem from behind, arms folded close around his lover's shoulders. Willem's head was laying back against his shoulder, almost pushed into the crook of his neck.

Clean, drying clothes and the scent of soap and no more itchy stubble. For a few days. And no one around to interrupt or pry. They could be themselves, share this time together without worrying about being seen by anyone else...they'd hear the other scouts before anyone could possibly get close enough to spy on what happened at the oasis' little stretch of beach.

Henry smiled to himself, listening to the deep breathing that vibrated through them both. Willem was utterly relaxed, loose and limber and so completely his. At times like this, it was impossible to match his lover to the strong, ferocious Colonel who commanded an entire garrison of Legionnaires.

Words weren't needed between them, now. He felt like the strongest man in the world, holding Willem this way. Just being quiet together, loving each other without any need for questions or answers or games. The desert, beyond the oasis, beckoned and he admired the blue gleam of moonlight on the sand.

Lightly, he kissed Willem's cheekbone and squeezed gently. It just pulled his lover even tighter into his chest. He sighed, inhaling the smell on the other man's skin. Sandalwood and lilacs. The soap didn't have that scent. It had to be something else...and he didn't care, right now.

They were always going to be together. Always.

Chapter Twenty-one

On an overstuffed divan, Daniel rested alone on the verandah, in the dark, and listened to the rain as it fell on the tin roof over his head.   He had stayed on the edge of the Jackson Square park long enough to see his partner leave with the young Creole fille.

It was nearing midnight and he was aware now of the evening's end; Rhys perhaps did not intend to return to the house tonight.   His gut instinct, something he had learned to trust after several centuries, whispered that the sly tchatcha was staying with Tennyson Beaulieu and he wondered if the situation was sexual or if Rhys did this only to ensure the fille's compliance with the assignment.

He lifted his glass of Jim Beam and swallowed the last of it.

For hours he had lain here, smoking cigarette after cigarette and drinking bourbon.

Ashwin.   Henry Ashwin.   His long-lost Legionnaire.

He tried hard to not think of his Legionnaire; more than sixty-five years had passed since he had seen Henry last, in Egypt, in 1939.   He had gone to the French Resistance, after that last ill-fated meeting.   Henry Ashwin of the English tomb-robbing nobility, with a Misrene wife and an infant son.   Why would Tennyson Beaulieu choose the name *Ashwin* for her use?   Could it be simply a coincidence?   Non, that was too easy an answer---the answer one would give oneself when one could not face the alterative possibilities.

He needed to find out who Tennyson Beaulieu was.   He knew, from his previous efforts, that her mama was a New Orleans native, a metal-working artist and professor with a rather intriguing family history.   But, what of the papa not mentioned?   To learn anything more, he would need to see a copy of Tennyson's birth certificate or speak with the girl's mama.

Refilling his glass from the bottle which sat on the faded wooden porch floor, Daniel reached for the cell phone beside it.   He knew someone who could give him answers quickly, once the true search was begun.   With a press of a button, the phone began to speed-dial Dante's voice-mail.

The message on the other end was humorous and he smiled, indulgent.

'This call may be recorded for quality and training purposes. If you don't wish this call to be monitored or recorded, then please let the answering machine know when you leave your message.'

With a deep breath and a second after the beep, he began to speak in a concise, business tone.   "L'Epee D'Mort.   I need a background search on l'fille, Tennyson Beaulieu.   Find everything you can on her past and send the information to me.   To be specific, search out any references to Ashwin and-or Egypt and-or London.   I have concerns about her and cannot, in good faith, continue trusting her in this assignment until I have been answered for those concerns."

Daniel clicked the phone off once more and lay his head back onto the cushions of the divan.   It occurred to him to wonder if Mattie Curran could be to blame for where Rhys was spending the night.

He drowsed and let the pattering rain send him into sleep.

An hourglass full of sand...the sand was pouring down into the bottom half, seeming to go faster and faster.   The sand turned to blood and then opened up to become an endless, red-tinted desert.   Across this desert came a man.   He slogged onwards, fighting his way through the fine, heavy drifts of sand. But, it was obvious that this man was losing the battle. The man was Rhys Lorraine, the young malakh he adored.

Above the sand, a set of scales hung. On one side, a huge golden feather lay. On the other side sat what looked like the world, as seen from the surface of some distant planet or moon. Below the sand, something waited...dark and terrible and cold, like an ocean of blackness. But, he knew, in some vague manner, it was not merely a black void. There was some thing in the black void, something hungry and hateful. It wanted to destroy Rhys and all that Rhys loved. It was gunning for Rhys in particular and knew what needed to be done, to utterly erase Rhys. From Rhys, he understood a strange emotion---a sense of powerless despair.

He could see a room made of carved stone where white and black statues stood, painted in gold trim. All the statues had erect chinois, even the figures with female breasts. They seemed to be gods, from Egypt---half-human, half-animal. A white stone altar glowed almost translucent in the firelight which burned in a bronze brazier before it. A giant man with long, black hair in thin, tight plaits sat on his knees before this, raising a knife to his left arm, cutting down the length of it, from wrist to elbow.

At the small of the man's back, at the top of his wrapped, black linen shenti was a mark; the giant man was tattooed...a strange, black tattoo.

The inner arm was laid open on the knife and then held over the fire; the blood dripped into the flames, hissing and spitting and making the smoke rank and sour with death. The large man did not seem to notice; he was naked except for the black linen shenti he wore belted at his hips. The man was a warrior; he had the proud, strong body of a dark-skinned fighter and the handsome face of a fierce god, but there was such sadness in his coal-black eyes, a grief fresh and new.

There came the knowledge that this warrior prayed and bled, had done so for seventy days, waiting for his beloved to be readied, for a dead love's body. He was now married to death; this warrior grieved silently, unable to even weep anymore, only waiting for everything to be finished so that he could complete his prayers and his sacrifice. For...in truth, his life was over with this dead love.

The image flickered, became the blood-filled hourglass again, dripping grisly minutes.

He blinked and when he opened his eyes, he found himself in a new place.

He was in a recessed stone pool of warmed water. The room was small, but beautiful. Stone walls, furs and pelts lay on the floor and hung from the carved pillars that held up a ceiling of what looked to be interlocking pieces of slate. Everything was painted; murals of detail that stole his attention when he focused on them.

To his left, there were swaying pieces of linen hanging from the very ceiling; beyond them, light...a great balcony of some kind that showed trees and bright sunshine. He could see, past this, the stones of what appeared to be an immense temple. To his right, several meters away, sat a giant bed made of stone with furs and linens on its flax pallet. It was surrounded by more linens that hung from the pillars, dancing slowly in the breeze.

Where was he? Why did this seem familiar and strange at the same time?

A noise startled him; he looked up.

Across from the bath where he sat, a stone panel of the wall opened and two young girls came in. They were naked and could be no more than seven or eight years old. Beautiful Khem girls, with their long, black hair in a single pigtail that was caught up on one side of their small heads. Each had gold in their ears and wore a bronze cuff on their left wrist. On the outer side of their right thigh, each was branded. A shen oval, bearing ancient hieroglyphs he did not remember, could not read. Their eyes were lined in kohl, their skin gleaming with sweat and oil that smelled like...lotus or lilies. Like the scent that Rhys' flesh gave off.

Each of them carried over their tiny arm a pile of folded white linens. These were laid on a stone table near the bed. Neither spoke to him or seemed surprised to see that he was in the bath. He stared, feeling as if he should cover his naked body in their presence, despite their own nudity.

'Where am I?' Daniel asked and then stopped, hearing the voice that came from his throat. It was soft, higher than he was accustomed to. The voice of a boy in late puberty. He hissed a breath of worry and went on, staring at the two dark-skinned girls as they came to the recessed pool where he sat. 'Who are you?'

They went invisible with a blur of colors and light that he recognized.

Tchachau. They were of Rhys' race.

Their hands were like flames on his skin. They began to wash him, to stroke at his skin with the oiled water. He protested, trying to wriggle free. 'Non---stop this. I can bathe myself, merci. I am...I am Medjay, I do not need your help.'

It was there, in his mind...a knowledge of who he was, what he had come from, and of his history. He was eighteen years old; in this time, that was parallel to being older, in the modern world. He was Medjay Nubian, born and bred, but he had not taken his warrior-hood tests. He was unmarked, in body and spirit. As pure as he might be, given the era in which he lived.

His father had bought this purity with his life, in battle for Pharaoh. He had been raised by an aunt, fostered by her brother, his uncle. He had never been outside the walls of this city, had never seen anything but this great realm of...

Thebes.

The two slender girls washed his body, leaving nothing untouched. He felt crazed, wanting to escape their hands. He had never been handled by a tchatcha, did not know what to think of how they moved, felt. These girls were no older than his sister, who had not received her first red moon yet. But, unlike Yeva, these were girls being trained as warriors. He was in their grasp, in the House of Maahes.

He had been sent a summons. Two tchachau, older than these---older than him---had come to his aunt's home. He was summoned to the tchatcha master, the commander of invisible infantry soldiers. He had not dared to disobey, even as his aunt had cried and protested, swearing that she would send for his warrior-guard uncle, in the House of Pharaoh...

Why was he here, being treated as a guest? It was obviously someone's private chambers. But, the tchatchau girls refused to speak, to answer his questions. At last, an unseen hand offered him a moon-shaped piece of bronze that faded into nothing at the handle, where the invisible fingers held it.

He took it in his wet hands and stared at the polished bronze surface, examining what he could see of himself. He was dark-skinned with long hair that fell below his shoulders. It was coarse, wavy. His face was that of a young, beardless boy. His ears were pierced, each with a small bronze ring. He was beautiful...his mouth full and expressive, his nose a little wider, his eyes large and dark with long lashes that gave him a soft, feminine appearance. His cheeks were rounded, his chin firm. His skin was darker than mulatto...it was truly Nubian, dusky and brown.

Dieu. He was very nearly a boy still.

He laid the mirror down on the stones that this bath had been created within and felt like his world might spin upon its axis, throwing him loose from reality...what was going on? This was Thebes...of the ancient world. He had often dreamed of this place, this time, but not for many years.

As he rubbed at his wet face and listened for the sounds that the two girls made---they made so very little noise, unnerving him---the panel in the wall opened again and he glanced up, from over the line of his fingers to see that the master was entering.

Tall. Broad-shouldered. He felt his tongue grow parched at the sight of this man who...he felt he should know this man's name. It was there, in his throat, where the desert had robbed him of breath and spit and words. This man was unnatural; it prickled in his skin, the awareness of the fact. This man was not like other men. He was too tall to be a natural man...too muscular and his skin was like dark gold, something between maize and bronze. Half-Nubian.

The man made him think of a lion, instantly.

The man's hair hung down his large back, in tiny plaits. Each plait was braided with gold strands that clinked in a musical way, drawing attention. He wore a black linen shenti that was buckled into place at his hip with a strip of lion-pelt and bronze tacks. The man's naked arms and legs were massive and seemed to be without hair of any kind. His chest was the same, gleaming with the oil and sweat of a tchatcha. On his right thigh, like every tchatcha, he bore Pharaoh's brand.

It was his face, though, that truly drew the eye. He wore a mask. The mask.

At the eye holes could be seen a dark, liquid gaze. The cheeks and nose were pure gold, as was the brow. The mask was held into place with the thinnest of gold chains that were wrapped under his hair, hiding their purpose. The face carved and formed in the mask was a god...beautiful and serene. At the bottom of both cheeks, the mask opened and showed the chin, the mouth of a malakh god. Yet...the mouth changed everything about the expression in that gold. The mouth was curved, firm and seemed to be the terrifying embodiment of intent; it lent a dark hunger to the mask. The silken mouth smiled and it was a fierce smile.

A frightening and beautiful smile.

On his hands, he wore two rings. One on each hand.

One ring was large, rare silver, with an oval moonstone. The other ring was gold and bore a red triangle of jasper. He knew what these rings were...one, the white ring that marked the tchatcha warrior as the heir of Apedemak, that dark Nubian god whose name was whispered with fear even when the name of Sekhmet was praised...for Apedemak was the unseen companion of Sekhmet and perhaps even her true father, if the Medjay stories were based in any truth. The other, the red stone ring, was the warrior ring of Sekhmet, given to the commander of tchatchau by Pharaoh for battles fought in the Kingdom's name.

This was a nobleman; if not born one, he had surely been made one through his service to Pharaoh.

The tchatcha wore a single bronze wrist cuff, on his left arm. Embossed on the broad, thick bronze cuff was a mark that electrified every nerve in Daniel as he stared. A warrior of Gods, a holy man, the sacred one...the protector of most ancient secrets and magics. The three triangles with an X in the encircled center.

He, in his deepest instincts, knew that this Guardian's mark was what had drawn attention to the young boy the warrior had once been, beaten and abused in the tchatchau pens for nothing more than his unusual grace and bearing, the manner in which he had been raised, away from the House of Maahes. This man was a half-Kemetian prince among the Nubian nobility of Meroe, never meant for life as a slave soldier in the tchatchau pens.

Daniel stared up at the huge, smooth-skinned warrior who seemed made of something other than flesh. The warrior stared back, eyes glistening like onyx stones, with a smile that both enticed his body and worried at his mind. This commander, this warrior...was no ordinary man. He was the Guardian.

He seemed to be more of a god than Pharaoh himself!

He was as forbidding and beautiful---even while behind his mask. This was a man who, if he aligned himself with a princess, could become Pharaoh with the darkest of choices...could overthrow the reigning House and bring in a host of Nubian royalty to re-make Kemet.

And indeed, there was talk of this strong commander taking one of Pharaoh's daughters as his bride---the strengthening of bloodlines could only ensure Pharaoh's House would reign forever. Yet, he knew nothing but the rumors...would Pharaoh marry his own daughter to a tchatcha, particularly one born to Meroe's ruling Candake, a malakh princeling sired by a Kemetian emissary on a diplomatic mission? It was unthinkable.

Perhaps this tchatcha would be bold enough to bid for the hand of a princess, a young goddess herself...become the protector of both the woman and Pharaoh. Something in his heart beat faster at the thought of Pharaoh's family becoming capable of the tchatcha power, to go invisible at will. They would need fewer guards, non? Who would dare to attack them, with such ferocious, fiery blood in their veins?

Daniel went on, staring breathlessly at the warrior who stood perfectly still at the stone edge of the recessed bath.   No muscles twitched and he could not be sure that he was hearing the tchatcha breathe.   When would the hands of the two invisible girls return, when would he be thrown out of this room...sent to his death or back to his aunt's home in the Medjay section of the city?

But, before he could stir himself and speak, asking for leniency, the man's eyes flickered and something changed in the room.   He felt the two girls leave his side; they walked, unseen and fiery like Amun-Ra's chariot, across the room and through the panel door...it closed. Now, he was alone with the fiercest commander of Pharaoh's army, the descendant of darkly protective, cruel gods.

He held his breath again, never letting his eyes wander from the gaze of the tchatcha master.   He could feel his heart thumping away, knew that this warrior might hear its drumbeat through his skin, for the world had become silent and without movement...as if time had stopped.   At last, he realized that the warrior was not going to attack him for being in the room, in this bath.   He released his breath slowly, being as quiet as he could.   And this changed everything.

The warrior spoke from behind the gold mask, his mouth forming the words carefully. His voice was soft, drowsy, musical.   'Abayomi. Born of the Medjay. Not yet of the blooded warriors, are you?'

He shook his head, his wet hair slapping at his back and shoulders.   'No.   I have not...I have not proven myself as a warrior in battle.   Yet.'

His host gave a different smile, now, showing a few teeth in the way that made him think of a half-tamed lion.   'Your sponsor, your uncle-father, he's done well.   Does he know you were brought to me?'

Daniel thought about it for a long moment and then shook his head again, being honest. 'No.   I did not have time to tell him of the summons.   I have not said anything, but I cannot be sure that my aunt will not send him word.'

'Ah.'   The word was drawled, accented by the knowing curve of the mouth that formed it. 'I do not believe she will do that and if she does, she will be told the truth.   Your uncle knew this day was coming.   That is as it should be.   I would have you decide for yourself, not rely upon the orders of your kinsman or the ways of your people.'

He had to fight the urge to cover himself again as the dark eyes moved over his naked body; he sat in the water, but he knew...he was visible, even through the oiled liquid.   He kept his voice low and flat as he asked.   'Why did you summon me?   Why did you ask your people to bring me to this room, to make a bath for me?   Have I done anything that displeases?   Am I to be---'   His cold strength failed him at the thought of what could happen to him here, in this House.

Tchatchau ate humans...his aunt had told him the stories, when he was a young child. He had learned to fear that which could not be seen, the invisible demons of fire.   Tchatchau tortured and killed, were fearless in every respect...and how could they love their human masters?   How could they love the god Pharaoh?   What would this warrior do to him?   He was unarmed and so much smaller...

But, now the smile returned and it was gentler, became friendly.   'No, Abayomi, you will not be punished.   You are not a blood sacrifice to Sekhmet.   Nor are you a warrior to be used as fodder to hone my children's skills in combat.   I summoned you to me for a different purpose.   You are an innocent, a trained warrior who has not seen his first campaign or taken a human life.   I wished simply to have you as my guest for the evening...to speak with you of your life and the life you want for yourself.'

He put his trembling hands on the sleek stones at either side of the recessed pool and began to stand up, to defend himself verbally.   'I am ready for my warrior tests, to prove my manhood.   My kinsman asks that I wait, that I not risk myself, that I not harm any.   I obey him, though I do not understand why he asks these things.   It's brought nothing but shame on me, as a Medjay.'

The smile of his host broadened as he stood in the water, defiant.   The voice was a purr. 'And will you obey me?'

He stopped in his movements, realizing that he was naked and gleaming with oiled water in front of a Lord who had been given much honor from Pharaoh. The perfume of the oils saturated the heavy air, soaking into his lungs as he sucked in a breath at the realization of how defiant he sounded.

The voice asked again. 'You know me? Will you obey?'

He splashed the water as he sat down hard and fast, feeling a blush creep up his face, as hot as the invisible hands that had washed him. He had not seen this man's whole face, yet he knew that he had pleased the warrior with his impudence...and he knew the tchatcha, somehow. Deeper than by reputation 'You are Bomani.' He stammered. 'Lion of Kemet. The son of our Mistress of Dread, Sekhmet, child to Lord Apedemak of Kush, born the youngest in the House of the Bayhas Candake in Ta-seti. You answer to none but God Pharaoh, to Pharaoh's High Priests.'

It was answered with a nod, the tiny plaits of gold wrapped hair whispering and chiming. 'Yes, I am that man. I am Bomani, born of Sekhmet. My tribe is in the mountains to the south, beyond the cataracts. The family's name is Bayhas. We know who I am, yes, but who are you, Abayomi? Do you know?'

He frowned hard, thinking, narrowing his eyes. He could not quite remember what he knew about himself. But, there was knowledge. 'I am Abayomi, of Horus, born of Medjay in this city. My kinsman Asi-Deruty speaks for me. He is a Captain of the Medjay, chief bodyguard to Pharaoh's beloved lotus daughter, Olufemeh, of the benu.'

Daniel felt his chest blossoming, as if a breeze blew over coals that he had forgotten about, at the mention of this princess. Green eyes. He could see female green eyes, in his mind. She was beyond him, a princess and a benu, but he felt love and longing for the girl who was eternal and several years older. He was simply Abayomi, a commoner...Medjay, trained but not tested as a warrior.

Bomani stepped down into the stone-lined pool and sat on the chiseled edge, long legs like tree trunks to the young Medjay. The strong hands began to move in the water, mindless of the two warrior rings. The tchatcha laughed, his tone much quieter and full of gentleness.

'You are this, yes, but you are more. You are the Light to my Darkness.'

He stared up at the smooth-skinned warrior who could suggest such a thing.

Again, the tchatcha spoke, his voice like a temple cat's purr. 'I have sought your light--- the light you alone show me---since my earliest memories. I have waited many Inundations for you to grow, to become strong like the tree I planted when I knew you were newly born among the Medjay.'

It was dizzying; he felt as if his soul was clawing to get free of his chest. He closed his eyes, daring to expose himself to a possible attack as he asked, whispering as his voice failed him. 'Why? Why did you wait so long, lord?'

'Perhaps I waited for nothing.' Bomani whispered back, as if this was some sacred truth that could not be said out loud, for fear that it might shatter the sanctity of sky and earth and bring down the wrath of the gods. 'Perhaps I waited for a different Inundation.'

Then, it hit him. He opened his eyes in surprise, to stare at the man who sat in front of him, large fingers dangling in the water as if to play. The mask hid the face, but he knew this man...he knew this spirit which spoke to him from behind the mask. He knew this mouth, these words, this voice. This was...

He was meant to become this man's servant, but more. He was to be this warrior's lover, a concubine or catamite, as he had been many times before. And Bomani suddenly did not frighten him in the least. He knew, in his heart, though he did not understand how he could know...ferocious and dark and terrible, Bomani would be tender and loving of him.

Crawling to his knees in the water, he pushed across the small pool and knelt up in front of the youthful-seeming warrior who had summoned him here to talk of a future that could belong to no other. Kneeling there, naked and shaking with the mix of apprehension at what he would choose, he lifted his wet fingers to daringly touch the mask of gold. He was allowed. Bomani smiled with the mouth of an angel, generous and accepting of anything he might do. He had kissed both boys and girls before, in games, but this was different, was *new.   He tipped his face up and held still.   He closed his eyes in offering.   Fever-hot lips ghosted over his cheeks, his eyes, the tip of his nose.*

Then, as he daringly slid his fingers along the length of gold-plaited hair, the lips moved on his mouth.   He opened his eyes in reflex to the searing heat, the tingle of recognition, the jerk of surprise, the rising of hunger in him that he had not sensed before.   In his chest, there was a bird that beat wildly with its wings, crying out to dance and to fly.   As the kiss ended, Bomani took his breath with the delicate, loving touch of fingers on his cheekbones and his jaw, cupping his face.   He stared up into the masked face of a man he would call Master and lover.

Bomani whispered to him, dark gaze full of happiness behind the eyeholes of the mask. 'Ieb, my Abayomi...little Medjay, you are my ieb, my ka, my beloved Nemat.   It is the promise I make before all gods and before my god.   It is my promise.   I will always come to you, always love you, until the wind blows no longer in the desert and even the stars die.'

Chapter Twenty-two

Now awake and sitting on the rumpled bed's side, Rhys watched the curvy, voluptuous figure distorted by the translucent glass of the double shower door. His beauty, his princess, his goddess, his Tenny. She bathed happily, satiated with their love-making.

He yawned, taking a drink of water. He wanted a cigarette. Getting off the bed, still naked, he found his coat in the living room; digging through the pockets, he turned up his Pall Malls and the Zippo. He shook a smoke out of the pack and lit it, inhaling deeply as he cleared his brain of drowsy contentment.

After making love, they'd fallen asleep together. Dozed off. He'd had dreams, again. The same weird dreams. He'd been dreaming that way all his life, as far back as he could remember. Dreams of other places and other times, people whose voices haunted him in the quiet dark of night. People whose voices made him startle awake on the edge of sleep. Whose voices brought the tight, ugly feeling to his chest. The feeling that always made him think he'd forgotten something integrally important; as if he'd forgotten the most critical thing.

Brushing strands of hair from his cheek, he went back to the bed and sat down, carrying the ashtray. His eyes instantly found Tennyson in the shower again, through the open WC door, as he delved deeper into his thoughts, frowning.

The dreams. He'd always dreamed that way and, often, the dreams were about a man who closely resembled Daniel. Strange. Even as a kid, in the complex outside Cold Springs, he'd dreamed of that man. And of other people who made him think of Daniel, whose voices all rang so clear and distinct in the still of the night.

He could remember, clearly, the night when he'd met L'Epee D'Mort. He'd felt a funny sensation in his chest and belly and the middle of his back, looking up at the man who was there to take him away from his Papa and his brothers and sisters in the Isosceles Labs. The research intern, Jimmy Tucker, had told him it was okay, that this man wouldn't hurt him...this man was there to save his life.

He hadn't possessed the voice, at that moment, to tell Tucker that he already knew this tall dark-angel of a warrior from his dreams...that he recognized the face and the smell of this stranger. A stranger who wasn't really a stranger, not in his instincts. His instincts had told him, silently, that Daniel was the one person in the whole world he could trust without conditions or proof. Daniel had only aged a little from the young man he remembered, from his dreams, and the name was different...but, he knew that this was the same man. Only, not a man...he'd known that, too, in a distant-vague way. Not a man, different from men and yet so impossibly beautiful to his heightened senses.

And, yet, even while knowing he could trust Daniel without rhyme or reason, he'd feared the leonine assassin and he knew where the fear came from...the knowledge that he possessed in himself the ability to hurt this dark-angel and that, in doing so, he would destroy himself utterly. The fear came with the knowledge of that terrible sensation in his body at the sight and smell of Daniel---*why* did he want to wrap himself into this stranger's arms and weep with the overwhelming myriad of emotions he couldn't identify, when he couldn't recall ever weeping for anything but the most intense of physical agonies?

Looking up into Daniel's face, that first night, had created a schism in his mind and heart; a schism he couldn't heal or quantify. How could a stranger feel like *'home'* when home was in the fenced lab compound?

Exhaling smoke from his nostrils slowly, Rhys scrubbed his forehead and gave a sigh.

It didn't do any good to chase the same thoughts over and over; it was unproductive, to constantly come back to the knowledge of those dreams. It was time to turn his mind to something else, something more pressing.

Tennyson.

He hadn't meant to go this far...he hadn't intended to let her get under his skin. From the first time they'd met, in the club, he'd found himself fantasizing about her. There was something about her...something intangible that he couldn't place. She wasn't the most beautiful woman he'd ever seen or the sexiest, even, but yet...something in Tennyson drew him in like a moth to the candle's flame. Like a bee to the flower. Her scent, her face, her skin...the mark on her shoulder.

Where did the mark come from?

He'd kissed it over and over, tonight, while holding Tennyson. Only because it was part of her.

His instincts told him to fear and hate that mark...he'd seen it before, but couldn't place the knowledge's origins. Somewhere, he'd seen it and he knew it and it meant trouble to him...trouble to him in the deepest sense of trouble. Something appalling would happen because of that mark, he was sure of it, but he couldn't grasp how he knew that.

Yet, he wanted to kiss those black lines buried under Tennyson's perfect, brown skin. He knew that she didn't know what the mark represented; he'd felt it from her flesh and her mind, the one time he'd commented on the tattoo. She didn't know if there was a purpose behind the mark. When he'd mentioned the tattoo, she'd shrugged and told him that she'd had it since she was twelve. Something her mom had gotten done...and that was a *strange* thing for a mom to do, from what he'd heard about moms. He carried a mark, himself, on the back of his head, under his hair, at the site of a particular surgery, but he knew that his childhood was far from what other people called 'normal'...he didn't even know what his tattoo looked like. No one had ever told him and he'd never mentioned it to Mattie or Daniel. He didn't know if they even knew Papa'd had him tattooed. And if Tennyson's mom was a normal woman, why would she have her daughter tattooed at twelve years old?

And why *that* mark?

Taking a last drag, Rhys put the thoughts away as he ground out the cigarette butt in the ashtray.

He'd told her his whole name tonight; he smiled, thinking on how her mouth had shaped itself around his first name. How *Josiah* had sounded, rolling off her tongue. She liked it, had said it a few times before kissing him again, cuddling close into his shoulder. She hadn't freaked when he went invisible, at the height of his ecstasy; not like Mattie, who had invariably gotten pissed at him for something he couldn't always control in orgasm.

Of course, it wasn't just the invisibility which had disgusted and annoyed Mattie.

He couldn't help what he was, the differences between him and other men.

He turned his mind to the change in his body. He had done something different tonight; suddenly, more than ever before, he felt protective of Tennyson Beaulieu. He felt possessive. At the edge of dozing off, earlier, he'd had a surge of anger at the thought of her previous lovers. She didn't belong to them; she couldn't. And the idea of other people touching her was still there, piquing him. He understood the emotion, now; he was jealous of those previous lovers. Anyone who had ever made love to Tennyson was an enemy and if they came around, he would eliminate the threat with prejudice. He didn't give a damn that they were females. Yet, she wasn't his to own, either. But, he felt real affection for her. The same kind of affection he'd always had for Mattie.

She was singing in the shower; singing without words. A vocal nonsense that chorded in his heart and was twinned by the song he had lived without, for so many years, but which he could almost hear in the very back of his brain once more.

On his feet, he swayed languidly, lost in the thought of Tennyson's flesh as he watched her small hands move down over ribs and broad, firm hips, smoothing soap onto her dusky skin. He throbbed for her touch, again, to lose himself in the sweet perfume of her love mingled with his own. Unique scents becoming something new and perfected. He ached to bury his hands in her long braids, bury himself eternally and melt away the cold core of his heart.

He walked to the doorway of the bathroom and then to the shower, never slowing as he pushed open the misty glass.

There, he stood in the thickly moist air, and stared at the woman who waited. She turned and gazed at him as he leaned against the wall, arms hanging limply by his side. She was perfection, wetly sleek and smiling.

Rhys felt he might go mad from the quietly babbling truth he could still hear coursing through his brain. He knew her most intimate memories---they were in his blood, now---and that made him no longer safe, no longer steady. No longer wholly himself. It had been changed with such a simple thing as a moment of physical touch.

Damn the gifts of his malakh birth, the empathy of being a sa-hekau with the fierce hungers of a tchatcha. Wasn't this how Mattie had become part of him? Wasn't this why he couldn't move past Mattie and how she had locked him out?

He was sweating heavy, scalding...and the wetness grew with the steam. Rhys hung his head, looking at the cream-white tiles beneath Tennyson's high-arched feet, letting his hair fold close to his face and throat. He had to outrun this weakness that made him feel such love and hope. If he couldn't...

"Rhys?" Tennyson moved towards him, in the shower, her husky voice full of concern. "Are you okay?"

He looked up.

Her pale green-gray eyes were wide, worryingly innocent. She was wet, slippery, her Creole flesh shining in the water and the light. And she was all he wanted, in this moment. She would make him feel safe, help him forget the sense of how *lost* he sometimes felt. He had to find some succor, to escape the grief Mattie gave him.

"Hey...you okay?" Tennyson touched his cheek then.

He responded instantly, stepping into the shower; pulling her voluptuous body close, he caused Tennyson to drop the shea butter soap she held. She giggled nervously, almost chaste in her surprise. It was a delicious sound to his ears.

Brushing the sweet wetness of her lips with his, he murmured. "Make me okay, ma reine..."

Daniel startled, his gaze taking in the wooden ceiling of the porch. It was dark, but not so dark as to prevent him from seeing where he lay. He breathed hard and smelled the bourbon, the cigarettes, the rain and the green wetness of his back garden.

The grieving warrior's image returned and, for a brief second, he felt his heart pause.

Something nameless in his soul cried out, bringing tears to his eyes.

He was dreaming of the unknown man once more...the warrior who had haunted him often the last century. For long years, he would not think of the dark-skinned man, and then find himself unable to escape the dreams and visions that occasionally came to drive him into horror.

He could see it, in his mind, the other images that came---that did not need his brain's restitude to find a lodging point. The warrior whose grief ate at him was someone he could identify, with stories he remembered from his time with the Misrene tribe in the El Faiyum oasis---especially those who carried the same name of Bayhas. He had dreamed of that warrior long before hearing the tales; being given the stories had only made the pain more real, gave him a basis of comprehension of where these images might rise from, within him.

It was Bomani he dreamed of and he could not say that the dreams came through his knowledge of the legend. He had often suspected this, in the long decades since that first night at a village fire when the words were spoken...words concerning a legend, a warrior whose blood had flowed like the Nile, up and out of Nubia, and whose blood had dwindled to nothing with the passing of centuries. There were none but the Bayhas who could clearly prove to be the descendants of Sekhmet's chosen son by Apedemak of Medja, this warrior called Lion of Kemet, and if the Bayhas of El Faiyum were his descendants, it was an extremely thinned bloodline.

The images came, now, bringing him to sit up and swallow at the sour taste of his mouth.

...Bomani, in the gold mask and leather shenti, in silent prayer before the alabaster statue of Sekhmet, preparing to leave; there was battle and Pharaoh was expecting the tchatcha at his side, leading the unseen infantry, and he could not accompany his master and lover, for he was to stay behind and protect the children left in the House of Maahes, and his Bomani had done something to ensure he would never go into battle---he was to remain behind while his love, his own master, prepared for what might be death approaching on darkened wings---Bomani offered up blood to Sekhmet in the hopes that these battles would not bring too high a price for the tchatchau...

...Before the giant warrior, on the altar, lay two swords and a shield, weapons that could not be broken, but would they be enough to save Bomani's life? He had stood at the temple's door, terrified this might be the last night he would see his master alive. Once the blood was given, his body and his pleasure had been offered up as an appeasement, but only for the first few hours of the night; after Bomani had given these devotions to the gods who might guard his life in battle, his master had taken him to bed and spent the rest of the night in private worship...

...He had woken alone, in the morning, to find the House of Maahes unusually quiet; the oldest students had marched out of the city behind their teacher and head priest, the Lord Bomani, leaving only a few to care for the young children. He had wept on his knees before the gods in the temple, offering his own blood in primitive sacrifice for Bomani's safe return. For what would his life be without the one who loved him so?...

Daniel breathed deep of the wet night air and felt his stomach lurch. He reached for the bottle that sat on the porch floor and lifted it to his mouth, taking a long drink. Swallowing the liquid fire of the Jim Beam, he let his eyes close as he considered the dreams. Could these images have come back through the idea of the job he had taken from the demi-benu Sterling? To steal the mask and artifacts reported to have once belonged to Lion of Kemet?

Stealing such items, could he give them up to the British man who had hired him?

There was no answer to be had without more information. He would simply have to wait and see what he uncovered, in Cairo, through the job itself. Settling on this, he rose and carried his bottle into the house, letting the screen door slam shut. Barefooted, he wandered through the kitchen and the large, warmly lit dining room, and into the dark study.

The house was chilly, but he did not feel it. In his daze, he felt only the heat he had known before, in the dream. He held the bourbon in one hand as he lit a few twelve-hour candles in the haunted room, bringing a golden glow to play. It was not haunted in the sense that any ghosts lurked in the corners, non...it was haunted through the memories he had bestowed upon its walls and in the decor.

This was the refuge of his childhood memories, the paintings and furnitures that his father had left for him, as master and lord of the family property. He had brought them from Neuchatel, in the last years, after Vivienne had left him through death. These were the trappings of a life he detested to remember, for the most part of his existence. Few ever dared to open the door, visit the D'Loup past. His children did not care to and Rhys preferred to leave the room locked up and ignored.

He walked with the surety of where each piece of furniture sat, carefully placing the bottle down on a table where animals made of blown glass waited to be some young girl's playthings again. Alba's toys, from their childhood. His sisters, Bintha and Alba, had played with these glass ornaments, centuries ago.

He was searching for something he could not quite put a finger on. Something that might make confessions easier to bear...for he knew, he needed to confess. He needed to find the words to speak with someone, to tell what he knew. He could not carry this by himself; it was beyond his grasp.

The emotions locked his voice away, took his words. Again, the silence threatened to steal into his brain. He had never been one to talk much of what he felt...not since his mother had died, when he was so young. His mother...his first Confessor. Oh, dieu, as if he had done much as a young boy that needed to be confessed. His thoughts and deeds had been so clean when held up beside what he became, upon his manifestation of the darkness, the benu malakh.

The study was small, when compared to so many others he had seen, in his life. The furniture was heavy, good for small children to romp on, even with its velvet and brocade upholstering. The walls were a dark, polished wood, but, he had hung the D'Loup portraits up once more, uncovered the chairs and the divans, polished the floor and the fine decorations.

Both his son and daughter, by Vivienne, refused to ask him about this room's significance, of the things that could be seen in the faces on the wall...the faces that only he could accurately identify, since many of the portraits did not have any notation on the back to give information about the subjects caught with oil paints.

Daniel lifted the bottle again and took a drink. What was he seeking here, in the room that mirrored a parlor of his once-happy childhood? The ghosts that never showed their faces, left no cold spots to be walked through?

His heart was broken and nothing remained of it but gleaming shards that pierced his lungs, stole his courage. He could not face his partner, Rhys...not yet, not now. He needed to confess, to find some method of mending his heart, finding peace with what he knew about the artifacts they were commissioned to steal for Sterling.

He walked along a wall, his bare feet instinctively skirting the chairs, the fine tables. He came to the first portrait he could remember ever *staring* at, when he was a child...it had been painted only the year before his mother's death. His frere, Robert, had, from early boyhood, been exceptionally skilled at capturing that which only he seemed able to see.

Robert had painted their mother's portrait and even Papa had said it was remarkable; he believed that might have been the first time Papa had admitted that Robert had any talents at all beyond that of heir, of tending the farm's business.

Daniel reached up, gripping the glass of bourbon in tight fingers and unmindful of his half-naked body, tugged at the white sheet that covered the large portrait, and stepped back to let the cloth fall away to his feet.

Oh, sweetest heavens, the face of his mother. His Mama.

His brother had chosen to paint Mama in the garden, on her knees among the plants. This was a familiar sight in his own memories, the image of Mama working with her plants; medicines, foods, and the ones that induced magical trances, magical knowledge. In the painting, Mama was not pregnant...was not yet gravid with the child that would kill her in the end. Had she known, then, that it would come...that she had perhaps a year left of life, a year to prepare her children for a life that was cold and darkened without the light of her beautiful smile and her generous hands?

He had Mama's smile...his children Julien and Seraphina, too, they had the smile of his Mama. The smile that seemed so alien and frightening at times, in his face, had seemed perfect on Mama. Her natural state---a small and round-bodied Berber immigrant from the sunny south with dark curls and dark eyes, dark flesh softer and more fragrant than any other he could remember from those lost childhood days.

Daniel took a drink of bourbon and studied his Mama.

In the long, dark red skirt, loose-fitting white blouse, and gray broadcloth bodice-apron she had favored, she sat on her knees, her legs showing bare and almost nut-brown from the knees downwards, this part being bared...her knees, her calves, her pretty feet. Her long, black curls hung free, despite the traditional styles women had worn at that time...Mama had, when at home, never followed the conventions of Suisse *or* Berber society.

Her arms, bare from the elbows down, were as nut-brown as her calves, ankles, and feet. Such strong hands...so small and delicate; he could remember seeing his father kiss Mama's hands even when they were covered in earth from the garden or flour from the kitchen.

His chest gave a spasm as something burst within him and he remembered.

He opened his mouth and tossed the last of the bourbon in the glass into his throat and swallowed, smiling sadly. His Mama had loved him with all the power of a wise goddess; she had said from his earliest memories that he was special, that he possessed a great gift in his spirit and must never let that gift be taken away...

Mama had died in agony, unable to give birth to her third son, the seventh child.

Her death had robbed their family of light, of laughter, of love. He could remember what had come, with that day...how he had seen his Mama dead in her nakedness, grown ashen and swollen and almost monstrous with the loss of that magnificent spirit too large and too powerful for the small female body it had been given.

He had stood there at the door and watched as his graying tantes, both D'Loup witches of true cunning, had washed Mama and his still-born brother. He had stood, unable to look away, until Jeanne-Marie had come to take him from the doorway, to keep him from seeing any more.

Out of everyone in the family present, he had felt the silence first. When Mama had cried out that last time, in the hottest part of the second day of her labor, he had stopped playing in their nursery. In that moment, he had no longer possessed the knowledge of how to *be*. His fingers had become as ignorant as his brain; he had made a discordant noise with his throat and stopped breathing, turning to stare at his sister Alba, where she sat beside him on the floor.

The silence after that last cry had broken something in him; he had started crying without sound, as silent as the house and as silent as his Mama. He had gotten up and walked to the room where she was, to peek through the crack in the door. He had felt a different emptiness in the air, something missing. He had stood there, watching his tantes move around the bed and around the room with the slowness of their own grief.

He had known, even then, that he had felt Mama die before his tantes had seen it. They had always been this way, he and Mama; not an empathy of any sort, just a constant awareness.

Jeanne-Marie had come to get him, to tug at his small, stocky arm, but he had refused to go. He had pulled away, snarling a curse at his eldest sister...a curse which should have gotten him slapped. But, no one had punished him for it; they had always whispered of him and Mama, smiling fondly as they did...he was Mama's favorite and no one felt the slightest jealousy over this.

He had broken the silence with his snarl, but the silence had not died.

He could never have destroyed the silence that had started in his gut, in his heart.

Jeanne-Marie had tried to pull him to her, then, to hug him as she knelt before the door...keeping him from the sight of what his tantes did. Robert had gone downstairs to the study, to get their Papa. Bintha and Alba had clung together at the door of the room where they had slept together...the nursery. Dark-haired Alba, blonde Bintha...clinging to one another and to Violette in their clean, white under-shifts, burying their faces in blonde Violette's shoulders, all three weeping.

Only Marie---his beautiful, strong Ree---had dared to approach him, to try helping him in any way. Caesar-like, almost mannish. His Ree. She had knelt in her plain blouse and petticoats---she claimed it was too hot to wear the full dress if they were only going to be in the house---and drawn his hands away from his chest, trying to pry his fingers to release the fists he had made.

He had been crying sobs that had no sound at all. His hair, hanging past his shoulders, had come loose from the ribbon he wore and fallen to soak itself in his sweat, in his tears and he had struck out at Marie with his fists, knocking her backwards from her crouched position into the floor just as Robert and Papa had reached the top of the stairs.

Robert had grabbed him, picked him up in his strong arms---so much the man, ten years older---and taken him away from the room, away from the hall. Robert had brought him down to the parlor, the room for which this New Orleans study was a mimic. Soon, Marie, Violette, Bintha, and Alba had joined them...but, he had said nothing, refused to look at any of his siblings.

He had sat in Mama's favorite chair and stared at the portrait of her that Robert had painted...this picture. He had kept his eyes on it, even as he heard his Tante Elisabette come down, telling Robert and Violette to go into Neuchatel and ask their oncles, the husbands, to come---that they could not convince Willem to let them prepare Deseseh for the grave.

A sound from upstairs had overridden the sound of Tante Elisabette's voice...

The sound of his father crying out, shouting at his sister, Tante Anne-Marie, to get out, to leave him be. Jeanne-Marie had jumped up at this, had gone up the stairs to help Tante Anne-Marie control Papa.

Papa had refused to allow them to wash and prepare Mama, refused to be parted from her...Papa's grief had been a horrible, mad thing, until Mama was buried in the ground and then, the grief had been shut away, turned off like a candle could be snuffed, in the same manner that Mama had died after giving that high, hoarse, bird's cry.

Mama had cried out and gone silent. Papa had done just the same, in his way.

He gave a dark smile and whispered to the portrait of his mother. "You walked with me, shaped my life, and left me...did you know, all along, what must happen? Did you know your death was to be the start of my silence? My inability to talk when I feel too much?"

He had sat in the family parlor and stared at this picture until the world had slowed down again and his mother was to be buried. He had not attended the burial. He had chosen, during that hour, to leave the parlor and climb the stairs to the bedroom where his mother had died. There, in her bed, he had stayed while the family crept around him in their grief, in their mourning...he had laid in his mother's bed and been swallowed by the silence in his heart.

He had cried for the rest of the summer, as his eleventh birthday had passed and his world had turned to autumn. Each night, he had climbed into Mama's bed and cried himself to sleep, had cried while he slept, had cried with each morning he was forced to rise and leave her room. He had stayed sick with grief for months and months, until Noel had come and his father had finished making the changes which would influence the course of his life.

His Papa had loved her so much...Papa had died with Mama. He knew this, now, though he had not truly understood it then. Robert and Marie, his benandanti siblings, had battled almost non-stop with Papa over all of their fates.

Robert was soon married to a sweet girl that he liked, even if he did not love her.

Jeanne-Marie had been harassed and threatened for several years, up until this point, concerning the thoughts of marriage...once Robert married, she had been pushed in acceptance herself, several years later. What could she do?

The air felt less chilly to him now, with the bourbon making his insides warm. The candles did little to dispel the sense of gloom in his study, but he had others to see...others to face. One by one, he pulled the sheets off the portraits of his sisters, his brother, his father. Each of them painted by Robert...even a self-portrait. At last, he came to his own picture, to the one that his brother had painted, just before leaving for the southern French coast, to be hired by the company that had given Robert the chance to travel as he had always longed to travel, working in imports and exports.

The only portrait or picture of him before his first death, he had been painted while standing on the long-lost path outside the front of the family manor, by the porch that few bothered to use. Sitting at his feet was his favorite mastiff, the one he had loved to hunt with. He had been dressed almost formally, at the time; for what purposes, he could not remember.

His long hair had been smooth and pigtailed, revealing the softer, gentler grace of his features...the features that had caused him pain for so many years as he was mistaken for a homosexual, for a child lord who could be taken easily by predators. It had not been until he joined the first troops of the first Foreign Legion with his fellow Suisse soldiers in 1831, that he had finally looked old enough for the role of soldier and man. More than two centuries after his birth.

Lucinda had told him often, in the years of their friendship during the last decades of the French Revolution, that he looked like one of the angel statues in the Cathedral...too gentle to be anything but good and portrayed, in marble, as the killers of demons and the slayers of evil. His petite, blonde whore's favorite angel, her patron angel? Fiery and fierce Archangel Michael, the warrior, who put the fallen angels---turned demons and devils---into hell with the use of a sword. Archangel Michael, whose marble face seemed too sweet to be that of a killer of anything, much less cruel and vicious demons.

He was of the opinion that if Archangel Michael was to be thrust into flesh and left alone in the world, as a mere human with that face and body, he would surely be destroyed by other humans. Men with boy's faces and boy's youth could never survive intact. Not that he had been a man, even then. He had not matured, inside, enough to be justified when he called himself a man.

Non...that had come with the Legion who had taught him how to kill in ways he could not have imagined, even as a soldier for the royal families of France...or the conflicts that had followed. The Revolution, when he had played both sides for the purposes of keeping his Everards safe, in Lyon. The battle he had taken up, in service to Napoleon, only to be betrayed by his commander with the end of that war.

He had been, at the time---formerly of the Suisse Army loyal to the Bourbon Kings, formerly of Napoleon's Grande Armee, formerly of the Royal Foreign Legion also known as the regiment of Hohenlohe---considered practically a mercenary, according to the new pacifist and bourgeois government. He was not alone in this, of course. There had been many men like him, at the time, who were considered dangerous to the new government. Many of his commanders had known what he was, had used it to their advantage in battle and in peace.

Louis–Philippe's accession to the regency was followed---as always in France---by a reorganization, which was no more than a purge of adherents to the old regime in favor of the partisans of the new. The army, both standing and retired, had not escaped this process. The creation of the Foreign Legion was intended to remove from France those officers and soldiers, French or foreign, who were felt to be awkward, excitable, or frankly dangerous subjects for the new monarchy.

He was not entirely sure which of those categories he had fallen into, but he had received a summons---upon asking to rejoin the active army and escape his ignoble retirement with the fact of his youth so blatant to witness---and the summons had claimed he was to be given a new post, a role to play in this, The New France.

Wiser after Napoleon's promises to---and betrayal of---his loyal soldiers and officers, he had accepted this offered position in the Legion Etrangere and been sent as a commissioned Suisse officer, under the command of Colonel Stoffel, to Algiers. Colonel Stoffel, a fellow Helvetian, had served Napoleon in Spain, had been a soldier for thirty years...had known of his abilities and kept his secret. He had flourished in the North African frontier.

The legionnaires in Algeria had served their apprenticeship in guerrilla warfare. The enemy, in a terrain which favored ambushes and sudden raids followed by swift retreats, had dictated the style of the fighting. It was not until the last of April, in 1832, that the 1st and 3rd Battalions---composed of Germans and Suisse, himself included---had recorded their first victory. On that day, they had stormed the enemy covering the approaches to Maison Carree, a large village some miles east of Algiers.

He had been given new honors for that battle.

Then, had come the conflicts of Oran.

The smoldering resistance of the Arabs burst into flame fanned by the courageous young Emir of Mascara, Abd-el-Kader. In early November, 1832, the Arab had arrived before the gates of Oran at the head of some three thousand cavalry.

Battle had been quickly enjoined. The first charge by the Arab horsemen was broken up on the slopes of Djebel Tafaraouini, a hill dominated by the little Arab shrine, or marabout, named Sidi Chabel. Then, the French had mounted a counter-attack. He had been put in charge of a unit for the first time. His unit was composed of mostly Spaniards---many of them guerrilla veterans of the Peninsular War against Napoleon's occupying army.

Fighting side by side with men he had done battle against, before, the victory had come sweet and hard. His Spaniards were uncouth soldiers, but crafty. They had known how to slip under a horse's belly and up on the rider's blind side, tipping the enemy out of the saddle to be stabbed to death. Disorganized, the Arab squadrons had started to break up. At nightfall, Abd-el-Kader withdrew. Oran was saved.

Again, he had been given honors for his work as a new commander while looking to be only in his late teens, perhaps early twenties. He had used a sister's married sur-name as his own, to disguise the truth of his age from the units who could not be allowed to suspect him. But, the leaders who did know of his identity had made sure he was safe enough to continue bringing honor to this, the outcast troops of a dozen armies in Europe.

He had fought with the first days of 1837, taking part in the second campaign mounted against the fortified city of Constantine. The previous year, a first attempt had failed to subdue this citadel, which was strongly defended, well equipped with artillery, and perched high on a rocky plateau surrounded by deep gorges.

The second attempts on Constantine began in foul weather in early October, 1837, and lasted for four days. On the thirteenth of that month, at the head of the storming parties, he had fought his way through a breach battered in the city's walls. All that day, he had fought in the narrow streets of the old Arab town, against a bitter resistance. At last, as night fell, the Legion finally captured the last enemy flag and declared a victory.

Even while standing firm in the bloody and oft-useless engagements which would follow, he had led his men in construction work. They had built entire cities and roads while marching back and forth over Algeria, working to keep the peace they had won. They had built forts, cleared and marked tracks, and set up the safe markets, which helped to reconcile the tribes to a more peaceful way of life. Often enough, though, they had been forced to lay aside the pick and shovel and take up their rifles once more.

He had traveled to the Crimea, to fight, then back to headquarters in Sidi-Bel-Abbes, where he could lick his wounds---emotional and psychological---among the brothers of the Legion. Other conflicts followed. He had mustered out, re-enlisted, served and fought under a dozen names, only to repeat the cycle. He had even fallen in battle several times, allowed himself to be declared dead, giving him new ways to change identities, names, places of service. Wars had come and gone.

He had been noted in the history of the Legion, in several places, his face used for enlistment posters. He had not cared for any of it...the Legion was his family; at the time, the only family he could claim to understand or love.

Still, he could remember the pamphlets that were given to the new recruits as they arrived in his small fort, in Libya, Henry Ashwin among them. The pamphlets had been designed to inspire pride; often, they intimidated, for what mere recruit could see himself doing the same deeds as might be written about, the numerous campaigns that had been fought so valiantly even when the odds were that no one would survive?

He smiled to himself, thinking about the first night Henry had spent under his command. After being fed and watered and having the rules explained to them, the new recruits had dismissed to general quarters and met the older men, the warriors who knew something of what they all must face. He had stood in a corner, dressed in a non-descript work uniform and ignored for the most part, and listened to the stories, the jokes, the sounds of men becoming acquainted.

Even while half-hidden and unnoticed in his corner, the young Englishman Henry Ashwin stayed in his line of sight, past the milling bodies of those other men. The young, blue-eyed Brit had sat at a table with three other recruits, talking about the pamphlets. They had, of course, no way of knowing that he, their commanding officer, was the soldier mentioned in one of the stories. He had even smiled quietly to himself as Henry read the pamphlet out loud, coming to the tale of Hermes Vaudois.

In World War I, at the entry of Monastir, the Legion had done battle alongside the Serbian cavalry. At that time, the battalion had been cut down---through death---to a mere two hundred infantry, the size of his current garrison. Leading this impossibly brave group was the battalion's adjutant chef, the cook, because all the officers had been killed or wounded. The battalion's cook had taken them to a victory the likes of which their fellow armies had never witnessed.

Henry Ashwin's fellow recruits sitting at the table, all of whom were French and more cynical, had said it was probably just propaganda, to enflame their belief in the Legion. But, he had seen the expression on the young Brit's face---he had, in the past, come to admire both Brits and Americans with just cause. They produced some of the most loyal, determined fighters.

Reading the tale of Hermes Vaudois, Henry had gotten a speculative gleam in his eyes. He had realized, then, that he was looking at a man who might prove himself to be the next Vaudois, even while the real Vaudois still lived and was currently in the commandership of the garrison, with the name of Willem Augustine.

He had always preferred the common labor and peace-keeping to the battle. But, he had never run from battle until nearly a century after the Legion was born, at the end of his service...in that sad, under-funded, peace-keeping border fort established on the line between Algeria and Libya, he had allowed a petty, glory-hungry officer to destroy his life of routine and stability.

He had run from the battle of a possible scandal, at the suggestion of two superiors in the Legion's main Headquarters of Sidi-bel-Abbes, Algeria, who knew the truth of him. They had suggested that he accept a lesser defeat, be sent to monitor French interests in Egypt. He had agreed to the retreat rather than be defeated and sentenced to having his command taken, his rank ripped away. He had not wanted to serve the remainder of his time in that fort as a cook or the lowest soldier, below that of even the newest and greenest recruits.

Was it arrogance or fear that had led him to retreat?

He did not want to think of what might have happened to him, if he had remained in that fort, being busted down to the bottom in rank and privilege. There could have been no guarantees that Henry Ashwin---or any other man loyal to him---might protect the newly demoted peon from the newly-promoted commander's wrath and hate.

The trouble had originated with a blackmail from his second-in-command, blackmail coming from the hissed accusation of his sexuality...of his 'unorthodox and repugnant relations' with a soldier under his command. He had taken the assignment to Cairo and left Henry Ashwin behind.

Daniel scratched his bare chest, smoothing his fingers through the curls there as he lifted the bottle by its neck to his lips, drinking several mouthfuls of bourbon in a desire to rid himself of the terrible cold that was once again trying to settle into his bones.

He studied his own painted face and smiled softly at the resemblance he could see, the resemblance to his youngest son, Julien. Had he really looked this way for a century? It was difficult to believe, sometimes. He had stopped aging as a demi-benu at seventeen, had looked so like his Mama. In the portrait, he had been captured in time by Robert's brush while wearing a rare smile. A smile that would soon disappear and become rarer still...in only a few years.

He knew better than most that the human mind did not look at passing time as something solid and fearsome. He was an excellent example of what a small sliver of years could do to the brain and body of anyone. Born in 1613, he had lost his mother the summer of his eleventh year...in 1624. He had died his first death at seventeen, in 1630. At eighteen in 1631, he had become the father to two sons, one of whom was illegitimate, and lost his own father. By the end of that same year, he had taken in the Scottish 'wife' of his dead brother and in the following year, become the adoptive father to her son, his nephew...while taking her as his mistress.

Five years later, in 1637, the love of his young life left him with his nephew to raise and disappeared from the world as he knew it, pregnant with his child. Twenty-one years later, in 1658, he was to witness the destruction of that world, with the death of his bastard son, Jean...which had set off the horror and despair that became his new life. In less than a half-year's time, he was with fifty other men in the main cell of an over-crowded prison. Nearly three years after that, in 1662, he was thrown into a windowless, solitary room where time became meaningless in the truest sense.

In 1721---after his first century had passed, unnoted by his mind---he was to be released from that terrible solitary room in the bottom of the prison. He had, at the time, not given any care of it. What did freedom mean to a man who had stopped being human? Freedom and time had meant nothing to his mind, then.

His first act of humanity had come in those first days...as he was leaving Geneva, to make a slow return into the canton of his birth, he had passed the building which had once housed the courts where his trials had taken place. In walking by them, he had spit on the steps---those steps where Adelaide had condemned Theresa. The mother of his dead bastard son had declared before the world to the mother of his living, legitimate son, that when all was dust, he would live and he would love Adelaide more.

He had not loved Adelaide more...not in 1721. But, he had spit on the steps of the great stone Courts building. Defiance weak and worthless, but defiance nonetheless...the first recognition of what he had survived. He had outlived the courts, had outlived the prison, had outlived the ones who stood as his accusers, his torturers, his betrayers. Defiant, oui, but human......non.

In the sliver of time---that first century---so few would consider worthy of note, he had been born, raised, loved, betrayed, imprisoned, forgotten, and finally left for dead. A century of time...what was this, compared to eons of consciousness? It was nothing...nothing but his first century, the life and death of that last Seigneur D'Loup.

A mere century. Nothing more, in the scheme of human events.

Tipsy now, he pulled the ghostly cotton sheet off the painting of Theresa that he had commissioned from some artist in Geneva. He drank from the bottle, sloshing the bourbon into his throat as he studied his dead first wife's picture. The work of the portrait was exquisite and showed her as she had been, early in their marriage...beautiful and cool and tiny in hand, waist, and foot. So delicate, his Theresa. He had despised her, almost from the first moment he had laid eyes on the girl who would become his wife.

Theresa Margrin-Rollet. Everything a merchant 'princess' could hope to be. Her father had been in business with his Papa, buying the majority of each year's surplus cattle and sheep and goats for resale in part to butchers for meat, their skins intended for the Margrin-Rollet leathers shop. He could remember the day they had met, in her father's house. He had traveled to Geneva with his Papa, to deliver the late summer's cull of yearlings---handpicked by himself, sold for prime livre. Finishing with Margrin-Rollet's foreman and eldest son, Marshel, he had been ordered to the family's large chateau.

He was broad-sided by his Papa's conniving duplicity while visiting in the well-decorated parlor with Marshel Margrin-Rollet, discussing the politics of joining a foreign army. He had been, since the recent birth of Jean, considering what he could do to escape his Papa's decisions.

He had decided that the best way he might do this would be to take the same route that Robert had taken, fleeing the farm and the canton. He had never been very interested in business or boats, but being a mercenary soldier---good work for any true-blooded Helvetian!---could take him out of his Papa's reach.

It was at this point he discovered the reason for his visit. If he had known he was to be presented as breeding stock to a merchant and his daughter, he would not have made the journey from Neuchatel...and his Papa had known this, had made all of the arrangements without telling him a single truth about the trip to Geneva.

His Papa had known that, once he was broad-sided with the situation, he would be too unnerved and overwhelmed to do anything. He would go silent and not speak in his own defense. It had worked exactly according to the plan...except for his wounded, cruel comment on the matter, which had soured any possible affections that could have developed between himself and his bride-to-be.

Theresa's mother and father had come in and were introduced; he had been mild and polite, doing his family proud. Minor nobility or not, every child was educated in the proper manner in which to greet others of similar background or class or money. Settled there, with her parents and her brother and his Papa, he had talked quietly with them of what he would do, following in his own father's footsteps, expanding the wealth and progress of the canton by bringing more commerce to Geneva, where a wider base of variety in business was available.

All lies, coming from his tongue...he had been intent on running away to join an army!

Then, a servant had announced Theresa.

A smarter man would have run for his life, at that moment.

Fourteen years old, with a better education and the arrogance to match, the only daughter and youngest child of those rich merchants who would have disdained to have him into their house on any other occasion...if not for that little, unimportant notation at the end of his name in the French royal court's records.

He was a 'cousin' to the King.

What he had not realized was that he was considered one of the most marriage-worthy boys in the nearest cantons. He was strong, beautiful, young, unmarried, of a good age, healthy, not a raving lunatic or an idiot or a filthy, useless pédéraste. This had made him worth a great deal. His Papa had been auctioning him off to the highest bidder out of several dozen potentials.

One of his greatest assets was the whispered proof that he was fertile and capable of producing heirs...his illegitimate son, Jean, was mentioned in the parlors of every doting set of parents who had aspirations of marrying their daughter into the D'Loup family. It was a sin, of course, to have a bastard, but when considering what might become of him---breeding stock, good provider, et cetera---that small sin was forgivable. It was, after all, proof and the Helvetian people of both German and French blood lived within fences built of proof.

Theresa, apparently, had known as little of the situation as he. This should have made them allies instead of enemies. When introduced, he had agreed that she was beautiful. She had sung a pretty song for him, for his Papa, recited a poem...he had gotten quickly bored. Then, his Papa and her Papa had decided that they were ready to know the situation...that the marriage was agreed upon, would take place as soon as decently possible.

They should have been allies, not enemies.

Embittered by his Papa's previous decisions concerning his life, he had turned in the silence to stare at Theresa, whose face had pinked with anger at being given to this rough, uneducated farmer. As she began to protest, to argue with her Mama, he had laughed to himself in absolute horror of what he was facing...his laughter had caused Theresa's brother Marshel to ask him what he found so humorous about the nuptials.

His reply had embarrassed and shamed every ear that heard him.

'Why do I laugh? The titled land-owning farmer and the rich merchant's daughter, we make a handsome pair---we should service well in the pen.'

From that moment on, Theresa had said not a kind word to him...of course, he had not encouraged kindness. Upon reaching home, on the farm, he had started drinking to constant excess for the sole purposes of becoming a sot. Which, with his malakh blood, was impossible. He had been drunk on his wedding day, drunk on his wedding night---had stayed drunk for months. This, of course, was an endless source of animosity between himself and his father.

Daniel looked at the portrait of Theresa and wondered if things could have been more amenable between them if they had met under better circumstances. Things might have gone differently, in their marriage, if not for a mutual abhorrence of each other. Perhaps she would not have helped him destroy their son.

He gave a scowl, muttering. "Bitch."

Daniel gazed at the gold of Theresa's gown---so fashionable---and fell.

Chapter Twenty-three

The music pounded through the floor, a Steve Miller song remixed into drum and bass.
'You make me hot, you make me sigh.   You make me laugh, you make me cry.'
He sat at the desk in his office, poring over the pages he'd spread upon the clean wooden surface.   He had to piece the fake puzzle together before he handed it to Misha---the clues had to look coherent, even if they were incomplete or incorrect.   He'd come into the club hoping to talk with Nico, after speaking with Dante Webster, but his childe hadn't shown up yet.   He imagined Nicolai was enjoying a long, convoluted hunt.   Well-deserved.

According to the clock, it was nearly one in the morning.   He glanced at it quickly to make sure and then lit another cigarette, letting it dangle from his fingertips as he refilled his glass with warm beer from the pitcher he'd brought upstairs with him.   Golden Wolf hadn't bothered to ask him if everything was okay---she wasn't that kind of employer.   He'd noticed that neither Lorraine or D'Loup were in the club.   Nor was Tennyson Beaulieu.   Most of the players present had been congregating in the bar, not the dance floor.   Mathilda's younger son, Rugby, was playing DJ---a stretch for the young, handsomely blonde teacher and researcher.

He returned his attention to the papers in front of him.   This clue linked this page to this clue on this page.   Slowly, they were compiling themselves into a definite shape.   He'd chosen the mistakes he had made twenty-four years ago---the last time he'd been in the real dark concerning the Guardian.   He was convinced that murder and mayhem and an utter disregard for human life had kept him from discovering the truth---his lack of purity had sullied his chances of finding the Sang-rael, all along.   It had taken a young American scientist's voice, on the other end of the phone, to start a deeper change in him.

Drag of the cigarette, sip of the warm beer, and then a sigh.   Did the pages lead to Tennyson Beaulieu, by any long shot?   He had to consider what Dante Webster and Julien D'Loup had told him, concerning the dinner meeting at Arnaud's.   Mishenka was traveling with a benu older than Daniel D'Loup, someone who had seen several thousand years if Dante was correct in his guesses.   Someone who spoke with a lightly Greek-toned British accent and who carried himself like a king.   Who was this Ulysses Ithaca?   Why was Misha consorting with such a malakh?

He was jealous, of course, and would never admit such out loud.

Dante has said, in an unusually delicate way, that the relationship between Misha and her benu companion was far from platonic.

Fighting the slow burn of his jealousy, he studied the office.   It had been given to him and Nicolai upon the start of their contract to Mathilda Curran.   It was appointed with a sturdy wooden desk and several rugs, a couch, and two Queen Anne chairs in burgundy. Nico had brought in several paintings and a handful of sculptures that his childe had purchased in Jackson Square.   These items did little to assuage or distract his mind from the matter at hand.

He knew, logically, he had no *reason* to be jealous.   Misha had offered to come back, once, and he had turned her aside for the sake of Nico.   All for the fact of how Misha would not have allowed him to continue loving Nico at the time.   But, he had kept Nico with him ever since, disregarding Misha's feelings.   What right did he have to be jealous if Misha had found herself a lover?

But, his greedy nature would not allow him any peace.   He was jealous.

He had never felt any jealousy concerning Misha until now; it was a novel experience.

He was accustomed to his attitude towards Nicolai's friends---the constant possessive fear that someone might come along and take his childe from him. But, he instinctively knew why he made a distinction between Misha and Nico, as well. Misha had chosen to love him, had existed at his side for several years as both companion and mortal wife before being brought into the Undead state. Nico had lived as his victim, mortal and resisting; what choice had Nicolai been given? It would make a great deal of sense if Nico decided to bide his time and find someone else, someone who was capable of real and un-punishing love.

A quick glance at the level of his pitcher told him that he'd have to get a refill soon, within the next two glasses, if he continued to drink so quickly. He topped off his glass and smiled at the foam that crackled softly---audible to his vampiric ears. He wondered if such dark, desperate worries for the state of Rhys Lorraine's behavior were the reason for Daniel D'Loup's nightly over-indulgence in bourbon. The Suisse benu malakh drank like a fish and showed very few ill effects. Perhaps he should try such a method, practically inhaling bottles of scotch and corn-mash whiskey and brandy.

If he did so, perhaps he would be more condoning of Nico's taunts.

His hands were steady as he began compiling the pages, clipping them together with a small stapler according to sections of importance and chronology. Several of the pages were crinkly and faded in a few spots but still legible. He hummed along with the music that could be heard from the dance floor.

He wasn't so immersed in his thoughts that he missed the scent. His enhanced power of smell picked up the odor of two vampires as they came up the stairs. One was Nico...he'd know his childe anywhere. The other...not familiar. He immediately stopped what he was doing and set the stapler down, reaching to open the desk drawer to his left. He watched the door as he easily found the sharpened stake. It was smooth in his fingers, made of whittled cypress.

Every hair follicle on his body was rising in alarm at the feel and scent of something so unnatural approaching. This wasn't an ordinary vampire---this creature had active magic in its veins. Magic was always a danger, always a possible problem. Who was this and why would Nicolai bring them here, to this safe haven? Perhaps his childe was being forced---

Well, he would put a stop to it quickly.

The footsteps in the hall were soft, inhuman, and then the door opened. He didn't blink, careful to keep his eyes trained on the threat of an unknown predator. Nicolai entered, dressed in a leather jacket, a maroon shirt of silky Lycra, and leather pants with his sunglasses pushed up to the top of his head in a sexy way. And right on his childe's heels was...a girl.

A woman, actually. He saw this when he focused completely on her. She was small and underweight, wearing excessively baggy clothing and a pair of scuffed work-boots. But, the thing that instantly caught his eye was her head...and her face. She was bald and it appeared to be a natural thing. As if her hair had fallen out. And she had the most intriguing face. Her eyes were bright and sharp and intelligent and she wore an unnaturally calm, easy smile. As if nothing in the world could upset her deep sense of balance.

She was most definitely a vampire, though. He could smell the blood on her. She'd fed recently. And she was so new that her blood odor was mingled with the scent of her recently dead mortal flesh. It made his skin tingle even more. She was a lovely creature, almost boyish in her lack of breasts and her slim hips. The curve of her cheekbones and her jaw were nearly masculine, but not so much so that her gender was in question. She was clearly female and it was in her scent and in the expression of her clear brown eyes. This one had given birth to children, had known both the joys and the pains of womanhood and the agony of disease and the creeping cold shadow of death.

Rare, to find such wisdom and pain mingling together and so visible.

It stayed his hand, the surprise.

Yet, *why* was she with Nico? There was no scent of sex on the female newborn---and she was most definitely newborn. He could scent no sexual attraction between his childe and the magic-blooded woman.

Nicolai came across the office, talking at him, while the newborn female stood motionless at the closed office door. "Joseph, we gotta problem. I just saw Misha."

He didn't relax his grip on the wooden stake that he held in his lap, hidden behind the wooden surface of his desk. He reached with his free hand to lift the glass of beer and take a drink, keeping his gaze steady on the strange interloper who seemed so confusing. A threat and yet...not a threat.

"Joseph? Did you hear me?" His childe's tone was impatience.

"I heard you, Nicolai." He said it flatly, never even glancing at his Rom lover. "You've seen Misha. Did you see, by any chance, the benu that she travels with?"

He was itching to ask about the newborn in the baggy flannel shirt and jeans who remained at the door, watching him with a strangely curious expression in her brown eyes. She was not making any attempt to guard herself from him, physically or emotionally. If he'd been a mind-reader, he imagined her brain would be an open and welcoming novel. She wouldn't attempt to hide anything...or so her eyes claimed.

"No, but I smelled him on her. When she first found us, she caught me by surprise. I didn't realize she was there. You were right about that, Joseph, she smells strange now. My guess? He's a big fucker with some age. Misha said he's been searching for the Sang-rael for thousands of years." His childe paused, narrowing his brown-black eyes in consternation. "I thought you said there weren't any more benu older than you."

Joseph went on, eyeing the strange vampire. The woman was bold, staring right back at him with frank and open approval. She seemed to like what she could see of him. Her slight, sweet smile had grown. She now wore the expression of a woman born to power. He could scent that on her, the power. It was in every fiber of her being and unchanged, even with the death she had so recently endured. DNA-deep, as he'd once heard Lorraine say.

'Some things are just innate...DNA-deep.'

He was slightly off-balance and it was on his tongue, to demand an explanation about this newborn standing in his office. But, he answered Nico instead. "No, Nicolai, what I said was that I had killed a great many of them in my youth. They were on the same search and how could I know which were harmless? That doesn't mean that I killed them *all*. If I had, where would people like D'Loup and Curran come from?"

"Who cares?" Nico sneered, turning sideways to sit on the edge of the desk. "Misha's new boy is one. She says he's able to track the Sang-rael. That's why they're really in New Orleans. He knew to come here and he knows that the chosen one is associated with Pandora's Box."

Joseph felt a cold chill run over his skin now and he took his gaze off the female newborn in order to study his own childe, staring with surprise and a growing horror. This was something Dante had *not* mentioned! He whispered, his voice harsh as he sat up straight in the chair, gripping the stake in fingers that trembled with the shock. "Are you *sure*? Nico, don't play games..."

"It's no game. Not according to Misha." Nicolai began fiddling with the large Crocodile Dundee knife that lay on the desk as a paperweight, turning it this way and that on the wooden surface. It made him think of a compass, abstractly. "She said that she wants the info you've got, but I think she's really wanting you to just verify what she already knows. Maybe she believes you'll give away the secret by accident."

He drained the glass of beer and bit his tongue in the process. The taste of blood made his head swim and he closed his eyes, blotting out the sight of the office and his childe. And the strange vampire woman with the bald head. She didn't matter in this moment...she wasn't being an overt threat. And he would deal with her once he'd handled Nico. Whoever she was, she wasn't leaving his office on her own two feet. He hadn't let a vampire continue existing in New Orleans yet.

Misha had managed to track down the Sang-rael and was now trying to play him for a fool. The benu she was traveling with...a threat he'd not discovered before tonight. Where had this information come from, that his wife and her malakh friend should have tracked it here? How did they know he was aware of the Sang-rael's true location? Was it mere supposition---could Misha have really believed he would recognize the chosen one, if he found it?

"Joseph, there's more. I know..."

He opened his eyes to study his childe. Nicolai was watching him with worry creasing his youthful brows into a hard knot. It made the gypsy seem darker, somehow. He refused to give the vampire woman any attention now, focusing instead on his lover. The newborn was unimportant and he was a master. Besides which...she hadn't moved yet from her post at the door.

"What more?" He was concerned for the expression on Nico's face.

Nicolai licked at the corner of his mouth, dark eyes moving around the room restlessly before coming back to him. "I think you know who the Sang-rael is. That's why we're here in New Orleans. It has to be. It's okay. I like this place, I like my friends. You're here to watch over the chosen one and that's cool. But, I need to know something...do you think the Sang-rael is in a lot of danger from Misha?"

"I don't know." He admitted. "Misha intends to use the Sang-rael's blood. I think that constitutes a fair amount of danger." Now, he focused on the female Undead at the door, studying her in consideration. What he needed to say to his childe wasn't for the ears of just anyone. Should he kill her now or wait a few more minutes? She obviously wouldn't leave the room, not without orders or by force, and---*why was she here*? He sighed, capitulating. "It's time to consider some safety measures for the girl."

His childe blinked at him, mouth moving silently for a second. "Girl? What girl?"

Joseph sighed, unwilling to play that game. "The chosen one."

"The Sang-rael's not a *girl*." Nicolai leaned a few inches forward, still perched on the edge of the desk. His long, straight hair was like a sheaf of black silk. "It isn't a *boy*, either. It's both."

He considered that for a second. "And you know this how?"

"Misha's info."

"*Misha* told you this?" He couldn't stop himself from sounding doubtful.

Could she have discovered that much of the ancient stories, without his help?

His childe blushed a pale pink, the stain of blood rising to give just a hint of the embarrassment he'd caused. Nicolai blustered, then managed to answer without stammering. "No, she didn't say that. But, Alvie's able to hear it. It's not empathy or telepathy---she's got magic. Alvie said that Misha was sending it off, kinda like a scent, all these secrets. The chosen one is some kinda hermaphrodite with big, black wings."

He frowned hard, reaching for the pitcher to refill his glass as he agreed. "That's an accurate description of the fallen midael on this plane of existence. The chosen one is, according to legend, a midael sleeping in the body of a mortal. It's believed that, when the Guardian of the Living breaks free of its mortal prison, it will be androgyne once more." He paused, deliberately raising his head to pin the newborn vampire woman with a cold stare, finally admitting to her presence. "You would be *Alvie*?"

Of course she would be. She *reeked* of magic.

Nicolai looked caught, defiant and frightened, but the newborn was exceptionally calm. It was his childe who answered him. "Yes, that's Alvie. She's a witch. She said it was there, in Misha, and I believe her. What's more, Joseph...she described something about the chosen one that fits someone we know."

Alarm rose in him like a fast-moving flood. Could Nico be aware of what Tennyson Beaulieu was? Would his childe unwittingly betray the girl? He reached for his cigarettes now, where they lay on the desk, working to keep his voice calm as he lit one. "So, you believe you've discovered who the Sang-rael is. This is dangerous information, Nico. If you care about this person, you must never let it escape your lips or your mind. You must learn to bury the truth so deeply that not even the most talented malakh mind-reader can find it. If you value the chosen one, you must do everything you can to protect her."

His mind circled the hermaphrodite question. It was true that the legends talked of the Sang-rael being both male and female---and that was something Nico had never been told, as far as he knew. But, the body was female this time. Tennyson couldn't be anything *but* female.

His lover nodded impatiently, as if it was common knowledge that they would all work tirelessly to protect the chosen one. "Alvie says that the Sang-rael was raised in a lab or a doctor's office."

At last, the newborn vampire moved from where she stood at the door. She began moving along the wall to the left in what could only be described as a swagger. He gripped the cypress stake tightly now, preparing himself for the coming attack. He'd destroy this arrogant woman here and then have Nicolai use the Dust-Buster to clean up the mess. It was only right---his childe had dared to bring the creature to Pandora's Box.

But, when she spoke, her voice took him by complete surprise. Husky, broken china. "Your wife found us in an alley and she admitted to what she was looking for, Mister Snowden. She also admitted the stuff Nicolai said. But, there was more. She was thinking real hard about what the creature is. The imagine I got concerned a man with blondish, brownish hair and wearing a lab coat. He was holding a little kid on his lap. She's seen a lot of pictures of them, the man and the kid. She was thinking real hard on how the kid's been traced to New Orleans, to this bar. If her sources are right, your wife thinks the creature would be in its early twenties now and easy to recognize. There was also all this jumbled up crap about some scrolls she's seen recently."

Her Appalachian voice was cruel, like the chilliest full moon hanging in a perfect, star-filled velvet sky...so clear and musical and full of magic. He liked her voice, even as he knew she was a threat. All vampires were predatory. None of them could be trusted. He'd made a job of it, keeping the Undead out of this city. He wasn't about to make an exception for such a beautiful newborn...even one with such half-hidden talents and gifts. He'd taught Nico to leave other vampires alone---to not run with their own kind. What was this woman doing in his office?

She was now standing at one of the windows, her frail-seeming fingers holding back one heavy black curtain; he couldn't see her face now, but imagined that she must be examining the house's side garden in the darkness outside. Her voice, as she spoke again, caught him off guard. "You don't need that piece of wood, Mister Snowden. I'm not gonna hurt anyone here. I'm not interested in devastating any innocents or stealing your territory. I'm a witch and a musician...that's all."

No, that was not all. She was *Undead.*

But, still, it floored him. She knew about the cypress stake he held in his lap, even without having seen it. He stared at Nico, silently and angrily questioning. His childe looked proud and sheepish, grinning lopsidedly at him. What was Nicolai up to?

In the silence between them, in the office---as he considered what she said, curious and yet absolutely sure that the newborn would have to die---the music from downstairs became an intruder. It sounded like Rugby Webster had started pulling out his half-brother's best remixes. The song that played now had a strangely ethereal, dirty quality, thanks to the Tin Pan Alley clarinet that repeated its song over and over, crackly and rasping like a broken 78 record. But, the song itself was a gay-boy's anthem and that was evident in the techno rhythms and synth.

'Now I know your heart, I know your mind. You don't even know you're being unkind. So much for all your highbrow Marxist ways. Just use me up and then you walk away. Boy, you can't play me that way. Well, I guess what you say is true, I could never be the right kind of girl for you, I could never be your woman.'

He risked a look at Nicolai, keeping his face neutral. How many times had his childe sung this song at him, in retaliation? He had to wonder how much influence Pandora's Box was really having on Nico. He'd never really had any problems out of his lover until they'd arrived in New Orleans. Was it the club or Lorraine?

'...I could never spend my life with a man like you, I could never be your woman.'

At the window, Alvie gave a shuddery sigh, then, drawing his attention once more. She still breathed, apparently. She had her skinny back to him and he grimaced at how very ugly her taste in clothing seemed to be. The flannel and baggy carpenter pants were grungy and ill-fitting. Who had told her such things were attractive?

She muttered something that was more breath than words and it eluded him.

Arching a brow, he drawled, determined to be nasty to the newly Undead witch who had dared to enter his office at the heels of his reprobate Nico. "Please, girl, enlighten me. I'm not yet accustomed to translating your mumbles."

She shifted on her toes to glance at him, her thin smile enigmatic once more. "I was just saying that the one you think is the chosen isn't. It's not the hot little black chick."

She was most definitely a witch---or she knew more about the club and his affairs than was good for her. She was either a spy or she was able to read minds. Either way, she was too dangerous. He made a decision as he stubbed out his cigarette---she couldn't be allowed to continue existing. He would fix the situation immediately. Rising, he gripped the stake in his hand harder. As he moved around the desk, his body in battle mode, Nico stepped into his path with raised hands, talking fast.

"Please, Joseph. The clues all point to Tennyson---I know they do. Right up to and including the mark on her. You *have* to be thinking it's Tennyson. And if...if I wanted to believe in something holy and savior-like, *Tennyson* would be the one I'd want to believe in. But, I don't think it's Tennyson." His childe faltered, staring up into his face with eyes that seemed bottomless and full of inhuman terror---Nicolai feared what he would do, now. Pushing on his chest with both hands, Nico stammered. "I think it's...it's Rhys Lorraine."

He opened his mouth to protest, his mind swirling with the idea of how absolutely impossible that was. Rhys Lorraine was dark and cruel and if there'd ever been a mortal born to be the Anti-Christ, it was that particular malakh. How could it be possible that Rhys might, even in the wildest speculation, be the Lion, the chosen one? Rhys didn't possess any redeeming traits---the boy wasn't even capable of real and all-encompassing love. One of the defining traits of the Sang-rael.

Nico pushed him backwards, as if trying to shoo him away. His childe's black hair was sexily disheveled from a night's hunting, but he could care less. His whole brain was fizzling with the concept of a tchatcha savior. Was something like that even *laughable*? No---not to him. To him, it was not only an impossibility, it would be a joke from the darkest, most evil mouth.

His lover was talking at him. "You have to understand something, Joseph. I know it sounds crazy. Rhys is the last likely angel of judgment, right? Only, he's...well, there's some stuff about him I know that...only, well, I shouldn't know. And you gotta forgive me for it, okay? But, listen to me first, hear what I'm talking about."

He sat down once more and Nicolai perched on the desk, his backside planted on the notes and papers he'd been working with. Right in front of him, one leg brushing against his crotch in a way which would normally be soothing. But, it wasn't soothing at the moment. His mind couldn't wrap around the concept of something so wrong as Lorraine. The boy was the worst sort of malakh---an empath with the genetic potential for becoming a man-eater. A cannibal.

Nicolai forged on, babbling away. "Rhys has wings. I've tried to tell you that before. They're right against his shoulders and they feel like a cold fog. You can't see them, they're invisible, but they're definitely real. Only someone who's touched him there would know. Rhys says they've been there as long as he can remember. And he was raised in that medical lab complex in California...remember when I told you about that? Rhys wasn't raised to be human. He was meant to be an assassin. A warrior. The scientists that altered him were after a certain idea, right? They named the project Isosceles, but the name they gave to Rhys---and to the others like him---was *DeathAngel*. *Mortis Angelos*. Modern malakh offspring genetically altered to be more like the ancient malakh, then raised to be outside human morality. Rhys told me all about it. And you know it's true, you've seen Rhys in action. He's not capable of understanding all the little subtle parts of what it means to be human or mortal. Even after all the years he's been away from the project labs. At least, that's what I was told---"

He nodded, gripping the stake in his left hand. He was slowly starting to take it in, the things his childe was trying to impart. The vampire woman was forgotten for a moment as he stared at Nico, who was still talking, explaining what he believed. What he'd started piecing together, from whatever clues Nicolai had managed to find on his own. Wrong or right, it was intriguing to see his childe and lover so impassioned about something he'd never shown any interest in, before.

"And, Joseph, it's hard to talk about, okay? Something else you gotta know. Rhys isn't completely a boy. At least, that's what I believe. It's like his body got confused in the womb or was altered to be part female. I've spent so much time with him---and look at what *you've* seen. Put him in a dress and make-up and he'd be the most convincing drag-queen you've ever laid eyes on. He's got more than a cock, alright? I think he might actually be both girl and boy. Intersexed or androgyne or...maybe hermaphrodite. We've never talked about it, but I know. He's got a mark on him, too. Kinda like Tennyson's mark, but---it's on the back of his head, right in the hairline. I've seen it."

He could see the point his childe was trying to make. But, a seed of rage began to germinate; how would his lover know what Rhys Lorraine had, in his skin-tight leathers? Forcing himself to relax, to let go of his anger, he posed the relevant question. He ignored the idea of how Nico might know that Rhys was of the third gender, neither male nor female. It raised too many questions and not all of them were kosher.

"Do you think *Misha* has pinpointed Lorraine as the one she's seeking?"

"I don't know, but if she's seen pictures of him as a kid, she'd probably be able to pick Rhys out of a line-up." Nico admitted, the fear twisting his childe's features into a mask. "If she thinks she's looking for Rhys, she'll come to the club. It'll be a bloodbath, Joseph. Too many people here would fight to keep him safe. Rhys, by himself, could---"

"Kill." He nodded, tasting the familiar copper-iron flavor of blood in his mouth when he chewed on the inside of his cheek, thinking. He could quell his anger, the suspicion that Nicolai and Rhys had been fucking around---that Nico had learned the gender difference via a very intimate road. "If I ask the Golden Wolf, would she tell me that the father of her child is intersexed?"

"She has to know about it." Nicolai had pulled his sunglasses free and was playing with them, now. "D'Loup might know about it, too. I'm positive Lorraine's both genders."

He saw the sense in it, but still knew...it couldn't be correct.

Lorraine *couldn't* be the chosen one.

"Alvie thinks that we should be protecting them both, Tennyson and Rhys---"

Joseph gave a wintry smile, cocking his head to the side in order to stare at the female newborn. She still stood at the window, her back turned to the room. It was as if she'd ignored the entire conversation.

He whispered his thoughts on the matter. "This one's been very useful, Nico. With magic in her blood, she might help us do what's necessary to protect the Sang-rael. If she's not a spy for Misha or another vampire master..."

His childe reached out and touched his hand, gripping at it tightly. Nico was hopeful. "Please, Joseph...can you give her a chance? She's not a spy. Let her prove that she deserves to exist?"

Alvie was resolutely silent, her fingers light on the curtain as she went on, staring out into the night. He kept his voice slow and careful, when he finally answered. "It's not my habit to allow blood-drinkers into my territory. I understand why you brought her to me, Nico, but *who is she*? If her Sire is here in the city, he's trespassing. Where is he hiding, that he could create this childe so recently and not be visible to me? Why would a Sire allow such a valuable, newly risen childe out of his reach for even a single night?"

He saw the way his own childe's eyes flickered, the way Nico bit at his lower lip. Nervous, wanting to be defiant but not quite managing it. "She's *mine*, Joseph."

His spirit jerked, fiery in every vein, at the idea. The thought that Nicolai could know a sexual secret about Rhys Lorraine was not nearly as ugly. Nico would leave him for this woman---the moment had finally arrived, just as he'd imagined it must. She was more than just a small threat to his territory---she was a threat to his existence. He couldn't smell sex on either of them, but that didn't mean *anything*. Perhaps it simply hadn't happened, yet. Perhaps it hadn't happened tonight but on some other night, previously, when Nico was supposedly hunting alone.

He pulled away from Nicolai's grip and straightened himself, raising the stake in his hand to point it at his miscreant lover. "So. You would take your inheritance and leave me? Do you think I should suffer a *cuckold* to go on?"

The jealousy he'd felt earlier now returned, changing directions.

True, Misha had a lover...but, at least she hadn't come to flaunt it in his face. This was intolerable, the mere concept. Nicolai was brazen. But, what could he expect? He'd taught his childe the nature of pain and degradation. How could he imagine that Nico would want to stay with him forever? He'd always suspected that it was only for lack of options that they continued on together.

But, before he could build up a real head of steam and rise to stake them both---or stake the woman and then take his childe someplace where no one would be able to hear Nicolai scream his blood-soaked apologies---his gypsy huffed a deep breath and stared at him with a steely calm. All the fear was gone. And he felt the fire in his veins ease off and become chilly. *This* was no mere catamite childe. Nicolai had become a man of great worth under his tutelage and now the results were before him, ready to be declared.

Nicolai's voice was firm, steady. He prepared himself for the blow that came. "No, that's not it, Joseph. Alvie has a lover and I don't wanna leave you. But, she's mine. I wanted her and she wanted us. *She's my childe.*"

That was not what he'd expected. He couldn't help but gape, his dignity forgotten.

Alvie, unmoving at the window, snorted, her tone low and mocking. "Hi-ya, grandpa."

Suddenly, his suspicious jealousy at the mere idea of Nico fucking Rhys Lorraine didn't seem half as enraging.

Chapter Twenty-four

Abayomi walked through the temple, prepared at last.

He had spent twelve days in the company of Bomani, eating at his master's side and sleeping in his master's bed. During this time, the tchatcha had done nothing more than kiss him, tend his needs with the care and ritual of a priest. He had been instructed to not relieve his sexual hunger, but to let it build...let the coals be fanned to flames. Bomani, the tchatcha commander, had brought him into this world of sacred savagery where he was the only innocent over the age of consent.

For twelve days, he had been bathed and carefully anointed by the two young tchatchau girls. His body hair had been shaved away each day, he had been pierced with gold rings, his skin enlivened with oils and salves that heightened the physical sensations of even the river-scented breeze that swept through the long sheets of linen.

Each night, he had been given time to listen to the tchatchau musicians who were also warriors of great skill. They welcomed him. During the time he ate the honeyed sweets and drank of spiced wine, delighting to the sounds of such music---they played songs that inspired the other tchatchau to dance with whirling, stomping abandon---the master, Bomani, had made devotions to the gods in the temple. This temple.

It was in his mind to know that Bomani did not believe as others believed. Bomani was of the belief that the gods they served were only ancestors and not something beyond human or malakh comprehension. Bomani seemed to believe that the jewels, the flowers, the offerings, did little to assuage the spirits of those deities and were really only of any use to the ones who made the obeisance. They worshipped the gods for their own sakes, to find the divinity within themselves.

He feared for Bomani; what manner of man would dare to challenge the gods in such a direct way? Did this Nubian not know that to disobey and anger the gods would bring down disaster on himself, on these children he trained?

As of yet, he had not seen his master's face. There was no moment he possessed in memory to give him an awareness of what Bomani looked like, under the mask. Each meal, Bomani wore the mask...each training session with the tchatchau that he witnessed, Bomani wore the mask. As the young tchatchau girls bathed him and shaved away his body hair, brushed his long silky curls, Bomani sat near in attendance and wore the mask. When Bomani called him to come to the bed, he was blindfolded and so he did not see the naked face of his master.

In his life, he could not remember ever seeing the tchatcha priest of Sekhmet close enough to have any knowledge of what might be under the mask. Twelve days now, he had visited in the House of Maahes and he was not allowed to see this man's face. When he mentioned it---only that first time, as Bomani kissed him in the water---the god-like malakh had told him that he would be allowed to see soon enough.

But, each night, he was called to the bed and he wondered if this would be the night when Bomani would do more than embrace him, more than stroke at his skin chastely...more than those kisses which made him feel bolder than he could recall ever feeling in his life. Each night, he answered the summons and walked through this temple to the bedchamber where Bomani waited, naked but for the small triangle of black linen that could barely contain the immense hardness of an erection that mystified him, scared him, intrigued him.

Something else that intrigued him was the tattoo on Bomani's lower back, at the top of his shenti. He knew that it was the Guardian's sigil, but he had yet to ask any questions about the mark. The tattoo looked large enough to fill the palm of his hand, but he did not dare touch it.

The tchatcha commander was built on a size that defied the scale known for average men. He stood more than a head taller than any other man that Abayomi had seen in his life. His master's skin, before sleep, was clean and smooth and when he came to the bedchamber, he was ordered to kneel before the malakh, who wore only the black linen pouch and the gold mask. Naked and shaking with mixed fear and anticipation, he always knelt and received the cloth around his eyes.

Blindfolded this way, he was lifted bodily as if he was a child and placed into the bed. Then, he would hear the mask being removed...followed by the whisper of the black linen dropping to the stones. Naked and trembling, he was held in hot arms against a large, hot body until sleep claimed him at last. Chaste and virginal he remained despite the hard erection that pressed into his thigh every night.

Bomani was gone from the bed each morning before he awoke. He never failed to find his master at devotions, in this temple to the gods. The tchatcha, serving the gods in white linen and gold mask, could have been another of the statues...come to life and moving among them, bringing wine and meat, bread and flowers.

He had witnessed the blood-letting...Sekhmet demanded blood and her servant Bomani would kneel before her alabaster statue and cut tiny slices into his own flesh with a bone knife to feed the mother goddess of the tchatchau, the deity that this warrior was rumored to be descended from.

Twelve days, he had been taught what to expect by watching his master. Bomani was kind and gentle and tender to him, but did command respect and obedience without a word. As of yet, it seemed he was simply a hopeful acolyte to the love that had been promised. And with each day that passed, his hunger grew.

He had started as fearful and breathless, worried for what he was to know about this giant of a malakh who whipped tchatchau children for failing...who held court among the invisible as if he might be a god himself. After twelve days, he no longer feared what might come to him, to his body...he eagerly awaited the moment when his master would consummate their love. For, yes, he loved Bomani now. How could he not love the one who claimed him?

Today, Bomani had instructed the two little tchatchau girls to prepare him.

Today, he was to join the master in evening devotions.

He had been bathed, his flesh carefully anointed in oils that glittered with gold. The gold rings in his nipples and his manhood had been examined for strength, to ensure his skin was not infected or likely to tear. He had endured the touch of the two invisible children without complaint; he had become accustomed to their presence---they were his near-constant companions, now.

His eyes had been painted gingerly with kohl, to outline them. His erection was thudding with blood, heavy between his legs, overly sensitive due to the way he had been shaved of each last wisp of hair and thoroughly anointed. Then, he had been presented to the large bronze mirror that was kept covered when not in use. In its wavery reflection, he had glimpsed his fully naked, prepared flesh.

His nipples had been erect from the breeze that wafted from the balcony, tingling with the gold rings in the pebbled skin. The growing sense of expectancy had aroused him to a heightened state of awareness, making his blood race as if he was being prepared for battle. His first battle.

But, the preparations had not stopped there. The two invisible tchatcha had adorned his body with gold in the form of new earrings and then a necklace of tiny links that was clipped into place around his throat. The chain did not end here; from the throat, a chain extended down his body to the gold ring in his manhood, threaded into the loop. At each nipple a chain ran from the main links to thread into the gold rings that kept his chest constantly aware of movement.

Abayomi savored the slender weight that hung from his throat, that tugged at the rings in his nipples and in his foreskin with each step he took.   He walked into the temple and towards the stone altar that sat between Osiris and Isis.   On either side of him, the invisible girls were silent.   The temple was lit by torches, the flickering glow making each statue seem more than alive and aware of the new body that came to offer devotions.

On the pelt of an ibex, he knelt before the altar in a single, fluidly graceful move.   Here, he put his hands behind his back in respect, clasping them at the top of his backside...his knuckles touched his heels.   The two tchatcha knelt with him, on either side and a step behind.   He thought of them as his honor guard because of their attentive silence; never once had he heard either of them speak a single word.

He lowered his head, closing his eyes in quiet prayer to the gods.

It was some time before he heard anything.   But, he felt Bomani enter the temple.   It was no rustle of curtains or footsteps but something instinctive and primal in his soul that seemed to awaken and turn blindly, inside his body, to look for the master.

Bomani stood immobile and silent behind him for several minutes.   Abayomi did not look up or shift to see the malakh commander.   He sat still, becoming like the statues he knelt for, his hands behind the small of his ram-rod straight back in the submissive position of a slave.

As he waited, patient even as his heart leaped faster at the knowledge that it was today, the only movement was the slight rise and fall of his chest as he breathed.   Then, the two girls were leaving.

At last, Bomani spoke.   His voice was rich, low, like the pelt of a black panther from the deepest jungles of the south.   'You have done well, Medjay.   Your open heart is a greatness I intend to honor.   You choose to leave behind the life you have known, coming to me at last...my ieb.   You cannot live your entire life behind these walls, but you must trust me in all things, at all times, under all circumstances.   That trust shall be earned, I promise you; you will live your life as you choose, but you are to be my mate...my most beloved.   You are strong, beautiful, and born of a proud people.   I am honored to claim you as my love, my succor.'

Abayomi wanted to speak, to tell the tchatcha that he was honored as well, to have been given a chance to learn this world...to be loved so deeply.   But, he held his tongue, kept his silence, did not open his eyes.

The unseen warrior continued, now.   'You are the Light of my very world, the sun that I must turn my face to in love.   I worship with the knowledge that the darkness would be eternal if not for your grace, your existence.   I have fed you with my hands, clothed you as I saw fit, and given you the time to prepare yourself for what must come to your life.   Is this what you know?'

'Yes.'   Answering at last, he did not nod.

It was true; often, when dining, Bomani fed him with the care of a parent.   The wine or beer was given to him in sips, from Bomani's cup, and morsels of food were put into his open mouth by Bomani's fingers.   He had been pampered in the manner of a pet or a child and learned to accept what no Medjay could ever have allowed or fathomed.

'Abayomi of Horus, you are about to offer me a great gift.   You are to be the concubine, my only love, a slave.   But, to me, a slave is not the pitiful creatures that often are forced to submit.   You can never be one of those, my ieb.   Many believe that a true master imposes his dominion on the slave and that the slave is an unwilling captive to the master's whims.   In many cases, this is the truth.   With you and with me, it cannot be remotely possible.   All control ultimately resides with you, the concubine.   You freely and willingly grant me permission to the love offered.   The permission can be revoked at any time and a true slave understands this, takes joy in eager and unhesitating submission to the will of Master.   Being given the opportunity to take this supreme control over a slave's life is a gift beyond comparison.   It is a responsibility not to be taken lightly and I desire to expand and enrich your life.   I will lose myself in your existence...I will live for you.'

This was not what he had expected.   He listened, the flames in his blood crackling at the sound of the magic in his master's voice.   His nipples throbbed, pleading to be released from the weight of the tiny chain that lay motionless between them. He could feel the slick wetness of oil between the cheeks of his naked backside.

'Pain and pleasure are what is offered to us in this world. Pain and pleasure shall be with you always, together and inseparable. They are often as one to me; their duality is a strength. I ask for your love, your devotion, your life. I offer you these same gifts---my love, my devotion, my life. Abayomi, do you accept the gifts; do you give them freely to me?'

There was no doubt in his heart. Breathing deeply, he answered the warrior tchatcha who stood behind him. 'Yes, master, I do. You may possess me in every way, both mind and body. I am yours, my lord.'

His belly jerked inside at the thought of belonging so utterly to another. Medjay were loyal to none but Pharaoh, to the gods. He had just given himself over to the hands and body of a warrior, a commander and trainer of the tchatchau...the man who was little more than a stranger. The man who had held him with the gentle hands of a friend, who had fed him as a parent feeds a child, who had never shown him anything but kindness...but whose face he had yet to see in its entirety.

The breadth and totality of the promises were breathtaking in scope. The only escape possible was to denounce what he knew to be true...to revoke the promises made. He could take back what he gave to Bomani, but the loss would be total, absolute. He possessed the power to destroy this warrior, who worshipped him...whose very life was built upon the love he might give.

Abayomi knew, then...his commitment would be permanent, without exception.

Who would dare to destroy a god?

He could feel the chain that caressed his glittering skin, cool and golden, chafing ever so slightly against his manhood, the flesh of his smooth abdomen and chest. His heart was beating a rapid crescendo in his ribs as he took a deep breath and let it out in a sigh of finality.

He was Bomani's, as utterly as any marriage and as binding...in spirit and body.

He was overcome with emotion, feeling as if his throat must burst from the tightness there. He spoke, without being asked to talk. 'I want more than anything to serve you, to be the one you give your passion. I feel more alive than I have ever felt before. I will live within your realm as you want, immersed in the love you offer. Please, master. Take me. I am yours to command, to do with as you wish.'

'You are, to me, the most beloved...for the world could never know what you give with this.' Bomani answered, sounding happy...relieved. 'I would offer you as a sacrifice. Do you wish the love you offer me now to be a sacrifice to the gods who bear witness?'

He felt a tortured nervousness now. He was to be sacrificed? Surely not!

But, then, he knew...if this man saw no better use for him, he could die.

Abayomi whispered, his skin overly sensitive with fear. 'Yes.'

He heard a rustling. Then, from every direction came a rain of lashes against his flesh, on his arms, legs, backside, abdomen, chest, feet, hair, everywhere he could be touched. He was being flogged, but...he had never felt anything like it before.

He shouted out at the surprise, opening his eyes and shifting to turn, but the lashes were not painful like those of a whip and he saw no one in the temple's flickering torchlight. No one was touching him, yet he was being whipped by invisible hands with something that smelled green which rippled in the air, too fast to be seen clearly.

'Do not fear.' Bomani told him, from behind.

He gathered his alarm and closed his eyes, lowering his head once more.

As the flogging continued from all sides, a strong flowery scent filled the temple. He was being whipped with flowers...lotus flowers. As the stems touched his skin, they bent and broke, the blossoms disintegrating in a cloud of flying petals as they sacrificed themselves on his oiled flesh.

Abayomi could feel the dismembered flower petals clinging to him, feel himself being plastered with the remnants of broken blooms and pollen. Who was doing this? How many unseen bodies moved to pick up more lotus, destroying beauty in sacrifice to him and to the gods?

He cried out in pleasure as the gold chain was whipped with the stems of the lotus. It pulled at the rings in his nipples, at the ring in his foreskin. His erection was whipped with the soft flowers, making him writhe and twist on his knees.

It threatened orgasm, this flogging. This sacrifice.

As he strained to stay motionless in obedience, he cried out again as he felt the broken flowers replaced with unseen hands that pulled him to his feet, unseen mouths that placed reverent kisses on his flesh, leaving nothing untouched. He was being gifted and adorned for his submissive devotion to Bomani.

A hand teased the heft of his sac, cupping him there as his mouth is kissed by a fever-hot tongue. His backside was stroked feather-soft as his throat was grazed by teeth strong enough to destroy it, take the blood and his life. The flowers continued to slap his back, his belly, his legs and arms---which were lifted and held out straight to either side of his body, making him vulnerable.

Each kiss was a white-hot brand, each flower a perfumed welt. His nipples were tugged, sending a fireball through his brain as the pain and pleasure exploded and sent aftershock waves through him...excruciating, exhilarating. The sheer intensity of the worship was devastating and he opened his eyes, to seek the ones who would love him so wholly as to devour his soul. He was surrounded by hot bodies but could see only mirage ripples in the air as tchatchau moved, constantly shifting him from side to side, lavishing his body with their primitive attentions. He was being consumed.

The last phantom hand left him, the last stem and blossom delivered the last stroke to his spine. He trembled, weak in the knees, and weeping shamefully at the crowd of invisible teenagers---it was difficult to tell, but he was fairly certain they were all close to his size from the feel of fingers and hands and mouths---these young warriors who had stripped him of the last expectations. Sacred moment, it was over and he wept from the enormity of it all.

He lowered his arms, wanting to curl up in a ball on the ibex pelt. But, he stood, hands at his sides, and stared up into the faces of Isis and her brother-husband, Osiris. The gods had paid witness to a sacrifice...if that was what had happened. He was not sure.

Silence was all he felt, heard.

He was alone, before the gods.

He could not tell if his master was still in the temple, unseen.

Abayomi closed his eyes, unable to bear the sight of gods staring back.

He felt the tickling caress of his hair where it lay on his shoulders, freed. A few strands stuck to his cheeks, fluttering as he inhaled and exhaled. He could feel the texture of the pelt under his bare feet, the fold of two pelts where they met...layered.

He breathed and smelled spices and wine as they burned in braziers along the stone walls. He calmed, slowly, heady with the scent of the lotus on his twitching skin...his skin was a thing separate from him, now, alive in ways that made it an entity of its own. There was air blowing on him, from the doorways that led into Bomani's private bedchamber, where the balcony lay. He could feel the breeze circulating across his naked flesh, shamelessly exposed this way. Every wetness---the kisses, the juice of the lotus, the oil--- seemed to be seared by that tiny wind.

The steady beating of his heart and the sensation of blood coursing through him, through his erect and aching manhood; these things he felt. The loss of sight and movement made his ears much more sensitive to the sounds around him. He could hear the ceaseless, rhythmic 'tick-tick-tick' of beaded water falling on metal somewhere close by. Perhaps by the door that led into Bomani's bedchamber. What was this? He had never noticed it before. Was there water in that space, water he had not seen?

He heard everything.

The flutter of birds passing the balcony in the other chamber. The distant sound of voices---from the training courtyard, where the young tchatchau played during the evenings, when the hot chariot of Amun-Ra descended from the highest heavens. The opening and closing of a door in the Hall of tchatchau, not so very far away...just on the other side of the main corridor from these rooms. The crackle of flames, from torches and braziers. His own breath as he continued to live, solitary in a void. His belly gave a gurgle.

Nothing else.

He went on, in that void, for what seemed like an hour. He flexed his chest muscles, causing the golden chain to slip on his skin. The metal shifted, making a light, metallic sound as the links connecting in the middle of his sternum rubbed against their neighbors and settled once more.

Abayomi wondered if someone watched him. He had heard no one leave the temple, had heard no one move. Was his master even with him anymore? The thought of someone watching him as he waited in voluntary submission was intoxicating, fearsome. If someone was watching, would they be masturbating lazily, dark fire-lit eyes never moving from his naked form?

He remained immobile, a statue of flesh; his legs were shoulders-width apart, arms lax at his sides. He twitched, fighting a shiver of wonder at how deep and lonely this void was. He stood, devoted to being in this place and at constant attention for what must surely come...he had become Lord Bomani's mate.

Surely he would not be left untouched, at the altar.

His body was chilled, from the breeze; the air was warm, but yet he felt cold.

Then, suddenly, a touch. He nearly jumped out of himself at the sensation of fire in the middle of his back. He might have shouted in reflex, he was not sure now. Holding position, he breathed fast, his nostrils flared at the scent...the familiar scent of his master. He held still, only the tiniest tremor betraying the surprise.

Soft, flexible...a finger. On his back. It rested there lightly on the flesh between his shoulders. Then, the fingertip traced a course upwards to his neck, ever so gentle. Before he could grow accustomed to this, the fingertip changed directions and slid oh so very slowly down his spine to the cleft of his backside.

It rested there for a moment. Then, the touch eased down, to tease the flesh that parted before its insistent push. But, instead of invading him, the fingertip moved away and over his hip, to slide along the line of skin where thigh intersected groin. It was joined---on the other side---by another finger. Back and forth, the two fingers tantalized the soft flesh, a torturous light touch.

Then, the fingers were withdrawn. He was trembling again, waiting and anticipating. After another long pause, Abayomi felt the fingers again...this time, against the insides of his knees at the tender skin that never grew hair. The two fingers became ten fingers and moved from his knees to his ankles and back up, going onwards and up to the top, brushing like feathers over his backside.

Again, the fingers were withdrawn. Another torturous wait.

Without warning, a finger moved along his erection, from root to the golden ring at the tip, in his foreskin. He drew a ragged sob, unable to help himself. But, the finger never stopped...it slipped on the oil, just barely grazing the tight skin. A low moan escaped him now as he realized that perhaps he was being seduced so languidly for the pleasure of the gods...perhaps this was the sacrifice.

After being withdrawn, for another agonizingly long time, Abayomi felt fingers return---hot and almost too large to be human. They glided along the length of his hardness, from tip to root to sac. He was dripping an early release, his body begging to be sated. The fingers that touched him were coated in oil, in this release, the nectar of physical desire.

He remained as motionless as he could, feeling the heat at his back, the heat at his naked groin. He was surrounded by Bomani in his void...and this was what he wanted. He was exposed, scrutinized, inspected, his body examined and tested. He was vulnerable and did not fear what the tchatcha might do...though, he could not be sure how he knew Bomani would never hurt him intentionally.

His master moved, came around him...and knelt. He did not look down, did not open his eyes. He felt it happening. He moaned as the large, flame-hot hands touched his hardness again, removed the chain that tugged just for a moment at his nipples.

This was a tchatcha, a sin-eater, the monster of those stories he had been told, as a child...someone who could know his flesh better than his own mother or father might have. The tchatchau were known for their sensual hungers, their brutality, their primitive natures...both animal and childlike.

Opening his eyes, he finally looked down at the man who touched him.

The fierce warrior was unmasked, wore only two gold rings in his ears. A delicate kohl gave accent to dark eyes as wide and tranquil and mild as those of a dove. But, in such a face! It was the face of a cat---broad, angular cheekbones and a straight nose, a long upper lip with that mouth he recognized...a strong, curving bow of lips that were a few shades darker than the golden-brown skin that covered every inch of the malakh's muscular, hairless body.

This was a man whose very life was battle, but whose face, in this moment, was not the face of a soldier. His mate, his master, his lover...the one who would claim him, who offered his pleasure to the gods in thanks for happiness, the one who might love him the whole of his life. Bomani, master and soldier, was quite possibly the most beautiful man he had ever seen. His long black hair was now unbraided, tumbling in soft waves over the widest part of his shoulders, gleaming with red in the flames from the nearest braziers and torches. His taut, firm skin held the flickers of light, became something new and holy to see. Was this what a god might look like, if made flesh?

It was impossible to believe this man would age, would die. Could he be a benu and undiscovered yet? Could that be possible? Men such as this, they did not die...it would be enough to make the heavens weep for three thousand years!

The malakh was looking up at him with awe; he knew his own expression must surely match the flushed, breathless gaze of his master, Bomani. Something in his heart stirred and he realized he had seen this face before...but, also not before. No, it came as if a ghost passed through him. He had seen this face, many years later. Thousands of years later, when all he knew now was dust. The name was there, in the back of his throat, and disappearing just as quickly as a phantom might. Another soldier...a man with eyes the unlikely bi-color of the sand and the sky. The knowledge of a distant future made him momentarily dizzy.

This was to be his lover. He would gladly die for such a man's love; to know he was treasured and precious in the sight of a conquering god such as this son of Sekhmet, a child of the Unseen. Bomani was no monster, was no dark cannibal of souls.

Joined for eternity, wheel inside a wheel circling in endless eterne.

Abayomi fell into the hot dark of Bomani's love, where time had no meaning.

He had given himself to the nameless love.

Chapter Twenty-five

Daniel stumbled, sitting down with a thump in the chilly floor.

"Dieu---!" It escaped his lips in a stammering cry.

The empty bottle fell from his nerveless hand as he folded both his naked arms over the top of his head, shaken by what he knew...by what he remembered. It roared through his brain with the speed and noise of a locomotive.

He shouted at heaven, roared for what had been lost...for what had been done. For what went on even now. For he did not doubt that connection, now. It was no mere dream.

He *was* Abayomi, the boy.

He had been the consort of that malakh, the one with eyes and hair like liquid night. What should have destroyed his life and ruined his body, had given him the only pleasure he was ever to know...and it was still going on, under his skin. In his blood and in every cell. Thousands of years later, with the blink of an eye, his bones still begged to be crushed in that giant's arms.

The binding had been weakened many times, but it could never be broken...

His wings sang, rising away from his spine, flexing in time with the internal rhythms of that love-making, the claiming he could see in his mind. It made him want to weep---for three thousand years, since that sacrifice, this had been going on. It had never ended, never finished between them. It would never be finished---

Clutching at his head, he sobbed and shouted wildly for the sheer magnitude of what he felt.

He was in hell. His chinois was so hard and tight, he felt as if he might burst from the sheer need that came with the memory of Bomani's touch. With his arms over his head, his knees drawn up to his naked chest, he cried at the harrowing knowledge of what went on, continuously, under his skin.

In his gut, a fire still burned---it filled him with the tears he cried.

"Papa? Papa, what's wrong---"

Julien was coming to him; he could feel his fils' footsteps, light and quick on the hardwood floor, in his wings and on the floor under his backside. With his arms wrapped up over his ears, his head---with his eyes closed---it was difficult to tell which direction his fils was approaching him from. At first. Then, he felt it. Behind. He found the intense knowledge of it through the awareness of his wings, unseen and too alive. His beautiful, brilliant fils was behind him and moving in fast.

"Papa, what's wrong? You were shouting---ah, mon Dieu, you drank the whole thing?" Julien's voice broke off, sharply, and he heard a murmuring from across the half-lit parlor.

Someone---Dante Webster, perhaps---asked. "Is he okay? What happened? I'm just getting all kinds of jumbled noise from him."

His short, genteel fils stopped moving and he felt the boards shift under him as Julien turned and answered the husa-hekau malakh. "I don't know---at least he's stopped shouting, now. It's okay, I've got him."

"If you're sure? Maybe I should try taking a peek up close."

Then, Julien was crouching in front of him, arms folding in around his head, pulling at his hands. With a nearly dispassionate tone, his fils spoke softly with a hybrid French-American accent. "Papa, shhh, you're safe. Shh, calm down. Fold your wings in, Papa. You're making so much noise with them, we heard you out on the street before we even got out of the car."

He rocked back and forth, letting Julien embrace him; his hands fell away limp as he cried into his fils' shoulder, open-mouthed, too weak to be the dominant, strong *pater familias* in this moment.   Through slitted, watery eyes, he realized Julien and Dante were both dressed in a noble style---they had been out to dinner, no doubt.   Their romance had never truly died, only grown stronger in the years of their friendship.   They might 'date' others, but the love affair still blossomed between his fils and Mattie's step-son, even after a decade.

He felt emotionally devastated in a way he had not known since the death of his beloved Vivienne, Julien's mama.   He swallowed, tasting the dryness of his screams where they lingered in his throat; bourbon and the acrid sourness of fear.   He uncurled, letting his fils pull him closer.   His fists were tightened as he fought with something in his brain which shrieked, begging to find its way back into the Dream.   The memories were heavy, racing through him...so real that he could feel every drop of sweat, see every flicker of firelight, smell the flesh of an aroused tchatcha.

"I cannot do this.   I can *not*."   He hissed the words, through his teeth as he pushed his face into Julien's shoulder.   "I am ripped in two---I am lost---"

The arms that held him were warm, the lips at his ear were warm, but the floor under him was cold.   "You *can*.   You can do this.   This is me, Papa...Jules.   You *can*."

Julien's voice was low, as quick as his footsteps.   Almost as velvet on his frayed nerves. He unclenched his fists and his fingers shook, eyes sealed shut on the images he could not escape, did not want to let go of.

His fils tugged at his hands, Julien's voice making his wings vibrate and stretch.   "I love you, Papa, we all love you...just take a breath and remember who you are.   Talk to me."

His wings were on fire---he could feel the flames crackling through each tiny tendril that reached for the spirit of Bomani.   But, with each word from Julien, the pain lessened and the memories slowed their insane whirl. He trembled yet, sobbing like a child into his young fils' shoulder as he had sobbed into Bomani's shoulder...

His words were hiccupped, forced through the gasps of his breath.   His voice sounded as if it came from some other throat.   "It's too loud---why?   Why am I remembering this now? Why do I dream of these things *again*?   Is it a punishment?"

Holding him as Jeanne-Marie had held him, in the hall, on the day their Mama had died, his winsome and gentle fils gave a sigh, loud in his ear.   "I don't know.   I don't know what you're dreaming.   Papa, it'll be okay.   Maybe you're ready, now, to know.   Maybe you need to know."   His fils' lips nuzzled at his stubbled cheek and he could feel the tightness of Julien's arms on his shoulders and ribs as his wings began to quiet and pull back into his screaming spine.   "You won't go mad, Papa, we can get through it...we need to sort through what you see.   We'll help you, don't be scared."   Then, his fils spoke to Dante, across the room, his tone more serious.   "Maybe it's about Mama?"

It felt as if he was peeking through the crack in his Mama's door again, staring at the truth of what came to those who were the beloved.   His mind circled on it as his wings slowed, folding inwards, becoming calm.   This was far too much to wrap his brain around...he had glimpsed Eternity.

He was no longer drunk.   He opened his eyes, peered through strands of his hair to see the dark wood of the wall beyond his fils' shoulder.   Daniel gave a small sob, mouth twisting on the pain of his throat, uncaring that his child and his fellow player might see him in his weakness.   "I cannot make it leave me.   I dream and it is real, as real as...you are real."

He pulled back from Julien and stared up into his fils' eyes, shameless of the tears on his face.   His knee was touching something made of ice.   Blinking at the sting in his eyes, he reached for it and discovered the heavy bottle he had dropped.   It was unbroken and empty.   He sighed; a small sound of human annoyance as he set it up-right, only nominally glad that it was safe.   Gathering himself, pushing at the memories that worked to overwhelm him in their clamor, he turned his head to stare at Dante, who stood in the study's doorway.   The young hacker looked afraid, apprehensive.

He whispered it.   "You know, husa-hekau.   You know where I have been...what I have done."

Dante was an empath who possessed the ability to read the output of malakh and humans alike and influence the emotions of people; how could Mattie's step-son not know?

Dante gave an apologetic smile, tilting his broad-jawed, handsome face; in the moment, the young hacker most resembled his dead papa, Robin Webster. "You're kinda loud with it, Daniel."

He glanced around at the mess he had made of his study. White sheets lay in the floor before almost every portrait of his family. All portraits but one. The picture of his son, Louis-Francois.

He imagined in his mind, the painting; his legitimate son, at eighteen, golden-haired and angelic, too lovely and strong to be anything but a saint......if one did not look at the devilish curve of his mouth or examine the emotion found in those green eyes. He knew...he dared not uncover the portrait yet. He could not face that beautiful monster's steady gaze; even with the difference in coloring, the expression in Louis-Francois' eyes was too much like the look in his own, at the same age. He did not want to face any images of the dark-natured child whose embittered cry for love had gone ignored...whose terror of being alone had led his long-dead fils, in arrogance and hate, to destroy those he loved the most.

Daniel drew himself together and out of Julien's arms. He shuddered a deep breath and remembered that Rhys was not at home and he had called Dante before falling asleep on the back porch's divan. He brushed a hand through his tangled, dark hair, pushing aside the horror---he was L'Epee D'Mort and he was more than a frightened child whose memories seemed to include an impossible lifetime, thousands of years ago. He must be L'Epee D'Mort.

He leveled a serious look at the hacker, past his mulatto fils Julien, and spoke in a steady voice. "Mon ami, you came here for some purpose. What have you discovered about our young fille, Tennyson Beaulieu?"

In the dim sunroom, among the plants on their shelves and pedestals, Daniel listened quietly as Dante Webster spoke. His eyes were on Julien as his fils poured coffee into three sturdy mugs.

"When I got your message, we were...kinda busy." Dante gave a lop-sided grin and used his thumb to push up the glasses he wore. The hacker was dressed in fine clothing, including a blue tie which hung loosely from the collar of Dante's shirt. "But, I started in and dug around and came up with some stuff. It was well-hidden, but for the wily cyber-cowboy, nothing's impossible."

He nodded, accepting the coffee from his mulatto fils as he settled more deeply into the chair he had dragged from its place in the corner. He watched as Julien finally took his own seat and lifted a mug of the steaming brew to his delicate mouth; for a moment, he was startled by how very much like himself his fils looked, but for the hue of his skin. Both of his children had taken after their mama, a New Orleans mulatto, in that respect.

"Tenny-girl's mom put a name down for the father, on the birth certificate, but the guy's been out of the picture since just before Tennyson was born. His name was Khalil Bayhas. I found that. His mom, Tennyson's grandma, was Egyptian from the El Fayim oasis, and his dad, Tennyson's grandpa, is named William Ashwin. How's that for ironic?"

"More ironic than you know." He murmured. *Bayhas*, his own family from the oasis villages. *Ashwin*, the name of his lost friend and lover.

"But, I also found some banking records for a legacy in Tennyson's name. She gets a monthly allowance check from a company out of London. The solicitor who handles the checks is a guy named Richard Hawthorne. He's one of the solicitors for King-Hobbs, Incorporated. The group that King-Hobbs represents, who signs off on the legacy, is called Nasir al Asad-Din. Which means, in Arabic..."

"Protectors of the Lion's faith. I know of this company, but I was unaware that the Ashwins were so intricately involved. The name comes from a nom de guerre used by the native Bedouins and Misrene to identify one of the Ashwins---Henry Ashwin, to be exact. Nasir al-Zarqa, the blue-eyed protector." He recalled the words with ease.

How very droll that life should have delivered into his hands the descendant of Henry Ashwin, in the form of Tennyson Beaulieu. It could not be mere coincidence. More than droll was the name Bayhas, which he immediately remembered, as well. He knew members of the Bayhas family, when he had lived among the villages of El Faiyum. They were *his* family.

Bayhas meant, in the old tongue, *'name of the lion'*. It was the name of the Lion of Kemet.

In the times he had journeyed back to Egypt, to visit with the people he knew, he had often come across members of Nasir al Asad-Din---including his own son, Alexander---but he had never heard a single whisper which might suggest that the *Ashwins* were so completely integrated into the families he had once lived among.

He had, of course, known that the villagers had called Henry Ashwin by the name of Nasir al-Zarqa. He had heard it said, in 1939, just before he left his home and family in El Faiyum. He had a suspicion, now, that his long-lost Legionnaire had made sure of an involvement. Could Henry's guilt have inspired such an act? True, his friend had named a son after him---the eldest son, an honor---but, could his words and the bold truth of what he was, as a malakh, have inspired the forming of a company dedicated to the protection and preservation of malakh genetics and history?

In his mind, he could picture the last time he had seen his blue-eyed English friend; the year had been 1939 and he'd been shot to death, by accident, mistaken for a potential thief or assassin. He could still remember the way it had felt, staring up into the horror-stricken face of Henry Ashwin as he bled to death in front of that man's Misrene wife and toddler child…William.

To think…less than a year later, he had left his own family there, in El Faiyim, intending to find some way of a permanent death in the war. He had left his young son, Alexander, and his wife, Muhjahri, never to return as their beloved. He had seen Muhjahri several times, over the decades, but they had agreed between them that, until he could return to the desert and the oasis with his heart fully undivided, he should not attempt returning to her tent or her bed. She was dead, now; dead for eight years. Vivienne had known of Muhjahri and of his love for her, had understood why he possessed a separate bank account for the upkeep of his Egyptian wife, for his Egyptian son.

His stubborn and angry son, who would have nothing to do with him at all, because of the callous manner in which he had abandoned the village and their family. He had seen his son only a handful of times in the last half-century; Alexander would not allow his calls or his letters or a visit of any kind. He did not know if he had grandchildren.

Considering both this and the situation at hand, of who Tennyson Beaulieu was, he nodded, continuing. "It is ironic, non, that our young fille is of Egyptian blood, as I am, as L'Fils D'Ange is. It is more than ironic that she is the grandchild of William Ashwin. Perhaps the gods choose it to be this way. Did you discover anything else about this company…Nasir al Asad-Din? Anything I might not be aware of? Is there any other mention of the name Ashwin to be found?"

"Not right off the bat, no." Dante looked around at the sunroom, avoiding his gaze. "But, I did find out something else. Tennyson's mom signed papers, when she was born, giving up the rights of a wife to her husband's family legacy. She can't claim anything from Nasir al Asad-Din herself and she's never supposed to tell Tennyson a thing about Khalil Bayhas. The legacy Tennyson receives is contingent on her mom's silence. If Tennyson ever comes to the representatives of Nasir al Asad-Din, asking questions about her father, the legacy will stop immediately."

"And what of Khalil Bayhas? Did you discover anything of him or his parents?"

"Only that…and this is weird, Daniel…there's no record of Bayhas' death. No death certificate, no proof that he died. And that doesn't fit with what Tennyson told me." Dante still refused to meet his eye. "She told me that her dad died in a shoot-out, trying to protect the pharmacist in a drug store. It was a robbery gone wrong and the guy bought it just a month before she was born."

"There'd be records, then, right?" Julien frowned and he could see the gears in his fils' mind turning. As a lawyer, Julien was quick to think in terms of legal documentation. "If Tennyson's papa died, there'd be a death certificate, police paperwork, records of the investigation."

"Oui." Daniel swallowed a mouthful of the coffee and considered the contradictions. "This suggests that either the fille has lied about her papa's death or she has never been told the truth. If the Ashwin legacy is based upon her mama's silence, then it may be the latter. Tennyson Beaulieu might be truly in the dark concerning these matters. If he did not die, where is he? Were you able to find anything on this missing papa, Dante?"

Dante did not speak at first, refusing to look at him.

"Mon ami." He said, letting a hint of frustrated anger tinge his words. "I pay you excellently for the information and I would know what you have discovered, in this matter. What do you know of Tennyson Beaulieu's papa?"

After a quiet moment which seemed to last for several minutes, Dante Webster made a sour face and shrugged, muttering behind his coffee mug. "The guy's alive and well, in Egypt. At least, that's where he was a few months ago, the last time a check was sent to him from his own legacy, in Nasir al Asad-Din. Get this...he's a bioanthropologist. Like Steve Rose was. Going deeper, looking at uni records, I found out they went to university in Cairo together. My bet? They knew each other."

A twinge of pain went through him at the mention of Rhys' papa, the dead man whose friendship had meant so much to him, in the years they worked together---he the subject of a study in malakh genetics and Steven the scientist. "Why do you mention Steven? What does Steven have to do with this?"

"Only that Ashwin and Steve were involved in the same branch of bioanthropology, the study of malakh evolution...but, it's not Steve that counts here, not in this one." Dante grimaced, still making the same sour face. "It's Roan Bashiyra Ata'din that counts."

"Rhys' mama?" He felt his skin grow cold. "What did Roan have to do with this matter?"

The young, hazel-eyed hacker would not meet his eye again and instead studied the mug he held. "Roan's parents were Egyptian, right? From some big village. Well, according to what I found, it's the same village that Tennyson's family came from, on the Egyptian side. Roan's parents are still alive, living in Egypt. I found Roan's name on a list of people associated with Ashwin Nasir al Asad-Din. She was also on the legacy list, connected with the Ashwin family. But, the craziest part was that,..Roan's maiden name was listed as Ashwin on the legacy papers, even though no one knows who her real father was. Her *adoptive* father's surname was Ashwin."

He breathed his shock. "What? This is impossible...non?"

"Well, maybe not." Dante shrugged, not meeting his eye yet. "According to the records I dug up, Roan was Egyptian, father unknown, but her mom married an Englishman named Ashwin. A man named William Ashwin, who adopted her as a child. The same William Ashwin. Khalil and Roan were made into step-sibs, through all that. It makes Rhys and Tennyson both part of the Ashwin family, but not through blood. Tennyson is an Ashwin, by blood, and Rhys is an Ashwin through marriage. They're cousins, but *not* cousins."

He stared at the hazel-eyed hacker in silence, the coffee turning bitter on his tongue.

William Ashwin...the name of his lost Henry's son.

Dante continued, ruthlessly explaining the truth. "So, they both come from the Nasir al Asad-Din people, connected to the same tribe *and* the Ashwins. Rhys is supposed to be receiving a legacy of his own, because of who he is to them, only...because the records state he died as a little kid in California, they don't know he exists."

It was quiet...and for the first time in a long time, he felt okay.

He lifted the glass of Courvoisier to his mouth and sipped at the ice-cold cognac. It was late, after one in the morning, and the winter night was cloudy, obscuring the moon he could feel in the sky. The light that slipped through the open doorway of the bathroom brushed everything within its reach and softened the visible colors and shapes.

Tennyson was sleeping.

Naked, luscious, sweet, and innocent.

She was in the same position he'd left her in, on her side and curled up under the seal-gray, velvet-soft duvet. The tumble of her braids was *right*, the silver-white gleam of light outlining every ebony plait on both slim throat and rounded shoulder. He'd never thought he could have her, that she might be his in any way. She was a lushly round and drowsy-limbed goddess.

She was a nubile queen who sucked her thumb.

Rhys smiled, watching her.

She slept like a sated baby. Her beautiful, dark face was slack with a gentle look. Long, dark lashes. The fine, delicate curve of her brows, the unlined and untroubled planes of her young forehead and cheeks, the push and angle of her high cheekbones and the curve of both jaw and chin. She was delicious when awake, but now, in the helpless hands of sleep, revealed by the night, Tennyson was eternal and ageless.

It might have been a solemn, sacred sight, if not for the thumb.

Here he sat, his hips wrapped in only a sheet, at her bed's side, and kept watch over a girl that had shown him something half-forgotten. It was laughable, it was worrisome, it might have been worth crying for. He had nearly abandoned the memory of what it meant to hold someone like that, to be lost so utterly in the moment of making love.

He knew how long it'd been since he'd made love to someone who could make him lose control, make him forget everything as if he'd been flung into the mythical Lethe. He knew how long it had been since he'd felt so wondrously empty and purified by the flesh of another. Mattie had made him love and then crushed his heart...and now, here, he found the seeds of a renewal.

His smile grew larger and he lit a joint, studying her closely. Genetics or spirit? Which one could possibly cause this reaction? Perhaps, it was the mixture of both. But, he could let that pass...he could just enjoy what he'd been given.

She sucked her thumb.

It hung loosely from the corner of her curved, thick lips, pulling the soft flesh slightly out of shape, but it only perfected the innocent look of her. He suspected that the teddy bear which lay on the floor, at his foot, was something she slept with. She'd never admit to *that*, would she? He could imagine what that could be like...her sweet, chocolate-skinned arms tight around the fuzzy white toy, her cheek and throat rubbing at the snowy, plush nap, the red satin ribbon.

Was the toy a gift from an ex-lover?

Tennyson had burned like a wildfire at his touch...had trembled and wept with each orgasm. She had the right physical and emotional release points for what he'd come to think of as being a malakh sexuality trait. She could smell his under-scent. The touch of her hands and mouth...the way she used her skin to find new sensitivities...the quick, decisive way she learned. She'd worn him out, really, and that had never happened. Ever.

It was difficult to believe she knew so little about sex with men when every step she took was heavy with sensuality. Yet, the truth had come out in the moment of revelation. She possessed a mysterious prowess and unconsciously erotic grace he'd been drawn to, finally unable to resist tonight. It made him feel intensely protective. What if there might be someday another? Someone who could use Tennyson's secret inner nature to hurt her in some way? It took nothing to betray; just a willingness to judge between the means and the ends.

Look at what *he* did, for a living...what he'd been trained and bred to do.

He squelched his possessive need to protect the young woman. He had no real claim on Tennyson. He couldn't have a claim, yet he wanted it. He didn't love her with the very core of his bones, but the affection was an abiding one, built on their friendship and the strange sense of trust he felt for her. He didn't love anyone with the whole of himself and Tennyson seemed to understand that without words. Not like the others he'd fucked. Who always wanted him to stay, who wanted to lay claim to what could never be owned. Tennyson's loyal affection mixed with his would be enough. She was like him, loved both men and women, but he had a duty to fulfill and even if he couldn't remember what that duty was, he still had work before him. It was whispered in his brain, too low to understand, every morning of his life.

And she completely forgave and accepted his true gender.

Rhys smoked, quietly, and drank more of the cognac.

He'd discovered the fine, French liquor in the kitchen, while searching for a water glass. It was something that happened---he still could not sleep through the night. Invariably, he woke every night, between eleven and twelve. No matter how little rest he'd had, he woke. Always with the dreams, strange shadows, whispering voices, and the sound of someone crying softly in the distance.

As a young boy, he'd thought the crying was a sound from some other room in his 'house', the lab. It had always made him feel bereft---something he didn't really understand, the emotions---as if he'd lost his way. Usually, he crept into Daniel's bed, but not tonight. The moment of internal panic and disorientation had passed quickly, waking up in Tennyson's bed, holding her close. But, like always, his mind wouldn't slow down long enough for him to go back into sleep.

So, he watched her...and enjoyed the knowledge of what she was, revealed to his mind by his skin.

With a sigh, he rubbed his nose with the fingers of one hand, smiling to himself again. He could smell her on his skin. That awe-inspiring scent. In her sleep, Tennyson stirred and gave a drowsy smile around her thumb and one of her little hands moved along the empty space he'd left behind. Unconsciously, she became aware of the cooled sheets and the lack of his damply hot flesh against hers.

He reached out to stroke at her hair, wrapping a braid around his fingertip. She gave a sigh, her smile grew in a subtle way, she tightened her lips around the curve of her thumb. Then, the sweet Creole girl settled back into a deeper rest.

She loved him as a friend...perhaps as more.

"Tennyson, Tenny..." He murmured her name a few times, tasting the syllables with clean happiness.

It would be easy to love her. To know that, no matter what became of his world or the work he did or the duty he didn't understand, this young and vital woman would be here, believing in him. A natural, honest relationship...as honest as he could allow it to be, anyway. Still, she believed in him, believed in their friendship. And, like Daniel, she could see the reality he hid behind layers of learned behavior and mannerisms. It was there, in what he'd picked up from her skin---she sensed the darkness in him and said nothing.

Recognizing the chord that rang true between them, Daniel had seen both the light and the dark and accepted in the way that only a centuries-old benu malakh could. Daniel had, from the very start, realized what no one else could see...a startling, spiritual-mental contrast that he'd been taught to protect and hide. Only Daniel could find it without having to pick his brain with empathy. Daniel's primitive side, the animal within. But, here, in Tennyson, he found someone who didn't need to be a benu malakh to understand him.

So different from Mattie...Mattie, who saw the truth with empathy and condemned him out of hand for how his abilities and truths could live internally side by side and without conflict. She'd thrown him aside, feeling justified in her dismissal, and yet...yet, she still got under his skin.

But...now...Tennyson's breath was calm, her mulatto skin was cool to his touch and soft and scented and willing. In less than two days, he was gonna take her to Egypt for a job and he'd have to stay professional about everything.   But, until then, she was his lover.   And it was breathtaking to love her.

At last, he was unlonely.

Epilogue

It was five miles of corridor, steel and stone, kept at a mere sixty degrees at all hours of the day and the night. Night and day could never exist there; without windows, the only measure of time came from the computers' incessant awareness of hour and minute and second. Sound carried with the precision of echoes, distorted and half-captured. Halogen bulbs hung hidden behind frosted globes every ten feet of every hallway and every room. The lab was sterile, cold. Processed air came from grills, piped in from above through aluminum pipes only ten inches in diameter.

Each lab was fifteen hundred square feet, containing computers and testing equipment. Each lab held a large, Plexiglas tube which cradled and nurtured a specimen...an experiment in progress. Ten of the labs held gene alteration experiments. Consenting adult humans who had signed all the necessary papers. Adult humans who worked dangerous jobs for dangerous people in dangerous agencies. Secret, clandestine, hush-hush. Male, female, black, white...aboriginal and Asian. Within four walls of gray, unpainted steel, each lab was a room designed for the alteration. Operating theater, bright lamps, counters full of equipment designed for measuring and mixing and examining.

The tubs were ten foot long, modern-day Frankenstein wombs. The birthing place of genetic frame-shifts. Dark gray, burnished steel, each tub had a rounded window that ran the length of the apparatus. Long, rectangular coffins made of steel and Plexiglas and body-shaped foam innards. Tubing ran from steel boxes and computers and poles that held plasticine sacks of fluid. Saline, glucose, vitamins and the Doctor Moreau elixir which changed a human into something else. Tubes that ran through the steel and the Plexiglas and the foam, pumping chemical enzymes. Tubes that recycled placenta-like fluids and oxygenated plasma.

The patient would lay down into the foam pad inside the tub. The patient would have an oxygen-rich air-feed mask sealed over the nose and the mouth, a catheter inserted into the bladder. The patient would have a sedative injected, to be put into a medical coma as needles were implanted into his spinal cord, the artery at his groin, and into each wrist. Needles would feed him everything needed to keep him alive through the veins. Needles would slowly---very slowly---feed gene-altering enzymes into him, each and every cell.

The patient would be sealed into the tub by hydraulic spring and rubber liner. The Plexiglas lid, rounded and clear, would close and make him distinctly alone. The patient might hear, faintly, in his dreams, the voices of others as they worked over his tub.

The patient would sleep for four months and then be brought up out of the medical coma slowly, pulled from the mechanical womb in the belief that...if his genes were strong enough to take the frame-shift in a coherent fashion, his body would show new phenotypes. The patient would be soft-muscled, soft-stomached, and baby-like for several weeks. It often required several months to put a newly altered agent back on his feet and capable of functioning in society, at the job, at assignments.

Once, in the mid-eighties, this particular experiment was run by the CIA, as its linked project series had been for five years before, since inception. The very first time the tubs were used to awaken the sleeping genotypes of agents who possessed differentiated DNA in any workable amount, the entire project was almost immediately red-lighted and silenced.

Ten special agents, who presented large concentrations of demi-malakh DNA, went into the tubs for genetic alteration, to make them more than human. Less than half survived; four lived, six died. Of the four who survived, only one was deemed viably sane afterwards. The reasons for her retention of sanity were never understood, even after several years of study.   The experiment was put aside, shut down, only to be re-activated in 1996 by a privately owned company who held a contract with the government for the design of a perfected biological weapon.

Now, in ten of the chilly labs, government agents were being held in medical comas while their bodies underwent a corrected design of the alteration process.   For the last several years, the lab had produced a much higher rate of success.   For every ten specimen, all ten would survive.   Seven or eight showed very few or no negative side affects.

But…in labs eleven and twelve, something new and beautiful and terrible grew.

Lab Eleven

Something new and beautiful and terrifying.   Long, lean, Nubian dark.   Female.   Thick, curly hair moved in the amniotic fluids like a cloud of black wool.   The features of her face were blunt and soft, gentle in sleep.   She dreamed, but the dreams were unknown; muscles reacted, twitching fingers and toes, knees and elbows.   She lay curled in a fetal position, unaware of the world outside, a sleeping beauty in her early twenties.

She was the offspring of a dead malakh, identical to her mother in every respect.   An unfertilized ova from fM-09 of the Isosceles Experiment---a defunct government research and development program in the Malakh Principles project---was bathed in a gene-transfer solution and then treated to a unique chemical stimulus which created the spark of cellular life necessary for meiosis.   The resulting blastocyte was implanted on a placental bed in a growth tub.   There, she was fed and carefully maintained in this her in vitro environment as it began to develop into a female fetus.

The fetus developed into a child.   With special proteins and stimuli, she grew twice as fast as a normal fetus.   Two years for every one year.   She grew from child to adult, being nurtured in her watery womb by the umbilical cord that connected from navel to placenta.   Speakers shunted into the tub provided instruction by osmosis.   The process of cloning was far more advanced than the common public had been informed---and fM-09-12 was just that: the twelfth and final clone of fM-09.   She was physically perfect, but her status was yet unknown, as she was still in stasis.   Once released and trained, she would become a biological weapon of unimagined potential.

Her eyelids flickered and became slits, revealing the blind opal-white of cataracts beneath.

She was lovely…as lovely as the flash of light on a straight-razor in the black of a filthy alley.

Lab Twelve

In the dimness of lab twelve, mM-t02-07 slumbered within his tub.   His pale brown hair, long and lank, swished with the flux of thick amniotic fluids as they moved in the constant recycle system.   From head to toe, he was a dusky golden olive, as if he had lived his entire existence in afternoon sunlight.   But, that was far from truth; he, like fM-09-12, had never breathed…had never known anything but that watery, mechanical uterus.   He had never breathed, despite his continual accelerated growth…never looked upon the face of his creator. He lived within the Plexiglas world of his tub, receiving all his nutrients and oxygen from the umbilical cord that pulsed the red and blue and white of viscera.   He, like his counterpart in Lab Eleven, was physically flawless.   This was the results of biogenetic research and development at its finest cruelty.

He flexed and moved, his face showing the concentration of a dreamer.   His hand pushed at the clear, domed Plexiglas and then went limp.   His feet arched into a stretch, long and taut with the high-stepping grace of a dancer.   He was a clone of his father, mM-t02. The seventh such clone.   When he awakened and was trained, he would be capable of invisible death...for he was the world's third living tchatcha malakh.

His eyelids moved and then drifted open to reveal eyes like the void of star-less space.

In upstate New York, in a wild patch of Adirondack boondocks of Essex county---not more than a dozen miles from Saranac Lake, Doctor Ian Cowan drove along the narrow gravel road as it turned back on itself several times.   It was time to work; he'd been called away from his vacation and for one reason only.   Doctor Hochstetler needed him in Labs Eleven and Twelve on Level Nine.

It was dark, the night sky half-obscured by winter-bare trees whose claws reached for heaven.   He'd been enjoying himself at home, with his parents---not a common occurrence--- only to be informed by the familiar, accented voice of his boss that something new was happening within the confines of Eleven and Twelve.   His own personal section of the project.   At least, it was the part he was assigned to work on.

At forty years old, with a double Ph.D. in genetics and biochemistry, he enjoyed the work he'd managed to score.   He could congratulate himself---how many guys at his alma mater, ten years ago, had managed to get hired into private research companies who specialized in government contracts?   Big, expensive contracts that not only paid all the bills but paid out hefty bonuses to their developers for the secrecy involved in a project that would revolutionize the world of gene-skewing.

So what if it was night-time and he was being called back to work early, on vacation? Doctor Hochstetler wouldn't have called if there wasn't something important going down. And he got paid for this kind of dedication.   At forty years old, his ginger-colored hair pre-maturely balding, he was on the flabby side of big.   Cowan had become fascinated by genetics as a kid when he'd realized that he could pin down his physical foibles on one or both of his parents---and their parents before them.   If he tended to be overweight, he could understand why, after a good look at the people in his family.   If his brown eyes were weak and tended to water in bright lights, at least he understood which side of his DNA presented the trait.

He checked his watch as approached the first of three check-points.   It was just after nine in the evening.   He rolled down his window in the frosty air and showed his ID to the heavily-armed guards.   The gates were opened and he continued.   A mile up the road, through the hills, he went through the same procedure.   At last, he was within sight of the complex, at the last fences.   Again, he showed his ID and was waved through the wire-razor gates.   Now, the complex loomed like some museum to cold war architecture.

He parked his car and got out, zipping up his coat.   He had no briefcase to carry, since he was never allowed to carry anything out of the complex.   Nothing was allowed out, nothing was allowed in.   Not even a cell phone.   Not so much as even an ink-pen.   Only his security badge.   Which would deactivate if it was ever tampered with.

Under his heavy gloves and balaclava and coat---all of military green canvas stuffed full of goose-down---Cowan wore jeans and brown Timberland work boots, a black tee-shirt with CASH written on it in gray, and a flannel shirt in green, blue, white, and gray checks.   It was so old and threadbare that it no longer qualified as flannel.   Bundled against the frigid Northern winter, he headed across the lot and then up the wide granite steps, to the front doors.   He knew the procedure, after a decade.   As he reached the massive double metal doors, he pulled off his gloves and put them into his coat pocket.   He couldn't feel the bone-chilling cold yet; his hands were still warmed from the fleecy down.

In the metal doors was embedded a stainless steel box with three lights, no larger than M&Ms.   One red, one amber, one green.   Above them was a keypad and a card-slot, for the ID that he was given on his very first day of employment in the labs.   Below the keypad and the card-slot is a black grill speaker.   At the very top of the box was a circular recess only a quarter-inch in diameter that blinks white light. On, off, on, off, on, off---in the rhythm of a steady heartbeat.

Fumbling, Cowan removed his ID from a pocket and slid it into the card-slot.

The speaker crackled. The voice was female, sterile, computerized. "Doctor Ian Cowan. Level Nine. Labs Eleven and Twelve. Please place your finger on the DNA scanner for verification purposes."

He now gritted his teeth in instinctive hate and put his left index finger on the little circular indention. The box hummed and he felt a sudden stabbing pain. He jerked, but forced himself to stand still, his finger still in place. A wash of cold liquid---sterile alcohol which burned and then dried almost too fast to be noticed. The blood was analyzed and matched to his voice pattern and his ID card.

He counted his heartbeats; after twelve, the computer voice came back and he imagined the tone was warmer. More friendly. "Welcome back from your vacation, Doctor Cowan. Doctor Hochstetler is expecting you. Doctor Hochstetler is currently in Level Nine, Lab Eleven."

The doors gave a hydraulic hiss and parted, letting him in. He picked up the pace as his eyes adjusted to the change in illumination. Night sky and security lamps to halogen lights that were never extinguished. He pushed up the glasses he wore and began removing his coat and balaclava as he walked along the white-tiled floor towards the elevator.

He stepped into the steel box and pushed the button for Level Nine. He readied himself for the strange vertigo sensation that always began once he'd passed into the deeper underground of the labs. His mind went to work. If Doctor Hochstetler was in Eleven, working, after calling him back early from vacation...he needed to be present. He wouldn't even bother going by his quarters yet. It'd be best if he just got a lab coat on and went straight to his boss' side.

Doctor Hochstetler had said *'Something is happening. I believe 'mM-t02-07 is waking up.'*

~Finis~

George Bennett Fain has been writing science fiction and historical fantasy for more than twenty years, specializing in the gay and lesbian genre. She is a native of the Blue Ridge Mountains region, currently attending Marshall University, studying the field of Sociology. She is the proud single parents of two daughters.

She lives in a houseful of women who are sometimes less than indulgent where her obsessions are concerned. Her hobbies include co-ed naked karaoke, gardening at her friend Adam's house, and photography--she dreams of owning her own greenhouse. She's a devout pagan who participates in a local drum circle.

George's idea of paradise is to live on a farm in BFE where she can get stranded in snowstorms, sleep under a tin roof when it rains, and have coffee on the porch on early, foggy mornings---and yet still be close enough to civilization in order to commute to work during the week.

Photograph supplied by Marty Laubach

www.ingramcontent.com/pod-product-compliance
Lightning Source LLC
Chambersburg PA
CBHW031219290326
41931CB00035B/247